Famous Writers
Course

Famous Writers School Inc.
Westport Connecticut

Famous Writers Course

Fiction writing

Volume III

The Famous Writers Courses are published with the
editorial advice and contributions of the
Guiding Faculty of the Famous Writers School

Bruce Catton

Rudolf Flesch

Max Shulman

Faith Baldwin

Bennett Cerf

Red Smith

* Mignon G. Eberhart

Bergen Evans

Rod Serling

John Caples

J. D. Ratcliff

Mark Wiseman

Gordon Carroll, Director

Contents

I section

II section

III section

IV section

V section

VI section

Fiction writing

Volume III

Section I

Lesson one

Fiction writing
course

What
is
fiction?

Without thinking too much about it, you probably have a good idea what fiction is. You know it is an invented or "made-up" story as opposed to one that's true. You know that fiction writing, unlike *non*-fiction, is based upon imagination rather than fact.

But now that you've started this part of the Fiction Course, you should have more than a general idea about your subject. You should know how it differs from other forms, and you should also know the principles of good fiction writing, why fiction interests a vast audience of readers, and why it's uniquely valuable in today's and tomorrow's world.

The differences between fiction and non-fiction vary in kind and degree. The two forms of writing are alike—and unlike. They're alike in that both are taken from life, from the world as we see it. Both record the actions and reactions of human beings. Both appeal to the thoughts and feelings of the readers.

Yet they differ in that non-fiction does *not* depart from facts as the writer finds them in time, place and order. Fiction, on the other hand, takes liberties with facts, invents them, rearranges them, and through imagination creates inner responses in the reader. In short, one of fiction's chief aims is to enter the reader's mind and create an emotional adventure.

Why does this imagined adventure appeal so powerfully to readers? In today's world of challenging and fast-moving events, fiction might seem to be a pale counterpart of reality. The truth is, however, that people are always deeply interested in motivations lying *behind* the actions of their fellow men who, just like the reader, know what it means to hope, suffer, yearn, despair, triumph or fail.

· Readers find that when they become immersed in other people's lives, they not only escape some of their own frustrations but also learn they're not alone in facing the conflicts and disturbances of daily life. They gain a better understanding of humanity—and of themselves. During the time it takes them to read a story, they share the lot of other humans on this earth.

How has this principle of fiction been established? Not quickly or deliberately, but logically out of generations of story-telling. Many centuries ago, before the days of the written word, prehistoric man learned it was fun to embroider on the facts as he related his adventures. He found he could keep his listeners listening as long as he could interest them, and gradually, over countless years, he found out more and more about what interested them. By the time the teller could write his stories and the listener had become a reader, awareness of which flights of the imagination would hold the reader's attention had developed some fairly reliable patterns.

To this day the patterns prevail, the main one being that readers like to be thrilled, amused, terrified, angered, saddened —like to share the feelings of the characters they read about. They want to know what the characters look like, what adventures they encounter, how they are moved by inner struggles, why they act the way they do. A fiction reader wants to identify himself completely with the characters in your story. Because he puts himself in their place, he cares what happens to them. This, in turn, gives him the illusion of undergoing an experience.

When a writer gets an idea for a story, there are several yardsticks by which he may measure its worth. The first question is, does this idea hold *my* interest? After I have filed it away in my mind and taken a look at it later, does it *still* hold my interest—that is, do I *still* want to tell it to somebody? Does it provide a foundation for a story? Does it give me something upon which to build? Is it provocative to me? Does it suggest characters who will logically and convincingly take action and promote events? Or is it, say, only an entertaining coincidence, or an incident which may be lively and amusing in real life but is in fact isolated, and offers no foundation whatever for the creation of a story?

We come here to the danger of telling a story merely because "it really happened." Material for a story is all around you, but selection is another thing and in selecting the writer should remember that the story itself *must stand alone*. It must have its own life and being. It is something the author creates.—Mignon G. Eberhart

---

Now for another principle of fiction. Fiction interprets and translates as well as reports. It attempts to analyze life and to tell the reader the results. It does this by action and illustration— by moving characters and events around so that they do the interpreting for the writer. It allows readers to peer through a door or window into the secret lives of their fellow men: it satisfies the natural curiosity that all people feel toward each other.

Although fiction may create a story from true events and facts, the writer needs only scraps of them—a thread of conversation, a flash of action, a glimpse of a face, an isolated happening—and the rest he invents. In other words, he puts into a factual account all the imagined feelings and emotions that make it seem more a rounded-out portion of life.

For instance, a traffic accident takes place. The non-fiction writer—the newspaperman—reports the time, the place, the way the accident occurred, the people involved, what the people said, what the police did, how the crowd reacted. The fiction writer, however, will tell what these people *felt*. He's free to change the time, the place or the nature of the accident—to interpret the actions of the people, to speculate and philosophize, even to make the people totally different in name or in walk of life. Then through the writer's senses, the reader shares the emotions and sensations of the accident.

Fiction writing is one of our most valuable crafts because it puts thoughts and feelings into the human record. On its light side it entertains, relaxes and offers escape from the problems of daily life. On its profound side it reforms, uplifts and enlightens. A story, by showing the inner life of some person with whom the reader identifies himself, may increase the reader's understanding of himself and his own life.

For instance, we don't know what ancient man was really like. We have found physical signs of his existence, yet we can only guess about his problems, feelings, hopes and desires. But when the future man of this planet reads the fiction of our times, he will know what we laughed and cried about, what made us hate and love, kill and nurture, what we dreamed about, what passed through our minds in our memorable moments of danger, despair or joy.

Today, the influence of any widely read piece of fiction can hardly be overestimated. If it's cheap or vulgar, our lives are poorer for the shoddy ideals it puts into circulation. But if it's conceived in honesty and executed with integrity, if it brings to its reader a wider comprehension of the world in which he lives, then we are all indebted to it.

You must learn about people

Since fiction must affect the reader's emotions, the fiction writer must learn to use the materials of life which produce *feeling*. This in turn means you must learn about people—about the limitless subject of human nature that will be the chief foundation for your stories.

If people's feelings and the way they act upon them are to

direct the course of stories, you must learn how to get under the skin of your fellow man. You must be able to feel *for* him and *with* him, and yet at the same time stand off as a spectator and examine him in his own scene, time and place.

Faith Baldwin puts it this way:

All people the world around share life; it is from this material alone that you can write. There is no other. Even the wildest flights of science fiction must employ people. No one has evidence yet of what space people look like, how they dress, what they eat, what their beliefs, procedures and ethics are, so this has to be drawn from the imagination. Therefore science fiction characters, however strange their attitudes and appearances, are nevertheless based upon the people walking around upon this planet.

No matter what your subject, the same holds true: your source is life itself. I do not care what devices you use to make your characters speak and move, nor what setting they are posed against—your story may be set thousands of years ago or thousands hence; the scenery and the costuming is of little moment. What matters is that your characters behave like people.

Young writers often forget this; some are interested only in their plots, and their characters are jerked along by the not quite invisible strings of the marionette. Some writers are too concerned with propounding a theory, mounting a soap box, or putting into fictional form a psychological truth. In the mock-up there may be similarity, but it isn't the real thing.

The young have not yet shared the experiences of the old, but they will. No man can escape from living while he lives. Everyone on this earth has basic needs; each in his own way rejoices and suffers. All are born and all die. People experiencing similar events react in various ways. Some suffer physically more than others because of a difference in their tolerance to pain; some grieve more profoundly, others can let themselves go fully into happiness. It is the writer's job to build characters, give them common experiences and then see to it that they react to these as the writer believes they would—consistently inconsistent, as a rule.

Even what we call light, popular stories can have, if the writer so wills, the breath of life in them. What's wrong with young love? Nothing, unless it doesn't live for the reader upon the printed page, reminding him of his young love or sending him seeking for it.

The world about us teems with life: it is in the slum, the hospital, the prison; it is in the brownstone, the cottage, the penthouse, the country estate; it is always vocal in tears and prayers, in gentle words and harsh, in self-pity, or in compassion for others.

I don't care what you dig out of yourself or how. I care only that when you have managed to put it down on paper, it is alive, however raw, however imperfect. Those of us who have been in this profession for a long time usually learned the hard way. Only the very few have achieved success overnight. But all of us who have learned know that to create means to make something live.

Life is all learning. All you learn and feel can be used; all impulses of compassion and understanding; all the ability to identify yourself with your characters, no matter how different they are from yourself. Walk in their shoes awhile, *then* write about them.

The creative gift is given you so that you may learn to create. Dig into your experience and your imagination, employ your observation, look for your people, and then bring them back *alive*.

Quite often a fiction writer feels set apart from other people by the qualities so essential to his craft. He's set apart by his watchfulness: almost every action and event takes on special significance. The most trivial occurrence in your daily life may supply you with ideas for stories. From day to day you won't always know what reward you are going to reap from your experiences. You may be too busy, too worried or having too much fun to notice and record your feelings. But on some later day all these experiences, lodged in your mind and emotions, will provide you with many intriguing ideas for stories.

Perhaps it's true that a fiction writer never takes a holiday. Somerset Maugham once said plaintively: "Oh, to look at a sunset and not have to describe it!" Well, you may not be compelled to describe every sunset, but whatever you do decide to write about, you should experience it as intimately as possible. And you should try to *understand* that experience—if not at the moment, then in retrospect.

Because of this close involvement with life, much of a fiction writer's work is autobiographical to some degree. Since most of his material comes from feelings and experiences that he understands, he naturally puts himself into his characters and situations.

But remember that only your intimate understanding of them brings your characters and situations to life—not the amount of *yourself* that you inject into them. You must let your characters move and talk, think and feel as *they* would, not as *you* would. Make them individuals. Keep them individuals.

Also, because human nature is so full of inconsistencies, a character is often more believable when composed from several characters. You may use the face of one, the physical mannerisms of another, the personality of a third, the problems of still another. Here again is a major clue to your craft—you rearrange fact, truth and reality to make your story more understandable and more plausible than the fact, truth or reality itself.

There's no denying the work and tenacity demanded of the fiction writer. But there is no fuller way to live or any more satisfying career to enjoy when the results are successful. And, as long as your senses respond to life, there's no time limit to your production. You're never too old to write—as long as you can think and feel and imagine.

But an even greater joy lies in the fact that your work will never reach an end or become totally explored. Just as no two people are alike, so are no two stories: each is a new undertaking, presenting new problems for new solutions. As you go along, your growth will be reflected in your writing, creating in you an ever-increasing power of expression.

Lastly, as you proceed to learn your craft, remember that successful writers are people of substance and character. They possess the fortitude to work steadily, and to work alone. They make a major contribution to the world they live in by bringing pleasure, inspiration and enlightenment to countless other people. So—learn your craft well. We will teach you ways to express your thoughts and ideas clearly and vividly, but what you ultimately achieve in the imaginative realm of fiction depends on how earnestly you apply yourself to your work.

One definition of good writing

There are probably as many definitions of good writing as there are examples of good writing, but all the definitions add up to much the same general principle. To me, writing is good writing if it stirs my emotions, if it satisfies an intellectual need and, most important, if it holds my interest from the first page to the last. This general definition covers everything. But it is obviously easier to define good writing than to achieve good writing.—Mignon Eberhart

Lesson two

Fiction writing
course

Who is
your
reader?

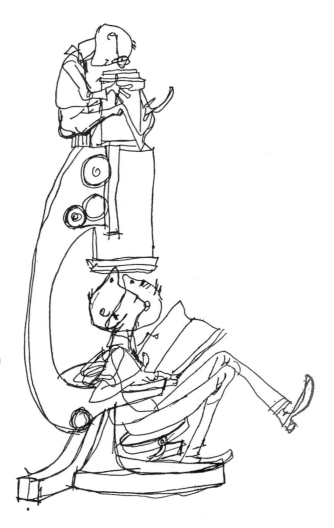

Who is your reader? What does he like? Where is he found? Already you know that he desires to be entertained or thrilled, to be made to laugh or cry, to feel anger or sympathy. You know that he wants to believe in your stories, to identify himself with your characters, to be taken out of himself while he shares the experience you create. But there's more to know about him.

The main fact about your reader is this: he is not you in reverse or you on the other side of the fence. He is someone quite different. He doesn't necessarily share your tastes and beliefs; he's probably had another kind of upbringing; his whole way of life may be quite opposite to yours. Hence you should never assume he knows what you mean unless you state it clearly, or that he can read between the lines of what you write.

You must study your reader and learn his fears, hopes, dreams, ambitions, what he admires and what he scorns, what he will accept and what he won't. Only by knowing all this can you attract his attention, hold his interest and make him feel what you want him to feel.

But you ask: Just how do I go about all this? In what way can I learn about people whom I will never meet personally? Well, we'll suggest a number of specific ways to you later in this Lesson, but first, let's consider some generalities.

Most people are grieved when a loved one dies. Most people feel fear if their life is threatened. Most people want to be loved, and to love. Most people become angry if unfairly attacked. These are emotions common to all of us. And there are also needs that most of us have, such as food, shelter and clothing, and the means to achieve them, through trade or work. With an understanding of such shared feelings you can be sure of finding a response in your reader.

Mignon Eberhart makes these points:

There is primarily one objective in fiction writing and that is—first and foremost—to catch the reader's attention and entertain him to the point of holding that attention. This is the means by which noble and lofty goals of fiction writing are reached. Thackeray moralized at great length, yes, but he told a story first. I doubt very much if anyone would have read Dickens' lambasting of social evils had he not been interested, for example, in how Mr. Micawber got into debtors' prison and how he would get out of it. Child labor was a monstrous thing and Dickens opened many eyes to its monstrosity—but those eyes were first caught and held by David Copperfield's appeal and adventures.

A fiction writer may hope to move the reader emotionally; he may hope to clarify some truth and make it stand out in blazing and memorable words; he may succeed in infecting the reader with his own ideals. But he does all this through the medium of a story. He is not writing a sermon. He is not writing a treatise. He is first and foremost writing a story as best he can. The sermon may come, but it is in a sense a side line to the story; the reader may be exalted, his eyes may be opened to some truth which affects his personal life in an important way, but these effects are achieved through the story.

A writer is frequently fired with a zeal to enlighten, to uplift, to show man's courage in the face of disaster or his loyalty to good in the face of temptation to evil. But he does this through the medium of a story. His writer's instincts tell him that his work will not be read unless it is, first, a story which captures and holds the reader's attention.

What characteristics do people share about reading in general? Today, with so many competing entertainments and so many demands on everyone's time, most readers are in a hurry. They're busy: they have little leisure. That's why modern stories start off with a sharp and arresting situation, why they avoid the slow and rambling style of past times.

Your reader is not only in a hurry these days: he is also better informed and less easily pleased or surprised. He's heard many more stories, is familiar with many more situations and plots, than the reader of past generations. He is, in fact, not easily won. That is why you must overcome his resistance and capture his interest quickly. Max Shulman adds:

What you want to do to your reader also depends, of course, on the kind of story you are writing. If you are writing *Little Nell* you want to make your reader cry. If you are writing *Auntie Mame* you want to make him laugh. When you can make your reader both laugh and cry, you are batting in the big leagues along with Shakespeare and Dickens.

Your reader's way of life

What else should you know about your reader? It's important to think of his way of life—the morals, manners, customs and outlooks he shares with many like himself. For instance, simple, hard-working people immersed in family life are quite different from a sophisticated group living on a luxury level.

What might be a hero to one group might be a bore to the other. What might seem wisdom to one group might seem "corn" to another. What might be a new thought to one group might be a cliché to the other. Hence you should always think about the cultural or educational level of your readers.

Now that you know you need this wealth of information

about your reader, how do you go about acquiring it—what are the specific methods we mentioned earlier?

The main method is to find out what publications your reader likes to read and what kinds of stories he's drawn to. You have many helpful guides for this research. Study the best-seller lists to see which novels are being read by the most people. Ask your local librarian which books are being taken out the most. Ask your local bookshop about leading items in the paperback field and in the rental library. Look at some of the popular magazines and see how they reflect reader tastes both in story material and in advertisements—magazines like *Good Housekeeping, Adventure* and *The Saturday Evening Post.*

Even the titles of stories in these publications reveal a good deal about reader interests. For instance, in *Cosmopolitan* a story title, "Mother of the Bride," tells you this magazine's readers like feminine subjects, with domestic complications and romance, while an *Adventure* title, "The Big Gun From Texas," tells you that its readers prefer action, danger and violence. A title in *The Saturday Evening Post,* "The Stranger's Family," indicates that the magazine is not exclusively for either men or women but appeals to both.

You'll know more about your reader when you find out whether he is part of a large or a small audience. If part of a large one, his tastes are wide and varied. If part of a small one, his tastes are special and he's looking for a particular kind of story. For instance:

One reader may never read anything but Westerns. You know, then, that he's interested in cowboys, in adventure, in a story packed with drama. You ask yourself how many people read Westerns, and then you know that this is a special yet a large audience. You wouldn't expect this reader to choose a story about two old ladies living quietly in a boardinghouse.

By the same reasoning, this reader's wife may like only stories of love and romance. Again, you'll know she is part of a large audience and a special one. You wouldn't expect her to enjoy a tale of rugged adventure involving daring and skill.

The above observations show why you should never try to fool your reader or take him up a blind alley, or—once you have his interest—let him down with an unsatisfactory solution. For he's not standing off and watching the character in your story as you are. He feels for the character. He lives with the character. He *is* the character.

"I think the reason people like my stories," says Faith Baldwin, "is that I like people. There's also something we call 'reader identification.' It means that when you are reading a story you can identify yourself with a person or persons in it."

If a tired, hard-working girl, for instance, is reading a light popular story about some other girl who has a million dollars, she identifies herself with the heroine because of wishful thinking. If the heroine is also a hard-working, tired girl, she can identify herself with her; if this character has sudden good fortune, the reader can think, "This could happen to me, too."

If, in a book, there is a problem or situation the reader has experienced, he or she thinks: I didn't solve it that way, or I didn't behave that way, or that's exactly the way I solved the problem or behaved in the situation, or, if I were in that situation, what would I do?

Who is your reader? That's the question you must always ask yourself before starting a story. When you've answered it as fully as possible, then you'll be better prepared to cope with any problems that your stories present.

The writer can never let down

The difference between learning to write and being a writer is guts, stamina, discipline, endurance, dedication, the ability to absorb punishment, and working at it twenty-four hours a day, always conscious of it, always having it going on inside no matter what is happening outside, when you're awake and when you're asleep, because it keeps going on and often you wake up with a scene, a character, a solution for a plot tangle or a way to shorten your telling that you didn't have when you closed your eyes.—Adela Rogers St. Johns

The search for the right word

Whatever one wishes to say, there is one noun only by which to express it, one verb only to give it life, one adjective only which will describe it. One must search until one has discovered them, this noun, this verb, this adjective, and never rest content with approximations, never resort to trickery, however happy, or to vulgarisms, in order to dodge the difficulty.—Guy de Maupassant

Lesson three

Fiction writing
course

Where
do you
get ideas?

Perhaps the question most often asked the fiction writer is:
"Where do you get your ideas?"

If the writer answers simply: "Ideas come from my imagination—from the world all around me," the non-writer is only
partly satisfied. Why? Because the writer hasn't told him *exactly*
how he uses his imagination, what he had to do to develop it,

and how he finds stories in life around him. Actually, this knowledge of his craft is something an author cannot communicate, for it's the result of his own understanding, study and practice.

Let's begin, then, by examining the chief source of ideas—imagination. What is imagination? The dictionary says:

The mental consideration of actions or events not yet in existence. The faculty of the mind by which we conceive the absent as if it were present. The power which the mind has of forming concepts beyond those derived from external objects.

You may see a man sitting at a desk, but in your mind's eye you can pick him up and toss him out the office window—you can put him on a throne and crown him king—you can fire him from his job or give him a promotion—you can see him becoming very fat or very thin—you can picture him sprouting wings and flying off. You can even see him creeping up on a victim with a knife in his hand or driving a chariot in ancient Rome! The only fact about him you have used is that he is a man—and there's nothing you can't do with this man in your imagination.

Just how is imagination brought to this point of productivity? There are many ways and they vary with each person, *but the best way to develop imagination is through observation.* Through our eyes we receive our keenest impressions of the world we live in. Our eyes show us life in action, show us what nature and people are like. Observation transforms our feelings from mere sensations into concrete forms. But we observe with our ears, too, and with touch, taste and smell. Therefore the fiction writer must deliberately observe as much (and as fully) as he can, with all his senses.

Look around you as you have never looked before—observe the colors of nature, the feel and look of weather, the shapes and textures of clothing, the colors of eyes, the tones of skin, the glints of hair, the fall of light on water. Watch people's gestures, mannerisms, facial expressions. Listen to voices, mark the differences of pitch, the varieties of emotions they convey. Note the way people walk (no two the same), the way they enter or leave a room, the way in which they hurry or dawdle.

Mignon Eberhart says:

The writer soon learns to observe everything that goes on around him and to use his observations as the threads of the tapestry which he weaves when he weaves a story. How he uses them, how he weaves these colors into the tapestry, how he designs its central theme, is a fiction process. For example, writers rarely use a real-life character in a story because the real-life character may not fit the design of the story—and the story comes first. But he does use a sort of composite character, one he knows well and one the reader too will probably recognize as being *like* someone he has known.

Somerset Maugham wrote: "No author can create a character out of nothing. He must have a model to give him a starting point; but then his imagination goes to work. He builds him up, adding a trait here, a trait there, which the model does not possess, and when he has finished with him the complete character he presents to the reader has little in him of the person who had offered the first suggestion. It is only thus that a novelist can give his characters the intensity, the reality which make them not only plausible but convincing."

A story takes on its own life. It is literally a creation. Therefore the characters in the story live within the story and they strike the reader as being real *only* as he sees them within their own frame.

There have been many times when some particular experience provided a writer with firsthand and dramatic material, as, say, a story with a background of war, written by a soldier. But there is material for dramatic and significant stories all around you. The events of everybody's everyday life are important; the writer sees and hears these events and then adds the color of his imagination.

Charlotte Brontë lived the quietest of lives in a country parsonage but she observed and reflected and added the richness of her imagination to the tapestry she designed and wove, with the result that to this day none of her glowing colors has faded. In short, there is writing material everywhere. But the writer selects designs and then weaves his own story.

A Chinese philosopher once said, "Time is a stream in which you dip but lightly." This applies directly to writing material; there is no end to it. Even Balzac, stunningly prolific in his writing, never ran out of writing material. His imagination seized upon the smallest incident, the slightest turn of character, and then gave it life and color and drama until it became a brilliantly revealing story of people and their struggles, their failures or their triumphs.

Take nothing for granted

Your imagination works when you daydream, speculate idly about people, predict future events, make decisions, hear gossip or tales of woe. But now, as a writer, you should use it all the time, until it provides all the "ideas" you will ever need.

Try to change your habit of overlooking the familiar and the seemingly uninteresting. Take nothing for granted. Never grow too old to wonder. A child is not afraid to ask, to investigate, to explore. He holds an egg in his hand and feels its shape with concentrated attention. He touches a woman's fur coat with delight, discovering it is gloriously soft. He observes that it feels like his dog or cat, and the fur seems to be a living pet.

A child examines shells on the beach, noting that they hold the warmth of the sun or the chill of the weather, or that they give forth a sound of the sea when held to his ear. He looks into people's faces and studies them with rapt absorption. What does he observe? You can be sure it's something genuine, uncolored by stale generalizations. As with a child, your powers of observation can contribute invaluable material to invigorate and strengthen your imagination.

There are other ways of limbering up your imagination and giving it daily stimulation. *Reading is a most important one.* The imaginative works of other writers revive your own memories and set off sparks of thought known as "inspiration." And don't worry who those writers are or where you find their stories. Your imagination is unique, and must be nourished in its own unique way.

Reading provides information that might otherwise remain unknown and unknowable to you. It not only draws the material of life together for your observation but illustrates and explains it as well. Experiences you might never have undergone are brought close through reading about them; strange facts inspire you to flights of fancy and wonder; the inner struggles of other people become real and fascinating.

No wonder, then, that we urge you to read as much as possible. No matter how much we tell you about the principles, techniques and elements of your craft, you must turn to reading as the artist turns to the museum and gallery. Let the arrangements of words and ideas, the style of prose, the full effect of a completed piece of writing capture your mind, just as a painting captures the visual senses of the artist.

Exactly what should you read? The classics or a chosen list of authors? There are no official lists. There's only one guide, and that is to read what intrigues and entertains and stimulates *you* the most. For instance, if you feel drawn to books written out of pure speculation and fancy, read the authors skilled in these fields. Typical of such works, old and new, are:

20,000 Leagues Under the Sea by Jules Verne
Brave New World by Aldous Huxley
The Time Machine by H. G. Wells
Lost Horizon by James Hilton
On the Beach by Nevil Shute
1984 by George Orwell

If, on the other hand, you like the writing of people who based their work on observation or experience, who found that biographical material offered them the best themes, you would enjoy such volumes as these:

David Copperfield by Charles Dickens
God's Little Acre by Erskine Caldwell
A Tree Grows in Brooklyn by Betty Smith
The Old Man and the Sea by Ernest Hemingway

In the field of the short story, excellent collections are available in most libraries and bookshops. Here are typical anthologies:

The Best American Short Stories (annual)
Prize Stories: The O. Henry Awards (annual)
Saturday Evening Post Stories (annual)
Tellers of Tales, edited by Somerset Maugham
Ten Modern Masters, edited by Robert Gorham Davis

Varied reading like this leaves you free to choose stories that excite your curiosity, spark your imagination and make you feel creative—an old fairy tale of your childhood, a book of light verse, a prize-winning biography, a short story in a magazine, a carefully documented history, an ancient classic or a modern best-seller.

What you get from reading

Find your reading wherever you can—at home, at the library, on the bookshelves of friends, in a secondhand bookstore—but keep at it and make notes. Written stories are far more valuable to you than stories acted or spoken out. They train your eyes for the look of words on paper, their patterns and rhythms, the timing of sentences, the pace of action. They familiarize you with a writer's use of language, his means of moving persons about, of introducing and characterizing them, of making word bridges between their experiences, of marking the passage of time. They enrich and enlarge your vocabulary, give you ease with grammar, and emphasize the sense of continuity in a story's progress.

And always when you read, remember that during the time you're reading, you are in the reader's shoes as well as the writer's. While being a reader yourself you learn best what affects a reader's emotions, what stirs his sympathy, what arouses his feeling of identification, what interests him, what bores him, what keeps him reading.

Faith Baldwin elaborates on this point:

Ideas don't come entirely from other people's stories. Sometimes they come from a news report. I take a dim view of a newspaper story when tricked up to seem like fiction, though many writers have done this successfully by creating other motives and characters. But if he has a retentive memory, your reader will remember that this exact situation took place, say, in Timbuktu ten years ago and was on the front page. Newspaper stories of actual events, however, can provide you a jumping-off place.

Or suppose you see an old man sitting on a park bench in the sun, feeding pigeons, and another old man sitting beside him—they are real people. But where did they come from? What are they thinking? What was their past? Have they a future? How do they differ?

A girl at a cocktail party, a woman at a matinée, a child crying on his way home from school . . . these are *people*. You see them. And from them and everyone around you, you draw your fictional characters. In order to do this you use what you know about people, what you think and have learned, and your imagination.

In addition to reading for ideas, go to police courts and listen to trials; watch shoppers, or people standing in lines at movies or restaurants; observe men at work on a building, children playing, the faces that whisk by you on a train or bus. Wherever you are, whatever you do, observe all you can, and let your imagination roam free. Don't rein it in because it seems improbable or foolish. For instance:

You see a man and a woman sitting in grim silence in a restaurant. Observe their faces, their mannerisms, the way they're dressed, the way they look at each other, take a guess at their ages. Then ask yourself: Why are they grim? Are they deeply unhappy? Have they quarreled? Do they bore each other? Have they received a shock? Some sudden family grief?

Try one of these explanations further. Imagine them at home. Perhaps they've had to save and scrimp to come to a restaurant, and it is the food that interests them tonight. No—they don't eat with enjoyment. Then perhaps their young daughter has just eloped—and they can hardly touch their food. They've come out to eat because everything at home reminds them too much of their hopes for her, now blasted.

Under the table the man's hand reaches out for the woman's, but she pulls back. It is his fault for not keeping a firmer hold on his child, for losing the child's respect. The woman is tired of his attempts to apologize. But it's too late now—the daughter is gone . . . and so on.

Keeping your imagination alive

You might want to take this situation still further. Perhaps it reminds you of one you have known or observed. What do you remember about it? What were some of the complications and emotions involved? Can you remember any of the later events? Was the eloping couple happy, or did they come to grief? Maybe you've read a newspaper story based on an elopement of this kind. Perhaps, by weaving all these observations together, you have a story!

This random exercise is the kind that keeps your imagination on the move, making it stronger and more active all the time. Create your own exercises and keep at them, so that when someone asks, "Where do you get your ideas?" you can answer truthfully: "Ideas come from my imagination—from the world all around me."

Bergen Evans says:

You find most to say on subjects of which you have personal experience—a change in your fortunes, a new idea which has altered your outlook on life, an event or chain of events which has affected your character. Yet your experiences are arches through which you can glimpse other possible experiences, and it is not merely permissible but desirable that you let your curiosity carry you into the unknown, that you sometimes let it control your choice of subject. It is not absolutely necessary to be a sailor to write convincingly about the sea—as Samuel Taylor Coleridge and Robert Louis Stevenson have shown us.

Keeping track of your ideas

Now that you know about imagination and how to get it working, how do you keep track of all this material before it escapes your memory? This brings us to one of the writer's most reliable sources of supply—the notebook. Again, Bergen Evans makes some good points:

As a writer, you *must* carry a small notebook with you at *all* times. Nothing is more perishable than actuality. An absurdity that delights us is spoiled, somehow, when we try to recollect it an hour later. The exact wording or intonation—which is everything—has faded and the next-best-thing won't do at all. You see something ludicrous or amazing or frightening or delightful—you must set down at once *what it is* that made it so.

Ideas, too, as well as observations, come unexpectedly and must be captured at once. Thomas Hardy said that one evening after sundown he was pruning a tree when an idea for a novel flooded his mind. He saw the whole thing—plot, action, characters, incident. Even large fragments of dialogue poured into his mind. He *knew* that he ought to stop work at once and go directly into the house and write it all down. But he was sure that so vivid and complete a thing couldn't fade in the remaining half-hour until dark and he wanted to finish the job he was doing.

When he went in, half an hour later, it was all gone—faded like the sunset, utterly lost. Every writer, I think, has had a similar experience, perhaps not so vivid but vivid enough to make him regret that he didn't set it down while it was fresh in his mind.

The writer ought to read the notebooks of other writers to see how the germs of stories are caught and preserved, how a trifle often grows into a significant scene or whole story. For example, he ought to read Chekhov's *Notebook* and Samuel Butler's.

Faith Baldwin continues on the same theme:

Now and again, when I have finished a day's work, a thought for tomorrow's work comes to me and I write it down. I sometimes write down titles and skeleton ideas. I suggest that students do this, too—a little notebook suffices. What do you put into it?

You put into it the scrap of conversation you overheard on the bus which left you dangling . . . why was the woman berating the older woman? . . . who was Joe? . . . what did she mean by the hundred dollars? . . . had she lent, given it or asked for it? . . . why were the two men quarreling there in the restaurant? . . . what about?

Or you see a face so intriguing you think about it. Describe it in the notebook. What was a girl with that face, that expression, doing walking by herself on a spring day in the Zoo?

Frederic Birmingham, in *The Writer's Craft,* tells how one woman novelist uses her notes:

I know a young author, Peggy Mann, who is particularly successful at restoring the moods and feelings of her readers. She has written fiction for all of the big magazines and her first novel ran through its first printing in a week. Her dialogue and her scenes are almost photographic in the "rightness" of accent and shape. And she has a most interesting technique of keeping the world in her handbag, as it were, after taking a squint or a squeeze at it. Here is what she says:

Scene: A fiction writer sits in a smoky bistro on the Left Bank of Paris and—wishing to capture the café for possible use in a future novel—he takes out a stub of a drawing pencil and scrawls several sentences on a corner of the grease-spattered paper tablecloth. His tablemates look on in full approval. The Creative Soul is showing.

Yet, let that same novelist take from his pocket a small alphabetized spiral notebook, let him turn to the letter "C" for "café," and make his description-entry in legible longhand with a sharpened pencil, and his café compatriots are likely to regard him as something of an ass.

But why? It is accepted, even expected, that the article writer should surround himself with card files, manila folders, filing cabinets. Why should the fiction writer not be entitled to the same techniques, the same tools of the trade?

I feel quite strongly about the matter because it was due to 31 spiraled and indexed notebooks that I was able to go ahead on my first novel, *A Room in Paris.* Before I left for Europe I stopped in the stationers and bought the above-mentioned notebooks, plus a supply of 10-cent pencil sharpeners. Then, during a year of Left Bank living, I went about always with a notebook in my purse or in the pocket of my dungarees.

If I happened to be standing by the Seine in the evening, and wanted to write a description of lamplights drowning in the water, out came a notebook and in went the entry under the letter "S." If I was sitting in the Café Flore on a rainy winter's morning, I might turn to the letter "F" in my notebook, and in would go a brief description of the Flore as I looked around.

I must admit that I felt rather a fool taking these notes in so mundane and orderly a fashion. And I certainly garnered a number of supercilious stares and smiles while doing so. Yet when, some six years later, the editor of Doubleday called me in and asked me to do a novel based on my Paris short stories, I think that I would never have dared attempt the job had I been forced to rely for my Left Bank color upon a scattered collection of illegible descriptions scrawled on match covers, the margins of menus, and the backs of old envelopes. But with a suitcase full of well-filled, well-organized spiral notebooks, I was able to say, "I'll try."

In fact, when I looked through my notes I knew that not only could I write the book, but that I must. For the notebooks carried me back to that special postwar period on the Left Bank, and my characters came along with me.

Then I bought another notebook! It became my master index. I labeled each of my 31 small spirals with a number, indexed every description in all of them. And I began to write.

If I had not had my well-ordered notes, I would have struck something of a block every time any of my characters entered a bistro, strolled down a Left Bank street, went to a life class, walked to the top of Notre Dame, or down narrow stone steps to a crowded *caveau.*

Length is of no account

In preserving your thoughts in a notebook, be careful to write enough so that when you go back to your jottings, you will recall what you had in mind. Give yourself sufficient clues to recapture at least your point of entry and, most important of all, the *feeling* you had at the time.

Here are a few headings and categories you can use for your classifications. And to make them more helpful you can list these subheads:

Situations: Romantic—Tragic—Dramatic—Amusing— Strange—True—Frightening.

Problems: Physical Descriptions—Interesting Characters.

Places: Physical Descriptions—Atmosphere—Locations.

Complications: Accidents—Emergencies—Predicaments— Obstacles.

Nature: Seasons—Weather—Vegetation.

Many writers build their stories around *Themes*—that is, around general truths about life or human nature. So if you have a philosophy you want others to share or a moral you would care to elaborate on, then make a list under the heading *Themes.* A phrase like "People are wonderful when you arouse their sympathy" could serve as a worth-while story foundation. So could phrases like: "The sacrifice of parents for their children seldom pays"; "Discipline makes a person happier than indulgence"; "A true giver doesn't seek reward"; or "Strangers are banded together by common danger."

Many college-bred aspiring writers I know are looking for a breakthrough into print. They can write—so they believe—but no one appreciates their efforts. No one gets the message—especially editors, that is, if they are bold enough to send their pieces out. Often afraid to think and read and write alone, they gravitate toward one another, shake Beethovian fists at destiny, sneer, snarl, poke fun at "hacks" —in short, do everything but plunk themselves behind a typewriter to write and learn, and rewrite and learn some more. And in between, to be rejected and rejected. They prefer to ramble on the sad state of current literature and how they managed to wrangle B's and A's in English from Professor So and So. They harangue each other on the virtues of *Harper's,* the *Atlantic* and the *Saturday Review* and blithely announce plans to write for these publications. But secretly, they are afraid. For these magazines have rejection slips, too.

They rarely do anything but talk and yammer. The *Post?* The *Reader's Digest?* Crass commercialism, they say. The newspapers? Rank journalism. The pulps? Beneath comment. Television? Philistinism. American movies? Juvenilism (only foreign movies are good). Trade journals? Nothing but tripe and unadulterated materialism.

Let us hope these literature-starved persons find enough literary pablum in letters from sweethearts to make life somewhat tolerable. —Al Amenta in *The Writer*

In addition to definable categories, there are many vague but workable forms of reference, such as *Turns of Phrase—Figures of Speech—Witty Observations—Items of Information—Experiences and Adventures—Incidents.* Since these cover large and small areas, your observations may take a few moments or considerably more to jot down, according to their importance.

Then there are notes that are more like sketches—such as *Scenes*—in which you depict a chance encounter, a wedding, a quarrel, a parade, a dance. You might describe various feelings you've experienced, or watched others experience, under *Emo-*

tions. Memories could give you an abundant supply of future material. Such listings as *War—Sea—Animals—Children—Fantasy—Space,* may help you to separate story possibilities.

Also, in writing, there's no substitute for authentic details noted on the spot. For this, you might have a heading *Details*. A visit to a circus, a fair, a theater, an auction sale, a night club, will ring true if you set down all you see, hear and feel at the moment.

Let's take the night club as an example. You're sitting at a table with a companion, looking over the place. While each writer in your position would have different reactions and find different things to jot down, your observations might be entered this way:

Setting: Night club called "Lenny's." Small, square room with low ceiling. Burlap trim on walls doesn't hide need for paint and repair work. No dancing. Candles in bottles, tablecloths soiled, chinaware chipped. Waiters tired, indifferent, uniforms dirty. Musicians play frantically. Their faces sallow—or is it the light? Music raucous, too loud, but people applaud Lenny's clarinet solos. Men guests pale, sly-looking; restless fingers; women cheaply dressed, untidy, too much make-up, too much dyed hair. Other people are alone, moving around edges of room. They mill around, then leave. Why? Looking for excitement—trouble? Food is bad, drinks watered, but no one cares. Customers listen to Lenny, smile, beat time to prove they understand music. Escaping from dull and unsatisfactory lives? Dead sort of place—everyone looks dead. Think about this later.

Now, just to show how another writer might see this same scene, suppose your companion jotted down these notes:

Lenny's. Air of excitement. Lively group in candlelit atmosphere. Good jazz music. No fancy trimmings. Small, functional room. Even waiters listen to Lenny—lean and dedicated musician. He will be discovered by columnist. Has ardent following here. Nobody eats or drinks much. Young people letting off steam, enjoying sound for sound's sake. Floating group looks in. Obviously fans of Lenny's. Two men in corner look like cops. Thin, sad-looking girl sits by herself, hunched over drink. Everyone keeps looking at her. Is she Lenny's girl? Good setting for love story.

Fortunately, taking notes has a way of sharpening your powers of observation. The more you see, the more you note. But try to avoid talking with others about what you have observed. When writers talk about their ideas, they tend to dissipate them.

At least keep them to yourself until you're quite sure of them. By that time you will probably be so busy writing that you won't want to stop to talk.

No matter how you finally decide to keep your notes (and you may change your mind about this from time to time), be free and experimental in your approach. Remember, notes are nothing more or less than your private warehouse. What you keep there is to interest and stimulate you alone—to give you ideas for stories that will ultimately be your own.

The curiosity of James Joyce

In Sylvia Beach's book *Shakespeare and Company,* the story of a famous American bookshop in Paris which made literary history in the 1920's, the author describes James Joyce's limitless curiosity about the world around him and the people in it.

"He treated people invariably as his equals whether they were writers, children, waiters, princesses or charladies. What anyone had to say interested him; he told me he had never met a bore. Sometimes I would find him waiting for me at the bookshop, listening attentively to a long tale my concierge was telling him. If he arrived in a taxi he wouldn't get out until the driver had finished what he was saying."

Everything, then, was grist to James Joyce's mill. Through courtesy, consideration and intense curiosity about other people, this author accumulated an overflowing supply of writing material which gave him a world audience and assured him a permanent place as a literary explorer.

All manuscripts get a reading

One of the things everyone asks me—are the manuscripts sent to the magazines read by the "proper people"? Practically every beginning writer harbors the delusion that his manuscript isn't read. You can't make people believe that every manuscript *is* read. Only a few, comparatively speaking, reach the editor-in-chief. But each is read by someone who knows his business and who can tell after three pages, or less, if it is worth reading completely.—Faith Baldwin

Lesson four

Fiction writing
course

How to
begin
writing

Now you are close to the point in this Course where, with your understanding of fiction, you will put actual words on paper. It's an exciting thought—for although hard work lies ahead of you, the heart of your chosen craft is the *act* of writing. But before you place your first word on that blank sheet, you must set up your working environment.

What does this entail? First of all, a place—a room or part of a room; a surface on which to write—a table or desk; a chair that is comfortable; good light; manuscript and carbon paper, pencils, eraser; and a typewriter.

The typewriter should be set at the proper level for your eyes and hands, should have clean keys and be in good working order. Within easy reach should be your notebook, index cards or whatever you use for keeping track of your ideas. Equally important, your reference books should be close at hand.

The spot you choose to write in should fit your personal and individual needs. Perhaps you should experiment and see how you respond to various working surroundings. Every writer differs in his choice. But we suggest you steer a course between being too indulgent of your whims and being too stern with yourself.

For instance, if you begin fussing with views and certain positions, you're probably stalling for time. On the other hand, if you're rigidly worklike, you may set a mood too austere for your imagination. In general, most writers prefer a relaxed and uncluttered setting.

Once your place of writing is established, select the best time for your work. Some writers like to get up at dawn, have coffee and, before talking to anyone, start writing. Others work best in the late morning, or in the afternoon, before dinner or late at night.

If you have only one hour a day to write, you'll get the most out of it by sitting down and writing at the same time every day. If you do this, you'll soon find that this is the hour when you feel the strongest urge to write.

Don't surrender to whims

A writer's mind can be very perverse. He may want to write, and yet at the same time invent all kinds of excuses to keep from starting. He'll make phone calls, sharpen pencils, have another cup of coffee, think of something that must be repaired, a letter that must be written. He'll develop headaches or strange ailments; he'll decide that his windows need washing or his eyeglasses need checking. It is so easy to procrastinate, to fall asleep, to read instead of to write. Then the writer begins to envy everyone who has a job in which the discipline comes from outside himself.

At this point, many writers get the idea that they're totally ungifted, are deceiving themselves and their families, are getting away with something by sitting here while others have to scramble to the office or factory. And even when they don't torture themselves this way, they find some legitimate reason for abandoning work—at least until tomorrow.

This demon within the writer must be defeated before it takes control. Right from the start, fight to be its master, to work when you can and want to, and with the minimum amount of strain or delay. Recognize your demon for what it is and utilize some device that brings words out and starts putting them on paper. Faith Baldwin has solved the problem this way:

> I love to write but I hate to get to work. I answer phones, write letters, pull down shades, empty ash trays and, when all else fails, I work. I sit down and reread what I have written the day before. Very often I tear it up. Sometimes I revise or rewrite it. But if I have an idea, even a skeleton for a short story, I start it.
>
> It doesn't make any difference if I tear that up and begin again. I must put something down on paper. If I can achieve a thousand or a hundred words, I've made a start. I'll probably rewrite them several times, but it's a beginning.
>
> Books are different, naturally, but I try to set myself a stint of so many words a day. Sometimes I exceed this—sometimes I don't meet my own requirements. The point is: *start now*—preferably at the beginning—and *keep going*. Next working period you have something to start from even if you destroy it.

In time you'll find your own device or method, but meanwhile here are some suggestions. If they don't work for you, at least you will understand their principle, which is simply this: Write words on paper—any words that aren't complete nonsense. Get the habit of putting down words at the time you've chosen to write. What the words are doesn't matter—it's the habit that counts.

Now what might these words be? Well, you can put down whatever wanders into your thoughts. It doesn't have to be well-phrased or grammatical—no one's going to see it. You may have a repressed desire to make someone suffer, to tell him some truths, to get the better of a rival or to come off best in a contest or job. You may want to be very rich or very "good" or very powerful. Write out the way you could fulfill one or the other of these wishes. Or you might start a personal history, beginning with all the facts that you can remember about yourself.

As we said in Volume I, some writers use an amazingly simple device to get going on the typewriter. They merely put down the word "the"—then follow it with another word. Then they follow that one with another word, then another and another. And so on. Soon they have a sentence. It may be a bad sentence—it may make little or no sense. But the point is, the writer has actually started to write, has forced himself—through a mechanical and physical trick—to put words onto blank paper.

If what he writes is incoherent or meaningless, he tosses the paper away and gets on with what he originally wanted to write, because his fingers and brain are now warmed to the task. If, on the other hand, the words he forced himself to write do happen to have some meaning and order, then he can try to build these into the beginning of a piece.

Another way to get going is to tackle a regular writing exercise, such as descriptions. (You can file these away, as you can all kinds of writing, for possible use later on.) Describe some people you've met recently. Put down every detail you can remember about their physical appearance, how they walk, talk, laugh, eat—and all you can recall about their character, how they react to things, what makes them happy or miserable and how they express themselves. Put down what you like best about them, or what irritates you most.

Or think about a particular place you have visited. Describe the color of the sky, the sweep of the countryside, all you saw going on. Make it so vivid that a reader looking over your shoulder could see this place and feel its atmosphere.

Or try setting down an experience you once had, an incident you witnessed, an emotion aroused in your daily life, a show you saw on television, a book you read, a theater you visited, a conversation you overheard.

Using adjectives for practice

Another good device is to write a paragraph depicting a mood. You might take a funeral, and by using adjectives like bleak, rainy, tearful, mournful, somber, create a short scene of a very depressing nature. Then, in contrast, write about a scene that's gay, perhaps using such adjectives as bright, lively, laughing, sunny, colorful.

In the same way, try describing the aromas of a house in which a festive meal is being cooked, or the colors of a flower garden on a summer day, or the sounds of a railroad station, or the feel of various textures in a clothing store.

You can never be placed in the perilous position of writing *entirely* about what you don't know. With exceptions so few that they are negligible, all fiction deals with people; and while people may differ in their customs, their surroundings, their age and gods and history and every aspect of their minds, their basic emotions remain the same. Whether they worship beast-headed gods or manufacture atom bombs, they all get jealous, feel lonely, love or hate each other, laugh, fret, weep. Moreover, you know exactly how they feel when they do these things.

Touch universals and your characters will seem close and real to a reader in any land and time, because you're writing about human beings. And you know all about human beings. You're one yourself.
—Eloise Jarvis McGraw in *The Writer*

In each case, practice using adjectives that emphasize the mood or sense of your paragraph. You can keep these exercises for later use, and you'll find they give you facility in creating effects for your future writing.

Some writers get their work underway by choosing a passage from a book—a book that appeals to them—and carrying on the scene or description in the same way the original author might have done. This may be difficult work, but it can also be rewarding, for it forces you to get on with the task of putting words on paper. But be careful not to settle just for easy imitation: use your imagination and talent to the utmost.

Still another device is to clip items from your daily newspaper and enlarge on the routine stories they tell. For instance, an item says:

Alice White, age 17, of 12 East Lynn Street, was rescued from a capsized rowboat this morning by a fisherman who heard her cries from Basic Wharf and rowed out to investigate. The fisherman, Richard Fraser, 21, is from nearby Wennington.

You then fill in the explanation for the incident. For example, you might say:

Alice White had been fishing from the wharf when she got the idea of going out rowing. Her boy friend had warned her that the boat leaked, but then, he was always trying to curb her adventurous spirit with threats or warnings. He meant to be kind, but he angered her. Now she was determined to show him, so she started out in the boat. Soon, water began coming in faster than she could bail. Suddenly she began screaming for help . . . and so on.

Using any of these devices is simply like starting a habit, and habit, once entrenched, will lead you strongly to overcome your reluctance. *A set time, a chosen amount of words per day, generate their own demand.* You will write more and more at each sitting, until you finally achieve the standard of daily wordage that seems to be your average.

Try not to set this standard too high or too low at the beginning. Find out by trial and error your comfortable best, then try to exceed it gradually. Your main objective is to set up and maintain a regular schedule.

A helpful hint from Hemingway

In a candid interview about writing, Ernest Hemingway remarked that "when I'm working on a book or story, I write every morning as soon after first light as possible. There's no one to disturb you and it's cool or cold and you come to your work and warm as you write. You read what you have written and, as you always stop when you know what's going to happen next, you go on from there."

Whether you work early in the morning is not important: each person must pick the best time for himself. But Hemingway gave an important clue to writing discipline when he said he stopped when he knew what was "going to happen next." If you, too, stop when you know what's going to happen next, chances are you will return to your typewriter next day in an eager frame of mind. Knowing what you're going to write gives you a keen sense of anticipation, a desire to get to work swiftly, and before you know it this momentum has gotten you over the hump of starting again and well on your way to finishing the work in hand.

What about inspiration? Should you depend on it to get your writing started? Mignon Eberhart answers:

Inspiration is a mysterious and ticklish word which is not easily defined. I find it far pleasanter to write when I happen to be in exactly the mood and the keys of the typewriter seem to take on a life of their own and gallop away. The trouble is that this does not always happen; as someone astutely said, "Inspiration may be late for her appointment."

A writer cannot wait for the spirit to move him; the spirit may be having a lazy spell that day. So the writer must train himself to plow ahead, follow his course, with or without that whimsical lady, inspiration.

What makes a story memorable

Stories remembered most are those in which people come alive rather than the moral or political points they make. That is why we remember Naomi and Ruth from the Bible, or the Prodigal Son. It is why, when we think of early American writing, we remember Ichabod Crane, the Yankee schoolmaster in *The Legend of Sleepy Hollow,* or the rapscallion Rip van Winkle, and the doomed brother and sister in *The Fall of the House of Usher* and consider their authors, Washington Irving and Edgar Allan Poe, our first really great short story writers.—Martha Foley in *The Best American Short Stories*

The eternal danger of inaccuracy

Even slight contradictions will destroy a story for many readers. I shall use the word "contradiction" as a general term to cover errors of fact, inconsistencies, inaccuracies in observation and research, and similar disturbances.

In his *Arch of Triumph,* Erich Remarque permits a character to see the constellation Orion in the summer sky over Paris. To a bookseller whom I knew the year the novel came out, this was an insupportable error, as Orion is not visible in the summer sky over Paris. The error prejudiced the bookseller against the whole work.—Edwin A. Peeples in *A Professional Storywriter's Handbook*

Section II

Lesson five

Fiction writing
course

The
short
story

In fiction there are four main forms for stories: the novel, novelette, short story and short-short. The novel is the longest form, the short-short the shortest. In between come the novelette and the short story.

Although there's always a margin for variance, the novel is generally from 30,000 words up, the novelette from 10,000 to

30,000, the short story from 2,000 to 10,000 and the short-short from 500 to 2,000. The longer forms will be explained in later Lessons. Here we will discuss the short story.

While there is no rigid form for the short story, no fixed writing rules, one precise definition is possible: a short story is not just a matter of length. It is a story shaped by its own special requirements and designed to achieve its own special goal.

What are these requirements? And what is this goal?

First, let's consider the requirements. Within a flexible range, they are:

1. The story must fit the chosen length completely and logically.
2. It must be based on an idea simple enough to be told clearly in this brief form.
3. It must proceed in a direct line from beginning to end, confining its characters, settings, complications, descriptions, dialogue and action to a single outcome.

Second, the goal of the short story is this: It must create one mood in its reader, must have one emotional effect. Or, to put the rule another way:

A short story, in order to satisfy the reader fully, must present a single effect derived from a single cause.

Because of these principles, writers have learned not to cover too great a passage of time in a short story. There is more opportunity for the development of character and plot if the time span is kept to a minimum. Hence, a short story can begin near its climax, cover a week more easily than a year, and a single day more easily still.

Use of the flashback

This enforced economy of time, however, leaves the writer with some explaining to do for the reader. A story that begins near the end must indicate a great deal of what went on before. This is why storytellers use a device called the *flashback*. The term means an explanation of, a return to, events and situations that have led up to the present one.

For instance, let's say a story begins with a situation in which a girl must decide between marrying a man she doesn't love and exposing her role in a shady transaction she had previously shared with him. He is waiting for her to get into a car and drive to the justice of peace, his eyes reminding her of what he will do if she backs out. The smiling parents are standing nearby, but they are clearly sorry to see her marry this particular man. She hesitates at the door of the car, her face reflecting inner conflict.

The reader now wants to know what her trouble is, how it came about, and, in order to sympathize with her and care about her fate, what sort of girl she is. So the writer, as quickly and economically as possible, flashes back to a point in her life when the trouble began. He does this by means of a verbal bridge, such as:

In the instant that Mary's hand left her mother's, she seemed to see the whole incredible nightmare of the past six months. It had all started simply, the day that Dan Bennett came into the bank, pushed a check at her under her teller's window and smiled as he asked her to lunch. . . .

The writer will cover these past events as briefly and vividly as he can, then rejoin the story at its opening point and carry it to its quickest possible resolution.

If a story will fit into the length you have selected without a flashback, and can progress directly from one point to another in a short time, then it must tell us all about character and situation as it goes along. The action must carry it forward in a straight line, each step being an outcome of the one before, moving onward with increasing suspense and finishing with a climax that has the same goal as the flashback kind of story.

This emotional impact can be created by a surprise twist—an unexpected result from the events of the story—or it can arise logically out of the story's sequence of events. And the effect can be anything you choose—amusing, tragic, ironic, uplifting or frightening.

The short story is not limited in subject matter or style, and can appeal to any kind of reader you want to reach. It demands only that whatever you write must comprise a unified, harmonious whole, must not sprawl or wander into irrelevant details or side plots, and must present at the end a compact, single impression.

Because of all these factors, great economy of language is needed in the short story. The writer can't afford a leisurely preamble or the use of words for their own sake. Adjectives must be carefully chosen, for with the right ones you can bring a character to life for the reader, sum up a situation or speed an action. Every sentence must be necessary to the story and its plot, theme, situation or character; every line of dialogue must make a definite contribution to the story's progress. It's as though you were keeping a vigilant eye on your reader's attention, knowing that to ensure its continuation you must provide him with constant intrigue, curiosity, identification, enlightenment, sympathy, surprise and feeling.

In designing this Course in Fiction Writing, we were aware of the ever-changing trends in magazine styles and audiences. In recent years the differences between the slick, the quality and the pulp story have been narrowing, so that it's increasingly difficult to be dogmatic about which type of story fits which magazine. We suggest you keep aware of trends in the fiction field by constantly reading the magazines which print the kinds of stories you're most interested in. In this way you stay abreast of editorial tastes and requirements.

Because you can't bring in new characters or changes of scene and situation to create fresh interest, the length of your story must depend on how long you can keep the reader interested in your chief character, your one situation, your one main plot, and the single emotion you want him to feel.

The pattern of the short-short

The short-short story calls for all the requirements above, as well as the same aim. The only difference is that the time element must be even briefer—a day, an hour, even a few moments. The situation must be even more simple and direct, the complications fewer, any flashback more compressed, the language reduced to bare essentials, and the outcome almost always a surprise or an unexpected twist of plot.

Because it requires precise and skillful writing, the short-short is a difficult form for the inexperienced writer. A character must be given identifying traits and mannerisms immediately, without a wasted word. Description and dialogue must create an instantaneous effect. Action must begin without delay to bring about the story's final outcome.

There is, however, much license of form in the short-short.

The story can be in the shape of a letter or it can be entirely flashback between the first paragraph and the last. It may transpire almost entirely in a character's mind. But here again, the writer must create one emotional effect in the reader. And the effect should strike hard. The story mustn't mislead or attempt to fool the reader, yet must achieve an impact on his mind.

Examples of the single effect

So far in this Lesson we've talked about the short story in broad terms. Now let's take two examples that specifically illustrate the *single effect*. The two stories are "The Lark's on the Wing" and "And the Arrow Sped." They are reprinted here just as they appeared in two well-known magazines of mass circulation.

In each story there is one main character with one main problem. There's no confusion about this, since other characters in the story merely contribute to the main character's development and support him or her in the chief role. You will likewise see that all the other elements in the stories are contributory, too, never overshadowing or detracting from the main character's problem or conflict. Dialogue, settings, the various complications that create suspense, are never irrelevant to the progress of the plot.

The main character goes from here to there, from beginning to middle to end, in a straight line. Throughout the story, the reader is held in concentration for the emotional effect of the ending. Nothing in the story diffuses his feeling or lessens his one over-all impression.

No matter how short stories are written or what their subject matter may be, this singleness of direction, this shaping of material into one main line, is essential to their structure.

We ask you to read each of these stories *twice*—once just to see what the story is about, and then again to weigh our comments in the margins. We have purposely confined these comments to what has been set forth in the contents of this Lesson. We have deliberately avoided comments on the techniques or mechanics of writing, for at this point they might distract you from the importance of fundamental elements.

Later in this Course, when these elements have been fixed in your mind, we will take up the mechanics of your craft in detail.

We will analyze stories sentence by sentence, paragraph by paragraph. Meantime, we want to make sure that you fully understand the basic points discussed in preceding Lessons.

The first story reprinted in full below is Stella Blount Hyman's "The Lark's on the Wing" from the *Ladies' Home Journal*. We have put Mary's thoughts into italics to show you how her fear and conflict are used as counterpoint to the action.

One main character—Mary Fields—is introduced.

The kitchen was full of smoke from the frying fish. Mary Fields raised a window impatiently. *I wish they hadn't insisted on having fish tonight,* she thought. *The scent'll be all in my hair.*

She turned the creek perch in the long iron skillet and wrinkled her nose in distaste. Creek fish always smelled like mud. Then, going to the window, she looked out. It had been a windy, cold day, a real March day; but now the wind had fallen, and the sun's pale gold, spread out over the western field, had that elusive look of spring.

Tomorrow'll be a pretty day, she thought, and shivered, half in desperation, half in anticipated happiness. "I can't believe I'm going to do it," she said aloud, cooling her face in the sharp air that came in through the open window. *But I am,* she went on to herself. *What have I got to be afraid of? I'm not a child. I'm forty-five years old, and papa and mamma can't forbid me. After it's over, all they can say won't make any difference.*

She turned around and pushed the skillet to the back of the stove, opened the oven door, and looked at the little corn pones browning in the big pan. The kitchen table was already set for supper. Mary looked at the familiar red-checked tablecloth and the old blue dishes they used for every day, and her heart ached. She was terrified to find that she was homesick already.

We learn her problem—that it's going to be difficult, perhaps impossible, for her to break away from her family and home.

I mustn't think about home and papa and mamma; I must think about Jim, she determined, standing in front of the stove and pressing her trembling hands together.

Now supper was ready. She dipped up the turnip greens and cut them up fine as her father liked them to be. She put the fish and the corn bread on the table, lifted the heavy agate coffeepot and poured the coffee, strong as lye. Then she opened the door and went through the cold, orderly dining room to the hall beyond. Her father and mother were in the living room on the other side of the house. They heard her coming and, like two eager old children, met her as she opened the door.

"Seems like supper's mighty late," said her father querulously. "Gettin' later every night."

"I had to fry fish. That takes time," said Mary, going before the old people and leaving the doors open behind her.

"It's soon enough for me. My appetite's poor," said Mary's

mother. She sat down at the table, sniffing the food daintily with a slight supercilious lifting of her upper lip.

Mary moved restlessly. She felt as if she might fly out the window from pure nervousness.

Her mother said, "Mary, I wish you'd boil me an egg. I can't eat this fish tonight. It'll give me heartburn."

Mary got up and dropped an egg into the kettle of boiling water. She thought, *What'll they ever do without me? How'll they ever get used to my not being here?* She returned to her seat to wait for the egg to cook.

Her father was eating the fish greedily, taking big mouthfuls and chewing noisily.

Mary warned, "Don't swallow a bone, papa. You know what happened the last time we had perch."

"Lemme alone," he said rudely. "Can't you let me enjoy my vittles?"

"Billy," admonished his wife, "I wish you wouldn't say common words like 'vittles.' Say 'food.' " She turned to Mary. "Don't you reckon my egg's done? I don't want it hard-boiled."

Mary jumped up guiltily and dipped into the kettle for the egg. "I'm sorry, mamma; it's hard," she said, offering the egg in a cup. "But you can cut it up over your greens."

Her mother shook her head obstinately. "I'll eat the fish," she said with the air of one going to the stake. "What made you forget the egg? Why didn't you stand by the stove and count?"

Mary thought, *I can't eat, and they'll suspect something's the matter.*

But the two old people were so occupied with their own food that they took no notice of Mary's untouched plate. They finished, and Mary set about scraping plates and washing the dishes. When she went into the living room her mother sat near the lamp knitting, and her father was fiddling with the radio dial.

Her mother said, "Hold this yarn for me, Mary."

Mary obediently held out her hands for the wool and sat looking at the older woman as she wound off the stuff in a ball. *She's not really cross and hard to please,* Mary thought, fixing her gaze on the thin crumpled face opposite. *She's spoiled, as Jim says, and so is papa.* She watched the alert little figure bending slightly from side to side with the exigencies of the winding. *She's only seventy and not a frail old lady; she's strong,* decided Mary. *But she's so particular. I don't know what she'll do when she knows I've hired a colored woman to come every day to help her after I'm gone.* Mary sighed deeply.

Her mother looked up inquiringly. "You tired?" she asked. "How was school today?"

Mary compressed her lips to still their trembling. The small solic-

Although Mary's parents are sharply drawn, they remain in a supporting role to her major one.

itous note in her mother's voice pierced her heart. She said, "No, I'm not tired, but I do get fed up with teaching." *I'll try to prepare her,* she thought.

"Fed up! You ought to be glad you got a job at your age," her mother replied with asperity. "You ain't forgot you're going on fifty, have you?"

Mary flushed. "No," she said faintly, "I haven't forgotten my age —nor the fact that life is passing me by."

The old lady looked at her shrewdly. "I guess you wish you'd married some no-'count man," she said.

Mary's lips quivered, but not from hurt. She was on the very edge of confessing to her mother what she was planning to do.

Then the old lady said surprisingly, "Ain't that new principal at your school about your age?"

Mary's heart fluttered with apprehension. She hadn't the courage to tell, after all. Could her mother suspect something? Could she have heard anything? Mary replied carefully, "I imagine Mr. Matthews is approaching fifty."

"Widower, ain't he?" she persisted.

Mary rested her elbows on the arms of the chair. Her hands were beginning to flutter. She said, "Yes, his wife lived only a year."

"Well, he won't stay single much longer now he's in the school-teaching business. Some little snippet'll grab him up."

Before she could bite back the words, Mary said, "I don't think he's the kind to be grabbed up by some silly girl."

"Yes, he is too," her mother said perversely. "His name's Matthews. Didn't he come from the lower part of the county? I used to know some Matthewses, and I didn't know no good of 'em."

Mary was silent. She knew it wouldn't do any good to defend Jim Matthews. He was the type that both her mother and father despised. Easygoing, bookish, satisfied with small blessings, gentle and rather slow.

The old lady went on relentlessly: "I got no use for a schoolteaching man. A fine farmer he'll make—in the schoolhouse three fourths of the time."

Mary said to herself, *I told Jim this was how it would be if I talked to papa and mamma.*

Her mother looked at her sharply. "I heard he liked that yellow-headed first-grade teacher," she said.

Mary smiled a little and replied, "Yes, I think he does."

A little flicker of relief passed over the elder woman's face, and Mary thought, *She was suspicious.* Then unaccountably she felt sad. *This time tomorrow she'll know she was right,* she thought.

Her mother wound off the last of the yarn, and Mary looked over at her father. He was sitting rather disconsolately in his chair, having been unable to get his favorite hillbilly music on the radio. The open

---

The reader isn't asked to keep track of side issues or other problems which Mary might have.

paper was in his hand, but he wasn't reading. From pure obstinacy he would not wear his glasses, and without them he could not see.

Mary said, "Want me to read the paper to you, papa?"

He held it out to her mutely. For half an hour she read the news, then she put the paper down and got up.

"You ain't going to bed a'ready?" he asked.

"Yes, sir, if you don't want me for anything," she replied, her heart sinking. There were so many things she wanted to do upstairs.

The old man searched around in one of his pockets and produced a button. "Sew this on for me," he said peremptorily.

All the dialogue is relevant and contributes to the progress of the plot.

Mary got a needle and thread and scissors and sewed the button on the frayed coat. The coat smelled of stale tobacco and faintly of the barn lot. Tears swam in Mary's eyes, and she looked yearningly at her father's slumped figure. He was a little older than her mother, a small man, wiry and hard-looking. Mary dropped her eyes to her sewing. She thought, *There's really no need for me to feel as I do. He's well and able to look after himself and after mamma, too, if she would let him.* She handed him the coat, put away the sewing materials, and paused a moment, looking at the old couple and the familiar room. The carpet with its sprawling red roses was faded to a subdued mellowness. She had done the pale yellow walls herself to correspond to the woodwork of sallow ivory. On the high mantel was the old clock with the picture of the green windmill on its front. The tarnished gilt frames on either side of the clock held the pictures of her mother's parents—the mother in a plaid hoop skirt and mittens on her folded hands, the father with high stock and staring, prominent eyes. They had run away to be married, Mary knew. Her grandmother, a young girl of seventeen, had climbed down the honeysuckle vine from the top of the porch and had gone off behind her lover on his horse. In her staid life with her parents, Mary had treasured this romance in her heart.

The old clock ticked with a measured, solemn sound. Mary's mother folded her knitting and yawned delicately behind her hand, the light glinting on her silver-rimmed spectacles and touching her thin, parted hair. Her father bent over, grunting, to untie his shoes.

"I'll do that, papa," murmured Mary, kneeling at his feet.

The old man did not thank her. He got up and stumped out without even saying good night. Mary looked after him sadly. *He doesn't even know I'm here; he takes me for granted,* she thought, *but how will he feel when I'm gone?*

She looked at her mother, who was taking her hair down and plaiting it into a thin pigtail. "Good night, mamma," she said, and her voice broke.

Her mother yawned again, "Wha'd you say?" she asked. "I don't know what makes me so sleepy. Probably won't sleep a wink when I get in the bed."

Mary climbed the steep flight of stairs that led to her room off the little landing. She opened her door, felt for the two steps that went down to her floor, and stood still in the darkness, sensing the atmosphere of the place that she had slept in since she was a little girl of six and had been moved out of her parents' room. She remembered how she had sobbed there all alone and how in the middle of the night she had crept down again in the piercing winter cold and slipped under the cover next to her father's warm back. Feeling her there, he had muttered:

"Can't get along without your ole papa, can you, daughter?"

The warm tears gushed to her eyes and rolled down her cheeks. Why should she be pulled apart between Jim Matthews and all she had ever known and loved? *I hadn't even seen him seven months ago,* she thought.

Stepping forward, she turned on the little pink-shaded lamp by her bed, then sat down in a low rocker and opened the table drawer. *I'll write the note while I'm in the notion,* she determined with a sort of reckless abandon. She took out paper and a pencil and wrote rapidly. It took only a few minutes, for she had rehearsed what she wanted to say many times in her heart. She folded the paper, put it in an envelope, and laid it on the table. Quietly, almost stealthily, she went to and fro in the low-ceiled, shadowy room, making her simple preparations for flight. From the closet she dragged a suitcase, laid it on the bed, and proceeded to pack swiftly.

Just enough for two days and nights, she thought breathlessly. *Jim and I have to be back at the school Monday morning. I'll be back to get the rest of my things—if papa and mamma will let me. Jim says he doesn't see how they can be so angry or consider themselves deserted. I'll be right down the road at his place and can come any time they need me.*

She closed the suitcase and stood petrified. Was there a sound of creaking on the stairs? She turned out the light and stood listening in the darkness. After five minutes of suffocating suspense, she turned the light on again and began to undress. She hurried with her preparations for bed and got in between the cold sheets. Stiff and unrelaxed she lay there. *I can't even say my prayers,* she thought, almost in a panic. Closing her eyes resolutely, she listened to the soft murmur of her little alarm clock. She had set it for four-thirty. After half an hour, she reached out and turned off the alarm. *I don't think they can hear it up here, but they might; and if papa gets up, I'll never get away.* She drew a deep breath, and on the end of it fell asleep.

She slept dreamlessly and awoke suddenly, knowing that a sound had aroused her. She sat up in bed half terrified. *Maybe I've overslept and papa is already up,* she thought. She turned on the light and looked at the clock. It was just four o'clock. Then eerily through

There's no digression from the main problem. Other elements of the story don't distract you from its single-track development but merely add to its complication.

the darkness she heard the sound that had awakened her—the queru-lous call of the old Rhode Island Red rooster in the chinaberry tree by the smokehouse. It was too soon to get up. Mary lay there, think-ing of Jim Matthews across the fields in the old farmhouse—"the old Wood place," it had always been called. He had appeared there last fall, and it had been noised around the neighborhood that he had bought it.

Then when school started at the big consolidated schoolhouse up the road, it was discovered that the former principal had resigned at the last minute. Calls of distress were sent out, and one day Mary went into the principal's office and found a big sprawling figure in the chair behind the desk.

"You know, I liked you straight off," he told her afterward. "A little Jane Eyre sort of creature. And from the first, I knew I needed you, Miss Mary."

Mary remembered the day she realized he meant to marry her. He had been sitting on top of one of her third-grade desks in her schoolroom. He said in his slow drawl, "That's a lonely old house I live in. It needs a woman."

She sat still at her desk, and slowly, in spite of her unbelief, a tide of pure happiness flooded her whole body. *Why, he means me!* she thought. But even then she remembered her father and mother. They would never agree to her marrying and leaving them, she knew.

You follow Mary step by step, from one point straight toward another—from beginning to middle to end.

His courting was of the most unobtrusive kind—a look, a word, a line scrawled on a piece of paper—"Come to my office for a moment after school, please, Miss Mary"—brought to her room by a student. He had never said he loved her.

Perhaps he doesn't—not in a romantic way, Mary thought, and sighed. What she felt was that she couldn't give him up, not even for duty's sake. In the end it was she who suggested running away.

"Won't they be terribly shocked?" Jim had asked, meaning her parents. "And isn't that cowardly, Miss Mary?"

"I can't help it," Mary had replied doggedly. "I'd never marry you if I had to argue with them about it first. There are so many reasons they could bring up against it. First, you are a stranger in the neighborhood. They don't know who you are. As for being a schoolteacher and a farmer, they never heard of such a thing. And it hasn't crossed their minds since I was twenty-five that I might marry. They would make me feel I was doing something wicked."

Jim shrugged in his lazy way. "Have it your own way. You know best, I suppose, but it's not cricket, do you think?"

Mary gazed wide-eyed into the darkness, turning on the lamp at intervals to look at the clock. At four-thirty, she rose cautiously and like a thief tiptoed around the room, dressing. She looked out the east window. No sign of the dawn yet, but she must hurry. Her father would be stirring as soon as light showed. What was that? A real creak on the stairs this time. Footsteps stopping at her door and her mother's low voice:

"Mary, you'll have to get up and take your papa to the doctor." She turned the doorknob. "What you got your door locked for?"

Mary hastily threw on her old bathrobe over her clothes and unlocked the door. "What's the matter with him?" she asked.

"Got a bone in his throat. Had it ever since supper, but he's so stubborn, he wouldn't say a word about it. Now it hurts so he can't stand it."

Her mother went on back downstairs, and Mary stood still in the middle of the room, her thoughts in a whirl. Jim wouldn't wait for her if she wasn't on time, she knew. He had said he wouldn't be made a fool of even for her. *He'll think I've changed my mind, and he'll be done with me,* she thought distractedly. *What on earth am I going to do?*

Then she had a daring inspiration. Purposefully, she finished her preparations and then stood a moment in front of her mirror looking at herself. The little dark figure in the blue suit and small veiled hat looked back at her.

I'm not good-looking; I never was, she decided. *I'm just a little brown woman, but Jim wants me; he needs me . . . I've done all I could for papa and mamma all my life.*

She took up the note from the table and put it in her bag, put on her heavy coat, and lifted the suitcase from the floor. If she could get as far as the kitchen before her parents saw her— Hurrying softly down the stairs, she hardly breathed. The door on her left was closed as she sped down the hall, but from it she could hear high argument, and for once in her life she was glad that her father and mother always bickered about everything. The thing to do now was to get the suitcase safely deposited on the path to the big gate. It was still quite dark as she stepped out onto the back porch from the kitchen. Then she ran around the house and dropped the case under a big oak in the grove. Back to the shed now where they kept the eight-year-old car.

I hate to tell a lie, she thought, standing just inside the shed to catch her breath, *but papa could drive to town himself if he wanted to.*

After a minute or two, she went back into the house and called to her father, "Papa, the car won't start, but I'll go down to the road and catch somebody going to town. You know today's Saturday, and people will be going early."

Your concentration on whether or not Mary will join Jim is never interrupted but prepares you for the emotional effect of the ending.

Before she could hear any protest, she was out the front door. She hurried down the steps and out into the yard. Already the light was beginning to change, and there was a faint stain of rose in the east. Mary looked up through the bare branches and saw that the stars had paled. But just above the rosy glow in the east a big planet burned.

I wonder if it's Venus, she thought, and she could hear her heart thudding. Birds were calling and chirping all around her, though the air was cold and crisp. They knew it was spring.

Mary hurried down the path toward the field gate. The smell of freshly plowed earth arose in the cold air. The ground under her feet was crusty with frost. The soft rose began to fan out in the sky, and beyond the thin line of trees on the other side of the farm she could see a black object moving slowly.

That's Jim, she thought gladly, and hastened so that she would be at the rendezvous on time. When she reached the gate opening into the main road, the car was drawn up, waiting. Jim Matthews came to meet her. Mary looked at the tall, heavy-set figure. *I've never really hesitated,* she decided. *I knew all the time I loved him.*

He looked at her closely as he took the suitcase from her. "You all right, Miss Mary? You sure you won't be sorry?"

"Oh, Jim," she said huskily, "something's happened. You'll have to go up to the house and get papa. He's got a bone in his throat and wants to be taken to the doctor."

Jim smiled wryly. "Then the romantic escape is off?" he inquired.

"No," said Mary, her voice quivering slightly. "I'll go along, and we'll get married while he's having the bone out. We'll have a taxi waiting to take him home, and I'll leave the note I've written with the driver. You see, he thinks our car won't start."

"That's a mighty daring scheme," said Jim, and now he was laughing.

In Mary's pointed little brown face two red spots glowed. "Maybe you don't want to marry me," she countered.

For answer, Jim opened the car door and helped her in.

"I was only kidding you," he said in his soft drawl.

They drove back through the fields with the first warm rays of the sun at their backs. The frosty, upturned earth glittered under the fingers of light. As they stopped at the big gate, a flock of robins flew up nearby. He got back in the car after opening the gate and, turning to her, said, "Now I know why you want to run away." He gestured toward the birds. " 'The lark's on the wing.' "

"But those are robins," said Mary, though her eyes shone.

"Yes," said Jim. "But 'The year's at the spring.' "

"Now you're making fun again. You think I'm trying to act young."

"No," said Jim, taking one of her small hands and holding it under his on the wheel. "I think you want what you've never had."

"And what's that?" asked Mary.

"Romance." And then he added, "I'm thankful to romance, Miss Mary, also to the fact that you want to mother the whole world. If you hadn't thought I needed you more than your papa and mamma do, you wouldn't be here with me this morning."

You are given an over-all impression, a from-here-to-there feeling about the story. Each incident has led you in a straight line.

"You think you're smart, don't you?" said Mary. She looked toward the house and saw her father's obstinate little figure waiting on the front porch. And suddenly teardrops trembled on her eyelashes.

Oh, heavens! she breathed. *It would be terrible if Jim saw me cry!* She swallowed hard and concentrated on the thought of her grandmother, who had descended to her lover by means of a honeysuckle vine. "I wonder if she was wearing her hoop skirt," she said to Jim, smiling at his puzzled face through a rainbow mist.

Here is another short story, this one built around the character of Grandma as seen from the viewpoint of her grandchild. Laurence Critchell's "And the Arrow Sped" is reprinted as it appeared in *This Week* magazine. As you read it, note our marginal comments on the author's handling of his material.

It was a day like this, not many years ago, that I learned my Grandmother's secret. She didn't really tell it to me, though. I had to piece it together out of little fragments, a tone of voice, a look in her eyes, a moment of tenderness in the midst of shelling peas. But when it was all complete, I then knew that Grandma would never grow old . . .

Grandma is still alive, you see. She's ninety-six. You wouldn't believe it to look at her. She's active and sprightly and full of fun, and she has four great-grandchildren, with another on the way. She doesn't live in the past, the way some people do. She told me once that when you're young you live in the future, and when you're old you live in the past, but when you're very old you live in the present, and that's when you find out what happiness is.

Grandma is a happy woman—clear-eyed, bright-faced, always ready to help. I look at her sometimes and marvel at how young this country is. For you see, she went west from Illinois, years ago, in a Conestoga wagon.

She was a girl of sixteen. She doesn't remember much about dates or places or trails. I know, because I've pumped her—it was long after the great migration, but close to the time when Custer died at Little Big Horn. What she remembers will tell you mostly about Grandma: she remembers the beauty of the plains in the mornings, setting out, and how the wild creatures were so plentiful and tame. To Grandma, that journey west in the Conestoga was like a journey through the Garden of Eden.

"I remember the creak of the wagons," she said to me one time. "That was a sound that went with you all the way—that and the flap of the canvas. We had lots of little children. You know, I think they loved those wagons. It was a kind of gypsy life. And the distances came up so slowly. Oh my! Maybe in the morning there'd be a rise

Marginal notes:

This direct progression has achieved an ordered, compact, single effect.

Grandmother is the main character. You're introduced to her immediately and learn that she has a secret.

You're not confused by other characterizations. It's Grandmother's story only, even though it's told by the invisible granddaughter.

of land far off. By noon it hardly seemed any nearer. And by sunset maybe it was a little higher, that was all. And birds . . . you've never seen so many birds . . ."

"Were there Indians, Grandma?" I said. I was sixteen.

"Oh," she said, and a strange look came in her face. "Yes, there were Indians. Once. Just once."

"What was it like?"—eagerly.

"They were Sioux," she said slowly. "And they killed him."

I didn't know what she was talking about. "Who?"

"He was your age," she said in a soft, faraway, tender voice. "Maybe older—seventeen. And the arrow went almost through him. It was very quick. That was something to be grateful for." She looked off through the porch screen to the west. "I went and knelt beside him and cradled his head in my arms. I thought it was I who had died."

"Oh, Grandma," I said. "Who was he?"

"A young man," she said in the same tender voice. "Going west. Like me."

"Tell me about him."

But she wouldn't. "I married your grandpa," she said, patting my hand. "He was a wonderful man."

That was how it went. There was a little mystery here. For always, when she thought of that boy, her thoughts quickly turned; they turned to Grandpa, whom she had loved, or to one of us, whom she loved, too, and the present and the future came flooding back. But little by little, as time passed, I learned more about the boy who had died with an arrow through his heart.

He was seventeen. His name was Jeff Beal. He came from Saugus, Massachusetts, and he was tall and lanky and plain, and he had a great thatch of blond hair. He carried a Winchester and he played the guitar, and he loved to walk beside her when she was riding in the wagon, and play and sing. Old songs that seemed to have come from England—I heard Grandma sing one of them once, to herself:

"I did but see her passing by
And yet I love her till I die . . ."

It was funny to hear Grandma sing it. She had such a sweet, young, tender voice—like a girl's.

And then one day I learned a good deal, and afterward I realized that I would never know anything more; this was all the story that Grandma had to tell. It was a spring morning, I remember, and I saw her going up the path to the fields and ran after her. She gave me a funny little look as I came up, but she didn't say anything, and we walked on together in silence—slowly, of course, because she couldn't walk very fast. Then I stopped and cut her a stick, and when I gave it to her I could have sworn a little pink color came into her cheeks.

There's no digression from her story, no side issues or problems.

"Funny," she said. "After all these years . . ."

"What, Grandma?"

She put the stick down firmly on the ground. "He cut a stick for me, too," she said. "And I was just sixteen."

"Were you beautiful, Grandma?"

She laughed. She had a wonderful, happy laugh. "Yes, I was beautiful," she said. "To him . . ." She looked down at herself. "I wore a long white dress and a bonnet. A poke bonnet. And it was the very early morning. Before the wagons had left."

"Did he kiss you, Grandma?"

The stick trembled a little. "I kissed him," she said.

She told me the story, then. And it was strange, but as she talked we seemed to be, not here, but there . . .

It was just after dawn of that other day. The sky to the west was clear and flawless. A little crystal mist lay on the land. Birds sang everywhere. She and Jeff walked side by side across the low, soft grass. Presently they came to a little rise of land, and he put his jacket down for her. Then he sprawled down beside her and plucked the grass.

"You're pretty," he said, not looking at her.

"Oh, no," she said, blushing. "I'm plain. I'm plain and ordinary. There's lots of girls prettier than me."

·"You're pretty," he said. "To me."

Something lighted in her heart. For a moment it seemed as if all the birds in the world were singing at once. His hand touched hers. Her cheeks burned. She was so happy she could hardly breathe. But she couldn't think what to say, so she just looked off to the west and said, "I wonder if we'll ever get there?"

He sat up. "We'll get there," he said. "And I'm going to have me some land. And build me a cabin. And have me a family. That's what I want. I want a family."

"Do you?" she said softly.

"Yes," he said. Still not looking at her, he plucked a blade of grass. "Do you?"

"Yes," she said, so low it was almost a whisper. "I've dreamed of that."

"We're young," he said. "We're strong. We're not afraid of work. I'd work for you. I'd work hard."

The sun was suddenly brilliant. The mountains danced with light. All the birds in the world were singing in her heart. "Oh, Jeff . . ." she said.

"Would you?" he sprang to his feet. "Would you?"

She dropped her head. "Yes," she said softly. "Oh, yes!" . . .

That was long, long ago. Now Grandma awoke as if from a dream. Her eyes were infinitely tender. For a moment, there in the morning, on the farm, in Ohio, she was a girl of sixteen again.

The flashback tells of a single incident. You're not required to follow other incidents that undoubtedly occurred on that fateful day.

All the dialogue and action lead you in a direct line toward the revelation of Grandmother's secret.

"But you said you kissed him," I said.

She smiled. "I did," she said. "The next day."

We turned back to the farm. "Was it nice, Grandma?" I said, smiling.

"It was beautiful, my dear," she said, and raised my hand to her cheek. "But the arrow had gone through his heart . . ."

That was all. And yet it wasn't quite the end of the story. For as we reached the farmhouse, one of her great-grandchildren, Jamie, came running as fast as he could to greet her. And that was when I learned Grandma's secret and when I knew that she would never be old. For at the sight of him a little shining light came in her eyes. It was the light of a love infinitely fresh, infinitely young, infinitely renewed. She pressed my hand quickly—and threw away the stick.

The story's time lapse is contained in a single day within the area of the flashback. The thoughts of the granddaughter are simply a framework around the single action.

You're given a single outcome from a single situation, and thus an over-all single effect is achieved.

Keeping your characters constant

There is an act that the competent writer may not commit, and yet is frequently committed by the beginner and the amateur. It is to say something is so, and not make it be so in the story itself. The clearest example is when a character is declared to be witty and yet never, within the story, exhibits that wit. A more complicated example would be the creation of excitement or tension in a story. It is never created by a statement, but by a whole series of happenings and remarks and descriptions that build up to tension and excitement in the mind of the reader.—Christopher La Farge

Solutions that come in the night

One of the most helpful discoveries I made long ago is that there is a part of the mind, which the psychologists call the subconscious, that works while you are sleeping or even while you are relaxing or are engaged in some other task far removed from writing. I have found it possible to train this part of the mind to do a pretty organized job. Very often I have awakened in the morning to find a problem of technique or plot or character, which had long been troubling me, completely solved while I had been sleeping.—Louis Bromfield

Lesson six

Fiction writing
course

The
slick
story

The terms "slick," "pulp" and "quality"—descriptive of three different kinds of stories—originated long ago with the types of paper used by magazines. The slick story was printed on shiny, coated paper in magazines such as *McCall's, The Saturday Evening Post* and *Cosmopolitan*. The pulp stories appeared on rough uncoated paper in publications like *Dime Detective,*

Argosy and *Adventure.* The quality stories were confined to the more costly, soft-textured pages of *Harper's,* the *Atlantic Monthly* and other "intellectual" periodicals.

Because of the great popularity of the slick magazines, the short stories they contain are written to please the widest reading audience in America. For this reason you should learn as much as you can about their distinguishing characteristics.

Who are the people that make up this huge reading public? What are they looking for in their reading? The audience is so vast that it includes almost everybody from every walk of life. These readers are alert, intelligent and perceptive: they want well-written stories with sound ideals and morals, presented in a concise, entertaining style rather than a subtle or psychological one. They want to see problems they can recognize and appreciate brought to a satisfactory solution. They want release from their daily troubles, as well as some ideas of how to solve them. They want to lose themselves, to escape into a world more exciting than their own.

Reader identification is so strong in these stories that even when the tale seems to take flight from reality, it doesn't leave the reader behind, unable to imagine himself taking part in it. The reader likes a bright, original approach to the situations, characters and events of these stories, without departures from normal, everyday behavior—and he accepts neither overly heroic nor starkly true outcomes. Max Shulman says:

When writing for the slick magazines, you should believe the stories you write. If you find they're either too contrived or lacking in robust story values, then you'll likely run into difficulty. There are, of course, professional writers who can deliberately and skillfully contrive the situations and characters that create a good slick story, but for the most part if you aren't in sympathy with the sentiments and ideals of your characters, then the chances are you can't write convincingly. The slick story reader belongs to a mass audience which shares the common human emotions: he wants genuine warmth and sentiment in his stories and quickly recognizes their absence.

Readers of slick magazines like stories of love, of conflicts between married people, of behind-the-scenes acts of neighbors, of important moments in lives similar to their own, or of glamorous places and happenings in which people like themselves are involved. Subject material isn't limited except by good taste. Offensive or controversial topics are to be avoided, although almost any subject can be presented if handled with tact and consideration of the feelings of a vast part of our population.

Two examples of the slick story

In the following slick story reprints—"Meeting of the Clan" and "Company Cast-Off"—you'll find that each has not only the *single effect* but also a clear-cut illustration of style, choice of subject matter, method of treatment and type of emotional appeal to the reader.

The characters are all recognizable people, faced with recognizable problems. Nowhere in these stories is the reader's credulity strained. He might disagree with the way in which the problems are resolved (and so might you), but not with their logic and probability.

Mignon Eberhart feels it's impossible to pay too much attention to credibility and plausibility. She adds:

Credibility is particularly important in the slick story because, as one editor said to me, a reader could believe almost anything before the story opens, but then things take place on scene, so to speak, and every event must be credible, every motivation, everything must be believed. This is particularly true of the slick story. The characters must be recognizable people faced with recognizable problems.

You'll note that the ideals on which the following stories are based are neither profound nor superficial, but warm with sentiment and perhaps a little enlightening. Here are events and situations which might happen to any of us and to which most readers can easily relate themselves.

The first of these examples of slick stories is Mary Bolté's "Meeting of the Clan," which came out in *Cosmopolitan*.

As the car rounded a curve and the glittering lake came into view, Ted reached over and squeezed Claire's hand. "Almost there now, baby. Got your armor buckled on?" It was an old and, to Claire, a somewhat bitter joke between them, for after six months of marriage Claire's attitude toward Ted's family was still a source of conflict, conflict that usually led to tears on Claire's part and irritation on Ted's. When Claire was among the rest of the Herons she felt, as she had often told Ted, "like a purse made out of a sow's ear."

Claire tried to make her voice gay. "All buckled on."

"That's my girl, that's my *wife*," said Ted, smiling and running his hand lightly over her shoulders.

Claire smiled back at him, touched by his concern for her. That he should, in the midst of grief over his father's death, be able to consider her feelings seemed a wonderfully generous and compassionate gesture. Although she had determined to overcome her shy dread of the Herons today, Claire felt it mounting steadily. The Heron clan always terrified her, and even now, when there had been a death in the family, when she should have been feeling sympathy, fear was still the uppermost of her emotions.

The Herons were known as a "wonderful family," "remarkably talented and so charmingly natural" ("snobbish" and "smug" were words of Claire's substitution), and on that Saturday in April when Claire had married Ted she had been congratulated more for joining the family than for marrying Ted. One aged Heron uncle had said to her, "You are pretty, my dear, and I daresay spunky and talented enough to keep up with any one of 'em." The remark had haunted Claire ever since, for she was not, and never would be, able to keep up with the Herons. How could anyone keep up with Sis, who had babies one after the other, while at the same time heading every organization in town? Or with Molly, who every day combined painting and singing lessons with teaching physical education? As for Ben and Ed, doctor and architect respectively, Claire simply could not understand their boundless energy. They would work all day, attend community meetings at night, and then drive two or three hours so as to be ready in the morning for a day of skiing. And often Claire had heard tales of the exuberant life Colin, the youngest and wildest Heron, had led. But Colin was dead now, killed in Korea.

Actually, Claire supposed Ted was the nearest to shiftless of the lot; all *he* did was work in a law office by day and study Arabic by night!

Claire looked at him now and sighed. Within ten minutes he would be gone. For whenever Ted got together with his family, he became one of them, vigorous, gay, and impersonal, and, so it seemed to Claire, completely lost to her. Among the rest of his family he took on what Claire called "the Heron look," which, although she could not say why, somehow obliterated the personal physical features that endeared him to her—the cleft in his chin, the wonderfully proud set of his head. But then, all Herons held their heads high. Seeing Ted alone, Claire saw something touchingly courageous about the pose, but when the rest of them were nearby, she saw only arrogance in the unbending head.

Claire said, "I wonder if everybody has arrived already. Everybody *is* coming, I gather."

A brief frown, which Claire did not understand, flickered across

The main character is an easily recognizable person. Claire's conflict is understandable and real, and therefore you can identify with her.

The author's style is clear, natural and intelligent without being "literary." It moves along thoughtfully but not too deeply for the understanding of a wide audience.

Ted's brow. "All us Herons are coming, anyway," he said to her.

Us Herons! There it was again. At the mention of the word, Claire pictured an impenetrable wall of dozens of Herons, all engaged in some activity, and herself, a Little Miss Muffet, sitting apart.

The pace of living for the Heron children had been set by their parents. Until his death a week ago, Mr. Heron had skied and played tennis regularly, crossing the Atlantic every other summer to take walking trips in Scotland or slalom down the slopes of Austria and Switzerland. Of all Ted's family, it had been Mr. Heron to whom Claire had got closest. It had happened two months ago, in August, when Claire, seeing him return from early morning bird watching, had shyly told him that her father, too, had shared his passion. Old Mr. Heron had blinked and looked down his long aristocratic nose at her in a curious, amused way, as if seeing her for the first time. But he had invited her to walk with him the next morning and afterwards had taken her to his cabin in the woods where he kept his bird books and several stuffed specimens. Later in the day, when Claire and Ted had been leaving to return to the city, Mr. Heron had said, "Well now, son, your lady and I and some scarlet tanagers had quite a nice little visit together"; and Claire had thought, "At least now he knows I exist. Maybe next time he'll call me by name."

Ted spoke again. *"Nous sommes arrivés."* Claire, turning, saw that his face bore the usual anticipatory expression that came over it whenever they returned to the family homestead.

As they drove past the tennis court, Claire found it almost impossible to believe that Mr. Heron, in old white ducks and green eyeshade, would not be springing around the court soon, swinging at the ball in his elegant 1910 tennis style. No one was playing, and, of course, no one would be, for today was a day of mourning. At least, Claire assumed so, even though there had been no funeral. Mr. Heron had been cremated. Claire had heard many people say that funerals were barbarous, and remembering the nauseating masses of flowers and food at her own father's funeral, she had to agree. But not to have a grave somewhere—that she could not understand, for she knew how much comfort it gave her mother to visit her father's burial place.

They had reached the porte-cochère, and Claire saw that her husband was looking eagerly around for other members of his family. Why, she thought, he really seems more happy than unhappy. At that moment Mrs. Heron stepped from the big, elegant front door, smiling.

"Claire, dear." Mrs. Heron held out her hands. "I'm fortunate to have one daughter-in-law here at least." Linking arms with the girl, she mounted the steps, explaining, "Ben's poor wife has the grippe, and Aggie, unfortunately, can't travel when she's pregnant."

Mrs. Heron, Claire noticed, was dressed in a knitted suit that

Character conflict comes ahead of physical background.

The characterizations are visually sharp but not exaggerated beyond reality.

The situation and background are credible. Even if you don't know a place like this or a family like the Herons, you won't find either beyond your imagination, and can picture both without straining your sense of reality.

must have been twenty years old. Before she and Ted had left the city Claire had put on a plain black dress, but Ted had said, "You're not going to wear *that,* are you? We're not going to a *funeral.*" So here was Claire in a spandy new lilac dress and Mrs. Heron in her old suit.

Shabby clutter, Claire had long ago decided, was a point of pride with the Herons. Like a socially-at-ease millionaire attired ostentatiously in threadbare clothes, the house and everything in it seemed dedicated to carrying out the theory that rickety disorder was the best backdrop for quality.

Claire's ideals are neither profound nor superficial.

Today, as she entered the house, Claire noticed that everything was as usual, and although she did not at first know the reason why, this startled her. Then, remembering her mother's house stacked with flowers and wreaths, she realized that she had expected some change, however slight, to signify that death had passed this way. There was nothing. The shredded sheet music on the piano and the ski trophies were in their usual disarray.

"Molly and Sis and her children are here," Mrs. Heron said, "and the boys should arrive soon." Smiling at Ted, she added, "The girls are upstairs changing for tennis. I know they're counting on a game with you."

Tennis! At the mention of the word, Claire's mouth fell open, but Ted said spiritedly, "Good! Come on, Claire. Let's get ready. We ought to be able to finish off our tournament today."

"Hi, there, you two!" Molly stood in the upstairs hall, already in shorts, brandishing her racket. "Well, I guess Sis and I can polish you off today."

"Is that so?" Ted cuffed his sister good-naturedly on the ear. "You've got a surprise coming, Mol."

From the opposite bedroom Sis called, "Don't be so cocksure, my boy, I'm in top form today. And when I'm in top form—well, too bad!"

"What conceit," Ted laughed, taking a pair of chinos off the hook. "It happens my wife is in top form, too, so you haven't a prayer." He bent and kissed Claire quickly on the neck. "You are in top form, aren't you, honey?"

There's plenty of warm sentiment in the story, and the characters' motives are sincere.

Why, he *wants* me to be in top form, Claire thought. He's counting on me. She tried to smile and said, "I hope so."

When Claire and Ted reached the court, Molly and Sis were already batting balls back and forth, laughing and yelling insults at each other. They were behaving exactly as if Mr. Heron were still alive; they were acting as though he weren't dead at all. But I can't, thought Claire miserably; I know Ted wants me to, but I just *can't.* She and Ted lost the first set—or, rather, Claire lost it. In the second set, when they were losing 0–3, Ted suddenly came over to her. "Please, darling," he pleaded. "Put a little more into it, okay?" But

Claire could not, and Sis and Molly won the season's family tournament with ease.

According to custom, cocktails were served on the porch overlooking the lake. Molly played her mandolin while Ted, Ben, and Ed argued about the approaching football season and Sis's children climbed over tables and chairs.

Ed asked, "How's the job going, Claire?" It was the only question her brother-in-law ever asked her, and Claire, nodding and replying, "Fine, thanks," felt that for all Ed noticed she could have answered that she'd been fired for stealing.

Claire had a good position at one of the downtown libraries, but whenever she spoke of it to the Herons, it somehow didn't seem like much.

Ed shuffled his feet, and, looking away from her, said vaguely, "It must be interesting work."

Claire smiled more to herself than to Ed. "The people are interesting."

"It's true of hospital work, too," Ed said, turning to her. But Claire, busy trying to imagine Ed or any other member of "the clan" confronted by one of her library customers, did not comprehend his remark.

Ed had gone on talking, but seeing that Claire was not paying attention, he turned back to his brothers; and Claire sat alone, finishing her drink in silence.

Mrs. Heron, appearing in the door, called, "Come along, everybody, there's Heron hash for lunch."

Heron hash, an aromatic mixture spooned onto baked Idaho potatoes, was the traditional Saturday lunch in the household, and Claire, sitting down to it, was again shocked by the usualness with which everything about the day was being handled. She looked at the familiar food, the familiar smiles around the table, and the greedy, busy fingers of Sis's children. At the end of the long table Mr. Heron's chair loomed up, huge and empty.

The meal progressed in the usual fashion, with everybody talking at once, telling old jokes, arguing about politics and books, reporting on friends, genially contradicting each other. Once or twice Claire saw Ted glance at her miserably. I'm letting him down, Claire thought, and I can't help myself.

Suddenly Mrs. Heron rose in her place.

An absolute hush fell. Her children lowered their eyes, as if they knew what she would say. She spoke quietly. Looking directly at the empty chair opposite her, she said, "Now I think we will have a hymn." Silently, everyone followed her in to the piano. Scooping the scattered sheet music from the rack, Mrs. Heron sat down, struck an opening chord, and raised her head. Together she and her children and her grandchildren began to sing, loudly and clearly. With-

There's enough action to create a balance of interest, to keep the story moving.

The portrait of the family is real, without being analytical. The author doesn't probe too deeply into whys and wherefores but gives the characters sufficient motivation for their acts and thoughts.

There's strong emotional appeal in this type of slick story.

out faltering, the children as well as the adults sang two verses through. The third came in clear sopranos from the women:

> A thousand ages in thy sight
> Are like an evening gone;
> Short as the watch that ends the night
> Before the rising sun.

And then, powerfully from every open throat, the last:

> O God, our help in ages past,
> Our hope for years to come,
> Be Thou our guide while life shall last,
> And our eternal home.

The room swam before Claire's eyes. Goose flesh prickling her back, she broke away from the group and rushed through the dining room, the pantry, and into the big old wooden kitchen. In an anguish of humiliation and shame she pressed her fists down hard on the dented copper of the sink. She had been wrong, wrong, wrong!

A sound made her turn. Ted stood at the door, regarding her sadly. "Claire," he said, coming toward her, "what are you thinking? Are you thinking that the way we're treating our father's death is heartless? Couldn't you stand to be in the same room with us insensitive Herons?" He put his arm around her waist. "I know it must be hard for you, remembering your own father's funeral, but listen, baby, not everybody does things the same way. I don't mean to sound brutal, but you know in a way you're a worse snob than any of us ever was, because you don't think any way is the right way unless it's your way. You've got to learn that just because people live differently from the way you live doesn't mean they haven't got hearts and feelings. It doesn't mean they can't cry even when they seem to be laughing." Putting both hands on her shoulders, Ted turned her toward him. "Am I making any sense to you?" Claire shook her head numbly. She tried to speak, but could not. "Stop feeling sorry for yourself," Ted said gently. "My family's not going to eat you. You're as good as any of 'em, and if you'd give them half a chance they'd be crazy about you." Pulling her close, Ted whispered, "I'm going now, just for a few minutes, into the woods to Father's cabin. I'll be back soon. Remember I love you more than anything. You'll never know how much your being here today means to me, to all of us."

When he had gone Claire stood for several minutes absolutely still. The house was silent. Through the window she saw the children running single file down the path toward the lake; off to the left Ted and his brothers were walking three abreast into the woods. In the perfect stillness it was the house that seemed alive, as if waiting for someone. "Is it waiting for me?" Claire asked herself. She looked

---

The events are not contrived but move along in natural succession, so that you can believe their probability.

The characters are not all black or all white. They all have human faults, including the main character.

around the old-fashioned kitchen. Now that she was alone in it, it looked dimly familiar. A memory, all bits and pieces, came into her mind. Torn linoleum and brown cupboards, and a gingham-covered back bent over the stove. Claire had begun to cry and she did not hear Sis come up to her.

"Forgive me, I don't usually eavesdrop. But, Claire, is what Ted said true? Do you really think we're going to eat you? I thought the tables were turned the other way. I've always felt you were so self-possessed, so darned aloof. And Molly, well, Molly says you make her feel like an ugly little match girl." Claire sat stunned, unable to move. After a moment Sis continued softly, "Do you know what Papa's favorite joke was? It was about his death. He used to tell us, 'If I get up there first, I don't want to hear any blubbering down below.' He meant it, too. He meant we weren't to weep for him. So now we're trying, in the only way we know how, not to. You must agree," she said gently, "that's at least one way for people to show respect for the dead."

Claire did not stir. Her cheeks were burning with shame. Sis put a hand on her shoulder. "You're not the only one who finds fault with our family. Don't you think it strange that you are the only daughter-in-law here today? Yes, Helen *does* have the grippe, and Aggie *can't* travel when she's pregnant, but Mother is glad of those reasons for their not being here; she knows, deep down, that otherwise they would have made less genuine excuses for not coming. You see, when Colin was killed we all acted just the way we did today, and Helen and Aggie thought it was barbarous." Sis hesitated a moment, and then continued, "Listen, every family, big or little, has its habits and proud traditions. I bet yours did, too. Each family's different from another, but oh, don't let those differences make a wall. As a daughter-in-law you're Mother's last—and best—hope."

For a moment both women were silent. Then Claire looked up shyly. Passing her hand over the wooden sink board she smiled at her sister-in-law. "Do you know, Sis, this kitchen is almost exactly like the one I remember in my grandmother's house?"

In the living room Mrs. Heron was standing before a mirror adjusting an old felt hat.

"Oh, there you are, Claire. Would you care to walk to the cabin with me? There are some things there your father-in-law wanted you to have."

For an answer, Claire linked arms with Mrs. Heron. As they went out, a scarlet tanager cut through the air above them. On the path ahead Claire saw the three brothers coming out of the woods, a slow smile spreading over Ted's face as he watched Claire and his mother approaching him.

From *The Saturday Evening Post* comes another typical slick

Your sympathy for the main character is consistently maintained through your knowledge of her problem and her attempts to cope with it.

You are enlightened by the way Claire reaches a change of heart and learns something about herself as well as the Heron family.

The outcome may not satisfy every reader, but it's logical and plausible—a soundly based resolution according to the nature of the problem. As we said in the text, "Here are events and situations which might happen to any of us and to which most readers can easily relate themselves."

story, "Company Cast-Off" by Williams Forrest. The main character, Talbot Brand, is a person you might know, and his problem is a common one which the reader accepts as true to life.

It was like a silent tempest, devised only for him, experienced by him alone. It raged in his fortieth-floor office, sweeping around him and entering his head and rushing about his brains until he felt the roaring shake him. There was a moment of infinite hesitation, and he sat rigid, fearful of a breakdown.

But then there was a bounding rap, tap, tap on his door and he knew who it was. Even as he happily called out, "Come in, Joey! Come in, come in!" the incipient collapse shivered and moved back into the recesses of his ordinarily resilient nature.

The door opened and slammed behind the red-headed gnome carrying the shoeshine box with fierce insolence. "Hiya, Mr. Brand!" cried Joey. "Hiya!" He sat on his box and selected a foot. Joey was the mascot of the company and probably of many others. "What goes, Mr. Brand," he declaimed, "a man with your dough, your position, why ain't you in Florida?"

"I'm thinking about it, Joey; thinking about it."

"Think spink," said Joey. "You been spendin' your life thinking. Me, I never gave a hoot. But you look nervous, Mr. Brand, nervous; get me?"

Talbot Brand smiled, not offended. He relaxed under the prattle and the dub, dub, dub of brush and rag, and the oddly refreshing motion of the polishing, that sent a soothing release sliding as far as his nape and opened the vise that gripped it. He didn't know what he'd do without Joey's visits. Joey breathed life and vigor into the office. With the exception of Miss Quise, the secretary, he was the only one who had visited Talbot since he was installed here, when the reorganized company moved into this soaring new building from downtown.

You are introduced to a main character, Talbot Brand.

Florida. He supposed it had come to that—picking up the retirement plan he and Belle had had for years. The only trouble was it was five years ahead of the date when retirement was mandatory. But his hand was being forced, and he had just had a terrific scare. Yes, it had better be Florida, and with no further delay. He'd have to explain it all to Belle, make her see it his way, let her know they had defeated him, or rather, allowed him to defeat himself. He'd retire with the let-down feeling that comes from crawling away to the pasture instead of walking away in the proper due time, feeling justified after a career well done right up to the end.

Talbot Brand is a recognizable character: his problem is true to life. It's easy for you, the reader, to identify with him.

The spell of loneliness and frustration disappeared from the room as Joey filled the corners with irreverent sound.

Quieted, Talbot asked, "Why don't you go to Florida yourself? I bet you have a bundle."

Joey's face came up like a hatchet. "With them bangtails I bet on? Nah. Anyway, I don't want to retire, and down there I'd have to give pedicures only." He brightened. "Is that bad?" Then he flip-flapped away, rolling with the work, humming ribaldry.

Now Joey was gone, but his peculiar melody lingered on, and, chuckling, Talbot felt sane and adjusted to his situation. He decided to forget the good, stubborn fight. Searching through his desk, he found the copy of the company's annuity-and-insurance plan. His slender pencil clicked from his lapel pocket and he prepared to figure what his benefits would be if he retired now instead of waiting out the additional five years.

Silence flowed deeper in the room, but he was comfortable in it, and surrender was under his hand. Now he could look with pity on the struggle of the past months. Could look with irony on himself and with tolerance on the new and young president and his "team" of marketers, engineers, lawyers and Ph.D.'s. All the more power to them; it would come to them someday, too, the end—or maybe even the old absent treatment; that silent, hurting rack on which they stretched an old buck they wanted to get rid of, but couldn't fire because he had been too loyal and too big in the company for too long. All the more power to them, he thought, with bitterness edging in.

It all came back to him, each humiliation jarring him. The president, J. C. Tanner, and his office. His executive secretary had been formidable. Talbot supposed many executive secretaries were, but he had never noticed it before. Her gray suit was like a sleek coat of armor, and her face was lean, strangely cool and lovely, but almost masculine in its authority.

"I'm very sorry, Mr. Brand," she had said, "Mr. Tanner can't possibly see you this week."

It had seemed incredible, but Talbot hadn't faltered; he had realized he was one of the old crew, not really a part of the "team," but his assurance, tall and easy in his shoulders, engraved on the lean planes of his face, calm in his eyes and given mature power by the handsome sweep of his iron-gray hair, had made him positive after a good healthy talk with the "boy," they would find a meeting of the minds.

"Have him give me a call," he said easily; "I'll keep the office fire burning."

He smiled at her, but she had already murmured politely and gone back to her work.

It was then that the first premonitory chill ascended the buttons of his spine.

He had been persistent, even huffy at length, and finally he had found himself sitting across from J. C. Tanner in the big round office. He felt strangely diffident, and he knew it echoed in his pre-

The background, the world of big business, is familiar enough so that your credulity is not taxed.

The author's style is neither too simple nor too complex, but literate, clear and direct.

tense at laughter. "With all this big reorganization, J. C., a little item seems to have been overlooked."

"Oh, so?" Tanner's face was round, bland. Beneath thick skin, there was an intellectual glow, and a padded force was concealed in his short, smooth appearance. He was heavy-lidded and spoke in purring tones, but he was capable of beaming laughter and a startling display of physical presence, as if only deft self-control kept him from being a hungry tiger. At least that was the way Talbot saw him now. He hadn't seen him so at first when he was made president; he had seen a hard-driving, rather pudgy, pleasant young man who he thought might be fine presidential stuff.

Talbot found himself bantering, but gripping his hands until the trimmed nails began to dig into the flesh. "Somehow or other, in the shuffle, my desk has remained clean. Stark, naked clean. Why, I don't even get a phone call any more; there seems to be a spook in the switchboard." His banter was playing against a dead coldness out of which two heavy blue eyes watched dispassionately. "I've been thinking of sending myself a post card a day with some pleasant squib on it."

Brand's characterization and inner conflict come ahead of the story action.

Tanner reflected. "You choose to make an issue of it. Perhaps that's better." He looked into Talbot's eyes squarely. "I'll be frank with you, Tal. I don't know where you fit in."

"You don't know where I fit in?" What the devil could he mean? "You know my grasp of the industry. Why, we've had some fine talks when all this was first beginning. I was sure we saw eye to eye on many things."

Tanner shook his head. "We didn't," he said simply. Then he leaned forward with sudden intensity. "Tal," he said, "you did the talking. I listened. When I did talk, I didn't find the comprehension I wanted. I didn't see you with the team. You were carrying your own ball." Gently he said, "Policy's different now. And that will reflect right on down through management." He stood up, put out his hand and grinned. "But we'll iron it out. We'll send up a few moons and look around and find some space for you. Give it time, give it time!"

The ideals and morals expressed by the characters and conveyed by the author are not too lofty or too superficial for slick-magazine readers.

Talbot had assured himself that he certainly was not going to be treated in that fashion. Over the years he'd had literally scores of opportunities to take his ability and experience elsewhere. He would let the word be known, and it would not be long before the offers began to filter in.

But the word went out and vast silence closed upon it. Another word had gone out first—that he was through. The word did not go out spitefully, with any intention of harming him; it was unavoidably manifested at conventions and conferences. And all those past open doors shyly closed.

Then, if not this industry, another. His ability could be utilized in another field, anything where major marketing experience would be valuable, and that was almost everywhere, was it not?

On a day of wind and rain he found himself in an employment agency. He was surprised to find himself there, and glanced around with interest. He had never been in one of the places before. He was sorry he took so careful a look around; there were so many anxious, lost forms, and these were offset by the trim fire of youth and near-youth wearing confidence and even arrogance like wreaths of deserved laurel.

A Miss Laycraft interviewed him, snapping his file card between long fingers.

"We found your résumé very impressive, Mr. Brand; very impressive indeed."

Good, he thought, feeling warmer after the outside damp and chill.

"But I'm afraid at this time—You see, Mr. Brand, there are so few jobs in your bracket—"

Quickly, wanting to hold onto that sense of warmth, of accomplishment, "I would like to make myself understood, Miss Laycraft. I wouldn't expect my present salary. A challenge, Miss Laycraft; a challenge with a good progressive firm."

She looked at him as if she understood something for the first time, and his eagerness broke as he became marked-down goods.

"We'll let you know," she said, "in the event anything suitable— Of course, your age—"

He was in a nervous flurry of getting up. "Yes, I know. I understand all that."

"Don't call us," said Miss Laycraft; "we'll call you."

One Sunday night he and Belle were in the house alone. Cora was out to a church party with her current beau, and George had left for Princeton at noon. They were sitting in the pleasant second-floor sitting room, reading desultorily while a small fire gave an erratic but beautiful ballet.

Out of nowhere, Talbot suddenly felt jaunty and summoned Belle to his lap. "Listen, grand old gal—" he began, and she said, falling lightly against him, her hair faintly spicy, "Kindly leave out the old." She wrinkled her nose, that was still the most perfect he had ever seen.

"Well, we're not so young as we used to be," he put in.

"Tal Brand," she said, sitting up, child-small, woman-curved, "I thought you were being too quiet for your own good." She kissed him firmly and rumpled his hair.

"I'm serious," he protested. "Listen, why wait five years when we can start all that fishing right now? It'll cut down on our retirement benefits, of course, but we'll be buying time, and maybe it's a darn good purchase."

Although the characters are understandable, they are not deeply probed or analyzed.

You can accept Talbot's motives because you know they are sincere, therefore he keeps your sympathy.

She lay dreamily against him, but at length spoke sensibly, if in mock Irish tone, "It's a foolish man you are, Tal Brand. Why, it's a grand life we have, with our house and all our friends and watching our children come into man and womanhood. Anyway, it would scare the kids if we picked up our crutches so far ahead of time."

"I'm not thinking of crutches," he said angrily.

She stiffened, and he told her he was sorry and petted her. She said, "Tal, the children still need their home, and they still need us living, working, not fishing. We're still their background, taken as matter of fact." Irrelevantly, it seemed, she started up and boasted, "Do you realize that I beat Cora two sets in tennis not so long ago?" And it was not so irrelevant; he knew what she meant. To the kids, they were still active, productive, strong people—the kind that could be counted on until you got that degree or went through your first confinement. They were not the old folks at the resort, playing shuffleboard and bingo, whom you shouldn't bother with big grave problems that could bend dear but desiccated necks.

"Don't you agree with me?" Belle insisted. "Isn't this just a whim?"

"Yes," he had decided, "it's a whim. That's all. Didn't you know I get whims?"

The time had come, however, when enforced retirement could no longer be considered a whim. This morning he was sure he had felt the danger signal preceding crack-up. Oh, yes, a month ago he had decided that if the company wanted to pay him for sitting in this fine office without doing a thing, let it. Every month an excellent check was forwarded to his bank, and what more could a man ask? He had found out; his nervous system had shown him forcibly that he needed more than checks. Call it what you will—self-respect, a sense of belonging—it was necessary, and the lack of it could incapacitate you. A man could not ascend in the elevator each day with his associates, big and small, trade small talk with them, and walk through the outer offices and give and receive good mornings, and enter his own office, close the door and forget that they all knew about him. He felt like a thief or the recipient of alms. He felt himself becoming a toady, too hearty, too self-protective.

In short, he was stripping himself of every layer of manhood that covered his shrinking soul.

He scanned the thick annuity-and-insurance book that described the benefits that accrued to all categories of employees. The book contained over thirty pages of text and numerous diagrams. It had been made up, Talbot knew, by a dozen company attorneys and industrial-relations men, who had spent months on its preparation, and it had been proudly distributed to every member of the organization as concrete evidence of the value of employment with the company. Talbot had been so busy with his own work that he had

All the people in the story give the illusion of being lifelike, but not so true to life that they strain your belief and understanding.

The story moves forward, with enough incidents to keep it from becoming static.

barely glanced at the book before. Now, he read it, or attempted to read it, with increasing bafflement.

In disgust, he closed the book and shot it into one of the unused desk baskets. It didn't matter which one, incoming or outgoing, because no one bothered to look in his baskets any more. He'd ask Dahlgren to make up a set of figures for him, which the company would do anyway when he turned in his resignation. He could check for error at his leisure, between catching tarpon.

He put on his coat, and the elevator took him down the whistling shaft to the river wind pouring along the avenue. In ten minutes he was in the glow of the ancient and intimate tavern where he had made new friends since the days when his lunches were taken up with business talks. The semi-retired men he consorted with now spent long hours over their martinis, oysters and huge mutton chops, in a masculine atmosphere of cigar smoke and phlegmy jokes. Talbot, still dancing lean, but lonely, had learned to bask in the casual acceptance of their deep voices and ruddy cheeks. His restless mind had learned the art of wasting time with involved stories and salty humor.

Today the atmosphere of the tavern seemed too laden with paunch, pungent chowchow and personalities lurching in dim light and rich futility. He longed for the crisp of wind and the sight of a gliding gull. He escaped to the river and liked its musty piers and soiled escaping water. He felt the pulse leading to the purity of the sea; and he felt motion in himself, an escape from the thick pool in which he had been contained.

The events and scenes are natural outcomes, one of the other, so that the story has a ring of truth.

It was unexplainable until he remembered the annuity-and-insurance book. The darn thing was beckoning him, crying out, "Come wrestle with me, if you dare." It wanted him to take off his coat and fight the obscurity, the massive legality, and make it a human company document, lean and agile enough to make itself understood to the mail boy with the most pimples and most receding chin.

It was a dare from the past, when all problems had made him tingle. It would be his last combat in the tourneys of business, but it would be fun to see if his lance was sharp or blunted. The tarpon would still be there a month from now.

In the office he called Tanner and insisted on being put through to him. When he explained that he wanted to do a simplified version of the annuity-and-insurance book, Tanner replied tersely, "Our experts are satisfied with it." But Talbot's pure vision kept him to his purpose. He went on safari for his secretary, who had been lending herself to various departments, after having read every pocket book on earth.

"I have something for you to do, Miss Quise," he said.

"But, sir, the department wants to get these stencils out."

"Come along," he said, hearing a familiar, all-but-forgotten ring

You are able to imagine Brand's difficulties, even though you may not have experienced them in your own life.

of authority. He turned away and heard her pattering after him.

Miss Quise was his guinea pig as he struggled to rewrite the book. He had never thought that one girl could look so uncomprehending so often. He broke scores of pencil points making the annuity-and-insurance book clear to her. During that time, when her weary brain spun too heavily and she broke down and wept, he solaced her with a fine lunch. She would soon sparkle again, and once said, "I feel we are doing a great duty for each and every person in the company, like poor Charlie Decker, an office boy, even if he's fifty. He has both parents to support and a brother who isn't all there."

Talbot felt strongly that Charlie Decker should know exactly what was going on in relation to him and his future, and his resolve stuck with him even after silence followed submission of the revision to Tanner's office. He contacted Gordon Mapes, editor-in-chief of the main employee publication, *Colossus*.

Gordon brightened when he saw the popularized material. Talbot said, "I thought you might be able to use some of this as a basis for articles."

"Basis hell," said Gordon. "Let's serialize this thing just as it is." He looked at the pages again, and gradually his face fell. His voice was unsure. "The lawyers would never stand for it. If it's officially printed, it's binding, and they'll say it isn't exact. To them, it's only exact if you don't savvy it."

They sat there in joint disappointment, but Talbot's lance was still bright and sharp, even after jousting with the book. "Print this and the lawyer version side by side, indicating that this is an interpretation."

"Done!"

It was a mauve and smoky night when Talbot walked through to the train. He was unaccountably depressed. On the train, he realized it was Friday night. Week ends lately had been like those of old, gay and active, with spots of calm communication between him and Belle. But this week end would be different. His project was over, and Monday would once again find him in the doldrums with no entity of storm building around him again to carry him, hard and enduring, over difficult terrain. His bones felt brittle and the bleakness of the night in the suburbs aged him.

"You need a drink," said Belle at once.

"Double."

Cora came through the room. When she saw him she held her pert nose.

"Is that a comment, daughter?" he asked.

"Not on you, daddy dear," she said, "but I passed that place where you're building the new plant. The poor people."

This was lost on Talbot. Even the drink did not bring him from where he had gone. That night he slept a dead sleep for several hours

Brand's problem is kept clear to you through his thoughts as well as his actions.

The dialogue is intelligent but never "intellectual" or obscure.

and then paraded among the shadows of the house until dawn came, red-rimmed. His hand shook when he drank his coffee. Belle was watching him carefully, and he decided to leave the house for a while. He made a shopping excuse and drove off. It was when he was in motion that Cora's words came back to him. They buffeted in a curious way. He drove the ten miles to the plant area. At once he knew what she had meant.

The excavations were being made across the highway from a boxy development, and the ridgy hills of earth gave off a sour odor so heavy that Talbot fancied it caused his car some effort to push through it. He turned into the development and cruised the streets, seeing that much effort and expense had been used to distinguish the houses in themselves and from each other. Trees had been planted and gardens were shaped.

What he was going to do was decided before he himself knew it. He started to make his house-to-house survey on the blocks that curved against the highway and were nearest the pestilence of the plant area. What he learned drove him home on wings once more, his mind exploding with sound and the architecture of ideas. Borrowed writing and notebook paper were filled with the homesteaders' quotes about the company, bitter, despondent, acrimonious and vicious.

The conflict is chiefly inward, with outward results.

Talbot drove himself that week end, with no practical reason for doing so. The work could have been done calmly and easily during the week in the office. But he drew up a presentation on community relations between noon Saturday and three in the morning Monday, with only five hours off for sleep in between. He made a master plan of the screen of trees and shrubs that should be between the plant and the development; he wrote sample news releases that could be submitted to area papers to show the people that the advent of the plant could increase rather than diminish land and housing values because of the influx of personnel; he wrote sample institutional ads that would be placed in these papers and local magazines. He urged immediate removal of the sour waste earth, and backed up all his suggestions with quotes obtained during his survey of disturbed homeowners. When the whole presentation was in its glossy folder that Belle had gone out specially to buy for him, he went to the bedroom, to find her reading under a low lamp. She put her book aside and waited until he was in his pajamas.

"Put on your robe," she said, "and let's go downstairs for a cup of coffee or chocolate. You look too charged to sleep."

"I am." In the kitchen, he made a small-boy face and said, "Would you think I was nuts if I said I'd like a beer?"

Belle was tender. "I bought some today. I thought you might want it."

He was puzzled. They sat across from each other, Belle with tea,

Talbot with his beer. Belle put her hand over his. "Don't you remember?"

His brow corrugated. Then he drank. "Dee-licious and slightly wonderful!"

"That's what you always used to say."

No matter what the characters do, they remain believable people.

Then it all became clear. The road up, the young road, the mad and glorious road, study and work and week ends frenetic with labor, and gentle interludes, and work again, and the whole process of forging ahead, with Belle watching it all, sharing it and adding to his strength. And the crisp beer when his eyes, head and throat ached.

And he found Belle was wise. "You were recapturing something," she said. "Did you know that?"

He looked into the soft gray understanding of her eyes and lowered his head. And she said, "Is it that bad? Tal, Tal, you always told me."

The author's belief in his story shows in his handling of a realistic problem—and therefore you can believe in it.

He told her everything—how heavy and disgusting the belly felt after the mutton in the tavern, and how he was too hearty to too many, and how he had felt as if something were going to break and cast him into the wasteland of the old and the used, with occlusions or tremors.

She did not dispute him, nor try to dissuade him from his fears, nor did she hide herself from the truth. She accepted it with him.

"I've had my fling," he said. "I don't think I can stand more of the absent treatment. Not and have anything left that you would want."

She did not try to advise him. This was his—and would become hers, too, only when he had made his decision. He looked at her with hope naked on his face.

The emotions of the characters in this story are common to most of us and hence are plausible.

"I'm going to stick around," he said, "a little while. I'm going to see if I get any recognition. Then—then—" He did not finish, and did not have to.

The company's disinterest or oversight infiltrated his office like a pale mockery. He lived with it, stoically, only halfheartedly listening to Joey when he came in with his shoeshine box. Miss Quise was again selling herself to all departments that could use her. Spring light flamed against the windows, chastising the stone and burning the metal. The abyss between the buildings seemed to be acres of inviting light and rose shadows.

Brand has strength, but his strength is not physical. It comes mainly from his ability to reason and persevere.

The community-relations program had been bucked upstairs long before, and now Gordon Mapes brought out the first issues of the *Colossus* containing the interpretation and true text of the annuity-and-insurance plan. After a week, Gordon called and said he had a slew of complimentary comments from the rank and file. Nothing from on high. "We won't get any of that," he said, "unless the top makes a move." And the top didn't.

Talbot took to walking by the river as a religion, watching birds fly off into the wild blue. He sent placid reflections with them, only to feel them come back with stunning force, like stones too heavy to be carried into serenity. And then he knew.

He knew he was earthbound, in a sense, that he could soar only in productive work and not in mere contemplation; that he was not yet tired or had not learned the trick of dissociating himself from business life. He knew that forced to look upon birds or rest in an easy chair and cast his thoughts into blue oblivion, in Florida or elsewhere, he would die of loneliness peculiar to the active man. He would send his very flesh, ounce by ounce, into the yonder, getting nothing back, and would send his spirit, piece by piece, after it, and would become old and thin and lost in the attrition of a personal uselessness.

He stopped walking by the river. He sat at his desk and waited. And hope barely prevailed. Then it slipped away like a golden insect that catches the edge of attention, but is not truly seen before it is gone.

That was the way he was when J. C. Tanner came in one morning and spoke, "O.K., beautiful dreamer."

Talbot looked up blankly.

"How you fixed for lunch, brain trust?" asked Tanner.

Fixed? Lonely, lonely.

"Free," he said.

"Good."

The explosive word took a fix in the room. Gold and green, useless fantasy swept away. Talbot lifted his head sharply.

Tanner stood before him. "Let's take a long slackers' lunch," he said, "and throw some balls into the air. See what they look like." His heavy lids fell and came up over brilliant blue eyes. "Tal, what were you doing in marketing all this time? I've been thinking about your recent employee- and community-relations gambits—and now, you stubborn, independent so-and-so, we have you pegged. A new department, a watchdog, Special Projects!"

It was building, the big living thing that could collect in the doldrums, the storm, the entity that could surge ahead, devouring problems as a tornado took up land and things upon it. Building and flashing in Talbot, with a sense of joy, mingled with the fierce urge of an experienced man still lusty for his combat.

Tanner looked at his watch. "Let's go."

Talbot got up with a smooth springing of muscles, with a stretching in all his being, and his soul uncurled.

"As I remember it," said Tanner, "you're a martini man."

"Right."

"We'll keep it in common." They strode out together.

The heck with the tarpon.

As in most slick stories, the main character solves his own problem: it is not solved for him.

The outcome is logical to the problem and therefore maintains conviction and plausibility to the end.

Because sympathy has been sustained throughout the story, you are pleased at Brand's success and feel an emotional response. What might have happened to you, or someone you know, has been solved in a way you can believe. Although all slick stories are not as realistic as this one, most of the ends achieved by "Company Cast-Off" are common to the slick story.

Lesson seven

Fiction writing

course

The

pulp

story

Although the pulp story must be understandable and satisfying to its audience, it differs in many ways from the slick. Let's
examine some of these differences, starting with the general
ones and then taking up the specifics which set good rules for
pulp writing.

In recent years a number of changes have taken place in the

pulp magazine field. Better grades of paper have replaced the old-time coarse pulp, so that the term is no longer accurate. Furthermore, the once-popular pulp magazine has changed in format (many current publications are pocket-size) and it's gradually been giving way on the newsstands to the paperback and comic books, which sell in the millions. Thus, although the word *pulp* has undergone a variety of transformations, it still serves as a label for certain kinds of fiction.

Unlike the slick story, the pulp is practically limitless in subject matter. Themes considered too sensational or controversial for the slick magazines may appear in the pulps or paperback books as a "true" story—a blend of fact and fiction acceptable to the pulp audience.

The story may be told from the viewpoint of the hero or the villain, or may have no special viewpoint at all, allowing its characters to move around like actors on a stage. The reason is that in the pulp story, the idea or plot—that is, what happens—is more important than either the people in the story or the style in which the tale is told.

For this same reason, the pulp story doesn't pause to examine deeply the motives of its characters, to analyze their aims, to make involved pronouncements about life. It doesn't portray relationships or emotions too complex to grasp quickly. The characters don't become introspective about their problems, but are impelled by these problems into some reaction, usually physical. The pulp story writer tells a story, a yarn, a tale, and the form in which it's told is almost unrestricted, as long as it has a clearly defined goal and proceeds swiftly to this goal in an interesting and exciting manner.

The specific differences—the rules of the pulp story—are also few and flexible, but they are important. Mainly, *the story must have action*. From beginning to end the idea, the characters, the events, must keep moving without pause.

In a slick story, the main character may come to realize within himself some truth that resolves his problem. In pulp stories, this inward resolution wouldn't satisfy readers who value daring, courage, endurance or conquest more than psychological qualities. The reader wants something to happen— a fight, a showdown, a test of heroism, a risk of life—some *outward* crisis which brings about the resolution.

In common with the slick story, the pulp story outcome is almost always moral, proving that the highest ideals of society are triumphant. But because strict believability and identification are not primary here, the story doesn't have to prove any other point.

Wonder, intrigue, curiosity and excitement are more important to the pulp story reader than emotion. In brief, the reader enjoys an armchair adventure. He's not asking to be put in a philosophical frame of mind, but rather to feel that he has had an experience or adventure which real life may deny him. He doesn't want everyday life repeated, but seeks to share in outwitting a criminal, winning a fight, achieving a feat of daring, overcoming a formidable enemy, conquering the unknown or partaking in sensational situations that make him feel involved.

Different kinds of pulp stories

Now that we have covered both the general and specific points that differentiate the pulp story from the slick, let's look at the differences among the pulp stories themselves. While the slick audience is divided into two main categories, the Women's and the General, the pulp audience enjoys many varieties of stories. Some of the main categories are Western, Crime, Science Fiction, Adventure, Romance and Confession. While all of these emphasize action, they differ in particulars.

For instance, the Western. Aside from the obvious fact that it's a story with a Western setting, it is always based on a conflict between good and evil people, with a recurring theme of good triumphing over evil. The story is usually told from a main character's point of view. This character needn't be the hero, but if he happens to be the villain then he must get his punishment and lose out in the end.

The background of a Western can be very broad, such as the settling of frontiers, or it can be merely a trial of endurance faced by one man. Authentic details are extremely important, including the vernacular of the Westerner and knowledgeable descriptions of the garb he wears, the six-shooter he uses, the grub he eats, the sagebrush he rides through. His motives must be easy to understand and his actions based on simple, straightforward responses to his situation.

The reader of a Western invariably expects that the story will settle some worthy issue. Though he can usually anticipate the end, he likes to follow the developments that bring it about: he wants to see the "bad guys" get their comeuppance and the "good guys" win out. To create this wish is an absolute must for the writers of Westerns.

The Crime story has character and action, but it is told more objectively than the Western: it is based more on idea, situation, development and solution of a crime or mystery than on what the characters think or feel. The form is not fixed. The story may be related by an amused, angry or evil bystander. The reader wants to be challenged by a puzzle. He wants to know what happens, how the plot comes out. He isn't deeply involved with the feelings or desires of the characters.

In Science Fiction, ideas are of much greater importance than character. A strong idea, a free play of imagination about space and time, outshadows motivations or emotions of people. Action again is paramount, but it's an objective type of action, not based on a character's goal but on such things as spaceships or hordes of metal men invading the earth.

There is no restriction on viewpoint. In these stories it's almost as if man had lost individuality, traveling beyond it into anonymity. His thoughts seem feeble and helpless in the face of the limitless universe. If the goal of a main character is the foundation of the story, it must be a goal remote from human experience. Wonder and speculation take the place of emotion in the Science Fiction reader's response.

In the Adventure story, which makes up the widest pulp category of all, action might be called the hero. Here the yarns are told in any style that appeals to the writer. The characters are caught in situations based on physical events, physical prowess and physical resolution.

Ruggedness is the main ingredient for the characters—masculinity at its most masculine. Technical details identify a story on sports, the sea, aviation, war, jungle exploration, etc.—but a common foundation is plentiful action. Many of these stories, told in the first person, are so closely allied to fact that the uninitiated reader may feel he's reading non-fiction. There is a distinct difference, however, for the author is a specialist at building a sturdy story on a skeleton of truth.

The Romance and Confession story deals with love that deviates from social standards. It illustrates how it happened and why, goes into the emotions of its main characters and leads them through suffering or enlightenment to a moral outcome. This form of story, like the Adventure story, is separated into categories by the title of the magazine.

The writer of the Confession story tries to make the reader care deeply for the main character and his or her trouble. Through sympathy, the subject matter finds sanction, so that it may deal with intimate aspects of life often untouched by the mass magazines. Because the hero or heroine suffers so completely for his or her sins, the reader's condemnation is tempered. Above all, the Confession story gives the reader a sense of witnessing secret and dangerous transgressions of human conduct.

Many writers belittle the pulp story as being easier to write than others. In spite of its looser form, this isn't true. The pulp story calls for a special skill and special craft. Hence, if you want to write in this field, don't do so because you think it entails less work but because it calls for the kinds of stories you like best.

To show you how the principles of pulp writing are applied by professional authors, we are printing four examples on the following pages: a Western, a Crime, a Science Fiction and an Adventure story, each typical of the pulp category it represents.

Read them carefully, noting our comments in the margins. Compare them with each other, keeping in mind what we've said about pulp stories in this Lesson. Then read other examples from magazines of your own choosing, until you have a clear understanding of the different kinds of pulp fiction and the reasons why each has certain qualities that satisfy a particular audience.

From Frank Gruber's series, *Tales of Wells Fargo,* we reprint "Doc Bell." This is a typical Western story, filled with action and based on the theme that "Crime does not pay."

The two men in the gray prison denims floundered through the brush, scrambling, falling, sliding and plunging from brush clump to brush clump. The baying of hounds, closing in, kept them moving along, far past their endurance point.

One of the men, Doc Bell, was forty or more, a grizzled man, who had lived too hard and was long past his prime. Yet his endurance

Since this is the last story in a book of short stories about Wells Fargo, with Jim Hardie as the agent in every one, the reader is well acquainted with his name.

was greater now than Jim Hardie's, who was ten years younger and supposedly in better physical condition.

It was Hardie who panted. "They're gaining, Doc. We can't outrun those dogs."

"Maybe not," said Doc Bell grimly. "But we can outsmart them."

He took a shaker of cayenne pepper from his pocket. He had pilfered it from the prison kitchen for just such an emergency. He stooped and sprinkled pepper generously into his tracks, reached over and sprinkled in Hardie's footprints. Then, to make certain, he scattered pepper on the ground over a radius of several feet.

There are *two* main characters, Doc Bell and Jim Hardie. But Doc Bell knows Hardie only as "Jim Hollis," and the author is clever enough to have it mentioned once and once only.

"Man's advantage over beast, Jim," Doc Bell observed. "The ability to reason. When those dogs get a whiff of the pepper it'll spoil them for two days. Come on."

He turned and started off down the slope, with renewed vigor. Hardie, groaning, followed the older man. The brush grew heavier and for a moment was so thick that it almost stopped Doc Bell. He finally forced his way through a heavy clump and exclaimed, "The river, Jim! We made it."

Hardie made it to the river's edge, beside Doc Bell. They waded into the shallow water, walked downstream around a bend, then found a sand bar and walked quickly across to the far side, where they climbed out of the water.

Both these characters seem to be villains.

"The race is not always to the swiftest," Doc Bell observed then, panting heavily.

"We need clothes," said Hardie, "and horses. They take money."

Doc Bell looked searchingly at Hardie. "You wouldn't be getting ideas, would you, Jim?"

"What's that supposed to mean?"

"A man is apt to distrust in others the things he feels in himself," said Doc Bell, sententiously. "There's a price of three thousand dollars on my head, and there's a little bit of larceny in everybody."

Jim Hardie smiled easily. "It wouldn't be worth it, Doc. Figure it out. I turn you in and then serve my ten years. That's only three hundred a year."

Doc Bell looked thoughtfully at Hardie for a long moment, then clapped him on the shoulder. "That's sound reasoning. I like that in you, Jim. No sentiment. Just reason."

Identification with either of these men is not necessary. You're reading mainly to find out what happens to them, what the story idea will lead to.

A half hour later, the two escaped convicts broke through a fringe of brush and saw a chuck wagon, some fifty yards away. The tantalizing odor of frying meat assailed their nostrils.

"Manna from heaven," said Doc Bell.

"Just one man," said Hardie. "But he's got a gun and we haven't."

Doc Bell moved back into the brush. Hardie followed. Doc seated himself on the ground and took off a shoe and a sock. He began to fill the sock with sand. "A sock full of sand has certain anaesthetic value," he observed. He reached up and handed the sock to Hardie.

"I've noticed a certain grace of movement in you that I don't possess."

"You also noticed the six-gun he's wearing," said Hardie, sarcastically.

Doc Bell got to his feet. "It's root hog or die."

Hardie nodded and again stepped out of the brush. The cook's back was turned to him and he advanced cautiously across the level ground. He was within two yards of the cook before the latter heard him. He started to turn, then, and Hardie leaped in. The sock in his hand crushed in the cook's hat and thudded on his skull. The cook fell sidewards, missing the fire in front of him.

Hardie was examining the stunned man when Doc Bell padded up. "I hope he isn't hurt bad," Hardie said.

Doc Bell stooped over the unconscious man and examined the bruise on his head. He straightened. "He won't even have much of a bump." He looked at Hardie with new interest. "You did that nicely. I deplore a needless waste of life. Spent too many years saving lives, I guess." Hardie was already peeling off his prison garb.

A few minutes later, after a short rummaging through the chuck wagon, both men were wearing new apparel and Doc Bell was feeding their old prison garments into the flames of the cookfire.

Hardie nodded approval. "It's real pleasurable to watch that phase of my life go up in flames."

"And like phoenix," said the ex-doctor, "a new man rises from the ashes."

"It'd be nice to think so, but it won't be that way."

"Don't tell me you've changed your mind, Jim. Back there in prison you used to say if you ever got out you'd go straight as a string."

"And I would, too," Hardie said. "If I had a nest egg."

"What do you call a nest egg?"

"Oh, I don't know. Enough to go to Mexico. Live it up some."

"I like Mexico," said Doc Bell, nodding thoughtfully. "I was a surgeon in the Army there, during the war."

"So you told me."

"You don't believe me?"

Hardie smiled thinly. "Hardly."

"A man like you, Jim, one who has never known respectability, you can't imagine the pull to return to it."

"I suppose not," said Hardie. "All I know is it takes money to live up to my appetite."

"How much money?"

"What's the use talking about it. There isn't a town in the country we can get into, much less get out of."

"What if I were to tell you that I know where there's a great deal of money?"

The author's style is straightforward and objective, with no emphasis on writing as writing.

All the characters' thoughts are expressed aloud. There's no inward speculation or philosophizing.

Sympathy for any one character is not as yet possible, but may arise from the action of the story.

The background provides action as well as setting. Notice, by the way, that in this part of the story, Doc Bell introduces Jim Hardie as "Jim Hollis." Otherwise, he's addressed simply as "Jim."

The dialogue is straight to the point and spurs the action.

"Try me," grinned Hardie. "I might be interested."

"I'll do better than that. I'll show you."

Three days later, Doc Bell and Jim Hardie, unshaved, their clothing alkali-stained and travel-worn, rode tired horses up the last sharp slope of an incline and reached a small cove that seemed to have been gouged out of the mountain itself by a gigantic superhuman hand. At the far side of the semicircle a weathered shack stood with its back wall against the sheer side of the cliff.

A man sitting on a bench against the wall, got to his feet, sprang to the door and called inside. Two men came pouring out and the three lined up to watch Doc Bell and Hardie ride up and dismount.

A stocky brick-haired man who answered to the name of Brick, set the tone of the greeting. "Sure glad to see you again, Doc. When word got around that you was out, we was real pleased."

A tall curly-haired youngster with a mean look indicated Jim Hardie. "Who's he?"

"His name's Jim Hollis," Doc Bell said. "He made the break with me."

"So?" sneered the curly-haired one.

Hardie grinned. "Your friends don't seem very glad to see me, Doc."

"It's greed, Jim," opined Doc Bell. "Pure greed. Look at them. That grin on Brick's face has a dollar sign on every tooth. The big one's Tibbs. But Curly here, he's the prize of the lot. Right now he's trying to figure how much he'll lose if you're dealt in."

"Cut the fancy talk, Doc," snarled Curly. "Is he in?"

"You're a good student of human nature," Hardie said to Bell.

"I pride myself on it."

"I asked a question, Doc," persisted Curly.

"Maybe I can answer it better than he can," Hardie said, hard and even. "Doc and I crawled halfway across this state together. If he says I'm in—I'm in."

"That answer your question, Curly?" Doc Bell asked.

Curly's lips curled back into a snarl. "If a man's going to ride with us on a job we've got a right to know what he's like."

"That's reasonable," admitted Bell. "What do you want to know?"

"Doc," said Curly, earnestly. "You're smarter than I am and I know it. But he isn't . . . and I don't see why we should split with him."

"I do. Isn't that enough?"

"If you say so, Doc," Brick said, quickly.

"No, it's not enough," Curly said, doggedly.

Doc Bell turned to Hardie. "There seems to be some doubt in Curly's mind as to your usefulness."

Hardie nodded to Curly. "You're a fast draw, I hear. Go ahead and draw."

"You do, Curly, and we'll be short a man." Doc made a smooth movement and a Frontier Model appeared in his hand.

"Put it away, Doc," said Hardie. "I don't need help."

"Maybe not, but *I* need you . . . and I'm still running things. That right, Curly?"

Curly waited a long moment before replying. Then he said, "Yeah, that's right, Doc."

The little cabin was well stocked with food and the bandits were prepared for almost any eventuality—except boredom. There was nothing for them to do. They slept, they ate and they played cards and wrangled with one another. Tempers became testy.

Doc Bell was their leader. His words and actions could not be questioned. When he saddled his horse every morning and rode down the steep trail not to reappear again until late afternoon and sometimes even after darkness had fallen no one dared to question him. Jim Hardie noticed that the former doctor carried a pair of high-powered binoculars with him and assumed that he was not taking the glasses merely to watch jack rabbits from a distance.

Something was in the wind, Hardie knew that. What it was, he had not the slightest idea.

After several days in the outlaw hideout, Hardie watched Doc Bell leave one morning and, turning, observed that Curly was in turn watching him. He shook his head.

"For a man who likes to talk," Hardie said, "Doc sure can keep things to himself. Wonder what he's got up his sleeve?"

"He'll tell you when he wants you to know."

"I suppose so. Hope it's as big as that Marysville job."

Curly cocked his head to one side. "What about Marysville?"

"Well, Doc was doin' the time for it. You fellows must've cut up quite a hand."

"Matter of fact," scowled Brick, coming up in time to hear, "we ain't seen any of that money yet. Doc stashed it."

Hardie grinned. "He's smarter than I thought he was. You grind the corn and he gets the mash."

It was the following morning when Doc Bell finally assembled the members of the gang about him, in front of the cabin. Getting down on both knees he spread out a large sheet of paper. "Here's the lay-out," he said, "and this is what each of us will do."

He proceeded to elaborate on the plan and Hardie, studying the plan and listening to the doctor, found that his estimation of the bandit leader was all too meager. Doc Bell had not only figured out every contingency that could arise, but had worked out the solution.

He spent two hours discussing the plan, then answered questions for another hour, and later in the day called the men together again and once more went over the thing, in detail.

The *whoo-hoo* of the train whistle was the signal for Doc Bell,

No warm sentiment flows through the story. The motivations are neither moral nor commendable—as far as we know.

Emotional response is not asked, other than excitement over the physical crisis ahead.

Hardie and the others to ride their horses out of the patch of woods, onto the railroad right of way. Then, as the engineer began to apply the brakes when he saw the log barrier on the tracks, the train robbers put spurs to their horses and galloped down both sides of the right of way. They discharged their revolvers, yelled and made as much noise as possible. Before the train had come to a full stop, Brick was in the cab, threatening the engineer and fireman.

Tibbs and Curly caught up the log laid conveniently close to the rails and were ready to rush the log end at the door of the express car. Only Hardie held back and Doc, standing to one side, snapped at him: "What are you waiting for, Jim? Give Curly and Tibbs a hand."

Hardie trotted up to the battering ram and grabbing hold with both hands, fell into step with the other bandits. They rushed at the door of the express car.

Inside the express car a rifle banged. A splinter was torn from the log, inches from Hardie's hands. He promptly let go of the log.

Tibbs dropped his end and Curly, swearing furiously, let go of his own end. The three men took cover along the side of the embankment and began firing with their revolvers at the express car.

There's no internal conflict in one character—the conflict is between characters, or characters and elements.

Behind them Doc Bell roared: "Hold your fire, men!"

Crouched, he came up to the embankment. "Give me your shirt, Jim," he snapped. "You, too, Curly . . ."

Without question, Hardie peeled off his shirt. Curly sullenly tore off his own shirt. Doc grabbed the two shirts and, bent low, ran forward to the engine cab. He boarded it, grabbed down a signal lantern and unscrewing the fuel cap poured coal oil onto the shirts.

Carrying the oil-soaked shirts he climbed onto the coal car and negotiated his way along the top, to the express car. Ducking under the end window, he reached up and with the butt of his revolver smashed in the glass. Then, striking a match and applying it to the oil-soaked shirts he threw the flaming mass through the express car window.

Smoke began to pour out of the window. Doc Bell grinned, moved to the side of the car, then dropping down to the right of way made a short run to the embankment behind which Hardie and the others were still crouched.

"They ain't gonna open that door," Brick said, pessimistically.

"He's right, Doc," said Hardie. "Let's forget this one. There'll be a posse from town in no time."

"Go ahead, get out," snapped Doc Bell. "All of you. I'm staying. There's a hundred thousand in that car."

The bandits hesitated. The firing inside the express car had stopped. Smoke was pouring through the windows broken by the gunfire of the bandits. "You goin'?" Doc asked, nastily.

There's no letup of action. It gathers momentum.

Before any of the others could reply the door of the express car started to open. A Wells Fargo guard dropped to the ground. His eyes were streaming.

"It worked!" screamed Curly.

"Of course it worked," Doc said, calmly. "All right, Curly, you and Tibbs. Get in and haul out the box."

Tibbs and Curly clambered to their feet and rushed to the express car. Tibbs reached it first. He started to climb up. A shot inside the car rang out and Tibbs fell back to the ground.

Curly yelped, thrust his gun into the car and fired twice. He stopped, peered inside, then fired again.

"Two men in the express car," winced Doc Bell. "One thing I hadn't counted on."

Tibbs made it to the outlaws' hideout, but he lost much blood on the way and was pale and only semiconscious when his companions deposited him on his bunk in the cabin.

Doc Bell bent over the wounded man. He tore away his shirt and studied the wound. "No bones broken, but he's lost a lot of blood."

He looked at a shelf across the room, where a medical bag was shrouded in dust. Drawing a deep breath, Doc crossed the room and took down the bag.

Hardie, alarmed, stepped forward. "Now, wait a minute, Doc. This is no job for an amateur."

"We'll see who's an amateur," Doc Bell replied, crookedly.

Hardie moved back to the wounded Tibbs. "Nobody knows me in town. It'd be better to take you to a real doctor."

Tibbs stared at him mutely.

"If gangrene sets in, you'll lose that arm," Hardie went on. "Maybe your life."

Doc Bell came up. Tibbs' eyes met his. "Perhaps you'd better do like he says, Doc," Tibbs said, weakly. "Let him take me to the edge of town and dump me. I'll make it to a doctor."

"You still don't believe I was a real doctor," Bell said to Hardie. "During the war, I handled as many as fifty gun wounds like this in a single day." He turned to the other outlaws. "Curly, Brick, come over here and hold him down."

Hardie moved back and the other outlaws came forward. They gripped Tibbs tightly, but Brick, Hardie noticed, turned away his head. Doc Bell noted it. "Brick's squeamish, Jim. How about helping?"

Hardie saw there was nothing to do but fall in. He moved forward and Brick gladly stepped aside.

Doc Bell opened his bag and brought out a forceps and scalpel. With swift, sure movements he probed for the bullet, cut a little with the knife, then reaching in again with the forceps, brought it out.

A smile of triumph was on his face as he exhibited the bullet gripped by the tongs of the forceps.

Action takes precedence over characterization and all other elements in the story.

You are not presented with a gradually emerging theme or message, only the testing of physical endurance and resourcefulness.

"Who's an amateur?" he asked.

Hardie nodded. "You're a real pro, Doc."

It was later, when the patient, bandaged and under sedation, was sleeping that the loot of the train holdup was sorted out on the table in the cabin. There were five large stacks of bills.

"Twenty thousand apiece," Doc Bell announced. He looked at Jim Hardie and sighed. "Seems a shame, in a way."

"How do you mean?" asked Hardie.

"Well, this money represents a month's wages for all the miners who work by the sweat of their bodies. Curly, here, will spend his trying to make eight the hard way. Tibbs—he's got a weakness for women."

"I'm not spreading *my* share around," Hardie said.

"Listen to him, boys," said Doc Bell. "Jim reasons things out."

"This money'll be hotter than the mill tails of Hades," Hardie went on.

Curly grabbed up his stack of bills. "I'll spend mine while I'm young enough to enjoy it."

"You might not get a chance," Hardie said, pointedly.

"I'll sure try," declared Curly.

Hardie shook his head. "Wells Fargo's got the serial numbers of every one of those bills. They're just hoping we'll start spending it."

"You seem to know a lot about it," Curly said, sullenly.

"It's not the first Wells Fargo job I've pulled," Hardie said, evenly. "How do you think I wound up in jail."

Authentic details support the plausibility and mood of story, and Doc Bell's quotation about money and evil is the theme of the story.

"Suppose *you* worry about you," snapped Curly. "I'll take care of myself."

"The love of money is the root of all evil," Doc Bell quoted.

"I never knew you to have any objections to it," Curly snarled. "Your fancy talk don't go down any more, Doc."

"Pearls before swine, Jim," Doc Bell quoted again.

Hardie smiled tightly. "I've got a real respect for Wells Fargo detectives."

Doc started to turn away, but Curly put up a detaining hand. "We ain't finished, Doc."

Doc Bell gave the young outlaw a cool glance. "As far as I'm concerned we are."

Curly looked at Brick. What he saw in the other man's face, apparently reassured him. "I mean the money we got comin' from the Marysville job."

"Maybe you was figurin' on runnin' out on us, huh, Doc?" Brick said, cheerfully.

Hardie said: "You listen to Curly, Brick, and you'll wind up in jail. You know what that's like? They put you in a cell that's ten feet long and six feet wide. I've seen men bang their heads against the wall. Big men, just like you."

"You stay out of this," Curly said nastily to Hardie. "What you do with your cut on the last deal is your business. We're talkin' about something else."

Doc Bell smiled placatingly at the angry Curly. "Don't you think it would be better if I kept the money for you? You'll spend this pile and need more in a little while."

"I want it now!" said Curly.

Doc Bell heaved a long sigh of resignation. "All right. But it's not here, you know."

You want to see these outlaws brought down, and the wish carries you on to see how it will come about.

"I know that," said Curly. "We darn' near tore the place down lookin'."

"While you was away," Brick added.

Hardie smiled at Doc Bell. "Looks like they don't trust you, Doc."

"It has to be hid somewhere close by," Curly went on. "They caught you at the foot of the mountain."

"I'll have to go to town to get it," Doc Bell finally said.

"You hid it in town?" cried Brick.

"The obvious is sometimes the most advantageous. Right, Jim?"

"Leave me out of this one, Doc. I've got all that's coming to me, right here. I had no part in the Marysville holdup."

Two hours later Tibbs awakened from his drugged sleep and declared himself ready for anything. Doc Bell tried to tell him that he should take it easy for a couple of days, but Tibbs, when he learned that Doc was going for the Marysville money, insisted on getting up and going with the others.

As a result, the five men rode down the mountain trail. Reaching the valley below, Jim Hardie pulled up his horse. Doc Bell rode up to him and held out his hand.

"Good-by, Jim."

Hardie smiled ruefully. "Just 'so long,' Doc. I've got a feeling we'll all meet together real soon."

"I hope not," chuckled Doc Bell.

Hardie waved to the other members of the gang, then headed his horse across the valley, to the west.

He passed over a low knoll, rode into woods and then abruptly turned his mount eastward.

It was dusk when he rode into Marysville. He turned off at the first cross street and there dismounted and tied his horse to a hitch rail. He moved off into the shadow of a building and settled down for a wait.

At the other end of town, Doc Bell turned to Curly, the wounded Tibbs, and Brick. "From here, I go in alone."

And now what's going to happen? Whatever the answer is, it will be in terms of action.

"All right, Doc," Curly said, after a pause, "but don't try anything fancy. There won't be a rock big enough to hide under if you do."

Doc gave Curly a thin smile and, turning his horse, rode up the dark street at an easy canter. He continued down the street, out of sight of the gang, past the Wells Fargo office and on to the far end of Marysville.

He scarcely looked to the right or left as he rode and he never once stopped.

He was clearing the last building on the street, when he became aware of hoofbeats behind him. He swiveled in the saddle and made out a single horse coming after him.

He did not pull up his horse, did not put it into a gallop. Jim Hardie rode up beside him.

"Goin' some place, Doc?" Hardie asked, carelessly. His revolver was in his fist.

Doc Bell shook his head. "You disappoint me, Jim. I hardly expected you to rob a friend."

"What do you call what *you're* doing?"

"I told you before, Curly, Brick and Tibbs were acquaintances. Not friends. Now, I'm going to disappoint you. I haven't got the Marysville money."

"What gave you the notion I was interested in that?" Hardie asked.

"Then why are you here?"

"You're a smart man, Doc," Hardie said. "I'm not exactly stupid, myself. I thought with the others out of the way we'd make a good team."

"With you cutting in on the Marysville money?"

"Nope. I only want what we earn together. You and I could go a long way."

"You mean that? You don't want any of the Marysville money?"

Hardie put away his revolver.

"Then let's go get it," said Doc Bell, putting spurs to his horse.

Hardie was not too surprised when he found himself climbing the steep trail that led to the hideout. Doc Bell looked over his shoulder once or twice and when they reached the cabin and dismounted he said to Hardie:

"Remember what I said? That the most obvious is the most advantageous."

He walked up to the door, but instead of entering, grabbed the single-step doorstoop. He heaved back, moving the stoop forward a foot. A black metal box was revealed.

"They've been walking over this for six months," Doc said.

From the shelter of some rocks fifty yards away, came a blast of gunfire. It was hastily fired, in rage, and Doc Bell and Jim Hardie were able to throw themselves flat on the ground, without being hit.

From there Doc returned the fire, then suddenly rose and, crouching, ran for the shelter of a huge rock. From behind it he peppered the rocks concealing the other outlaws and Jim Hardie was able to

The physical action never falters, approaches its crisis.

The big moment of the Western pulp story comes: the showdown—the battle.

make it to the protection of the rock that shielded Doc Bell.

There was a moment of quiet and during it, Curly's voice yelled: "No deals this time, Doc. It's gonna be you and the money."

"Stay with me all the way, Jim," Doc said to Hardie, "and we split down the middle."

To the other outlaws he replied: "Go to hell!"

Curly's voice rose once more: "We've got no quarrel with you, Jim. Get on your horse and go."

Hardie said to Bell: "There's just a chance I can outsmart them."

"Go ahead, Jim!"

Hardie rose up to a standing crouch. "Curly," he yelled. "You mean it?"

"Like I said," Curly's voice replied. "Go ahead."

"You've already got Doc," Hardie said, "and I sure don't fit into this argument."

He started out from the rocks, moved toward the cabin, where his horse stood patiently. Curly rose up from behind the rocks that had concealed him. He started into the open, then Brick and Tibbs showed.

Hardie, watching closely, saw the wicked grin that came over Curly's face. He waited until the outlaw's gun began to swing toward him, then he whipped up his own gun and fired.

Curly's gun went off, a fraction of a second after Hardie's bullet struck him. It was that close. Before he hit the ground, Doc Bell was up, firing at Tibbs and Brick. In a moment it was over and Doc Bell came toward Hardie.

"That split still goes, Jim," he said, holstering his gun.

Hardie's gun covered Bell. "I'm afraid I've got to take it all."

Vast disappointment came over Doc Bell's features. "I knew I couldn't trust this scum, Jim, but you—I prided myself on my judgment of you. I thought you were honest."

"You were right, Doc," Hardie said heavily. "The only thing I lied about to you, was—my name. It's Jim Hardie. I also didn't tell you that I work for Wells Fargo and that I had myself put into prison to . . . well, to do what I did."

If you know Wells Fargo stories, you already know that Jim Hardie is the "good" man—the hero. But if you don't, you can only guess that he may have some other purpose in his partnership with Doc Bell than getting money. By not knowing his thoughts, you're made to wait for a revelation through action.

The hero is revealed! And through his courage and fortitude, good triumphs over evil: law and justice prevail.

"Dead Boys Don't Remember," from *Ellery Queen's Mystery Magazine,* is a Crime story by Frances and Richard Lockridge, who are also well known to readers and to radio and TV audiences for their "Mr. and Mrs. North" detective series.

The bus stopped at the head of Blueberry Lane and red warning lights blinked fore and aft. Behind it, two cars halted obediently, and then a third came round the bend of the state road and stopped, too. One car, with equal obedience, pulled up facing the blue and yellow school bus, and that was at 3:20 of a Friday afternoon in late May.

Like the Western, this story starts off with action.

A main character, Rodney Burke, is introduced and described outwardly, as if by someone watching him. His thoughts aren't given.

Rodney Burke got off the bus, carrying his schoolbooks. He was towheaded and sturdy and a few months more than ten years old. The boys and girls who remained in the bus made shrill sounds, as if something very exciting were happening.

There was nothing actually exciting under way—School Bus No. 3, of District No. 1, had made its scheduled stop at Blueberry Lane, so that Rodney Burke could get off and walk half a mile along a shaded, little-used road to the sprawling white house he lived in. It was the back way home; the conventional way was by the town road which paralleled the state road, and it was on the town road that the Franklin Burke house fronted—fronted distantly, as became so large a house, so deep in spreading lawns.

Several of the boys and girls yelled, " 'Bye, Rod!" as if he were going on a long journey from which return was improbable. Rod waved and yelled back—yelled " 'Bye, kids," as if this were indeed a parting. Then, bareheaded, the sun bright on his bright hair, he walked into the lane—walked out of the sun into the shade, into the flecked pattern of shadow and sunlight which moved gently on the road surface.

The road curved after a hundred yards or so and Rodney Burke—walking in the middle of the roadway, wearing a striped shirt and denim trousers and sneakers—went around the bend in the lane, out of sight from the state road. But the bus had pulled away by then.

It takes a boy of ten varying times to walk half a mile on a shady lane, depending on how much of a hurry he is in and, of course, on what shows up. If deer show up, for example, he stops to look at deer, partly because deer look so expectantly at people, partly because they are very pretty creatures, and when they finally decide to bound away the white of their tails is like froth on breaking waves.

But Rod was seldom a boy to dawdle: he was a boy of projects, most of which involved building something. Usually he came up the garage drive—sometimes running—within ten minutes after the bus stopped, and one could set clocks by the bus.

Janice Burke was working in her annual garden partly because it needed weeding—as didn't it always?—and partly because it was an experience of infinite sweetness to see her son coming along the drive, with the afternoon sun bright on his hair. Janice was a little flushed—it was quite warm for May—and she was a little older than most mothers of boys of ten.

Close identification with any character is not possible since the author switches from one to the other.

The Burkes had waited a dozen years before they had had a child, so that Rodney had seemed rather a miracle. He still did. They tried, of course, not to let him know it, nor make too much of an only child. "We mustn't fuss over him," they told each other, and usually managed not to.

Is it "fussing" over a boy to notice if he takes ten minutes longer than usual to walk half a mile through a lane in which there are no perils? There is no reason to be anxious if he is twenty minutes later than usual—probably the bus is late. But at twenty minutes of four, Janice Burke stood up in her garden and shielded her blue eyes with a grubby hand as she looked into the sun, since the boy would come out of the sun. And five minutes later she walked—to meet him, she told herself—along the garage drive and around the garage, where the field road ran down to Blueberry Lane. When she saw the field road empty, she began to hurry and then to call, "Rod, Rod?"

When she ran back from the empty lane, her breath came shudderingly. In the house she went to the telephone and drew deep, but still shuddering, breaths as she dialed, and tried to make her voice steady as she spoke. But her voice still shook. Rod had left on the bus with the others; they were sure of that at the school. And the bus had been on time, and Rod had got off at the usual place. Harry Bigham, who drove the school bus and had just returned to the garage from his last trip, was sure of that.

Janice Burke was reaching toward the telephone again, but it rang under her hand and she snatched at it. She said, "Yes?" in a voice not like her own.

"Mrs. Burke?" a man's voice said, and she said, "Yes. Oh, *yes!*"

"We've got the boy," the man said. It was a voice like any voice. "We'll tell you what to do tomorrow. You hear what I'm saying?"

"Yes," she said. "Yes! *Rod is*—"

"He'll be all right if you do what we tell you," the man said. "If you pay what we tell you." And then his voice faded, as he turned from the telephone. But she could hear him say, "Bring the kid here."

Then she heard Rod's voice—oh, his voice, *his* voice. "Mama?" Rod said. "*Mama!* They—"

She heard a click and the telephone was dead. She called into it —called the boy's name. Then she fainted. Franklin Burke, coming home early from the city, walked into the living room in time to see his wife sway in the chair and fall from it.

Janice came quickly back to an ugly world and clung to her husband, shaking—and told him.

It was not a decision which many have to make; it is a decision to be reached in agony. Nothing one does is better than any other thing, surer than any other. Franklin Burke called the State Police, to whom country people turn most readily. The police told him, when they came—not noisily and as much as possible by back roads—that he had done the right thing, and hoped they were telling him the truth.

They told him, too, that it looked like the work of professionals, and that the chances were better if that was so. Professionals wanted money; they wouldn't panic; wouldn't—they didn't finish that, or need to, and again they hoped that they were right.

The idea—the mystery and complications—are more important than any other element of the story.

"I'll pay anything," Franklin Burke said, "anything I've got . . ."

"Only," the captain in charge of Troop K said at Hawthorne Barracks, "only, the kid's ten, isn't he? Old enough to remember faces. Remember places. He won't remember if he's dead."

"No," Captain Heimrich—Captain M. L. Heimrich, whose concern is with murder—said. "No, he won't remember if he's dead. He may be already."

The author's style is utilitarian—the fastest and most economical means of moving the plot toward its goal.

They did not, of course, say that to the Burkes—to the tall, gray-haired man with face set hard, to the white-faced woman, whose eyes stared in terror and disbelief, and who would not let a doctor give her sedatives. "I've got to be here," she said, and said it over and over and over, "be here when he comes back." But the Burkes knew without being told . . .

The polish of professional crime showed in several ways. On that the various police agencies agreed—and by Saturday morning everybody was in on it. The police of the villages and cities of Westchester and Putnam counties were in on it, and the sheriffs of the counties, and the New York City police and the FBI. And, of course, the New York State police, with whom it began. They all agreed the crime was professional, and probably the work of city professionals, since professionals are, for the most part, city men.

There was the deftness of the kidnapping itself. It was not by chance that a car had waited at just the right time, just the right distance along the lane, for Rodney Burke. (The car had pulled to the soft shoulder of the narrow lane and left tire tracks.) It was not by chance that the boy was the son, and the only son, of people with the money the Burkes had, or that their house, and the lane leading toward it, were isolated in the town of Van Brunt, near the Hudson.

It was not by chance that the letter which came in Saturday's mail was typed (new typewriter, almost without idiosyncrasies) on white paper one could buy anywhere, or that there were no fingerprints to guide, except those of postal clerks on the envelope. The letter had been mailed in midtown Manhattan. The letter read:

Complications pile up and the story continues to move on a basis of action.

Price is $100,000. Raise it by Monday and you will be told what to do. It will be tough for the boy if you get new bills, or big ones.

All planned, the police thought—shrewdly planned, with no amateurs involved. Ruthlessly planned. They'll kill him, Captain Heimrich thought, one man in thousands hunting a stolen child—hunting with nothing much to go on, and nothing much to hope for, and haunted by the memory of a woman whose eyes looked and looked, and saw nothing. Probably dead already, Heimrich thought, on Saturday afternoon, as he followed a lead which would take him nowhere.

They had, after some thought, decided to let the newspapers have it. Professionals would know already that the police were in it; the outermost filaments of the web they lived in would have quivered that news to the center.

If enough people heard about it, somebody might see something, remember something. Many did, of course. Leads came from everywhere. Rodney Burke, age ten, fair hair, blue eyes, 84 pounds, was everywhere.

By Saturday afternoon he had been seen as far away as the West Coast. (The police doubted that. A car had been used, probably still was being used. But they checked everything, since anything was possible.)

A boy (surely Rod) had been seen running along a sidewalk in Mt. Kisco. They found the boy, who had been going to the grocery for his mother, and running because he wanted to run. (And who did not look at all like Rod.) The Virginia State Police closed in on a motel in Emporia because a boy was crying loudly in one of the rooms and sobbing out, "I want to go home." The boy was six. He was crying because he wanted to go home.

No inner conflict is depicted, no relationships examined.

Heimrich, alone in an unmarked car—the police were spread thin to spread wide—drove down a long, rough driveway toward a house secluded in the woods. He drove down the drive because somebody had seen a car drive down it earlier, and somebody was quite sure the people who owned the house were in Europe. They were going on as little as that.

The house, when Heimrich came to it, was a rather large house— a house which had accumulated largeness over years. It was set in a green cup of lawn, with woods edging it. There was a car, with city license plates, parked where the drive widened. Heimrich stopped close behind the city car and got out, and as he got out a man came to the door of the house, and then onto the flagstones.

He was a young man in a polo shirt and slacks—a pleasant-looking young man, who smiled at Heimrich pleasantly. Heimrich told him about Rodney Burke and the smile vanished and the man swore. He said that kidnapping was the dirtiest business there was.

"Yes," Heimrich said. "This is your house, Mr.—?"

"Baxter," the man said. "No. Friends letting me use it. Only been here a couple of hours. Drove up from town and—" He stopped. His eyes narrowed. "Empty house," he said. "You think—?"

"Now, Mr. Baxter," Heimrich said. "We're looking everywhere, naturally. You've been through the house?"

"All this?" Baxter said, and motioned toward the sprawling house behind him. "Must be a dozen rooms. All we need is a couple of them." He paused. "Got friends coming up later," he said, and then, "You want to look? Come on."

There's a challenge in the nonchalance of the pleasant young man, and you're not likely to put the story down until you explore the house with Heimrich.

He might as well, as long as he was there, Heimrich said. But it would be time wasted, as the morning had been time wasted, and now half the afternoon.

It was. They went together from room to room—looked into the attic and the basement, looked in bedrooms and kitchen and in three shining bathrooms. "Nice place," Baxter said, as they came into the living room, with the house searched and nothing found. "Lucky people. How about a drink?"

"No," Heimrich said. "I'll be getting on. Thanks for—" He stopped, as if listening. Baxter waited.

"Wish I could do more," Baxter said.

"Yes," Heimrich said, but not as if he were answering the pleasant young man in slacks and polo shirt. It was, instead, as if Baxter's voice had interrupted something, as if music were playing which Heimrich strained to hear.

"You hear water dripping anywhere?" Heimrich said. "Bathrooms? Kitchen?"

Baxter looked surprised, puzzled. Then he shook his head slowly, and listened, too. Listening carefully, he heard a faint sound which seemed to come from everywhere, and from nowhere—a kind of grating sound, rhythmical, with metallic pings marking the beat. The sound had just begun.

"I hear it now," Baxter said. "Just barely hear it. Something running in the house? Refrigerator, or—"

"Probably," Heimrich said. "Well, sorry to have bothered you, Mr. Baxter."

It might work that way. Heimrich went out onto the terrace, with Baxter in the living room, looking after him curiously. Heimrich looked around for what he wanted and found it. It was near the edge of the grass, a cube of cement blocks rising three feet above the lawn. It was capped by a heavy metal cover.

Heimrich started to walk toward it, and Baxter came out of the house and watched him. A pocket of Baxter's slacks bulged, heavily. So it wasn't going to be that way.

Heimrich whirled as Baxter reached toward the heavy pocket, and Heimrich was the quicker. "Now, Mr. Baxter," Heimrich said in his soft voice from behind a steady revolver, "we'll go have a look in the pump house. Good place to lock a small boy up in, wouldn't it be? Cover too heavy for a boy to lift and—*better drop it, Mr. Baxter*."

The man who called himself Baxter dropped it. He wasn't pleasant-looking any more. He went ahead of Heimrich toward the concrete cube.

"Get the cover off," Heimrich told Baxter, and Baxter got the cover off. It was heavy enough—far too heavy to be moved by a boy who, to push against it, would have to balance himself on iron rungs set close to the inner wall of the pump house.

The boy balanced himself on the rungs now and started to come out—and saw Baxter and started to go down again. "All right, son," Heimrich said. "All right, Rod. You can come out, now."

Good versus evil is the only moral issue involved, the only theme.

Your chief interest is to see how the details are worked out and whether the boy will be recovered alive—not the sentiment or emotion of the characters.

It was like hide-and-go-seek, and the game over, and everybody home safe. Rodney Burke came out, blue eyes wide. He shrank away a little from Baxter, who did not move, and looked at Heimrich and said, "Are you a policeman, sir?"

"Yes," Heimrich said. "How did you start up the pump?"

"Anybody knows that," Rodney told him, and was evidently surprised that everybody did not. "There's a faucet. So they can drain the tank to clean it. And when the water comes out, the pressure goes down and the pump starts and—"

"Of course," Heimrich said, gravely, and kept his revolver pointed at Baxter, who had never heard of this before.

"It's an old-style pump," Rod said. "Metal pipes. They use plastic now, mostly. Because with metal pipes the noise the pump makes telegrams—no, tele*graphs* through them and into the house—"

"Yes," Heimrich said. "See it now, Mr. Baxter? Water pumps don't start up until enough water's been run out of the pressure tank. And—*there wasn't any water running in the house, was there?*"

"I saw a car come up," Rodney said. "Through the little window. The venti—ventilator? And I thought I'd just try. Maybe somebody'd hear. Because when I yelled nobody could—"

He stopped. "Gee," he said. "I left the water running. Pump the well dry."

Before Heimrich could do anything, Rodney seemed to bounce to the top of the pump house. He went down into it. He came back out of it. "All right now," Rodney Burke, country boy, trained to country ways, said, and the sun was bright on his bright hair.

The country boy defeating the criminal from the city is the pivotal point, confirming the theme that crime does not pay.

Baxter, city man, used to city ways, looked at Rodney Burke. He began to shake his head slowly. It had looked like a perfect setup—a perfect place to keep a boy in until he decided what to do with him. How was a city man to know?

Imagination is given free rein in the Science Fiction story, but the pulp market requirements are still those of the Western and the Adventure types—physical conflict and physical courage. From *Amazing Science Fiction Stories* we reprint Henry Slesar's "No Place to Go."

There were four of them. Major Cato was the leader, because the gold leaves on his shoulder said he was, and because the others felt he was. Casey Strauss was the navigator, a big, gruff young man who rarely talked or smiled. Finney was the copilot, a slender, engaging man, popular with women. Bob Joyce was the youngest, and the most erudite. He knew rockets, and that was important to a rocket crew, even on their sixth journey to the Earth's neighbor.

They were the elite. They were four out of a squadron whose members numbered less than sixty. But out of the fifteen exploratory

Although a main character is introduced with the rest of his group, any close reader identification will obviously be subordinated to an idea.

moon trips to date, they had made six. They were proud, but not cocky. Space took care of that. It was too vast to sustain cockiness.

The sixth landing was the easiest one yet. They cheered Major Cato until he was forced into an embarrassed command that silenced them. They began the long, arduous preparations to establish a camp on the moon.

"Lieutenant Finney," Major Cato said.

"Yes, sir?"

"I want our radio gear set up before anything else. Command headquarters wants immediate contact, so we can't afford to wait until we erect shelters. That must be done first."

"Sure," Finney grinned, his handsome face obscured behind the plate of his helmet. "I'll set it up, Major. Wouldn't mind getting a message to Frisco myself; there's a little gal named Gloria—"

"Save it," Cato said, moving off towards the others.

He wasn't a big man, even in the bulky space suit. He was compact and thickly muscled, and his soldierly stride was almost comical in the lesser gravity. But his crew didn't smile.

Casey Strauss was removing supplies from the ship with the aid of Bob Joyce. He was mumbling through his helmet microphone all the time, as if in complaint. Joyce seemed to be elated; he tossed the supply cartons about like a juggler, exhilarated by their reduced weight.

"Snap it up," Major Cato said. "We don't have time for games, Joyce."

"Yes, sir; sorry, sir," Joyce said hastily.

"This isn't a kiddie picnic," the Major said.

"No, sir."

When he walked off again, Joyce tapped Strauss' arm and jerked his head in the Major's direction, as if to say: "What's eating him?" He couldn't say it aloud; the helmet communicators received all messages. There weren't any spoken secrets among the crew.

They worked hard, and diligently, and with a minimum of waste. They might have been detailed to a supply depot on Earth. It wasn't that they were inured to the mystery of space, but they were a taut crew, and it was business before pleasure, work before wonderment.

Four hours later, Cato called a halt to their efforts.

They stood around in the gray-white dust, in a valley of jagged rocks and craters, and looked at the magnificence of the sky. The stars, unblurred by the hazy clouds of Earth, shone diamond-hard overhead. But the eight eyes on the moon sought out only one object in the heavens—the awesome, beautiful greenish globe that had given them life.

"Earth," Strauss muttered. "God, it makes me feel funny, looking at it. I guess I'll never get over that feeling, if I see it a million times."

"I know what you mean," Finney said wryly. "Damn thing makes

Imagination is given free play: your credulity is strained but wonder and curiosity hold your interest.

Action and idea predominate over characterization.

you choke up inside, like it was a woman or something."

"That's because it's home," Joyce said. "You've got to feel that way about it. It's home."

"All right!" Major Cato snapped. "Let's stop daydreaming. Everybody back to the ship. We'll get some rations and hit the sack; we can't work if we don't eat and sleep."

They returned to the slim shaft of white and silver metal that had brought them there, and as they walked, without speaking, the three men in Major Cato's command exchanged looks that were as explicit as words. What was eating him? What was wrong with Major Cato?

They ate, and then they slept, and then they returned to work.

An hour afterwards, it happened.

Finney was fooling with the radio gear, and puzzling over short bursts of static. Strauss and Bob Joyce were stacking oxygen equipment, and Major Cato was inside the vessel.

Finney saw it first. He shouted so loudly into his helmet mike that he nearly burst the eardrums of the others. They came on a flying run to his side, and followed the direction of his pointing arm and horrified eyes. Then the light came to flood the universe with blinding power, a light so strong and incredibly bright that it dimmed the sun. Then there was the sound, reverberating through the cosmos and making the very craters of the moon tremble. But their eyes revealed the worst of what was happening, eyes that were riveted on the green world overhead.

The writing style is bold and vivid, well-matched to the fantasy it creates.

There, on the murky patch of land that would have been Europe (where, they couldn't say: France, Germany, Italy, Spain? A thousand images crowded their minds), there, like a monstrous white fist bursting its way out of the greenish globe, came a cloud whose deadly nature was instantly apparent. Then the horror was compounded, as the cloud grew greater and greater still, and was succeeded by a rending concussion that tore a gigantic hole in the very surface of the world. Enough! Enough! their minds cried, but the nightmare wasn't ended. Another blast came from north of the first, and then another from the east, and still another. The hole erupted fire, and mountains flew from the surface into space. And then there were no end of eruptions; volcanically they came, belching smoke and hellfire and debris, tearing the very heart from the hemisphere, and then encasing the globe itself in an envelope of blue flame that seemed to sear and shrivel it before their eyes, until the Earth ("It's home," Joyce had said), the Earth that had borne them, was a black, misshapen ember, reeking and loathsome and seemingly discarded by the God who had made it.

The four witnesses to the cataclysm stood sculptured in horror and disbelief, each suffering his own private hell. Then, as the mighty sounds diminished and the fires died in the night sky, they began to move. Casey Strauss lifted both hands to the cinder that had been

Earth and clenched huge fists, shaking them in rage, shouting curses. Finney dropped to his knees on the gray-white dust and went limp. Joyce, the youngest, wandered off in an erratic course, as if walking could take him away from the terror he had seen. Only Major Cato remained fixed to the spot, a rigid monument as solid as the rocks of Tycho Brahe.

In their helmet receivers, they heard only the unending sound of Strauss' invective, until his curses became unintelligible mumbling, and he stopped. Then they saw the big man, like a felled oak, fall to the ground.

Cato reached him first.

"Finney," he commanded. "Help me."

Finney didn't answer.

"Joyce!" Major Cato shouted. "We've got to get Casey into the ship. He's in a state of shock—"

Joyce turned in his wandering and stared back at his superior officer. Then he returned slowly, and helped the Major carry the unconscious navigator into the ship. They undid his helmet, and looked at his open, staring eyes and blue lips. They removed the rest of his rig, and Cato rolled up the man's sleeve and gave him an injection of a drug which would induce relaxation and sleep. They covered him with a blanket, and Cato ordered Joyce to his bunk.

"Take this," he said brusquely, handing the younger man two small white tablets. "Take these and hit the sack; that's an order. I'm going out to get Finney."

He returned to the surface, and hoisted the limp copilot by the shoulders. Finney looked up at him with a twisted grin and said: "Her name's Gloria, Major. From San Francisco . . ."

They slept, sedated, for almost twenty hours, with Major Cato watching over them from the pilot's chair until he nodded and slept himself. Then they began to stir and waken, reluctantly, and started to talk quietly among themselves about what had happened. They spoke tonelessly, dispassionately; it was the only way they could talk. Only Strauss seemed unable to make his lips and mind work; he mumbled senselessly into his microphone, until Finney suddenly leaped from his bunk in a cry of rage.

"Stop him! Shut him up!" Finney screamed. "He'll drive us all nuts!"

Cato shot out of his chair and went to Strauss' bunk. He unthreaded a bolt in the big man's suit and then reached in to yank a wire that silenced his mumblings.

"All right," he told them curtly. "Now we've got to talk. We've got to figure things out."

"Figure what?" Joyce said numbly. "What's there to figure? Earth's gone. We've got no place to go . . ."

"Then we have to stay here," Cato snapped. "And if we want to

---

Authentic details help to build the visual image of time and place, and convince you that this experience is not beyond probability in the future.

Thoughts of characters are not given, but are indicated through actions and dialogue.

While the predicament of these men is remote to us, their sense of insecurity at the loss of the Earth is a recognizable emotion which we can share, thereby increasing the strength of the story idea.

survive, then we've got certain agreements to make. The most important item we have to conserve is air, so that means we live in our suits until we can't stand our stink any longer. We've got food enough to last another six months, maybe even a year. The water tank will hold up more than that, if we're careful . . ."

"You're crazy," Finney said, his voice cracking. "It'll never last that long. And what's the difference if it did? We'll struggle along for a little while, and then—"

"Stop it!" Cato said harshly. "We can't afford any hysteria. If we want to stay alive as long as we can, we've got to use every minute and every ounce of energy."

"What's the use? What's the use?" Finney moaned. "We can't save ourselves here. And there's no place else to go—"

"Easy," Joyce said, swallowing hard. "We've got to make an effort." He fell on his bunk and put his head in his hands. "If only we had the fuel—if only we could make it to Mercury or Mars—"

"Don't talk wildly," Cato said. "There's not a chance for such a thing, we've got to make our stand right here, with what we have. It may be a short life, but it'll be a busy one."

"Look," Finney said.

They turned to watch Casey Strauss rise from his bunk, his eyes focused nowhere.

"Thou hast laid the foundations of the Earth," Strauss muttered. "The heavens are the work of thine hands . . ."

"He's praying," Joyce said.

"No." Cato took a step towards the navigator. "That's not prayer. Look at his eyes."

"They shall perish, but thou remainst," Strauss said, his voice rising, his hands lifting slowly from his sides. "They shall wax old as doth a garment, and as a vesture shalt thou fold them up, and they shall be changed . . ."

"Casey! Can you hear me?"

"Babylon the great is fallen, is fallen, and is become the habitation of devils . . ."

"He's mad!" Finney said. "He's gone mad!"

"It's only shock." Cato came closer and touched the big man's arm. "Casey, get hold of yourself."

"Rejoice over her, thou heaven!" Strauss shrieked, raising his fists. "In one hour is she made desolate . . . for God has avenged you on her . . ."

The idea is steadily emphasized through action and events.

"Casey!" shouted Major Cato.

The great fists of the navigator came crashing down on the Major's shoulders. He grunted and lost his balance, and in a flash the big man was upon him, the huge hands circling his neck; only the thick folds of the space suit kept Cato from strangling. Joyce shouted and leaped to aid the officer, while Finney stared stupidly at the scene.

Strauss' strength was of madman's quality. It took ten minutes of struggle to pacify him. Then Cato, breathing hard, said: "We'll have to chain him to the bunk, until he calms down. Finney—let's have that hypo again. We'll knock him out for a few hours."

Finney brought the needle. "Here," he said. "Why not knock him out for good, Major? He won't be any use to anybody now."

Cato looked at the copilot sharply, and then set to work.

Six hours later, wearied by thinking and by effort, they fell asleep again. But Major Cato was awakened by an unfamiliar sound in the ship's cabin, and he whispered:

"Joyce?"

The sound stopped.

"Bob, is that you?"

Joyce's voice, muffled by his pillow, answered.

"I—I'm sorry, Major. I couldn't help myself."

"Don't worry about it; I feel like crying myself. When I think about the stupidity of it—"

"But it's worse than that, Major. I—I can't describe how I feel. Just the idea that there's no more Earth—no more home. I feel so drained, empty; I never felt so alone in my life."

"It's the worst loneliness you can suffer." Cato's voice was gentle. "I know what you're going through. But we have to face up to it. All we've got left is our determination to stay alive."

There was a silence.

"I don't want to die, Major."

"Then let's live. For as long as we can."

The four men slept again.

The warning came out of Cato's dreams. Like an alarm bell, it rang in his unconscious and jarred him awake, his eyes flying open in time to see the shadowy figure standing in the middle of the floor. He shouted: *"Finney!"*

The copilot whirled towards him, eyes flashing wildly. Then he raised his arm and fired the weapon in his hand; the explosive bullet thundered against the bulkhead and ricocheted. Cato dove low and tackled his legs, bringing the tall, slender man to the floor of the cabin. Joyce was out of his bunk in an instant, clicking on the light that flooded the ship's interior and revealing the battle taking place between the senior officers. Even Strauss stirred and tried to rise, blinking at them, almost conscious again of his surroundings.

"Drop it!" Cato said gratingly, struggling for the gun. "Drop it, Finney!"

"Let go, let go!"

Joyce jumped to his aid, kicking at Finney's wrist until the copilot howled and released the weapon. Then Cato dragged him to his feet and shook him.

"What happened?" Joyce said.

> How the idea will be carried out, rather than what the men will feel or do, is the main interest of the story.

"Lieutenant Finney had ideas. He thought he'd increase the size of the rations a little . . ."

"I wouldn't hurt *you*, Major!" Finney blubbered. "So help me, I was going to take care of *them*, only them!"

On his bunk, Casey Strauss was looking at the chains anchored to his arms and legs, and his big face was puzzled.

"What's this?" he said gruffly. "What's the big idea?"

Joyce grinned. "Looks like Casey's snapping out of it. I only hope it's permanent."

"It doesn't matter," Cato said wearily. "He'll be all right in a little while. We'll all be all right. Even you, Finney."

"What do you mean?"

"The game's over. I'm supposed to hold out for another twenty-four hours, but I can't take that chance. So I'm calling a halt right now."

Joyce stared at him, bewildered. "What game, Major? What are you talking about?"

"Unchain Strauss and get the air locks open. We're going outside."

"Unchain him? But Major—"

"We'll take the chance. Let him go."

Joyce obeyed, while the Major held Finney's weapon pointed at the copilot. Then he dropped the gun contemptuously on his bunk and said: "You, too, Finney. We're all going out."

They opened the air locks, and stood about, waiting for Cato's command.

"I'll go first," he said.

They followed him out onto the moon's surface.

"Now look," Cato said.

They turned their eyes in the direction of his pointing arm.

They stood around in the gray-white dust, in a valley of jagged rocks and craters, and looked at the magnificence of the sky. The stars, unblurred by the hazy clouds of Earth, shone diamond-hard overhead. But the eight eyes on the moon sought out only one object in the heavens—the awesome, beautiful greenish globe of Earth.

"A miracle! A miracle!" Strauss cried, choking with sobs.

"The Earth," Finney said dully. "It wasn't destroyed. It didn't happen at all . . ."

Joyce couldn't speak. He turned to the Major and stared, unbelievingly.

"No," Cato said. "It didn't happen at all, not really. It was an hallucination, a delusion, and I created it for you. The food you ate the first night contained a drug, a hypnotic chemical. When you were asleep, and under its influence, I planted this terrible vision in your heads. I *made* you see the Earth destroyed.

"You've been guinea pigs in an experiment, a test to determine the reaction of men on another world, who are cut off completely

The action is objective, almost clinically observed for its support of the imaginative idea.

The outcome is a satisfactory twist that points out how precious the earth would seem if you were cut off from it forever. This outcome prevents the story from being unhappy and meaningless.

and irrevocably from the mother planet. We're going beyond the moon in a few months; plans are underway to send our first ship to Mars, to Venus, to Mercury . . . and before long, the stars. But they wanted to know how men like yourselves—trained, experienced, so dependable in all other ways—would withstand the shock of total rupture from Earth, how they would accept the certainty of loneliness and death, when the most important umbilical cord of all was cut."

"The experiment is over," Cato said. "Now we're going back. Lieutenant Joyce—"

"Yes, sir."

"You're second-in-command as of now. And Bob—"

"Yes, sir?"

"Take care of yourself. They are going to need you. On Mars."

There are Adventure stories of every sort in the pulp field— some are based on dangerous sports, others show the hazards everyday men must face as they earn their living, like the *Railroad Magazine* story below, Harry Bedwell's "Moonshine."

Firing a hog for "Big Boy" Watson was enough to give you the jitters. Big Boy's demands, like his hulking body, were enormous. When you rolled down the high iron in the cab with him, besides keeping the boiler hot you had to be conscious of everything else that went on.

Phil McKay did his best to avoid trouble. Phil was lean and wiry and naturally high-strung, and his efforts to please the overgrown engineer hair-triggered his reactions. The young fireman had been over the Cardigan Division so often that he believed he knew every aspect of it, day or night, calm or storm. He could tell by the flicker of a distant headlight or by thin smoke on the horizon the exact location of a train miles ahead. He could also determine whether or not it was standing still, as well as its speed if coming toward them.

He had, moreover, a keen memory for train orders and timetables, and he never overlooked any traffic that affected his train. In black night, without even peering outside, Phil could usually gauge from the lurch of his engine where they were. He was quick to catch signals as they hove in sight. All these instincts had been sharpened by his work with Big Boy. In fact, he was too much alert for his own good.

You reached Lakeland intersection from the west through a cut and on a curve, and when you got close to the interlocking tower your train straightened out. Phil knew that spot like the palm of his right hand. A bluff swung around to the left of the tower, and under it glittered a lake.

One April night that Phil would never forget, a full moon silvered the landscape but the bluff facing the engine as it approached lay in

---

Time, space and a speculative idea have been combined in this story.

Because so much railroad language is used in the opening of this story, and because the main character is a "young fireman," you know this adventure will involve a hazardous occupation.

its own shadow. An arm of the lake stretched into the light. At that precise moment when the interlocking plant's signals flashed on them, the moon-image shone brightly in the water against a dark background of shadowy bluff.

The plot action is launched by flashback and then moves steadily forward.

That particular aspect had never before greeted Phil McKay. It was new and startling. To him it seemed like the headlight of an engine that had just cleared the interlocking plant and was headed straight into them.

Action has first place in the story's elements. The conflict is based on it—so is the story's development.

Big Boy, who hadn't bothered to shut off and approach the intersection under control, became cautious at the sight of signal lights. He applied his brakes quickly, thus strengthening the illusion in Phil's sensitive mind.

The harsh screaming of the air plus the grunt of brake shoes sounded like an emergency brake application. Phil thought his hogger also had seen the locomotive right on top of them and had "big-holed her."

You couldn't reasonably take time to study a situation like this. Phil acted fast. The moonglow that looked like a locomotive headlight wasn't ten car-lengths away. He whirled to the gangway, dropped to the bottom step, and unloaded. All in one second!

The youth was flung headlong down an embankment ballasted with cinders. The cinders tore off considerable clothing in addition to skin from his face and hands and knees. He was also badly bruised, but the worst damage was to his prestige. This he would soon discover.

Engineer Watson hadn't seen him jump. The lights signaled clear through the interlocking plant, and the big fellow let off his brakes and rolled on down the main line. He had gone a mile beyond the intersection before it occurred to him that he no longer had a fireboy, and a half-mile further before he decided to stop and find out why.

It took Phil a limping forty minutes to catch up with his train, and the rest of his life, more or less, to explain what had happened. From the wisecracking callboy to the dignified Mr. Frome, road foreman of engines, the personnel of the Cardigan Division had a field day kidding Phil McKay, and Big Boy Watson himself led the pack.

The unhappy fireman found refuge from the tormenters for a few days while he laid off work to grow new patches of skin and treat his bruises. But when he reported back to the roundhouse, everyone apparently had forgotten his real name. "Moonshine," they dubbed him, and it stuck like a visiting mother-in-law. Merely to yell, "Hey, Moonshine!" was good for a laugh any time. Phil writhed in ignominy.

Big Boy led the pack and revived the epithet whenever it seemed to be dying out.

The conflicts are between Phil and the engineer, between Phil and the dangers of the job he is doing, not within Phil himself.

But Big Boy was no throttle artist. That lummox had his own

method of handling trains. He never moved the Johnson bar until he had to, and while he was seated at the throttle he looked like a cross between a zombie and an oversized kewpie doll. His placid, flaccid, assured air impressed the men who rode swivel chairs. Any one of them would have said offhand that Watson was a capable runner. Moreover, he had the craft to invent plausible alibis and the gall to put them over.

So the firemen assigned to Big Boy were pretty much at his mercy. Phil could not break away from him because of the incident at the interlocking plant. Any attempt on Phil's part to bid off the unwanted run was met with raised eyebrows and a not-too-veiled reminder of his skittishness.

The author's style is unvarnished and functional, in keeping with the background and characters. You can imagine a railroad man has written the story from experience.

Well, one day he had a Baldwin Consolidation lined up for Number 28, a mixed drag east, and that added to his woe. Big Boy would beat her, as he did all engines, but the mighty 1612 was temperamental and wouldn't take abuse without kicking back. Phil would have to bail coal all the way. The 1612 and Big Boy had lamed his back before. Plenty of firemen could testify to that sort of treatment.

The roundhouse was sighing and whispering with steamy locomotives. Machinists' hammers made an echoing uproar under the soot-blackened roof. A boilermaker backing out of a cold firebox pulled his tools after him and said, "Hiya, Moonshine!" That name still made the tips of Phil's ears burn.

Phil climbed the ladder to the cab of the 1612 and stowed his lunch morosely in the seatbox. There had been plenty of time for the gang to forget that moonlight incident, but it lingered on like a head cold and was blocking his advancement. He swung open the firebox door and squatted and peered. The fire, he decided, was no more than a slag heap smoking in a cave. Grimly and expertly he began to build up the temperature in that cavern.

Pretty soon he felt the deck vibrate as a large, heavy body moved up the ladder. Engineer Watson squeezed his bulk through the gangway into the cab like a man-mountain, moving with extreme deliberateness. Phil's secret ambition was to give him a stiff crack in the behind with a shaker bar.

The hogger breathed moistly. He glanced at the steam gauge. "See that you keep her that way," he rumbled. "I don't want to be set out till Christmas."

"Some guys wouldn't care if you stayed out longer than that," Phil muttered darkly.

"Heh, what's that?" Big Boy asked. "Never mind. Keep your damn mouth shut!" He trundled to his seatbox, raised the cushion, and peered within. "And try not to leave the cab on this run, Moonshine!"

Phil winced. He poised his shaker bar and looked wistfully at the bulging backside.

Passing footfalls below, with a familiar cadence, diverted him from the tempting target. He slid down the grab-iron to the ground and into the path of a rawboned man of unusual height, and blurted out:

"Listen, Mr. Frome, won't you please let me take the exam along with Kirk and Eldredge? I've got the same rights they have to a shot at the right-hand side of the cab."

The road foreman of engines studied him sharply. Phil did not like the look in those steel-grey eyes.

"You'd better stick to the left side for a while yet," said the official. "Mr. Grayson doesn't go for skittish engineers." Grayson was the superintendent of the Cardigan Division, a man as tough as a scarred old cat from the rimrocks. "You know what I mean—the way you unloaded at the intersection. Watson, for example, would never do that."

Phil glowered. *If you and Big Boy keep bringing up that Moonshine stuff,* he thought bitterly, *I'll be firing drags forever.*

"Better take yourself in hand," Mr. Frome continued, not unkindly. "Watson tells me that you're always looking for trouble and quick to find it. You're like the section hand who made a practice of watching to see that the rest of the crew got their tools off the track when a train was coming, but his shovel was the one that finally got run over. Take time to think about things, McKay."

"You can't always take your time," Phil protested. "If I'd really seen what I thought I saw at the intersection, I didn't move any too fast."

But Mr. Frome didn't get that. "If you'd had the right-hand side of the cab that night," he said bluntly, "what would have happened to your train?"

"I'd have stuck and cleaned the clock in that first second," Phil stated.

"I guess you've got to prove that to Mr. Grayson," the road foreman said, "and Watson's reports don't help you."

Now, the examinations to be set up to engineers were so stiff that many of the older firemen had fallen down or had declined to attempt them. Men with no more rights than Phil were being offered the chance to take them next. Phil had been studying and cramming for months, and felt sure he could pass. But they hadn't invited him to take the tests. The thought rankled.

Prove to Mr. Grayson that he wasn't too tense to handle a road engine, even in an emergency! Fine chance! Phil watched Mr. Frome climb into the cab of 915 as she backed out to tie onto Ten, an eastbound passenger train. There wasn't any test for that, except to build up a record, if he could. As long as they called him "Moonshine" he'd have the shovel tied to him.

Long Tom Quilty, the head brakeman, came and guided the 1612

No message or theme is being conveyed. It is simply a story—what happens to Phil McKay and how he copes with his predicament.

The relationships and conflicts are grasped quickly and easily—they're not complex or mental—don't require elucidation—are based on feelings.

The goal is clearly defined and simple: Phil must prove his worth.

out of the roundhouse. They clattered through switches and paused at the chutes for a dump of coal. Ten glided through the yard, headed for the open country. As she passed they could see Mr. Frome in the cab, standing beside the engineer, and Big Boy said: "Wonder what old Waters has done that the traveling grunt has to ride with him?"

The 1612 backed into her train. The conductor came forward presently with the orders. After they had read them over together Big Boy stuffed the tissues into his pocket, climbed back into the cab, and adapted his large person carefully to his seat.

The fireman held out his hand for the orders. Big Boy rumbled. He regretted the slight effort to dig them out of his pocket.

"Always scared somebody's gonna overlook something! A regular rule-book railroader!"

Phil eyed them briefly. He didn't have to check with the timetable to find how they worked. He knew all the items and how they reflected on his train's movements.

Engineer Watson whistled off, and they moved out into the country. The hot sun went down behind them, and they rolled through the long twilight into the dark. Big Boy beat the 1612 up the first hill. Phil had to work and connive with all his skill to keep her hot.

The action is consistently maintained in first place.

They set out three loads at Republic and picked up an empty. They took siding at Bolo and were delayed eighteen minutes on a meet with an extra west. At Frogtown they picked up two loads.

It was a stuffy night. Phil's jumper was plastered tight to his hard back. His scoop rang often at the firebox door. The track ahead moved under the beam of the headlight like a ladder as the long freight clanked through the night.

That night, Tom Quilty had elected to lounge on the fireman's seat by the hot boiler rather than ride the tops where it was cooler. He knew Phil would have a time with Watson and the 1612, and he stayed in the cab to give what help he could—to pick up orders on the fly and to keep the coal shoveled down in the tender. Tom was that kind. He was a good man to have along.

Big Boy jounced in his own blubber. He seldom eased a lever. He let the 1612 and the fireman do the work and most of the thinking.

Tom snared an order at Daley. At Lakeland intersection the hogger turned a fat, derisive grin on Phil. At Atlantic they set out more loads. The board was against them, and the conductor came forward with a "31" order. It read: "No. 28, Engine 1612, take siding and meet Extra 2714 West at Prosper."

Again Phil had to ask his engineer for the order. He nearly didn't. The struggle to keep the 1612 going under Big Boy's mishandling had tired him. It was well past midnight; they were getting on toward the end of the division and his energy had sunk to a low ebb. But an insistent sense wouldn't quite let him pass up reading the order. He should know what they faced. Meet Extra 2714 at Prosper. Twenty-eight to take siding. The 2714 would be a hotshot. They rolled on. The semaphore at Prosper was showing red when their train came in sight of it, but there was a dancing dot of white light on the platform below. That would be the night operator, Eddie Sand, signalling to them with his lantern that he had an order clearing the board. Evidently the dispatcher had changed the meeting point between Twenty-eight and Extra 2714, and they would go through Prosper without a stop. The lanky brakeman got down to pick up the order. Big Boy didn't arouse himself even to the extent of checking his train.

Eddie stood close to the track as the 1612 blasted down on him, expertly holding the order hoop aloft in one hand and his lantern raised in the other to silhouette it.

Tom leaned out from the gangway, ran his arm through the hoop, and snatched it from Eddie's hand as they swooped by. He detached the order and cast the hoop back into the night. Then he handed the paper to Big Boy, who glanced down and crumpled it up.

> You look for an act of daring and courage to bring about the story resolution.

Phil glared at him. The engineer hadn't bothered to accommodate him by offering the order. You only made yourself disliked by trying to do your duty in detail, got your shovel run over while looking out for the other fellow's tools. Phil bent over the firebox, then stood upright.

Extracting the wrinkled tissue from Big Boy's listless fingers, he unfolded it. There was, he saw at once, a fault here, something wrong with the order. His captious eye picked it out in the dim glow: the absence of three words, "instead of Prosper," that seemed to be trivial, but Phil knew instinctively that any flaw in a train order could be dangerous.

Little unheeded items grow ominous when you are shuttling fast traffic on a single track. The dispatcher hadn't put out a protecting order to Eddie Sand at Prosper when he made that meeting point between Twenty-eight and the 2714, because he'd been in a tearing hurry at the time. Twenty-eight had to stop at Atlantic anyhow, so the dispatcher gave them a "31" there.

> The technicalities of this occupation and life are carried through to the very end, and are both the foundation and chief interest of this kind of pulp story.

Meanwhile, he had started another freight westward, Extra 2728, behind the 2714, and then had aroused Eddie and issued an order for Twenty-eight, fixing the meeting point at McCormick for her and this new train. That was the order Phil held under his startled eyes. It did not change the meeting point with the 2714, which was still at Prosper, through which they were proceeding at an unchecked speed.

Eddie, unaware that Twenty-eight already had a meet at his station, had signaled them through.

All that Big Boy gathered from his quick glance at the order was the name of the new meeting place, McCormick. The similarity of the two engine numbers escaped him.

But Phil had instantly caught the absence of three words. If the order had changed the meeting place it would have read, ". . . at McCormick *instead of Prosper*."

His nerves ran in cold trickles when he got the meaning. As he saw it, they still had a meet here at Prosper with the 2714. He tried to yell at Big Boy to stop, but the bitterness of his past hasty experience choked his voice. Caution checked him. He wasn't going to be stampeded into another ridiculous error.

He might be wrong about their now having meet orders with two extras. Maybe his memory had slipped and it was only the 2728 they were to meet, and the dispatcher had merely neglected to add the "instead of Prosper" to the order. The taunt of "Moonshine" still rankled.

But confidence in his memory returned to plague him. Those two engine numbers had registered in his mind; 2714 and 2728. Phil McKay glanced back from the gangway along the train rolling through the dark. The caboose was already well past the station where Eddie Sand had handed up the order to the rear end. The caboose hadn't yet noted any error, or somebody there would have pulled the air.

Maybe, Phil thought, *my imagination has built another illusion. Take it slow and thoughtful.*

But you don't deliberate in the close ones. It wasn't possible to debate this situation. It was too imminent. If they were to meet the hotshot here, they'd have to stop at once and back into the clear, or the 2714 would be smashing into them.

He couldn't wait for Big Boy to dig the order out of the wad of them in his pocket to make sure there were two freights running against them. Big Boy would argue about that, and if Phil had the picture right, the hotshot was storming through those hills ahead, not far away, expecting a clear track at Prosper.

Delayed action would be the same as none at all. No matter who said so, you couldn't linger over a decision when a head-end smash impended in the cuts just ahead.

"Stop her!" Phil yelled. He couldn't hold back the warning longer. "Give her the big hole! We've still got a meet here with the 2714."

The engineer jounced placidly on his seat like a mold of jelly. He stared at Phil without concern. The 1612 rambled on. Big Boy's fat lips rolled up in a grin.

"Don't jump yet, Moonshine!" he called. "That order changed our meet from Prosper to McCormick. Don't unload! We ain't got time to wait for you to catch up with us again."

The cab of the locomotive pulling a long string of cars isn't a tranquil place for quiet reflections. The engine dips and sways and slews; there is a steady drum of exhaust and the clank and rumble of gear. It is easy for you to become confused.

Phil peered out over the hills through the front window. The first cut wasn't far ahead. He caught a flicker of light along the ridges, but

---

There is no introspection or philosophizing, no analyzing or psychological probing.

Phil's prowess and skill in his work are put to the test.

it faded as he glanced. That might be another will-o-the-wisp, or some light from the firebox still in his eyes. But it could be the 2714 coming close at hand!

He crowded the throttle shut against the engineer's restraining hand, and reached past Big Boy and flapped the brake valve handle to emergency. Compressed air howled. The thunder of brake shoes snatching at all those rolling wheels ran down the long train like an earthquake. The 1612 plunged and rolled and checked.

Engineer Watson bent forward on the retarded momentum like a captive balloon. His crooked elbow cracked on the window frame. He yelled angrily and clutched his arm. Long Tom Quilty slid to the deck. He didn't say anything, just watched the fireman.

Phil thrust the order at the brakeman, sprawled on his seat, and searched the darkness ahead. A dim glow out there flickered and died—a headlight turning on the curves.

Twenty-eight grunted to a stand. Big Boy clamored and swore.

Phil scrutinized the deceptive glow. But he couldn't get its location. Then a pink radiance reached into the sky above the hills. It caught some familiar contour, and Phil knew that the 2714 was storming toward them. Her fireman had opened his firebox door and sent that pink wedge into the sky. Phil gauged her position and could make a guess at her speed.

Your sympathy stays with Phil because his motivation and perseverance are commendable.

He glanced back along his standing train. The rear end was clear of the Prosper yard by more than half a mile. The 1612, the head end, was close into the hills.

Big Boy couldn't get the air pumped up and the brakes released, and that long train backing into the siding before the 2714 would blast out of the cuts and tear into them.

Tom Quilty was limber and quick on his feet, but not fast enough to run forward a sufficient distance to flag her down and prevent her from ploughing into the 1612. The hotshot, without excessive tonnage, would be turning them fast.

Phil was getting the picture in instant flashes without taking time to check for accuracy. He dropped to the deck and pushed Tom Quilty toward the gangway.

"Get down there and uncouple the hog!" he snapped. "Fast! Then come back here in the cab."

Tom didn't hesitate. He realized you had to be quick in the close ones. But Big Boy stared in a strangling fury, not having caught on yet to the peril they faced. To him it seemed that the young fireman was panicky over moonlight again.

What Phil did next could well cost him his job. Taking the engineer by one arm and bracing himself, he pulled Big Boy from his seat—an act equivalent in railroading to mutiny at sea. Big Boy's plump legs scrambled for a foothold on the steel deck. Phil slid into his seat.

Big Boy gurgled: "You gone crazy? You know what you'll get for this."

He still had no idea what was wrong but was already preparing an alibi. Phil yelled at him.

"The 2714 is just over the hill, coming to meet us at Prosper!"

He released the brakes and widened the throttle as Tom signaled from the rear of the tender. The 1612 snorted briskly.

"Well, then, where are you goin' now?" Big Boy shouted.

He was angry and confused.

Tom Quilty rippled up the ladder. The 1612 took hold and bellowed under the urge of Phil's hand.

You don't look for an inner truth to be revealed but for an act of daring and courage to bring about the story resolution.

If you figured this situation a month you would always get the same answer. Phil McKay believed he had it in one instant. If they tried to back up and at the same time sent Tom out to flag, the 2714 would come blasting out of the cut before the lean brakeman could get inside of it to stop him.

The safest thing for Phil would be to stand aside and let them do just that. He would be in the clear. It wasn't his responsibility. But as Mr. Frome had said, you looked out for the other fellows' tools at the risk of getting your own run over.

"Tom," he called, "the hotshot is too close for you to flag her before she hits us."

"Then why are you runnin' right into her face?" the hogger bellowed.

"Listen, Tom." Phil raised his voice above the engine's roar. "Right at the other end of this short cut there's a siding into the paint factory. We'll run up there, and you head me into the clear. That will get us far enough up the line so we can stop her before she hits our head end. Want to try it?"

The dialogue adds to the authenticity by supplying further technical details of Phil's occupation and its problems.

His thoughts were streaking, but his voice sounded calm and assured.

"Sure," Tom called back. "I'll get out on the pilot and be ready to run for the switch when we get there."

"It may be close," Phil said. "Don't forget to jump and get out of the way if you have to."

Tom crowded through the front window of the cab. He went forward over the running board along the boiler and dropped to the pilot.

Big Boy gathered up his sagging mouth. "You gonna try to make the switch before the hotshot gets there?"

Phil nodded from halfway out the cab window. The drivers ground into the rails and the tempo of the exhaust grew into a thundering roll. The 1612 had power. She picked up her speed with a surging rush.

"What if the hotshot gets there first?" the hogger shouted. But Phil McKay was not panicked and his answer was calm.

"I don't think she will."

The climax was only seconds away. Much as Engineer Watson disliked to hustle, he decided to move quickly now. He waddled to the gangway and backed down the ladder in a hurry. At the bottom he let go with one hand and stepped off. The train was going so fast that he lost his footing and rolled through the tall weeds into a muddy pool.

The 1612 grunted on the slight curve as they swung into the short cut. The spot of green light that marked the switch stand goggled at Phil from the other end. The main line curved away at the end of the headlight's beam into another slash in the ridges. The 1612 responded to the tug of his fingers.

By now the headlight of No. 2714 was spraying patches of light along the near ridge, and the glow from her firebox again slid into the sky. Phil knew he had to figure his moves in inches.

Ruggedness is stressed in Phil's lack of fear, his physical courage.

The green switch light dwindled as it bobbed near. Phil let off the whistle in short, screaming blasts. The cries slammed over the hills, reaching for the engineer of the 2714. He might hear them, or think he did, and that would at least make him more alert.

Phil shut the throttle. He dipped into the auxiliary tank for an accurate seven pounds of air. Just seven pounds exactly his fingers on the valve recognized as the brakes took hold of the drivers.

The 1612 checked smoothly as the blast died from her stack. Her brasses pounded in the comparative quiet. Bluish stars swung along the horizon. Night smells drifted in from the farmlands.

Tom Quilty's lantern came out to the end of the pilot beam. That limber man was coiled on the foot-iron like a wound-up spring. The switch light bobbed with the swaying engine. It seemed to fly at him, too close, as if he would overrun it.

Excitement is the chief emotional effect sought by the author.

Phil checked her sharply. Tom's lantern shot forward from the pilot. The brakeman lit sprinting. He would have to find his footing by the feel. He couldn't see the ground under him. If he stumbled, if he were thrown, he couldn't open the switch in time. It would be that close, that a jog would stretch time too far.

Then the headlight of the 2714 flared on Phil's eyes as the hotshot lashed out of the cut ahead. Tom was swinging his lantern in quick arcs as he streaked toward the switch stand. Phil let off the whistle in a half-dozen short calls. The 1612 chuckled as he released her brakes and let her drift toward the switch points.

Phil's hand dropped from the whistle lever to the throttle. His nerves tried to tighten as he listened for a signal from the hotshot. The yellow disk of her headlight swung at him like a racing moon. If they hit, it would be a grand smash and a great pile of wreckage.

Tom Quilty's lantern paused at the switch stand. A grim roar climbed up over the hills, reaching for the stars, as the engineer of the 2714 set all the brakes on that storming line of cars.

In the crawling light from the headlights, Phil searched out the rails of the siding where they came down and laced with the main line. He believed he could see the switch points in the reflection under the beams, but perhaps he merely thought he could because he was certain where they were.

He knew for sure they had not opened when they moved under the 1612's pilot, for the switch light still showed green.

Maybe Tom had missed his switch key's first stab at the lock. But somehow those points would have to open up while they traveled from pilot-point to the front trucks. The hotshot was still coming at breakneck speed.

Phil pulled out the throttle to the fraction his fingers felt would lift her into a burst of speed without faltering. His nerves did not flinch. They held steady while the grinding roar of the hotshot's set brakes, added to the glare of her headlight in his eyes, tried to tighten them. No. 1612 surged forward powerfully, with her tall stack barking.

When Phil faces the story's crisis, it is an outward one to be resolved by an outward act.

He felt the slight lurch as she took the curve of the siding. The switch light's beam had turned red now and it swam toward him as the engine made her try to avoid the hotshot. The 2714's headlight streamed into his cab.

Tom Quilty was coiled at the switch stand, ready to swing the points back if the tender cleared. He was calm-eyed and watchful in the shimmering light. If the 1612 didn't clear, Tom would be included in the resultant wreckage. He ought to be using his long legs to cover distance.

Phil gave a final strong pull at the throttle. She would have to take it all now. The 1612 roared and lunged.

The story provides you with the climax of an armchair adventure.

A blast of air slammed through the cab as the hotshot howled by. The gust spanked Phil as he leaned out of the window, and it nearly projected him from his seat.

The hotshot streamed down the main line, bucking and growling in the hard grip of brake shoes. A faint smile of intense relief flickered across Phil's lips.

Hours later, the young fireman came out of the roundhouse in the hot sun and slouched across the terminal yard to his room. All he wanted now was to sleep. Sunlight edged the drawn blinds as he crawled into bed. His back hurt. He tore the bed covers apart, tossing.

Footfalls in the hall had a familiar cadence. Phil's stomach chilled as someone knocked on the door. With a groan he got out of bed slowly and slipped into a bathrobe. There, silhouetted against the light, stood Mr. Frome, the road foreman of engines.

"Sorry to wake you up, McKay," he said, "but Mr. Grayson is in a hurry for your report on what happened last night. I've got to wire it to him."

The fireman rubbed his aching back. "You must have heard Watson's version by this time," he said dismally. "I couldn't change that."

"No, I guess not," Mr. Frome agreed. "I've got Eddie Sand's, too, and Tom Quilty's. What I want you to do is verify Tom's report. His facts don't agree with Watson's at all, and Tom's a mighty reliable man."

"Yes, sir, he is," Phil enthused, "and fast on his feet. Why, if the brass collars don't recognize the chances he took last night, and the fine way—"

"Now, McKay," the foreman soothed, "there you go, getting all excited. The division superintendent is really on your side. He thinks I misjudged you somewhat. Asks if I didn't confuse quick judgment with skittish nerves." A slight pause. "I reckon maybe I did."

"Oh!" Phil brightened.

"Now, if you'll explain about last night I'll send the Old Man a wire telling him how wrong I was. He wants you to go up for the engineer's examination next week and to see him just as soon as you can get back."

Phil walked across the room and raised the blinds. Golden sunlight streamed in. "What about 'Moonshine'?"

His lips curled in a smile.

"Oh, *that!*" Mr. Frome's steel-gray eyes twinkled. "I don't believe you'll hear it any more. Last night, you know, when Watson unloaded into a frog pond he came out all muddy and wet and mad enough to kill. The men of the Cardigan Division are calling him 'Mudhop.' "

Phil's grin widened. "Big Boy Mudhop!"

His back didn't hurt any more. He listened gaily to the clank of couplers and the rumble of a switch engine batting freight cars around the yard.

In summation, the story is composed of physical events met with physical prowess, which brings about a physical resolution—the primary aim of pulp adventure stories.

The outcome proves no special point. You simply observe that bravery triumphs over obstacles.

Suspense puts life in your story

All great fiction is great because suspense, that all-enduring substance, is present in it. Only suspense has the magic power to transform a work of fiction into a living and immortal piece of writing.
—Lajos Egri in *Your Key to Successful Writing*

Section III

Lesson eight

Fiction writing
course

The
quality
story

The quality story differs from the slick and the pulp in that it emphasizes thoughtful, philosophic content. It seeks to make the reader think. Together with the emotion it arouses in the reader, it attempts to convey a message, to enlighten the reader about a truth he may not have considered before, to arouse him to a cause, to leave him in a contemplative mood.

The quality story goes deeply inside its characters. It is concerned with the struggles that people suffer alone, the fears they don't understand, the loneliness they cannot break, the sudden discoveries and insights that come to them. It deals with the subtle subject material—and sometimes the stark realism—that other mediums tend to avoid. Sometimes it's referred to as a "slice of life" story, because it often takes the seamy or sordid side of life as a theme and doesn't soften or sweeten it for the reader.

Different as the quality story may be, however, from the slick or the pulp, it's first of all a story, therefore subject to all of the principles set forth in this Course about short story techniques. It differs, but only in approach, reader and purpose.

The quality reader, says Bergen Evans, likes fiction in which there's meaning in every action, in every line of dialogue, no matter how innocuous or wandering, as long as it deepens the characterization and gives it psychological dimension. Dr. Evans continues:

This reader doesn't demand movement and action, or a story in which many threads of plots are tightly woven. When he says, "What happens next?" he means to the character's inner feelings and resolutions as well as to the direction of events.

He doesn't want everything spelled out in plain words. He likes to grasp an abstraction without having it explained. He appreciates beautiful language, unusual phraseology, and any writing form that helps to create a significant situation. He'll accept unhappy endings if that's the way things are.

Outcomes don't have to be resolutions, but can be left hanging, explained only by the reader's own ability to understand. He will accept experimental writing, and it is in this medium that innovations of style and viewpoint are so often discovered.

Because the reader is usually at a high educational level, he's part of a relatively small audience. The quality magazines carry little advertising or artwork. Their buyers are reading readers—that is, they bring to their consideration of a story a sophisticated literary viewpoint. A quality reader is something of a philosopher to begin with, and looks to his reading for stimulating ideas, for nuggets of wisdom, germs of truth. Also he's intrigued by the persuasion of some large crusade or reform.

The quality story is the most difficult to write because it's not stereotyped, has no precise rules, springs most often from the writer's individual talent. But once more we offer a good rule—

study quality stories in magazines or in anthologies and write them only if you're in sympathy with their goals. To write quality stories successfully, you must have something to say, be determined to say it, and use all your craft to say it effectively.

A quality story should be satisfying to write for more than just the telling. You should find satisfaction from expressing some strong conviction, from communicating some aspect of life which you find significant. This is your place to teach, to judge, to criticize, to influence the minds of others with your ideas. Although your audience is small, your voice will be heard.

Two examples of the quality story

The quality stories presented below show the way in which simple subjects can be given depth and meaning. The problems are inner ones. There is very little action, only a struggle of varying intensity taking place within the minds and emotions of the main characters. All that transpires from the outside is used to emphasize what is happening to the inner feelings of the principal character.

Note that the values are subtle and searching. The story conveys a philosophic message, and the outcome is reached only by a change of attitude on the part of the main character: no physical crisis is used to bring it about. And the writing itself has a deceptive simplicity which is the essence of well-written prose.

Our first example of this type is "Bachelor of Arts" by Nancy G. Chaikin, a sensitive and thoughtful story reprinted from the *University of Kansas City Review.*

From the window of her dormitory room, Anne Lupoff could see across to the windows of the faculty offices in Mackey Hall, those little cubicles of light and dark that even in the nighttime smelled comfortably of tobacco and old books. She had got into the habit of looking across every night, as she sat at her desk, to see whether Russell Slater was working late; and now, on the night before graduation, she noted, with a sudden electric shock at her stomach, that the light was on in his office. She had promised herself that she would not go through the foolishness of trying to see him that night, that her eagerness was all out of proportion to what she had a right to expect from him—that there was, in fact, nothing to expect.

But as surely as she had resolved and known, even while she was doing it, that she was deceiving herself, she felt now the old, strong

A main character, Anne Lupoff, is introduced, and you're taken at once into her thoughts and feelings.

impulse driving over her; it was the last night, the very last night. Slowly she turned from the window and took the pins out of her hair, walking toward the dresser where she had left her comb. It had been a simple, if fond, professor-student relationship—absolutely nothing more. But now the comb was racing through her hair, and her heart was beating audibly, and she was thinking, "What if he leaves before I get there, what if he leaves, what if he leaves?"

The final, irrevocable, beautiful, warm spring night on this campus. The air flowed softly around her head as she left the dormitory, and there was the slightest sound of it in the trees; and over in the bell tower, a darkening shaft against the late spring sky, the carillonist was playing "Gaudeamus Igitur." She looked up again at the office window—she knew so well which one, counting from left to right until she hit number four—the light was still there, all alone, surrounded on either side by long dark rectangles, the windows of deserted rooms.

The others had all gone home—indeed, there was no reason for anyone to be there now; the grades were in, most of the students had left. Why should Russell be working at night in his office? Perhaps he knew, perhaps he had known all along that she would have to come; perhaps that was why he had said nothing, not a word, up to now.

The elevator was closed down for the night and she walked the two flights of stairs slowly, hearing the echo of her footsteps carrying hollowly into the halls, thinking that maybe he could hear them too, there in his office—would know that it was she, and smile to himself, that strange reluctant half smile that did not quite close his small dark eyes. But when she reached his office there was no sign that he had expected her. His head was bent over some papers—familiar, ugly balding head that inclined itself to one side when he lectured—and his chair creaked back and forth, back and forth as he read.

She knew that she could have stood there for some time while he read, could even have turned and left and he would not have noticed. But, having done the foolish, childish, inevitable thing, she wanted it now to be inescapable. So she stood there only for several seconds before she made the final, efficient, deliberate sounds which would give her away. It was silly—as silly as a grammar school adolescent waiting around the corner for her crush—but she was too close to the end of it to care how it looked, what he would think or had been thinking. She wanted only to know whether he welcomed it, whether there was anything there at all.

At last he looked up, and smiled the smile she had imagined, predicted, craved. At last the head came up from the papers, the eyes half closed, and the large dry lips said quietly, "Please come in."

"I can't imagine why you're working tonight," she said, annoyed

So far, there's no action.

Physical action only spurs her thoughts and feelings.

with herself because, as usual, the words came out flippant, intrusive
—not gentle, and softly sympathetic, as she had wanted them to
sound. "Everyone else has gone home."

"Everyone else has less to do," he said, offering her a cigarette
across the desk, then leaning back and waiting for her to speak.

She shifted uncomfortably in the chair she had taken automatically, and wondered what on earth, what in the name of heaven she
could possibly say now that would make sense. In a panic of foolishness, she realized that there wasn't anything at all.

"Out late tonight, aren't you?" he said.

"It doesn't matter the night before graduation—no hours at the
dorm. I could stay out and sleep anywhere tonight." My God, of all
the things to say! But he spared her any signs of misapprehension.

"Of course," he said quietly. "The night before graduation. At
last. Have you stopped mourning?"

She was determined to disregard his amusement. "I'll never stop
mourning," she said quickly. "I want to stay here, dammit all. I
don't want to graduate."

"So you've said. But, as I've told you, there's nothing to stop you
from coming back eventually. They might even give you a teaching
fellowship."

"Eventually," she said with disgust. "By the end of the summer
I'll have gone crazy."

He laughed out loud, holding his cigarette up in the air in front
of him, leaning way back in his swivel chair.

"This is most unwholesome of you, my dear. You're supposed to
want to graduate. But that's nothing," still laughing, with his ridicu-
lously short legs coming up in front of him, "you'll find out what you
want—one of these days."

She grew hot and red under his "my dear," his paternal amusement, his fifteen years of seniority, and hated herself for even hoping
that he might have known how important he was to the whole thing.

"I don't know," was all she could say. "I just don't know." And,
after a long silence in which he simply pulled on his cigarette and
she thought of all the crazy stories in which she might have thrown
herself upon his gentle, true, unrevealed love for her—"My parents
will be here in the morning. They'd like to meet you. Will you have
lunch with us after the exercises?"

"Of course I will, Anne. And thank you."

She got up and went to the door. "Good night then," she said,
turning for just a minute on the threshold. "Good night, Professor
Slater."

He blew her a kiss with his small hand, and she ran down the hall
like a little child, her head pounding, not wanting to give him a
chance to spoil that tiny, harmless gesture.

Back at the dormitory she stopped for a moment before going in.

When Anne speaks, she
analyzes what she has said.
Dialogue deepens the mental
content of the story.

Anne's feelings are more
important than her physical
description.

The air was cooler now, and the carillon had stopped playing. But she imagined that she could still hear the strong prophetic chords of its clear, sad music—"Gaudeamus igitur, juvenes dum summus . . ." She rubbed the remembered echo of it like salt into her consciousness and wished that she could cry loudly, uncontrollably, as she had cried in her bed when she was a little girl. But nothing would come, except the realization that this, at last, was it—that tomorrow she would have to leave, with her regret sifting inside of her like grey ashes—a strange combination of incomprehensible fears and longings.

She did not even know what she wanted from Russell; surely there was nothing she could rightfully expect. She did not know where along the way he had come to represent some sort of solution —a last desperate straw at which she might clutch. But that was what had happened, and now, looking back over it, she saw that it was an empty, innocent way—a filmy world of literature and abstraction— and that there was nothing she could hope for from it to sustain her. The world, the real world, loomed like an ugly impassable giant and now, after all the years of loving school, her only refuge from it, she was being cast forth against it—out of this balmy, unreal, spring-washed campus, into its evil, waiting arms.

Russell had refused to be the slayer—had he offered, she realized now, she did not know what she would have done. And she did not know now, what she would do, how she could bear it. Perhaps that was the way people died, too, crying to life "Keep me, keep me," but finding no refuge anywhere. Suddenly she felt cold and tired, so she opened the door to the dormitory and went in.

Inside, the halls were strangely quiet and empty, with the voices of the few graduates who were in their rooms scarcely able to break the unaccustomed silence. She knew that they were playing bridge down the hall on her floor, and one of the girls had a turkey which she had been invited to help eat. But she did not go down the hall at all. Instead, she lay awake for a long time, hearing their voices.

"I pass." The slap of the cards on the floor of somebody's room.

"Oh no you don't! That's my trick!"

"My God, fellers, think of getting out of here at last!"

"Tomorrow, no less, my fine-feathered graduate!" And all the others laughed loudly, genuinely, feverish in the excitement of having finished the four years.

You see, she thought to herself, I'm unnatural. I'm probably the only one in the whole place who doesn't want to graduate. They don't even *care,* they don't even care. They'd think I was crazy. I can't even explain it to myself—how could I explain it to them?

She fell asleep long after the bridge game had broken up, after the turkey had been noisily eaten. When one of the girls came down the hall yelling, "Lupoff, hey Anne—your turkey!" she closed her eyes

The prose has a precise, descriptive style that suits the story's introspective quality.

She probes her own thoughts and wants to understand herself, but can't.

and breathed deeply and loudly, until the girl went away. Finally it was all over, the doors closed on the other rooms, and there was only the heavy silence in which she fell asleep at last.

In the morning, with the sun slanting hotly across the floor of her room, she put on her cap and gown and stood before the mirror looking at herself, pleased with how right they looked on her—how sensible and bright and wise they made her seem. She could never remember which way the tassel went, but she'd see when she got down to the procession. Now she would only have to come back to this room to collect her bags—they were all packed—and they stood alone in the middle of the floor of the half-empty room, with its stripped bed and cleared, glass-topped dresser, and dust-covered study lamp.

She looked across to Mackey Hall, but the window glared in reflected sunlight and hurt her eyes—then, down to the street, where the black-robed figures were already hurrying to have breakfast before the procession formed.

When you say "what happens next?" in this kind of story, you mean to Anne's emotions, not to events.

She thought of calling the Union, where her parents had presumably spent the night after arriving very late, but decided, instead, to go directly over there and meet them for breakfast. They had said that they would be sitting in the lobby that morning, before the exercises, but she was afraid they would get mixed up and go to the wrong place.

She knew they would expect her to be excited and pleased and loving, that they would not understand. She prayed for patience with them, but knew, even before she went to meet them, that she would not have it. To them, her degree was their stamp of having succeeded in the demanding, difficult New World to which they had come together thirty years ago. She was their only child—the next best thing to a son; if she could not be a professional (my son, the doctor . . .) she could at least be a Bachelor of Arts.

In their letters to her—long, affectionate, awkward letters which begged her silently to fulfill their hopes and prayers—they had betrayed their longing for a tall capable son who would do them honor in a profession. And she, with the academic honors which came to her as a by-product of her furious love for the place and the life, had given them the next best thing. They were unbearably proud of her, and she was embarrassed by their open, unashamed European pride, their overstated affection, their naive conviction that in giving her a college education they had attained the peak of parental obligation. Instead, she thought sadly, they had driven her further and further from them—with their strange emotional way of life, their pathetic ignorance of everything she had come to love.

You're given every dimension of Anne's emotional upheaval. There's no black or white sentiment, ideal, moral or character—only the gray in-between of real life.

She was not ashamed of them—she had never attempted to cover up for their uncertain, fumbling ways—but they had widened the gap immeasurably, and she was ashamed, not of them, but of herself, for having betrayed them by growing so unattainable, by spending these years in slipping further and further out of their reach. And now, the cruelest blow surely, that she could not honestly say she was glad to be going home with them, could not even try to fool them by celebrating, savoring, loving the meaning of this day.

She walked slowly over to the Union Building, feeling the unfamiliar folds of the black robe about her legs, the pressure of the four-cornered hat upon her brow. And they were there in the lobby of the tall white building, huddled close to one another on a leather sofa, watching anxiously for her through the crowds of noisy alumni and polished, expectant looking fathers and mothers, and eager black-gowned graduates.

Setting, too, has an effect on her: it intensifies her state of mind.

Her mother looked beautiful—that dark Balkan beauty seeming out of place amidst the athletic trophies and plaidy, collegiate trimmings which characterized the big room; the dark blue eyes looking very deep and sorrowful under the pale brim of her hat, the black hair curling softly all around her face, the white of her blouse pointing up the incredible, natural foreign coloring. Her father, small and very white-haired, turning his summer hat around and around in his fingers, looked only worried and afraid, as he always looked in a crowd.

But when they saw her, when they saw her, they clasped their hands simultaneously in front of them, like one person, and smiled broadly, looking slowly down her, from the stiff top of her cap with its ridiculous displaced tassel, to her shoes, just showing from beneath the gown—their glance sweeping with love and wonder over her face, her body, her hands, tentatively outstretched to them. Then they were kissing her and saying the things she had known they would say.

"My Anna—" they would never call her Anne—"our own girl—to think this day would come, that we are here, so far away, to see you with your college graduation."

"Hello Momma—Pa. Did you have a good trip?"

"Such a long trip. You never told us how long—and we sat up all night." Her mother shook her head slowly.

"Well my gosh, you should have taken a Pullman. I *told* you to take a Pullman, Poppa."

"I didn't know. The man said the chairs were comfortable. It wasn't so bad, Momma, was it?"

"I don't know, I don't know. I only know we're here—and soon our girl will graduate." It was all that mattered. She looked eagerly around the crowding room. "You want breakfast first, yes Anna?"

"Yes, Momma, first we have breakfast and then I'll tell you where to go for your seats and where to meet me afterwards."

They had their breakfast in the big oak-paneled dining room of the Union, but no one was very hungry. Her parents kept shaking their heads and looking curiously, proudly, about the big room. And for Anne, it was an intolerable imposition of one of her worlds upon the other—they simply did not go together; they had nothing to do with one another. She did not even know what there was for her to say to her parents—but they did a good deal of the talking themselves. She had almost forgotten how odd their conversation could sound.

"You know, Anna, what a great day this is for us—our own daughter graduating. We want you to know how proud it is for us." Her father laid his cool, old hand over her perspiring one, then passed it swiftly, lightly over her cheek.

"Yes, Pa, I know, *I* know." She was stifling with their pride, their misplaced joy.

"And we want, your momma and I, you should come home now and rest and read and do whatever you want till the fall. All summer you shouldn't work. You should just stay home with us and be—" he laughed loudly—"a loafer!"

It was an attempt, a pitiful attempt. And an image of the long, unfilled intolerable summer days consumed her, filled her eyes with tears.

Her mother saw them and turned to the little man, with bewilderment in her own eyes.

"Leave her, Joe," she said, "plenty of time for talk later."

Later, later, later—the shocking, desolating recognition of how much time there would be, how much of later, sent her sobbing out of the dining room. After several seconds of hesitation, the other two people followed her, and they all walked together in silence to the point at which the academic procession was to start. She left them there, indicating the building to which they were to go and arranging to meet them again at the Union for lunch. She hoped they remembered that Russell would be with her—they had told her to invite him, as many as she wanted, they had said—but she did not want to bring it up now.

So she stood in line with the others, under the blazing sun, her head throbbing beneath the cap—and watched their figures disappear toward the doorway of Blane Auditorium, their legs very short, moving quickly, firmly, their hands clasped together between them. Then the procession started and she felt nothing except the burning of the sun through her gown, the hot pavement through the soles of her thin summer shoes.

She was grateful that, in the huge auditorium, with the visitors all sitting behind the graduates, she could not see the faces of her parents or hear their murmured wonder and pride when the honors were announced. But on the platform she could make out Russell's face, saw the familiar, noncommittal half smile when her name was announced for the work she had done under his tutelage. At least she had done him proud—at least that; it meant a lot to a man ap-

The author enlightens you about the difficulty confronting young people who have found college life happy and consuming, then must leave it forever. The story is intended to have a philosophical effect on the reader.

The characterizations of Anne's parents are penetrating and compassionate. They are not molded to the wishes of a mass audience.

pointed Special Studies Tutor to have his student come out on top.

Even now some silly, overeager, bright young sophomore was plotting to take her place. And maybe he was thinking that there would be others who would do just as well as she had—someone else he could treat to lunch and Aristotle. She brightened a little—he *had* treated her to lunch, hadn't he—often. And today, today at least was hers. She would make the most of it.

Then, at last, they were singing the Alma Mater—and she sobbed as if she were a slobbering old alumnus at a reunion dinner who had too much to drink.

When the ceremonies were over, she stood outside in the milling mixed throng of graduates and parents, all of them kissing, calling, perspiring—caught in the only half-understood moment of having just received a diploma, a degree, the sad consummation of sixteen years. The high noon sun was incredibly strong, a summer sun now, sudden, uncompromising, with no hint of the balminess and promise of spring in a college town.

She stood there for some time, waiting for the faculty to file out, hoping to catch Russell before he started for the Union. Then she spotted him, talking over in a corner to Bill Daimler, a young teaching fellow who was always following him around. Wondering whether he had forgotten, she hurried over to them.

"Behold," shouted Bill, when he saw her coming, "the sweet girl graduate."

"Who mourneth as she comes," said Russell, holding out his hand in a congratulatory gesture.

She shook his hand, and Bill's. "My parents are going to go on ahead and meet us at the Union," she said. "I hope you'll have lunch with us too, Bill. They'd be happy to meet you."

"I'll come gladly—if nobody minds—provided you promise to smile all the way there." Bill looked at Russell sternly. "One thing you haven't taught your prize student, Professor Slater, is how to accept the facts of graduation."

Russell rolled his tongue over into one cheek and looked at her carefully. "She doesn't want to learn," he said at last.

Anne felt terribly foolish again now, and turned her head away quickly. But Bill grabbed her shoulder and was steering her out of the crowd.

"Enough of such trifling conversation," he said cheerfully, "on to the Union and the parents of the sweet girl graduate."

She looked around to be sure that her parents were not waiting in front of the auditorium, but she did not see them anywhere. So they walked together, the three of them, down the suddenly busy, crowded excited streets of the town to the Union Building. Now everything was beginning to lose its meaning, and the only thing, in all this strange turmoil, that seemed to have any real relation to her

The action and events are explored exhaustively for their effect on the main character's mind and feelings.

The weather, too, contributes to the mood of the story: it illustrates that the season for college is over, in actuality as well as in Anne's life.

was the sight of her parents, small and anxious, standing together near the front entrance to the Union lobby, looking once again for their daughter.

She felt a renewed sweep of pleasure in her mother's beauty, as she introduced them to her, and in the way her father, suddenly secure in the pride of his daughter's success, shook their hands quietly and firmly, looked brightly into their faces.

"We have heard so much about you—all of you professors," her mother said.

"The faculty, no less," her father said, laughing, his too even false teeth showing in the pink face. "If you love her like she loves you . . ."

"Poppa! Oh Poppa!" She made a gesture of impatience, and the rest of them laughed with the old man.

Then they climbed the marble stairs to the busy dining room and took seats together at a table near one of the big windows. The dining room was almost filled already, and it was some time before their orders were taken. Waiting there at the table, only half-hearing her parents' questions and answers, some flippant, some serious and respectful, which came from Russell and Bill, she began to feel again the misery of being wedged between two clashing worlds. They were all strangers now, and there was nothing she could say to any of them that would bring them together, or her closer to them.

Slowly she allowed herself to be wrapped again in self-pity, wanting to cry out to them that one of them—one of the two worlds, lives, homes—should claim her, keep her, hold her safe against the other. But there was no sign that anyone knew what she was thinking, could have understood what she meant; and the meal was miserable, confused ceremony of farewell.

"When does your train leave, Mrs. Lupoff?"

"Soon, I think. What time, Joe?"

"This afternoon, three o'clock. Maybe you and Anna should go ahead back for her bags, Momma, there's not much time."

Anne looked at her watch. It was true, there wasn't much time.

"No, no. We'll all go," her mother said.

But Bill had to leave before dessert had been served. To her great relief, Anne noted that Russell was making no move to leave with him. She wanted him with her until the last possible minute. And, thank goodness, he knew it.

"If nobody minds," he said, "I'll string along until train time. Can't see my best pupil leaving without a proper send-off."

Both parents laughed with pleasure.

"Mind?" her mother said, inclining her head slightly toward him. "Why I think we love having you. Isn't it, Poppa?"

"Delighted," said her father, with a funny little bow from the shoulders.

The values in the story are subtle and searching.

"Wedged between two clashing worlds . . ." The author makes a plain statement of the story's meaning. "Bachelor of Arts" is based on and developed from this inner kind of conflict.

The professor Anne has a crush on is not handsome nor is the crush worked up for the sake of having a big romance in the story, but is presented exactly for what it is—an attachment arising from the nature of college life.

Her mother and father waited in the parlor of the dormitory, while she and Russell went up to get her bags. He had never seen her room before—but now there was nothing of her left in it—not cute little cartoons she had tacked up on a bulletin board near the door, or the snapshots stuck under the glass dresser top, or the sonnet from Keats, framed delicately on the wall. Only her bags—sitting miserably, coldly in the middle of the floor—and a coat for traveling flung across the stripped bed.

Russell looked around the room carefully, as if he could see it all, all that had been there—then walked slowly over to her desk—empty, dusty, untelling—near the window.

"And this," he said, running a finger over the surface, "is where you sat, turning out those themes of yours." She nodded. "And there—" he looked out the open window and pointed across the street—"is where I sat and read them." He turned and faced her again.

"So you knew that I could see your window from here."

"You forget that as a member of the faculty, I know everything." He smiled at her—but softly, gently, touching her chin lightly with his finger. "Someday you'll know everything too. And you'll see what a little goose you're being and how important it is for you to leave now and give yourself a summer to think things through." He did not say what things—only "things . . ."

Then, unexpectedly, he drew out of his pocket a small volume—a thin edition of Shakespeare's sonnets, bound in rich red supple leather.

"From me to you," he said, handing it to her.

She opened to the flyleaf. "For Anne, my favorite," he had written, "to remind her gently of her salad days." Then, after watching her as she read the inscription, he walked out of the room. Slowly, closing the book without a word, she followed him down the stairs to where her parents waited.

Action is secondary to meaning, and Anne's sense of loss is the theme of the story.

In the taxi, on the way to the station, she watched her town rush by, wondering how she could be expected to throw it over, demolish it, forget it, after four years of living only from semester to semester, return to return. As the familiar streets and structures stretched out behind them, she found herself coping unsuccessfully with that incomprehensible prospect—that she would not ever see them again, and that they, in turn, would go on about their business of standing, being, again, as if she had never been there at all.

She remembered how ugly they had all seemed at first—the streets busier than she had thought college-town streets should be, and the buildings, old and baroque, spread out all over them. And now, how beautiful, with their smell of pipes, their old halls and rooms, their windows and mottoes and walls. She turned to Russell, who sat beside her holding her small traveling case.

"You're used to graduations by now, aren't you." He was something like the buildings—a permanent, steady figure, unmoved and unmoving against the incoming and outflowing tide of students.

"I'm used to them. But some I regret more than others."

"Oh—you'll have another Honors student. Next year it will be someone else to do you proud. You're used to that, too, aren't you?"

"Perhaps," he said. "But by next year that won't matter to you."

She wanted to say, "Will it matter to you?" But she only sat there silently, until the cab pulled up in front of the station house, at the foot of a long sweeping hill. From the bottom, you could see only the bell tower and the wonderful blue sky behind it. She had had her last glimpse of the buildings now, and of the town.

While her father paid the driver, her mother waiting beside him, she and Russell went into the station house with her bags. He set them down near the door to the tracks and pulled her over into a corner, near a candy machine.

"Never mind, Anne honey," he said. He put a nickel into the machine and pulled the plunger under a chocolate bar. "Sweets to the sweet," he said, handing it to her.

"Hardly worthy of you, that old cliché," she said. She could feel the tears starting to roll softly down her cheeks.

He swept his fingers lightly over them—first one side, then the other. "Or of you," he said.

They shook hands slowly, and she felt that his hand, like hers, was warm and sweating.

Her parents joined them, then, looking embarrassed and outcast, and there was the sound of the train, eastbound, rushing in upon the track. They all walked silently out of the station house and, as she mounted the steep little flight of steps to the coach, she could hear him saying good-bye to her parents. They were telling him over and over how much he had done for her, how he must visit them if he ever came east, how much, how very much, they knew she would miss him. He thanked them and helped them on to the train.

As the train quickly gathered its speed, she could see him standing on the platform—still waving—his small form becoming smaller and smaller—his hand at last going down to his side.

She pressed her head hard against the window then, sobbing softly, letting the wetness and the smooth pane of glass cool her flushed face. In the seat in front of her, her parents sat wordlessly together, looking at each other and at her. Finally, when the sobbing had stopped, her mother turned around tentatively, apologetically.

"Such a nice man," she said. "So brilliant. How lucky for you to have him."

And her father turned around too. "You are spoiled by such smart men," he said. "You only shouldn't look for too much now in the ones at home."

Identification is at its closest in a story like this, for you are kept intimately aware of the main character's thoughts and reactions throughout.

Depth of meaning is carried into every move, thought and word. The author's state of mind is thus very important to this type of story, which can say only as much as the author knows about the subject. In the quality story, the more known, the more conveyed.

"Oh Poppa, Poppa." It was too much.

"Never mind, never mind." Her mother slapped her father impatiently on the shoulder. "Poppa will see now if we can get berths for the night. Go, Joe. When we get home we talk—when we get home."

Anne turned her head again toward the window, renewing the effort to escape the bewilderment in their eyes. Now she resented having to cope with it, with any of it, and she tried hard to push herself once again back into the world in which she had so recently succeeded. Silently she reviewed the last few days and hours, flushing again under the triumph of her oral examination, feeling again the weight of her thick, careful thesis manuscript as she handed it to the head of the department, accepting again, from a high, crowded platform, the academic honors which had come to her.

She thought of everything Russell had said, everything he might have meant to say; and she stood with him again in her empty, bereft room, taking from his hands the smooth, leather-covered volume with his farewell on the flyleaf. But something had changed, thinned, lost its earlier impact; and against the even mechanical counterpoint of the noisy eastbound train, the meaning seemed to slip away from her. She was again strongly conscious of her mother's eyes upon her.

The older woman turned further around in her seat. "Anna," she said quietly, "Anna." She waited for her daughter to look at her. "We think now we should fix up the house for you—the way you want it. Then maybe you can entertain all your friends."

Anne smiled briefly at her. It was natural, after all, that even as she had been looking backward, in a last desperate effort to hold on, her parents, with the same measure of desperation, were looking ahead to home, the only place they understood, the only place in which she was—or seemed to be—wholly theirs.

Now she thought of her home, substantial, middle-class brick house that stood solidly on the corner of a city street, having nothing to do with classes or Honors or midnight discussions of philosophy —but only with the strong rich smells of foreign cooking, the sounds of steady, quiet domesticity, the small passing exultations of family life. It was, after all, the only place to which she had always been able to return.

Now, suddenly, she felt curiously relieved by its simplicity, its lack of complication, its demonstrative, basic, unashamed warmth. For the first time in her life she was not embarrassed by it.

She wished that there was something she could say to her parents to make up for the last few hours. But she knew that they did not expect any such compensation from her—and that their surprise and delight at getting it would be more than she could bear, would only push her back again into her shell of remorse and longing for something else.

This is a study of a common problem in America's growth, and how it affects one girl in particular.

No pat solution is offered. Anne struggles over the emotional bridge between her two worlds, and inevitably one of her worlds recedes—just a little. This is exactly as it would be in real life for a girl in Anne's circumstances.

So she sat there alone, saying nothing, struggling with the changing tides of her emotions, pressing hard against the images which had so easily brought tears. At last, after a long time, with the flat landscape darkening against the sky of summer evening, she was able to picture clearly and with a sudden sharp knowledge of how it felt to be there, her own room at home—with its windows wide and flung open over a long, green lawn, its bed, large and soft, that had stood there, in that corner of that room, as long as she could possibly remember.

In "An Arm Upraised," a *Scribner's* story by Alan Mac-Donald, we are taken right into the mind and feelings of the man driving. Like the preceding story, it is subjective in point of view and extremely delicate in its handling.

He saw the child for the first time on a hot morning in July. She was standing at the edge of the concrete highway along the only straight stretch between the two towns. He was driving fast, for he wanted to be at his work in the bank earlier than usual in preparation for mill payday.

You're introduced to a main character, given his thoughts and feelings.

He scarcely noticed her that first time, except for a faint irritation as he saw her arm go up stiffly, like the handle of a pump, just as his car was passing her. If she had wanted a ride, why hadn't she started to point when she saw him coming?

He didn't stop.

Two mornings later he saw her again, standing in the same place, as he came around the curve into the straight stretch. Unconsciously he slowed down a little. When he came opposite her, up went her arm again with clocklike rigidity.

There was something in the mechanical dullness of the movement that made him feel like shaking her. Almost against his will he brought the machine to a stop, reaching over to push open the door.

She didn't hurry to cover the few feet that intervened between herself and him. She seemed to move even more slowly as she approached. As she put one hand on the door handle, she paused for a second to look in at him, with no expression whatever in the dullest blue eyes he had ever seen.

"Park City?" she asked. Even her voice had an unpleasant thickness which grated against his ears.

He nodded.

"Get in. I'm in a hurry," he said, not unkindly. He tried to keep the quick distaste he felt for her from showing in his words. For the child was not only ugly, but inexcusably dirty.

As she sat down and he leaned over to close the car door, he became instantly aware of that peculiarly acrid odor which comes from a human body, long unwashed. Her clothing, too—dress, stockings,

Although there's movement in this quality story, it contributes to an inner meaning which will develop from it.

shoes, and the knotted handkerchief which she clutched in one hand —all were filthy with the crusty filthiness of repeated wear.

He could only guess how old she might be. Probably twelve or thirteen to judge from the size of her scrawny body. But the face, with its blotched unhealthy skin, might have belonged to a woman of thirty or more. It was a big face, too big for the rest of her.

The writing is on a high level, lucid and visual as well as economical.

Without reason and without pity, he instantly hated her. Hated the smears of chalky powder which showed on her cheeks and nose. Hated the way she settled back into the spotless cushions of his car. Hated everything she represented as opposed to the clean, precisely ordered design of his own existence.

As the machine gathered speed again, she sat beside him awkwardly, staring straight ahead, saying nothing, seemingly interested in nothing in the morning-washed countryside.

The driver analyzes his own reactions. He weighs his experience, tries to understand his mixed feelings of repugnance and pity, his inability to ignore the child.

He tried to analyze the instant revulsion of feeling her mere presence caused in him, to justify it by telling himself that the most poverty-ridden people can be clean. Like other children, she must have gone to school, for that was compulsory. She must have come in contact with other girls her own age, must have had teachers to tell her about herself, even if there had been no training at home.

He made a conscious effort, looked over at her, and smiled. "I've never seen you before along this road. Do you live around here?"

He knew she heard him, for her eyes blinked. But she said nothing. A moment later he thought he detected a slight nod of her head, although he wasn't sure.

He tried again. "Where do you want to go in Park City? I work at the Commonwealth Trust Company. Do you want to get out before that?"

This time she looked at him, a slow almost vacant turning of the eyes. "I'm goin' to a drugstore." She hesitated as if undecided whether to tell more, and then added "—to get medicine for my brother." She made a little movement of the hand which held the dirty handkerchief. He decided she must have the money tied in it.

"What's the matter with your brother?" This time, in spite of himself, his voice was sharp, almost hostile.

"I don't know," she said, and twisted a little in her seat as if restless at being questioned.

The stupid finality of her answer only increased his irritation. He felt like throwing back his head and laughing harshly to see if she would notice even that. Then he shrugged, impatient at the intensity of his own feeling about her.

Arriving at the Commonwealth Building near the heart of the business section, he stopped and opened the car door for her. She got out deliberately and stood looking in at him. Her face untied into a grimace which he knew must be meant for a smile. Then she said, "Thank you for the ride." Each word came out with equal flatness, like the slow dragging of a stick against a paling fence.

He pointed across the street. "There's a drugstore—over there," he said. "Don't cross until the light turns."

Anxious to be away from her, he drove quickly around the corner to the parking lot at the rear of the bank. As he stepped from the car, he couldn't help looking down at the seat which she had occupied. He was relieved that there were no soiled spots on the upholstery.

The characters are neither idealized nor softened, but portrayed as real people.

Entering the bank, he forgot about the child immediately.

But the next morning he remembered again, as he neared the place where he had first seen her. When he noted she wasn't there, he was glad. At least she didn't hitchhike to town every day.

Nor was she there on the following day.

On the third morning, he came to the straight stretch traveling in line behind two other cars. Each of the machines had only one occupant, young men like himself driving to work in Park City. As they all rounded the curve, he saw the child a quarter of a mile ahead. Again she stood on the same spot.

When the first machine passed her, he expected to see her arm go up. But it didn't. Nor did she move when the second car approached.

He suddenly leaned forward, steering with one hand, and busied himself with the radio dial on his instrument board, For months he hadn't played the radio on his way to work in the mornings. Out of the corner of his eye he saw the child look at him, saw the wooden motion of her arm rising upward. He went on.

After he had passed, he straightened in his seat and looked into the rear-view mirror. The child's face was looking after him, her arm was still upraised. But she hadn't turned nor stepped forward.

He didn't know why he stopped. He cursed the impulse that made him do it. When he backed up to the place where she stood, he was sorry he had. She seemed dirtier and uglier than before.

As he swung open the door, he said nothing. He couldn't look at her as she climbed in for fear that she might see the aversion in his face. Once more the odor of uncleanliness curled nauseatingly against him. There was no need to say anything this time—the radio with its music taking the place of words. He was glad for it.

During the remainder of the summer, the child rode with him. Sometimes every second day, sometimes at intervals of three days. Occasionally, she carried a basket, and he concluded she must be going for food supplies. Other times she had packages wrapped in newspapers, but she never divulged what was in them.

Any attempts he made at conversation met the same flat responses that he had encountered at their first meeting. Maybe by a nod or monosyllable he would know that she had heard what he said to her. Nothing more than that. Watching her as she rode with him time after time, he became convinced, perhaps not unwillingly, that there was nothing he could do to help her, nothing that he might say which would penetrate deeply enough to have any effect upon her or her condition of living.

He came to regard her as a symbol—a symbol of something to be endured with detachment instead of hate. A thing which should be studied to be better understood and reduced to undistorted proportions by that understanding. In this new pattern, he saw her as a potential breeder of all things evil, for in years to come she would spew from her womb creatures of her own kind to war against and impede the advancement of other humans like himself. Using her type as a common denominator, he found it easier to solve the problems of class strife, upheaval, and human brutality which splashed across the front pages of the newspapers he read.

He liked to dwell upon this new reaction he had achieved toward her. There was a warming broadness about it.

Then, one morning late in October, she told him she had taken her last ride with him. She didn't say it that way. She spoke three unhurried words as he was opening the car door for her in front of the bank. "We're movin' tomorrow" was all she said. She didn't add where she was moving nor why.

Somehow the unheralded announcement enraged him, for she stood on the sidewalk looking in at him as if expecting him to do something about it. He compressed his lips. If she had been able to find words enough to tell him she was moving, and had something further to say, why didn't she say it?

He waited, grimly. She turned to go and then stopped.

He didn't help her. Whatever she said now, or whether she said nothing, didn't matter. In another moment he'd drive around the corner and be free of her. At the prospect, he experienced an upsweep of relief, like a person who has shaken off an ominous pursuing presence.

Suddenly the child turned her eyes from him and stared fixedly at something above his head. Then she said, "Thank you for all the rides—it's the most fun I've ever had."

Even as the revealing implication of her words came pounding in on him, she had turned—and was walking stiffly away from him, down the street.

> The man attempts a symbolical interpretation of the child's life, and the action and background support his introspection, all characteristic of the quality story.

> An emotional jolt brings this realistic, unresolved story to a close, leaves a sad truth lingering in the reader's mind.

The cycles in storytelling

There is, in the entertainment world as in all other human pursuits, a sort of cyclical mania for first this delight and then that. The phenomenon has been studied at length in Mackay's *Extraordinary*

Popular Delusions and the Madness of Crowds. To the extent that Mackay draws a conclusion, it is that the mania is resisted by many even at its peak, that it speedily becomes a bore, and that, once its magic is gone, the mania is as detested and avoided as it was once adored and embraced.

Throughout the cycles of entertainment mania, storytelling has gone its steady course. And fiction that has brought the reader pleasures he could not get elsewhere has always had a good audience. Our problem, then, as storytellers, is to stop worrying about the transient effects of competitive media and to develop a high skill for making our stories bring the reader pleasures he can't get elsewhere.—Edwin A. Peeples in *A Professional Storywriter's Handbook*

An episode is not a story

Because the short-short story seems so easy to do, virtually every writer attempts one at some time in his career. After all, he has little to lose, either in time or in the expenditure of thought, in turning out four or five typewritten pages. The shock comes when those pages are returned with an editorial "Sorry!"

And why are they returned? In most cases—and I have this on the authority of the many weary editors who cope with so-called short-shorts—the writer regards brevity as an excuse for a slim story. More often than not, he doesn't produce a story at all, but an episode. And there is a great difference between an episode and a story—which brings us to a consideration of the basic requirements of a short-short story.

The important word in that phrase is story. Short or long, the story must be there. And what does that mean? It means that the short-short must have precisely those same qualities that we seek in longer stories: an interesting hero or heroine, a goal for him to achieve, obstacles to overcome, and at last a concise result for his efforts.

Finally there is this to say: the fact that a story is short does not mean it has to be shallow. Far from it. No theme is too profound for a short-short story. In Biblical days the prophets were able to encompass vast themes in brief parables, and that is still true in our time. No writer need hesitate to attempt rich and deep significance in the things he says through the medium of a short-short. The only thing he must bear in mind—if he is to have readers—is that primarily he is writing and must always write a story.—Oscar Shisgall in *The Writer's Craft,* by Frederic Birmingham

Lesson nine

Fiction writing
course

What goes into a short story

So far we've talked about the short story in a general way—the effect a short story should aim for as well as ways in which the writer achieves that effect. We showed you three types of short stories—slick, pulp and quality—designed for three different kinds of readers. Now it's time to look at the detailed parts which make up a short story.

These parts or elements have been given names by professional writers. They may appear in the story in any order the writer chooses, so long as they're all present. In this and succeeding Lessons, we'll examine these four elements one at a time. They are:

1. Character.
2. Setting.
3. Situation.
4. Theme.

But, you ask, what of the word *Plot* that you hear about all the time in writing? Isn't Plot one of the basic elements or ingredients? Just what is it, anyway? Later on we'll explain in detail the rules and techniques of plotting. *But plotting technique comes in the* development *stage of the story*. It isn't one of the static ingredients like Character, Setting, Situation and Theme. Plot involves them all; it is the moving story itself.

Let's illustrate this simply. Suppose a writer's eyes were recording life like a movie camera and suddenly stopped at a certain point. The picture caught at this point, if described and explained, would be Situation. When the camera started turning again and the action began to move ahead from the static picture, this would be Plot. Plotting, then, is really the whole act of storytelling, not simply one of the ingredients.

Now let's return to the four elements.

Because readers prefer to read about other human beings rather than about nature or inanimate objects, most fiction concerns people. Describing the people, giving them life, is the element called *Character*. The people also have to be placed. This is what writers call *Setting*. The people must then be in a position to do something. This is called *Situation*. And then, since most people's acts have some purpose or "meaning," we have the element writers call *Theme*.

Notice how author Frank Bennett balances the relationship of the four elements in his story "Upset!", which we reprint below from *Everywoman's Family Circle*. As you have done in previous Lessons, read the story through first to get its sense. Then read the Summary at the end where we analyze these elements as he chose them.

There was anger in John Lyman the day he upset the boat. It had first shown itself when he'd shoved back from his desk, saying, "The summer's gone! Wasted!"

"Not wasted, John," Doris had said gently. "It's been good for all of us."

"But not good for my work," he'd said bitterly.

Out of that, his anger had grown. Anger filled with hostility and resentment. However, Doris had laughed and kissed their child and had said to both of them, as if nothing were wrong, "You kids be careful with the boat while I'm gone."

A tall spare man, barefoot, in T-shirt and shorts, he stood on the porch of the summer cottage, watching his wife climb into the car and drive away along the lake road. She was going to the village for boxes in which to pack his manuscripts and books. Frowning, he laid his pipe on the porch rail, but he smiled faintly as Bingo, his old dog, hobbled over to sniff at it. Coming to sniff at the pipe was, he knew, Bingo's excuse to be near him, and he patted the shaggy graying head. Then, remembering his unfinished book, he asked his child hopefully, "Isn't there something you'd rather do than go sailing on our last day here?"

Johnny stopped wiggling her bare brown toes in the hot dust of the path and frowned up at him. "Do we have to go home tomorrow, Daddy?"

"Yes," he answered. "School begins Monday, you know."

She sighed deeply. She looked small in her swimsuit, and quite frail. Bingo nudged his hand, and John thought how he had had the dog longer than he had had Johnny, who was almost nine. And he remembered that Bingo had been his dog even before he met Doris, who had been 18 then and now was 29. For 11 years she had tried to be as old as John, and he had tried to be as young as she. Now, in his anger, he wondered despairingly if their love was worth the years of trying and so often failing.

"I can't think of anything else I'd rather do," Johnny said. And John felt his angry resentment grow . . .

He was a poor sailor. Doris was probably right, he knew, when she declared that he was always so preoccupied with his book on early Greek art that he let the wind and the boat take advantage of him. Today, however, he was preoccupied with his anger and bitterness when a gust of wind neatly flipped the light craft over.

He went under and knew panic, not for his own safety but for the safety of his child. Under ordinary circumstances, she swam well, but this was no ordinary circumstance. Breaking through the water, he looked wildly about for her.

He saw the boat first. It had swung to the right, a red-painted keel glistening in the sun. Then, to his left, he caught a glimpse of Johnny's bright hair. In her terror, she was fighting the water, gasping and screaming.

Calling assurance to her, he swam to her. She came up, sobbing, and he put an arm around her and held her close. She clung to him like a thin frightened animal, and he could feel her terror as something alive and insane. Suddenly he wanted to shout for help, too, though he knew there was no one to hear. And he wanted to fight against the water with all his strength. But he forced himself to remain calm.

"Don't cry, honey," he said gently. "We're all right."

He stayed there, treading water and holding her close and talking quietly. At last she heard him, and when he felt her arms relax, he laughed and said, "We'll never hear the last of this from Mother."

She laughed, too, then and asked, "Where's the boat?"

He finally located the red keel far to their right. "It's running away from us," he said.

Alone, he might have caught up with it and let it carry him to safety. Lifting his head, he saw how far they were from shore—almost half a mile—and again he felt a cold clutch of panic. But he said smilingly, "Think you can hang on while I swim?"

She laughed again and put her arms about his neck.

Clinging to him, she seemed light at first, and he told himself he could make it. Swim 100 strokes; then float and rest awhile. After the third rest period, she seemed to have grown astonishingly heavy.

He was too old for something like this, he thought—now he had lost count of the rest periods. He was not up to it physically. He had always preferred books to sports. And now he wondered if he had not spent too many hours of his life by himself, studying, writing, teaching. Too many hours of wanting nothing more than his pipe, his dog, his books.

Doris had come into one of his classes, a girl of 18, the oldest of a large family. A fresh lovely girl with laughter in her eyes. One day he had found her on the campus petting Bingo, and she had said he was a beautiful dog. Actually Bingo was a big ugly brute. Doris had said that Bingo had character. He had laughed and told her what a lazy no-good Bingo was. Then she had laughed too, and listening, he had known that she was what he wanted.

On their wedding day, she had declared she would give him a houseful of rowdy sons who would make him forget his books and fill him with laughter. The first was to be named John Jr. But she had succeeded in giving him only a tiny premature daughter whose chance to live at birth had been almost zero. But she *had* lived, and they named her Johanna and called her Johnny. Now he was swimming to shore with her, while a great weariness filled his body and despair gripped his mind. He was tiring fast.

He wondered what it would be like to die at nine and at 40. He wondered what would become of old Bingo. And of the pipe he had left on the front porch. He wondered how long it would be before

Doris would laugh again, and he knew how foolish it was to be angry because a book had not been written.

"Daddy," Johnny asked, "is our boat lost for good?"

"Oh, no. It'll wash ashore."

"And will we sail it next summer?"

"Of course. And probably upset it again."

She laughed, and he swam on.

When next he lifted his head, he saw they were quite close to land, but as far as he was concerned, it did not matter. He had reached a point where he could no longer make any forward progress.

"Now," he said, smiling, "I'll race you to the cottage. I'll count 10—and give you that much start. No fair looking back.".

Excitedly she struck out on her own.

John closed his eyes. His feet and legs were lead weights pulling him down. Slowly the water covered his chin, his mouth—and then his feet touched bottom! At last he crawled out on the dry hot sand.

"I won!" Johnny cried as she ran along the path toward where he lay. "I've been to the cottage already!"

He sat up to look at her. Knobby knees, skinny arms and legs. He had been like that when he was a boy of nine. Blond hair, blue eyes—that part of her was Doris's gift. Then he knew that if he had drowned, it would not have mattered much. But if Johnny had drowned, he and Doris would have been lost, and the whole pattern of the world's future would have been changed. Suddenly he knew why he himself had been born into this world. Not to write a book, but to father and protect this one particular child.

"There comes Mother!" Johnny cried and went racing away.

Somehow he managed to stumble to his feet and follow.

"Daddy and I upset the boat!" he heard Johnny say laughingly. "Then we swam a race to shore, and I won!"

Doris's startled eyes met his. Instantly, without being told, she seemed to know what had almost happened to him and Johnny and she sank down on the porch steps as if her knees had suddenly turned to rubber.

Dropping down beside her, he took her hand in his.

"You were right," he said gently. "It has been a good summer." And when she stopped trembling, he kissed her.

Summary

1. *Character:* The characters are John Lyman, his wife Doris, their daughter Johnny, and the dog Bingo.

2. *Setting:* A summer cottage and a lake.

3. *Situation:* John Lyman is a writer who's forced to go sailing instead of finishing his book.

4. *Theme:* This is summed up in mid-page above in these

words: "But if Johnny had drowned, he and Doris would have been lost, and the whole pattern of the world's future would have been changed. Suddenly he knew why he himself had been born into this world. Not to write a book, but to father and protect this one particular child."

Elements help you to outline

Most ideas for stories spring to the writer's mind in fragmentary form. Almost never do they arrive whole, with all the parts in place. With the four main elements in mind, however, a helpful initial plan can be made.

For instance, let's say the sight of a deserted railway station platform at dusk stirs the writer to write a story. This isn't too slight a fuse for story response. The subject might be a turn of weather, the look in someone's eyes. No one has yet solved the mystery of the kindling of imagination and creativity.

This station scene is only one element—Setting. The writer's first step, then, is to find the other three parts. When he has found Characters, and a Situation for them to be in, and a Theme or meaning for it all, he will have the skeleton structure of a story. The same thing would apply if the writer who saw the station platform saw at the same time a man standing at one end, staring up the tracks. The writer would then have two elements, Character and Setting. This time he would have to think up Situation and Theme.

If, on the other hand, he saw the platform and at the same moment a philosophical thought came to him about the broadening influence of travel, he would have Setting and Theme, and would have to create Character and Situation.

If this writer happened to glimpse a dispute going on at the station between a man and a woman, and he saw the woman strike the man in the face, then the writer would have a Situation, Character and Setting, and would have to provide only Theme to have a story foundation.

It doesn't matter how these elements are come by or what their relationship is developed into. If they're not there to begin with, the writer's idea will remain just that—the germ of a story, no more.

From this you will see how you can look into your notebooks

and test the ideas and thoughts, the observations and happenings that are entered there. You will find that some of these notes remain uninspiring entries for a while, but one day, because of some new experience, they suddenly begin to sprout and provide you with the nucleus of a story, *needing only your ingenuity and knowledge to make Plot germinate.*

The process of assembling the four elements becomes increasingly automatic with practice. Once this occurs, you can safely attempt a story with one or even two of them still vague in your mind. Every writer being different, there are those who, primarily inspired by Character, will have little difficulty creating Setting, Situation and Theme. Those who find Situations primarily exciting will have no trouble peopling them, setting them, and giving them a Theme. Setting will inspire some writers the same way, and there'll always be those who think philosophically and build the other parts of their story to illustrate it.

The main point about these elements is not their order, not their relationship, but your basic understanding of how they make up the framework of a short story, and why. As for the other ingredients of the short story, you'll see that they arise logically out of a deeper consideration of the main ones. So let's start this consideration with a more detailed approach to Character.

Getting the wrong compulsion

If you contemplate writing a short story or a novel, beware of the following frames of mind: the teacher's, the preacher's, the critic's, the lecturer's, the intellectual's, the scientist's, the lawyer's, the propagandist's. Beware of the feeling: I have to tell a story—to put my message across. Your first job as a fiction writer is to get out of such frames of mind, for they give the wrong compulsion to write a story.—Gorham Munson in *The Writer's Workshop Companion*

Lesson ten

Fiction writing
course

How to handle character

Just what makes story *characters* interesting to readers? Is it a list of the exact physical details of people as they look and behave in real life? Writers have learned that to portray people exactly as they are doesn't make for convincing characters. A reader would be bored by a precise record of the repetitious, inconsistent thoughts and behavior of real people.

The art of characterizing is to select the most distinct traits of people and from them create a character consistent enough to be believable to your reader. It is also to understand the real motives of your story people, *why* they do as they do, feel as they feel, think as they think. A sound knowledge of your character's motives makes for sound characterization. Faith Baldwin says:

Characterization is simply the gift of making people live—making them real to the reader. You can't just say: "Mr. Jones had a terrible temper." You have to show him in one. What he does, what he says and to whom . . . children, wife, friends, office workers. You have to show, too, why he's like that; what causes him to go off like a firecracker at intervals.

And you do not characterize Mrs. Smith by saying, "She was very unhappy," and leave it there. Show her being unhappy. It can take many forms—indifference to other people, complaining or keeping still, weeping tears or a face like a mask. So she's unhappy. Well, why? What happened to her? What is she afraid of? Was it in the past? Is it now? Does it threaten her future?

It's fun to tell a reader what people look like and wear, but you have to do more than exhibit a mannikin to characterize. The reader must know what a person has thought and is thinking, how he or she reacts to a given situation.

The fiction writer uses real people as models, but not as stamps. He has the freedom of the artist and none of the restrictions of the photographer. He must know his characters and make them known, but at the same time he must select traits from his knowledge that will keep the character recognizable to the reader. So his success will rest as much on what he leaves out of a person's character as on what he chooses to put in. Max Shulman says:

Always remember that characters in fiction, just like characters in life, are creatures of many dimensions, many facets. The more richly you endow your characters with genuine human traits, the more a reader will wish to follow their fortunes. But if you draw your characters from real life and put them down *precisely* as they exist, you will find yourself spending most of your time in courts of law being sued for libel. And losing.

Most characters in fiction have some basis in fact, but they are shaped and altered by the author's skill. They become amalgams of fact and fiction—or perhaps amalgams of several factual characters.

It isn't feasible to lay down hard and fast rules about where characters come from. Just bear in mind that there are laws governing defamation of character and invasion of privacy. If you are using a character from real life, change him enough so that he can't be identified.

In fact, the very changing of factual characters is an integral part of the writer's art and should give you pride and satisfaction.

Let's consider some of the evidence that people give of their individuality—the evidence from which you'll select what you need for characterizing. First, you know quite a lot about people simply from what is visible to you. Careful handling of appearance can help the reader "see" your characters.

On the one hand there's the static, physical evidence for which the character has no responsibility—such as size, weight, shape, age, coloring, nationality. On the other hand, you have to tell what people *do* with these inherited characteristics—what clothes they wear, the way they speak, laugh, stand, walk, sit, sleep, eat, the gestures they use, the mannerisms they develop, their facial expressions—all these create a sharp picture for the reader.

Bergen Evans makes this point about characterization:

You should know that if you don't visualize your character, your reader isn't likely to. You must therefore think the character into being and then convince your reader that the character is alive by presenting it through significant details, such as characteristic expressions or gestures, and through dialogue and action.

Your character will convey its vitality if it is complete in your mind —much, much more complete than it appears in the work. A good character is like an iceberg; it is seven-eighths submerged in its creator's imagination. Only a fraction of it appears above the surface of the action. Yet the rest is there. It must be.

Look at the way in which this O. Henry character becomes visually alive in a passage from "A Double-Dyed Deceiver":

A slim, wiry youth in high-heeled boots came down to the water's edge. His face was boyish, but with a premature severity that hinted at a man's experience. His complexion was naturally dark; and the sun and wind of an outdoor life had burned it to a coffee brown. His hair was as black and straight as an Indian's; his face had not yet been upturned to the humiliation of a razor; his eyes were a cold and steady blue.

He carried his left arm somewhat away from his body, for pearl-handled .45s are frowned upon by town marshals and are a little bulky when packed in the left armhole of one's vest. He looked beyond Captain Boone at the gulf with the impersonal and expressionless dignity of a Chinese emperor.

"Thinkin' of buyin' that 'ar gulf, buddy?" asked the captain, made sarcastic by his narrow escape from the tobaccoless voyage.

"Why, no," said the Kid gently, "I reckon not. I never saw it before. I was just looking at it. Not thinking of selling it, are you?"

This is outward description of a character. It tells you the boy's build, approximately what he's wearing, that he's old for his age and has had hard experiences. It tells you his coloring, and what the weather has done to it; the way his hair grows, that he has never shaved, and the color and expression of his eyes. Through facial description, you learn that he has dignity, is impersonal, and is used to expecting little and withstanding a lot. And when he speaks to the captain in a gentle voice, the dialogue tells you that he is controlled.

Here's an example of outer characterization from *Typhoon* by Joseph Conrad:

Captain MacWhirr, of the steamer *Nan-Shan*, had a physiognomy that, in the order of material appearances, was the exact counterpart of his mind: it presented no marked characteristics of firmness or stupidity; it had no pronounced characteristics whatever; it was simply ordinary, irresponsive and unruffled.

The only thing his aspect might have been said to suggest, at times, was bashfulness; because he would sit, in business offices ashore, sunburnt and smiling faintly, with downcast eyes. When he raised them, they were perceived to be direct in their glance and of blue color. His hair was fair and extremely fine, clasping from temple to temple the bald dome of his skull in a clamp as of fluffy silk. The hair of his face, on the contrary, carroty and flaming, resembled a growth of copper wire clipped short to the line of the lip; while, no matter how close he shaved, fiery metallic gleams passed, when he moved his head, over the surface of his cheeks.

He was rather below the medium height, a bit round-shouldered, and so sturdy of limb that his clothes always looked a shade too tight for his arms and legs. As if unable to grasp what is due to the difference of latitudes, he wore a brown bowler hat, a complete suit of a brownish hue, and clumsy black boots. These harbor togs gave to his thick figure an air of stiff and uncouth smartness. A thin silver watchchain looped his waistcoat, and he never left his ship for the shore without clutching in his powerful, hairy fist an elegant umbrella of the very best quality, but generally unrolled.

Young Jukes, the chief mate, attending his commander to the

gangway, would sometimes venture to say, with the greatest gentleness, "Allow me, sir,"—and possessing himself of the umbrella deferentially, would elevate the ferrule, shake the folds, twirl a neat furl in a jiffy and hand it back; going through the performance with a face of such portentous gravity that Mr. Solomon Rout, the chief engineer, smoking his morning cigar over the skylight, would turn away his head in order to hide a smile.

"Oh! aye! The blessed gamp . . . Thank 'ee, Jukes, thank 'ee," would mutter Captain MacWhirr heartily, without looking up.

Note the fullness of outer description, the vivid picture of a person whom the author has created from physical evidence. You know quite a lot about Captain MacWhirr, and the chances are you'd like to know more. The more important he's intended to be in the story, the more the author will tell you about him, because the more you know about him, the more you'll care what happens to him.

This is something to remember in casting the people you write about. A well-chosen name may sometimes be enough to characterize a person of no importance, and minor characters may be sketched in briefly. You'll regulate the extent to which your characters are made important to your reader. Once again, it'll be a matter of what and how much you tell about them, and of what and how much you withhold.

More examples of characterization

Just as we have given examples of physical features, now we give examples of how characterization is strengthened by including mental characteristics, and how a sympathetic identification with people can be added. Here's an excerpt from "A Thing to Remember," written by Hugh Beaumont for the *Ladies' Home Journal:*

Dr. Edward George White, Doctor of Divinity, pastor of St. Mark's Community Church, membership two hundred and forty-seven, had thought of his inadequate salary and spoken firmly.

"No, I think not. Have to think of expenses now, of course." He had risen to his feet and drawn a big breath of air into his lungs. "Well," he had said, "that's that. Thank you very much, doctor." Then he had shaken hands with the medical man and stepped out onto the autumn-clad campus with a briskness he was far from feeling.

He glanced about at the familiar university buildings and was vaguely surprised that they looked no different to him than they had a half hour before, when he had entered the School of Medicine building. It seemed to him that they should assume an unusual clarity, as though drawn into a super-focus when seen through the eyes of approaching death. Either that or they should have a blurred, unreal quality. It disturbed him that they should appear so perfectly normal and unchanged.

Slowly his mind began to fumble at his feelings to attempt an objective evaluation of his emotions. This was an opportunity that should not be overlooked. Sermon material here. He remembered a story told by a minister friend about having had to circle an airfield for forty minutes in a plane whose fuel was already perilously low. The friend had been able to turn the experience to account. He had, he had said, been able more than at any other time in his life to sort through his beliefs and feelings and to determine, once and for all, the bedrock of his faith, to sift out his unshakable convictions.

Doctor White was aware of no such inner clarity. Within himself he could find only emotional fuzziness and a desire to sit down.

In the case of this character, you have not been told what he looks like, only what he thinks, but from this you know what kind of man he is. He's been given individuality through his thoughts and feelings, through his reactions to his situation.

Now let's see what happens when outer and inner characterization are combined, as in this excerpt from "The Green Palms," by Robert Payne:

Dunhill lay on the long raffia chair of his porch, nursing his blood-poisoned hand, now heavily bandaged; the hot throbbing poison moved along his arm, festering the glands under the armpit, a sullen, endless throbbing like the rhythm of the whole island. The tapping infuriated him. He heard his servants clip-clopping at the back of the house, and once his wife called to him, but he paid no attention to her. He felt surly, ill at ease; he wished he could leave with the coastal oiler; the sea dazzled him, so that another kind of throbbing began to inflame his eyes; a four-weeks-old *Strait Times* lay in a crumpled ball at his feet.

He was thirty-seven, his face licked red by the sun, yet underneath the redness he felt worn out, drained by the malarial exhalations of the place, with no fight left in him. Every morning he had gone by buggy to the oil well in the interior; every afternoon he had returned, sick with loathing of the smell of the yellow-green oil, the sight of the drills and the derricks, the thud of the steam engines in the clearing. His wife had come from Singapore the previous year, and somehow her presence had only made him feel a more savage hatred of the place, the endless moist days broken only by the October monsoon, on this island off the coast of Borneo.

Here the author has told you how the man feels, what he thinks about, what he looks like, why he's in this situation, and what his emotional state is. You're now prepared to follow the story with a clear idea of the character as a living person.

Other methods of characterization

What about other ways of rounding out characters so that your reader will forget they are invented?

1. Characters as seen from other characters' points of view—that is, what other people say or think about them.
2. Characters in action—the way in which people behave alone, with others, or in reactions to situations.
3. What characters think of themselves. You can reveal a great deal by describing their feelings and philosophy as they express themselves in thoughts, actions or speech.
4. Their habitual poses, expressions, postures—things they always do, say, think or feel.
5. Their setting and environment. Either of these could be the cause of an ambition, a driving motive for action, the foundation of hope or despair—or a revelation of personal character.

Characters as others see them

Let's take up these methods of characterizing in order. A person as seen from another's point of view is well illustrated in this excerpt from a story called "The Muse and Mr. Parkinson," by James B. Gidney in the *Atlantic:*

I had known Mr. Parkinson for several years before he became a national figure. I didn't know him very well but only as everyone who rode the 7:51 knew him. We said "Hello" when we met and occasionally, riding together on the train or ferry, we exchanged the superficial remarks of two people who don't know each other very well and belong to different generations. He would talk mostly about his children, and, like many people who rode the same train, I followed Bob through Amherst, and Priscilla through Smith.

He would keep us up to date with such information as: "Priscilla's doing very well at Smith. A couple of A's this term"; or "Bob's running the mile this year. Seems to be pretty good at it. Surprised his mother but it didn't surprise me. The kid's not very husky but he's wiry." He would think this over for a moment and then confirm it with: "Yes, he's pretty wiry all right."

If I had been asked to describe Mr. Parkinson, I should probably have said that he was a "typical commuter." He was a sort of abstract of all the commuters in existence. He usually walked to the station in the morning, but when the weather was bad his wife drove him down to catch the 7:51. After a perfunctory kiss she drove off, leaving him to chat with other commuters or run an eye over his *Times*.

The *Times* was Mr. Parkinson's only departure from normal commuter behavior. Almost everyone else read the *Tribune*. He never read in the smoker and never played cards during the half-hour ride to Jersey City.

You have seen how Mr. Parkinson is brought to life, is gradually given character from which a story would develop, through the eyes of someone known so far as "I." Obviously this "I" will take on further identification as the story progresses.

Seeing characters from others' vantage points can be done by conversations in which opinions are voiced on someone who is absent. Or a character may read a descriptive letter from another or may recall others through memory. This is simply an indirect way of characterizing—one useful in keeping a story moving along.

A frequently used device for indirect characterization is that of the hovering eye of the invisible author, following people wherever they go and observing what they think, feel or do, without the characters being aware of scrutiny. A good example of this is the following excerpt from "Paul's Case," by Willa Cather:

His teachers felt this afternoon that his whole attitude was symbolized by his shrug and his flippantly red carnation flower, and they fell upon him without mercy, his English teacher leading the pack. He stood through it smiling, his pale lips parted over his white teeth. (His lips were continually twitching and he had a habit of raising his eyebrows that was contemptuous and irritating to the last degree.)

Older boys than Paul had broken down and shed tears under that ordeal, but his set smile did not once desert him, and his only sign of discomfort was the nervous trembling of the fingers that toyed with the buttons of his overcoat, and an occasional jerking of the other hand which held his hat.

Paul was always smiling, always glancing about him, seeming to feel that people might be watching him and trying to detect something. This conscious expression, since it was as far as possible from boyish mirthfulness, was usually attributed to insolence or "smartness."

Here, although the reader hasn't been told directly what the boy thinks or feels, he has begun to form a real picture of him, to know that there's a problem behind the boy's cocky manner.

Actions show character

Now we can look at the way in which characters reveal themselves by and through their actions. Watch this character in "The Lovely Day" by Jacques de Lacretelle:

Left alone, the old man walked carefully down the steps leading to the garden, went up to the lilac bush and slowly inhaled the perfume of the flowers, his hands clasped behind his back. A look of contentment appeared in his face and he stroked his little white beard. Then he seized a rake lying beneath the steps and began to rake one of the paths. Every now and then he stopped and then his expression was a mixture of happiness and resignation. From time to time he bent down to pull out a weed or turn over a pebble. In all his movements there was a sort of humility which gave them a certain grace. He looked like some rustic saint.

This man is unobserved except by the invisible author, yet without conversation, thought or explanation, he is sharply characterized.

Another way is to show characters in reaction to a situation or event, as in this example from "The Comeback" by Lee McGiffin, a story in *The Saturday Evening Post:*

The night of the big play-off the auditorium was packed. The bands came and went. The applause rose and fell.

Bill Bailey discovered butterflies in his stomach. Bill Bailey with nerves. What a laugh!

And then they were on the stage. Ten boys in dinner jackets, waiting for Bailey to give the downbeat. Bill Bailey with his gray temples, and his old tux, let out a bit around the middle.

They played a warm-up number. Then, just as he raised his hand, the boys shuffled around, reaching into their pockets and under their chairs.

Suddenly the lights went off. Bailey felt a trumpet thrust into his hand and heard Ken's hoarse whisper. "You'll have to take it, Mister Bailey, I don't feel so good."

Bailey had no choice. They were on regional TV and the audience was waiting. He closed his fingers on what he knew was his own trumpet. His big foot tapped out the downbeat. Then came the rhythm and the sound, the power and the glory of a sweet, hot trumpet.

Bill Bailey poured out of his horn the things he had never been able to say since he came to Brazos College.

Here you have watched a character put to a test, and have seen by his reaction that he is a musician who hasn't lost his touch despite his fears. The reader can see and know Bill Bailey by this form of characterization.

Characters reveal themselves

Now consider what can be accomplished by a character who tells about himself and thereby gives away his peculiarities to the reader. This is from "Bridewater's Half Dollar" by Booth Tarkington:

George Bridewater looked upon a certain bench in Garfield Square as his own. The Square, a smoky parklet in the shabby, oldest part of the city, had a small central space of gravel about which were twelve benches, three on a side; and it was the middle bench on the north side, facing the sun, that Mr. Bridewater looked upon as his.

The seven or eight other habitués respected his feeling, and, if a stranger loitered near, Bridewater yawned and extended both arms along the top of the bench, kept them there until the intruder either passed on or made another selection.

He performed this maneuver a little after five o'clock one afternoon of last May, to discourage an unknown saunterer whose appearance was that of a young workman out of a job; but, though he thus significantly stretched himself, Bridewater was interested in the conversation he was having with acquaintances upon other benches and didn't interrupt it.

"I'm fifty-four, Mr. Schleeman," he said, speaking loudly because he was addressing the seedy fat man who sat upon a bench across the graveled central space. "I'm fifty-four and I ain't never yet let no foreman work me to death. Who do you think I am? I'd say. Don't get talky with me, I'd say, or I'll put the heat on you! Give me my time and I'll go, I'd say, but don't get talky!

"I says just that the last job I had. It was in nineteen twenty-seven; and if they think they can take advantage of me now on account of the depression, make me work for nothin' and get talky with me, too, I'll show 'em!"

In this characterization the reader sees that a man is building up an image of his importance both for others and for himself.

The repeating of a trait

Now let's see how habitual poses, expressions, feelings or sayings can characterize effectively. This is usually done by having the person repeat a trait several times throughout the story. For instance, a man might always bow deeply to a lady and say "Ma'am" with a courteous flourish. If he does this often enough, the reader can almost "see" that he has respect for women. Suppose, however, that this same man adds a raised brow or a curled lip to his act. Then the reader would know that the flourishing gesture was not chivalry but mockery.

Since there are both conscious and unconscious traits of character, people may sometimes be clearly portrayed by a description of their sleeping posture. Or a person's expression when praying or concentrating can be sharply revealing of character. The innocence of a child is best told by unselfconscious reactions. Evil, grossness, self-pity, love—almost any characteristic can be clearly delineated by conscious or unconscious habits that people develop.

See the manner in which Edna Ferber bases a whole story on the habitual ways of two characters. Here are excerpts from "Old Man Minick":

His wife had always spoiled him outrageously. No doubt of that. Take, for example, the matter of the pillows merely. Old man Minick slept high. That is, he thought he slept high. He liked two plump pillows on his side of the great, wide, old-fashioned cherry bed. He would sink into them with a vast grunting and sighing and puffing expressive of nerves and muscles relaxed and gratified. But in the morning there was always one pillow on the floor. He had thrown it there. Always, in the morning, there it lay, its plump white cheek turned reproachfully up at him from the side of the bed.

Ma Minick knew this, naturally, after forty years of the cherry bed. But she never begrudged him that extra pillow. Each morning, when she arose, she picked it up on her way to shut the window. Each morning the bed was made up with two pillows on his side.

Then there was the window. Ma Minick liked it open wide. Old man Minick, who rather prided himself on his modernism (he called it being up to date) was distrustful of the night air. In the folds of its sable mantle lurked a swarm of dread things—colds, clammy miasmas, fevers.

"Night air's just like any other air," Ma Minick would say with some asperity. Ma Minick was no worm; and as modern as he. So when they went to bed the window would be open wide. They would lie there, the two old ones, talking comfortably about commonplace things. The kind of talk that goes on between a man and a woman who have lived together in wholesome peace (spiced with occasional wholesome bickerings) for more than forty years . . .

Usually, some time during the night, he awoke, slid cautiously and with infinite stealth from beneath the covers and closed the wide-flung window to within a bare two inches of the sill. Almost invariably she heard him; but she was a wise old woman, a philosopher of parts. She knew better than to allow a window to shatter the peace of their marital felicity. As she lay there, smiling a little grimly in the dark and giving no sign of being awake, she thought, "Oh well, I guess a closed window won't kill me either."

Still, sometimes, just to punish him a little, and to prove that she was nobody's fool, she would wait until he had dropped off to sleep again and then, she, too, would achieve a stealthy trip to the window and would raise it slowly, carefully, inch by inch.

"How did that window come to be open?" he would say in the morning, being a poor dissembler.

"Window? Why, it's just the way it was when we went to bed." And she would stoop to pick up the pillow that lay on the floor.

This study of habits has served the author well, for surely the reader can picture this old couple and feel that they are real.

The frame must suit the picture

In the case of Number 5—characterizing from setting and environment—here's an example of character given shape by a choice of setting. It is from "The Outstation" by Somerset Maugham:

He was gratified by the guard of Dyak soldiers who presented arms as he passed. He liked to sit in judgment on his fellow men. It pleased him to compose quarrels between rival chiefs. When the headhunters were troublesome in the old days he set out to chastise them with a thrill of pride in his own behaviour. He was too vain not to be of dauntless courage, and a pretty story was told of his coolness in adventuring single-handed into a stockaded village and demanding the surrender of a bloodthirsty pirate. He became a skillful administrator. He was strict, just and honest.

And little by little he conceived a deep love for the Malays. He interested himself in their habits and customs. He was never tired of listening to their talk. He admired their virtues, and with a smile and a shrug of the shoulders condoned their vices.

"In my day," he would say, "I have been on intimate terms with some of the greatest gentlemen in England, but I have never known finer gentlemen than some well-born Malays whom I am proud to call my friends."

He liked their courtesy and their distinguished manners, their gentleness and their sudden passions. He knew by instinct exactly how to treat them. He had a genuine tenderness for them. But he never forgot that he was an English gentleman and he had no patience with the white men who yielded to native customs. He made no surrenders. And he did not imitate so many of the white men in taking a native woman to wife, for an intrigue of this nature, however sanctified by custom, seemed to him not only shocking but undignified. A man who had been called George by Albert Edward, Prince of Wales, could hardly be expected to have any connection with a native.

And when he returned to Borneo from his visits to England, it was now with something like relief. His friends, like himself, were no longer young, and there was a new generation which looked upon him as a tiresome old man. It seemed to him that the England of today had lost a good deal of what he had loved in the England of his youth. But Borneo remained the same. It was home to him now. He meant to remain in the service as long as was possible, and the hope in his heart was that he would die before at last he was forced to retire. He had stated in his will that wherever he died, he wished his body to be brought back to Sembulu and buried among the people he loved, within sound of the softly flowing river.

Through reaction to setting, this man emerges as a distinctive character. Placed in another scene he might seem utterly different.

In the following excerpt from "Old Red" by Caroline Gordon, the author uses a home and family environment to characterize the cast of her story:

When the door had closed behind his daughter, Mister Maury went to the window and stood a few moments looking out. The roses that had grown in a riot all along that side of the fence had died or been cleared away, but the sun lay across the garden in the same level lances of light that he remembered. He turned back into the room. The shadows had gathered until it was nearly all in gloom. The top of his minnow bucket just emerging from the duffel bag glinted in the last rays of the sun.

He stood looking down at his traps all gathered neatly in a heap at the foot of the bed. He would leave them like that. Even if they came in here sweeping and cleaning up—it was only in hotels that a man was master of his own room—even if they came in here cleaning up, he would tell them to leave all his things exactly as they were. It was reassuring to see them all there together, ready to be taken up in the hand, to be carried down and put into a car, to be driven off to some railroad station at a moment's notice.

As he moved toward the door, he spoke aloud, a habit that was growing on him: "Anyhow, I won't stay but a week . . . I ain't going to stay but a week, no matter what they say . . ."

Downstairs in the dining room they were already gathered at the supper table, his white-haired, shrunken mother-in-law, his tall sister-in-law who had the proud carriage of the head, the aquiline nose, but not the spirit of his dead wife, his lean, blond new son-in-law, his black-eyed daughter who, but that she was thin, looked so much like him, all of them gathered there waiting for him, Alexander Maury.

It occurred to him that this was the first time he had sat down in the bosom of the family for some years. They were always writing saying that he must make a visit this summer or certainly next fall. ". . . all had a happy Christmas together but missed you . . ." They had even made the pretext that he ought to come up to inspect his new son-in-law. As if he hadn't always known exactly the kind of young man Sarah would marry! What was the boy's name? Stephen, yes, Stephen. He must be sure and remember that.

He sat down, and shaking out his napkin spread it over his capacious paunch and tucked it well up under his chin in the way his wife had never allowed him to do. He let his eyes rove over the table and released a long sigh.

"Hot batter bread," he said, "and ham. Merry Point ham. I sure am glad to taste them one more time before I die."

A reader can see Alexander Maury more clearly in his reactions to this home and his relatives than if he were to be shown, say, on an ocean liner. Maury would be the same man, but he wouldn't be as readily understandable as when located in his own familiar background.

Another way to characterize with environment is shown in an excerpt from "María Concepción" by Katherine Anne Porter:

María Concepción walked carefully, keeping to the middle of the white dusty road, where the maguey thorns and the treacherous curved spines of organ cactus had not gathered so profusely. She would have enjoyed resting for a moment in the dark shade by the roadside, but she had no time to waste drawing cactus needles from her feet. Juan and his chief would be waiting for their food in the damp trenches of the buried city.

She carried about a dozen living fowls slung over her right shoulder, their feet fastened together. Half of them fell upon the flat of her back, the balance dangled uneasily over her breast. They wriggled their benumbed and swollen legs against her neck, they twisted their stupefied eyes and peered into her face inquiringly. She did not see them or think of them. Her left arm was tired with the weight of the food basket, and she was hungry after her long morning's work.

Her straight back outlined itself strongly under her clean bright blue cotton *rebozo*. Instinctive serenity softened her black eyes, shaped like almonds, set far apart and tilted a bit endwise. She walked with the free, natural, guarded ease of the primitive woman carrying an unborn child. The shape of her body was easy, the swelling life was not a distortion, but the right inevitable proportions of a woman. She was entirely contented. Her husband was at work and she was on her way to market to sell her fowls.

Her small house sat halfway up on a shallow hill, under a clump of pepper trees, a wall of organ cactus enclosing it on the side nearest to the road. Now she came down into the valley, divided by the narrow spring, and crossed a bridge of loose stones near the hut where María Rosa the beekeeper lived with her old godmother, Lupe the medicine woman.

María Concepción had no faith in the charred owl bones, the singed rabbit fur, the cat entrails, the messes and ointments sold by Lupe to the ailing of the village. She was a good Christian, and drank simple herb teas for headache and stomachache, or bought her remedies bottled, with printed directions that she could not read, at the drugstore near the city market, where she went almost daily. But she often bought a jar of honey from young María Rosa, a pretty, shy child only fifteen years old.

María Concepción and her husband, Juan Villegas, were each a little past their eighteenth year. She had a good reputation with the neighbors as an energetic religious woman who could drive a bargain to the end. It was commonly known that if she wished to buy a new *rebozo* for herself or a shirt for Juan, she could bring out a sack of hard silver coins for the purpose.

Although this author gives us a good deal of direct information, the reader would have gained a vivid impression of María Concepción by her movements within a specific environment. The "white, dusty road—the treacherous curved spines of organ cactus" are the scenery or setting. The fowls she carries show her work and her relationship to surroundings, as well as her philosophy of life. Her home and living conditions define her even further, as do her religion, her clothes, her attitude toward the medicine woman. In other words, the factors that contributed to making her what she is also allow the author to portray her in the present moment.

Further helps to characterization

All the above examples can, of course, be carried further. For instance, hobbies may characterize a person, or a goal or an ambition, like mountain climbing or exploring. A religious calling certainly conveys to the reader a set of traits, as would the vocation of a sailor, soldier, doctor, actor and so forth.

The craft of characterization rests mainly upon the keenness of the writer's observation. You must not only watch and listen but also, from your impressions of people, select the traits that predominate. Choose those which make the most striking impression—the ones which, if you were to close your eyes, would most distinctly picture a person. And among these should be one that stands out most of all—the *main* or *dominant* or *basic trait* as writers call it. You'll be surprised how clearly your characters emerge if you endow them with one major trait, and then add two or three minor ones.

This way of bringing people to life is exemplified in a short paragraph from "Samuel" by Jack London:

> Sara, at the time I met her, was a buxom, phlegmatic spinster of sixty, equipped with an experience so tragic and unusual that though her tongue ran on for decades, its output would still be of imperishable interest to her cronies.

Here the author has deliberately stressed Sara's tragic experience and has given her three other traits—"buxom, phlegmatic spinster of sixty"— to create a quick, sharp picture for the reader. London did not go on to say, as he might have said, that she liked to cook, had a fondness for dogs, was afraid of storms, despised lazy people, and had a wart on her right hand. He chose certain sharply distinguishing traits and assembled them so that the reader didn't need more to form an image.

And again, in the following example, Conan Doyle in "The Red-Headed League" brings a character to life by the use of carefully chosen traits:

> Our visitor bore every mark of being an average commonplace British tradesman, obese, pompous, and slow. He wore rather baggy

gray shepherd's check trousers, a not overclean black frock coat, unbuttoned in the front, and a drab waistcoat with a heavy brassy Albert chain, and a square pierced bit of metal dangling down as an ornament. A frayed top hat and a faded brown overcoat with a wrinkled velvet collar lay upon a chair beside him. Altogether, look as I would, there was nothing remarkable about the man save his blazing red head and the expression of extreme chagrin and discontent upon his features.

Remember, too, that your reader likes to be led to his recognition of a character, likes to feel that he's made the discovery himself. It is a case of showing rather than telling him. The more you illustrate by the ways we have described, the better your reader will see your characters and feel that they live.

Another reason for showing rather than telling is that you avoid waste motion and keep the story moving. It's always important to make your character's traits contribute to your story action. This is what is meant by the saying: "Passions spin the plot." Through the traits of your character, your story is given direction. Out of these traits come the developments. It is the character's reactions to situations and events that make a story.

Any two characters placed in the same situation will react differently and therefore create a quite different story. This is why you must be sure to keep your characters consistent. If you have made a man stingy, for instance, don't suddenly change him into a generous person. People just don't change like that.

A good way to ensure consistency is to repeat the main traits in different ways—to keep characterizing for emphasis. For instance, you might choose a woman who was quiet and serene, with a calm smile. The first time you might say: "She entered the room quietly, with her serene brow and calm smile." Another time, you might say: "Her eyes reflected her inner calm, her mouth curved in a placid smile." And again: "Her quietness soothed us. There was reassurance in her deep serenity." The essential quality of this woman is thus impressed vividly upon the reader's mind.

The shorter the piece you are writing, the fewer should be the character traits. As we've said in earlier Lessons, the reader should be given only as much detail and plot as he can digest in the right space of time. The use of a dominant trait is therefore the best way of making characters come alive without too many words and scenes. A person of complexity, who must be illustrated in careful detail for the reader, should be kept for longer pieces of fiction.

One of the best helps in characterizing is for the author to have genuine interest in his character. The more you can put yourself into his thoughts and feelings, the more your reader will respond to him. Look at this excerpt from a story called "That Sister of Mine" by Camilla R. Bittle, which appeared in *McCall's*. It's a good example of an author having firsthand interest in a character and thus creating reality for the reader:

When the list of names came out in the paper, Louise knew she would not be asked to join the Young Matrons Club. Sick with disappointment, she crumbled the paper into a ball and threw it away; then she lighted a cigarette and started to heat up the coffee. "We never should have come back here to live," she thought. All of a sudden she felt something warm and wet on her face, her throat felt as though the collar of her blouse were choking her and she stood over the shiny electric range in the shiny modern kitchen and cried.

She poured herself a cup of leftover coffee, then went into the den and turned on the television set. The coffee was bitter and too hot, it burned her mouth. A giveaway show blared forth and girls with bright, brittle smiles praised a home-permanent lotion.

Louise didn't hear the program at all. Every girl on the screen reminded her of her sister Julie; she could see Julie over and over again, smiling too widely, laughing too loudly, driving too fast, drinking too much, stamping an imprint on the town so that no one ever saw Louise at all. She was only Julie's sister; even after ten years of living away from here, no one could see her for what she was. She had sensed unfriendliness ever since they'd come back; now she had proof and wished they lived anywhere but here.

Her tongue, which was almost blistered from the coffee, hardly hurt; but there was a terrible tightening in her throat from swallowing tears lest her boys come in from play and see her crying; and fury pounded inside her because she allowed herself to cry at all. She thought of the important things that touched her life, and the triviality of this one overwhelmed her.

She gulped her coffee, left the den and went into the bathroom, where she soaked a washcloth and held it against her eyes. She told herself that she wouldn't cry any more. She would be angry and indignant, but not hurt. Life was full of slights and snubs; it was foolish to be upset. She powdered her face, but the powder stood out on her fair skin like a mask of flour.

Emotion and sympathy have been evoked here by the author's

ability to *project*. This is a word for you to know for it separates fiction from other forms of writing. An effective writer projects or puts himself in the place of other people—he imagines what they would say, do or feel because of what they are. This makes possible reader identification, a main function of characterizing.

All these approaches to creating people about whom you write should help you in the beginning. But with constant practice they will become so automatic that you'll probably forget that you have learned them. For if you follow the three main goals—to observe keenly, to be interested in your characters and to portray their most distinguishing traits—you will soon combine the rest without effort.

Five examples from great writers

To round out your knowledge of characterizing, here are five more varied samples taken from the works of master craftsmen. Read them carefully, then find some samples of your own from stories you like. This exercise will not only broaden your awareness of how characterizations are achieved but will give you ideas for achieving them yourself.

From "Twenty-Six and One" by Maxim Gorky:

The frosty air, rushing through the door in thick smoky clouds, whirled round his feet, and there he stood on the threshold looking down upon us from his eminence, and from beneath his blond, skilfully twisted moustaches gleamed his strong yellow teeth. His vest really was something quite out of the common—it was blue, embroidered with flowers, and had a sort of sparkle all over it, and its buttons were made of pretty little pearls. And the gold chain *was* there . . .

He was handsome, that soldier was, quite tall, robust, with ruddy cheeks, and his large bright eyes looked good and friendly and clear. On his head was a white stiffly starched cap, and from beneath his clean spotless spats appeared the bright tops of his modish, brilliantly polished boots.

From "Orphant Annie" by Thyra Samter Winslow:

She was nicknamed Orphant Annie when I first met her, at Rutgers & Olds. I've no idea that the nickname stuck to her nor that anyone else remembers it. She was named, perhaps, because of the old jest—that she was not an orphan. At that, she had supposed orphan-like attributes. She was, as she is now, a little thing, slender, with grey eyes set wide apart. Although she is, in a way, even plump, because she is small-boned she has always given the impression of extreme fragility. She was, and is, pale, too, though her mouth is full and ripe-looking. Her face is a bit broad, her cheekbones a trifle high for artistic perfection. Her skin is smooth and delicate-looking and her hair an unnoticeable light brown and straight. Her nose is slender and straight, with just a suspicion of a tilt to it, and, though her hips and waist are slender, her breasts are well rounded.

From "Big Blonde" by Dorothy Parker:

Hazel Morse was a large, fair woman of the type that incites some men when they use the word "blonde" to click their tongues and wag their heads roguishly. She prided herself upon her small feet and suffered for her vanity, boxing them in snub-toed, high-heeled slippers of the shortest bearable size. The curious things about her were her hands, strange terminations to the flabby white arms splattered with pale tan spots—long, quivering hands with deep and convex nails. She should not have disfigured them with little jewels.

From "Turn About" by William Faulkner:

The American—the older one—wore no pink Bedfords. His breeches were of plain whipcord, like the tunic. And the tunic had no long London-cut skirts, so that below the Sam Browne the tail of it stuck straight out like the tunic of a military policeman beneath his holster belt. And he wore simple putties and the easy shoes of a man of middle age, instead of Savile Row boots, and the shoes and the putties did not match in shade, and the ordnance belt did not match either of them, and the pilot's wings on his breast were just wings. But the ribbon beneath them was a good ribbon, and the insigne on his shoulders were the twin bars of a captain.

He was not tall. His face was thin, a little aquiline; the eyes intelligent and a little tired. He was past twenty-five; looking at him, one thought, not Phi Beta Kappa exactly, but Skull and Bones perhaps, or possibly a Rhodes scholarship.

From "An Experiment in Misery" by Stephen Crane:

It was late at night, and a fine rain was swirling softly down, causing the pavements to glisten with hues of steel and blue and yellow in the rays of the innumerable lights.

A youth was trudging slowly, without enthusiasm, his hands buried deep in his trousers' pockets, toward the downtown places where beds can be hired for coppers. He was clothed in an aged and tattered suit, and his derby was a marvel of dust-covered crown and torn rim. He was going forth to eat as the wanderer may eat, and sleep as the homeless sleep. By the time he had reached City Hall Park he was so completely plastered with yells of "bum" and "hobo," and with various unholy epithets that small boys had applied to him at intervals, that he was in a state of the most profound dejection.

The sifting rain saturated the old velvet collar of his overcoat, and as the wet cloth pressed against his neck, he felt that there no longer could be pleasure in life. He looked about him searching for an outcast of highest degree that they too might share miseries, but the lights threw a quivering glare over rows and circles of deserted benches that glistened damply, showing patches of wet sod behind them. It seemed that their usual freights had fled on this night to better things. There were only squads of well-dressed Brooklyn people who swarmed towards the bridge.

Some wise words on writing

I write when the spirit moves. And it moves every day.—William Faulkner

I write as I walk because I want to get somewhere and I write as straight as I can, for that is the best way to get there.—H. G. Wells

What a writer should try to do is to make something which will be so written that it will become part of the experience of those who read him.—Ernest Hemingway

I find when I am writing a novel I'm dealing in a double life. I live in the present with my family at the same time that I live in the past with my characters.—John P. Marquand

Section IV

Lesson eleven

Fiction writing
course

How to
handle
setting

There are many ways to use *setting* in stories, ranging in importance from the barest statement of place and time to a strong force in the development of plot. There's only one general rule: setting should contribute to the story but never block or slow its movement.

Let's look at several of the ways to handle it. Here, in this example from "Meeting of the Clan," by Mary Bolté, which appeared in *Cosmopolitan*, the setting is sketched in lightly, at the beginning, merely showing where the characters are:

As the car rounded a curve and the glittering lake came into view, Ted reached over and squeezed Claire's hand. "Almost there now, baby."

The story continues for several hundred words without another mention of setting. It depicts the characters and their problem, employs a flashback within Claire's thoughts, then brings the couple back to the present. In the following excerpts, the phrases that have to do with setting are italicized.

Ted spoke again. "Nous sommes arrivés." Claire, turning, saw that his face bore the usual anticipatory expression that came over it whenever they returned to *the family homestead.*

As they drove past *the tennis court,* Claire found it almost impossible to believe that Mr. Heron, in old white ducks and green eye shade, would not be springing around the court soon, swinging at the ball in his elegant 1910 style. No one was playing, and, of course, no one would be, for today was a day of mourning.

And this is the way the family homestead is shown to the reader to picture the environment:

Shabby clutter, Claire had long ago decided, was a point of pride with the Herons. Like a socially-at-ease millionaire attired ostentatiously in threadbare clothes, *the house and everything in it seemed dedicated to carrying out the theory that rickety disorder was the best backdrop for quality.*

Today, as she entered the house, Claire noticed that *everything was as usual,* and although she did not at first know the reason why, this startled her. Then, remembering her mother's house stacked with flowers and wreaths, she realized that she had expected some change, however slight, to signify that death had passed this way. There was nothing. *The shredded sheet music on the piano and the ski trophies were in their usual disarray.*

These are all the details given to the reader, except for an occasional placement such as: "Molly stood in *the upstairs hall* . . . According to custom, cocktails were served on *the porch overlooking the lake* . . . The room swam before Claire's eyes. Goose flesh prickling her back, she broke away from the group and rushed through *the dining room, the pantry and into the big, old wooden kitchen.* In an anguish of humiliation and shame she pressed her fists down hard on *the dented copper of the sink.*"

In this scant yet effective manner, the writer leaves it to the reader's imagination to fill in the picture of the home. In this kind of description the writer has no use for setting other than as a background in which characters move about. On the other hand, the setting is an integral part of the story.

For instance, if the Heron family lived in a small city apartment, it would alter the atmosphere, problem and characterizations. Without undue emphasis, setting in this particular story is an important factor and has been used without halting the action or intruding upon the main story idea.

And here Ambrose Bierce establishes his setting and mood at the very start of the story, "A Son of the Gods":

A breezy day and a sunny landscape. An open country to right and left and forward; behind, a wood. In the edge of this wood, facing the open but not venturing into it, long lines of troops, halted. The wood is alive with them, and full of confused noises—the occasional rattle of wheels as a battery of artillery goes into position to cover the advance; the hum and murmur of the soldiers talking; a sound of innumerable feet in the dry leaves that strew the interspaces among the trees; hoarse commands of officers. Detached groups of horsemen are well in front—not altogether exposed—many of them intently watching the crest of a hill a mile away in the direction of the interrupted advance. For this powerful army, moving in battle order through a forest, has met with a formidable obstacle—the open country. The crest of that gentle hill a mile away has a sinister look; it says, Beware! Along it runs a stone wall extending left and right a great distance. Behind the wall is a hedge; behind the hedge are seen the tops of trees in rather straggling order. Among the trees—what? It is necessary to know.

Yesterday, and for many days and nights previously, we were fighting somewhere; always there was cannonading, with occasional keen rattlings of musketry, mingled with cheers, our own or the enemy's. This morning the enemy was gone. We have moved forward across his earthworks, across which we have so often vainly attempted to move before, through the débris of his abandoned camps, among the graves of his fallen, into the woods beyond.

There are other kinds of stories, however, where details count so much that the writer makes inventory of them. Typical is the detective story where objects or the arrangement of room or scene provide clues to solution of the crime. In this excerpt from "The Little Mystery," by E. C. Bentley, there is significance in the details of description (italicized below). It doesn't bore the reader, because setting is pertinent to the story:

This was an *old-fashioned, high-roofed, stucco-fronted house with a basement and three other floors;* like all its neighbours, *slightly dingy in appearance,* though not dilapidated. They mounted the steps, and Marion opened the door with a latchkey. It could be seen, as they went up the stairs, that *each floor had been partitioned off to form a self-contained flat;* and Marion's *own door, like the front door, was fitted with a Yale lock.*

"Well, here's my *top floor,*" she said as they entered. *There were four rooms opening off the landing, all fairly lofty and well lighted.*

"And a very good top floor," Trent observed when he had been shown *the living room, bedroom, bathroom and kitchen.* "Much better than the top floor in my own place; and furnished, as I think you said, with faultless taste. If ever you want to get rid of *that little tallboy,* you might let me know. And *that mahogany writing table—* it was a spinet when it was young, wasn't it? You want to keep that, I suppose."

Marion laughed. "Are you setting up an antique shop? But now, let me tell you what it was I wanted your advice about. To begin with, look at the top of *that table.*"

He bent over it. "You mean these faint scratches here and there —as if something hard and heavy had been shifted about on it. Curious? The scratches are in four lots—making the four corners of a square. Was it done when the furniture was moved here from Wallingford?"

"No, it was done fairly lately—three weeks ago, say; perhaps more. That table was as smooth as glass till then. I rub it over with a duster every day, so I noticed it at once. And it wasn't done by the maid who comes in two mornings a week. She is a very careful, neat-handed woman; and besides, I first saw the scratches on a Thursday, and her days are Tuesday and Friday. Of course, I don't like having my table scratched, but what I like much less is not knowing who did it, and how any one could have been here to do it. *The entrance door* is locked when I'm out, of course; and *the street door* always is. And don't look as if you thought I was worrying about a trifle. There are other things that tell me plainly some one comes into this place when I'm not here.

"You see *the velvet cushion in that armchair?* It's embroidered a prettier pattern on one side than on the other, and I always leave it showing that side, as it is now. But several times I have come in and found it turned the other way round. Any one who had been sitting in that chair, and had punched the cushion into shape again before going away, would be as likely as not to leave it wrong way round. Then again there is *that old writing table* you covet so much. There is nothing of value in either of the drawers—I keep father's notes for his memoirs in the left-hand one, and as much as I have done of the fair copy in the other—but three times some one has been at them."

As you can see, not only has the author been specific about the setting but it is vital to the action of the story.

Details establish a mood

Careful enumeration of a setting may include not only objects and surroundings, but the weather, the smells, sounds, tastes or sense of touch involved in the scene. Details can be used to establish a mood or some special atmosphere. In this excerpt from "Roman Fever" by Edith Wharton, an almost continuous set of details creates the feel of a place:

The clear heaven overhead was emptied of all its gold. Dusk spread over it, abruptly darkening the Seven Hills. Here and there lights began to twinkle through the foliage at their feet. Steps were coming and going on the deserted terrace—waiters looking out of the doorway at the head of the stairs, then reappearing with trays and napkins and flasks of wine. Tables were moved, chairs straightened. A feeble string of electric lights flickered out. Some vases of faded flowers were carried away, and brought back replenished.

A stout lady in a dust coat suddenly appeared, asking in broken Italian if any one had seen the elastic band which had held together her tattered Baedeker. She poked with her stick under the table at which she had lunched, the waiters assisting.

The corner where Mrs. Slade and Mrs. Ansley sat was still shadowy and deserted. For a long time neither of them spoke.

Now consider the next example, in which setting is made up of impressions skillfully chosen to carry the reader into the story. It is from "The Carpenter Goes Home," by Frank Laskier.

In Durban, we loaded coal and pulled out within a day and night Together, the carpenter and I prepared the ship for the impact of the gales that sweep the Cape of Good Hope. The anchor, raised and secured; the cable was coiled down in the locker, sealed from the deck with oakum, burlap and cement; this is so that we would ship no water below decks forward. The lifeboats were double-secured with extra lashings of rope; all the hatches were battened down afresh.

Immediately we hit the open sea, the breeze freshened to a head-on gale for the three-day trip to Capetown. We were thankful in those days for our strong, well-found ship, for she took a most violent pounding. Straight from the South Pole came the wind, churning seas to a height of well over fifty feet that tossed the ship about like a cork. Doing a steady eight knots, the *Tribesman* kept her course, drenched with spray, her decks awash. As the bow hit each breaking sea she would shudder under the impact, then the great green roaring seas would sweep her end for end; seething masses of water flooding the scuppers, burying winches, all as the ship rolled madly on her course. And the wind—all day, all night, a Niagara of fury, screaming through the rigging. Yet above this turmoil, the sun shone, and in the shelter of the lee, it was quite warm.

From this example, with the background of sea, weather and sounds, the reader is transported away from himself and into the story adventure. This kind of detail also shows the advantage of writing about settings which you know well or have retained in your notebooks, rather than those purely imagined. Max Shulman says:

The background of your story can be of enormous added value. If you can paint an exotic picture, if you can evoke a nostalgic mood, you cannot help but captivate a reader. Beware, however, of piling up detail for the sake of detail. Never let description get in the way of your story.

If you want to write about places you don't know firsthand, then your research must be thorough and careful, and done well enough to withstand the sharp scrutiny and often intimate knowledge of the reader. Remember, the entire feeling of a story can be shattered by one inaccurate detail of setting.

The following examples show just a few of the many ways that setting helps to make stories realistic and convincing. Note how it is always interwoven with the other three elements.

In "The Killing of Will Blake" by Charles Hewes, from *Saga,* setting is neither emphasized nor played down, but given almost equal stature with character and situation.

When Stede Bennet had ridden halfway through *the town of Canyon,* he reined up his horse. He stared curiously at *the empty town,* and *the vacant doorways of the stores and saloons stared back at him. A gust of wind sucked up dust from the street and whirled it higher than the buildings.*

Stede took off his Stetson and scratched through his thin black hair. It wasn't natural for *a town to be deserted at one o'clock in the afternoon.* He rode on *through the town and out the stage trail on the other side,* where he reined in sharply. There was a mob of people huddled together a quarter-mile west of town.

"Either we ride out there or go back to town," he mumbled. "I can't see staying out in this hot sun any longer."

He turned his horse, rode back into town and stopped in front of *the newspaper office.* Swinging his long, lanky frame to the ground, he walked to *the window where a copy of the paper was posted.* The paper was the Canyon *Clarion,* the date was August 3, 1883. Two huge words, boxed in black, filled up the front page: Funeral Today. *The whole town apparently was at the cemetery*—every man, woman and child. Stede rubbed his chin thoughtfully, then picked up the reins of his horse and walked *a half-block to the sheriff's office.*

Details for setting

In the next example, setting constitutes the problem and the danger, and also characterizes the man in the story. It is from "The White Silence" by Jack London:

Already penitent for his angry action, but too stubborn to make amends, Mason toiled on at the head of the cavalcade, little dreaming that danger hovered in the air. *The timber clustered thick in the sheltered bottom,* and through this they threaded their way. *Fifty feet or more from the trail towered a lofty pine. For generations it had stood there,* and for generations destiny had had this one end in view—perhaps the same had been decreed of Mason.

He stooped to fasten the loosened thong of his moccasin. The sleds came to a halt, and the dogs lay down in *the snow* without a whimper. *The stillness was weird; not a breath rustled the frost-encrusted forest; the cold and silence* of outer space had chilled the heart and smote the trembling lips of nature.

A sigh pulsed through the air—they did not seem to actually hear it, but rather felt it, like the premonition of movement in a motionless void. *Then the great tree, burdened with its weight of years and snow,* played its last part in the tragedy of life. He heard *the warning crash* and attempted to spring up but, almost erect, caught the blow squarely on the shoulder.

In the following example, James Joyce, in his story "Araby," shows how all the senses can be employed to create a setting, giving it the quality of real life:

When the short days of winter came, dusk fell before we had eaten our dinners. When we met in the street the houses had grown somber. The space of sky above us was the color of ever-changing violet and towards it the lamps of the street lifted their feeble lanterns. The cold air stung us and we played till our bodies glowed. Our shouts echoed in the silent streets.

The career of our play brought us through the dark muddy lanes behind the houses where we ran the gauntlet of the rough tribes from the cottages, to the back doors of the dark dripping gardens where the odors arose from the ashpits, to the dark odorous stables where a coachman smoothed and combed the horse or shook music from the buckled harness.

When we returned to the street, light from the kitchen windows had filled the areas. If my uncle was seen turning the corner we hid in the shadow until we had seen him safely housed.

If you study this example, you will see in it the use of weather, time, light and shade, color, touch, sound, smell and feelings. Though taste hasn't been described, the line "before we had eaten our dinners" suggests a sharp appetite soon to be satisfied, which evokes the image of food.

There's still another valuable use for setting. This is to arouse emotion, sentiment, nostalgia or sympathy for either the characters or the nature of the story as, for instance, in this excerpt from "The Nightingales Sing" by Elizabeth Parsons:

Upstairs, there was a light in her own room and one in her mother's dressing room. It was a family custom that when she came in late, she should put out her mother's light, so now she went into the *small, bright room*. With her hand on the light chain, she looked around her, at *the chintz-covered chaise longue, the chintz-skirted dressing table with family snapshots, both old and recent,* arranged under *its glass top, the polished furniture, the long mirror, the agreeable clutter of many years of satisfactory married life.*

On the walls were more *family pictures,* covering quite a long period of time—*enlargements of picnic photographs, of boats, of a few pets.* There was Joanna at the age of twelve on a cow pony in Wyoming; her father and uncle in snow goggles and climbing boots on the lower slopes of Mont Blanc, heaven knows how long ago; her sister and brother-in-law looking very young and carefree with their bicycles outside Salisbury Cathedral sometime in the early Thirties, judging by her sister's clothes. *In all of them the sun shone, and everyone was happy in the world of the pictures,* which was as fresh and good and simple as a May morning.

She stared at the *familiar little scenes on the walls* with love—and with a sympathy for them she had never felt before—and then she put out the light and went back along the hall.

The objects in this story have a special emotional significance for the character, and atmosphere is created from this feeling.

Different uses of setting

In the following excerpt from "Waves of Darkness" by Cord Meyer, Jr., see how an all-embracing setting contributes to the fear of a soldier awaiting possible death:

The blasted coconut trees cast deceptive shadows that danced in slow rhythm as the flare swayed to and fro in its descent. The unearthly, pallid light accentuated rather than dispelled the threat of horror that the night held. It was impossible to distinguish shadow from substance. Every small depression in the ground was filled with darkness, and the line of thick jungle growth some sixty yards ahead presented an impenetrable question.

He could make out nothing for certain. Each natural object assumed enormous and malevolent proportions in the shadows that lengthened toward him. He felt as if he were lost in the evil witch forest of some ancient folk tale and he shivered involuntarily.

And here, stretching imagination into the unknown, is the way a writer of science fiction, Alexander Blade, created a setting for his story "The Deadly Mission," which appeared in *Space Travel* magazine:

The strangest part of awakening in the luxurious cabin was knowing just three things about himself. Three and no more.

The first fact his own brain seemed to supply, as though he were familiar with the thought: he was on a starship, an exceptionally large starship. He did not know quite how he estimated the size of the vessel. Perhaps the distant drumbeat whine filling his ears the very second he awakened told about size in a language he did not understand. This first fact was easy. He was lying in a deep anti-grav berth, in semidarkness, while dimensional murals on two walls arranged their lights and shadows, their gleams and murk into a shifting, real-seeming picture of outer space.

The above example shows how effectively a setting can support a situation, give it plausibility, and pave the way for the movement of characters.

There's also a way to utilize setting to help the theme of a story. Read the way Willa Cather used it to give meaning to her farm story, "Neighbour Rosicky":

But this was open and free, this little square of long grass which the wind forever stirred. Nothing but the sky overhead, and the many-coloured fields running on until they met that sky. The horses worked here in summer; the neighbours passed on their way to town; and over yonder, in the cornfield, Rosicky's own cattle would be eating fodder as winter came on.

Nothing could be more undeathlike than this place; nothing could be more right for a man who had helped to do the work of great cities and had always longed for the open country and had got to it at last. Rosicky's life seemed to him complete and beautiful.

Another use of setting is to inject character into the objects, place and weather of the scene, as in this excerpt from "The Outcasts of Poker Flat" by Bret Harte:

The third day came, and the sun, looking through *the white-curtained valley,* saw the outcasts divide their slowly decreasing store of provisions for the morning meal. It was one of the peculiarities of that mountain climate that its rays diffused *a kindly warmth over the wintry landscape, as if in regretful commiseration of the past.* But it revealed *drift on drift of snow* piled high around the hut; *a hopeless, uncharted, trackless sea of white* lying below the rocky shores to which the castaways still clung. . . .

The wind lulled as if it feared to waken them. Feathery drifts of snow, shaken from *the long pine boughs, flew like white-winged birds,* and settled about them as they slept. *The moon through the rifted clouds looked down* upon what had been the camp. But all human stain, all trace of earthly travail, was hidden beneath *the spotless mantle mercifully flung from above.*

The above use of setting comes close to poetry—the kind of poetry that lends to stories an aura of kinship between nature and mankind.

Some examples from the classics

And now, in various approaches to setting, we give you several passages from the works of other exceptional authors. While the writing style may be alien to your present aims or tastes, the moods created by these settings are well worth studying, for there's always something for you, the student, to learn from the masters of your craft.

From "Henry Esmond," by William Makepeace Thackeray:

Then Esmond saw the great house which he had come to inhabit.

It stood on a rising green hill, with woods behind it, in which were rooks' nests, where the birds at morning and returning home at evening made a great cawing. At the foot of the hill was a river, with a steep ancient bridge crossing it; and beyond that a large pleasant green flat, where the village of Castlewood stood, and stands, with the church in the midst, the parsonage hard by it, the inn with the blacksmith's forge beside it, and the sign of the "Three Castles" on the elm. The London road stretched away towards the rising sun, and to the west were swelling hills and peaks.

The hall of Castlewood was built with two courts, whereof one only, the fountain-court, was now inhabited, the other having been battered down in the Cromwellian wars. In the fountain-court, still in good repair, was the great hall, near to the kitchen and butteries; a dozen of living rooms looking to the north, and communicating with the little chapel that faced eastwards and the buildings stretching from that to the main gate, and with the hall (which looked to the west) into the court now dismantled. This court had been the most magnificent of the two until the Protector's cannon tore down one side of it before the place was taken and stormed. The besieger entered at the terrace under the clock-tower, slaying every man of the garrison, and at their head my Lord's brother, Francis Esmond.

The Restoration did not bring enough money to the Lord Castlewood to restore this ruined part of his house; where were the morning parlors, above them the long music gallery, and before which stretched the garden terrace, where, however, the flowers grew again which the boots of the Roundheads had trodden in their assault, and which was restored without much cost, and only a little care, by both ladies who succeeded the second Viscount in the government of this mansion. Round the terrace garden was a low wall with a wicket leading to the wooded height beyond, that is called Cromwell's Battery to this day.

From "On the Road" by Anton Chekhov:

The "travellers' room" had a festive appearance. The air was full of the smell of freshly scrubbed floors, there were no rags hanging as usual on the line that ran diagonally across the room, and a little lamp was burning in the corner over the table, casting a patch of red light on the ikon of St. George the Victorious. From the ikon stretched on each side of the corner a row of cheap oleographs, which maintained a strict and careful gradation in the transition from the sacred to the profane. In the dim light of the candle end and the red ikon lamp the pictures looked like one continuous strip, covered with blurs of dull black.

When the tiled stove, trying to sing in unison with the weather, drew in the air with a howl, while the logs, as though waking up, burst into bright flame and hissed angrily, red patches began dancing on the log walls, and over the head of the sleeping man could be seen first the Elder Seraphim, then the Shah Nasir-ed-Din, then a fat, brown baby with goggle eyes, whispering in the ear of a young girl who possessed an extraordinarily blank and indifferent face . . .

Outside a storm was raging. Something frantic and wrathful, but profoundly unhappy, seemed to be flinging itself about the tavern with the ferocity of a wild beast and trying to break in. Banging at the doors, knocking at the windows and on the roof, scratching at the walls, it alternately threatened and besought, then subsided for a brief interval, and then with a gleeful, treacherous howl burst into the chimney, but the wood flared up, and the fire, like a chained dog, flew wrathfully to meet its foe, a battle began, and after it—sobs, shrieks, howls of wrath. In all of this there was the sound of angry misery and unsatisfied hate, and the mortified impatience of some-thing accustomed to triumph.

Bewitched by this wild, inhuman music the "travellers' room" seemed spellbound for ever, but all at once the door creaked and the potboy, in a new print shirt, came in.

From "The Gold-Bug" by Edgar Allan Poe:

Many years ago, I contracted an intimacy with a Mr. William Legrand. He was of an ancient Huguenot family and had once been wealthy; but a series of misfortunes had reduced him to want. To avoid the mortification consequent upon his disaster, he left New Orleans, the city of his forefathers, and took up his residence at Sullivan's Island, near Charleston, South Carolina.

This island is a very singular one. It consists of little else than the sea sand, and is about three miles long. Its breadth at no point ex-ceeds a quarter of a mile. It is separated from the mainland by a scarcely perceptible creek, oozing its way through a wilderness of reeds and slime, a favorite resort of the marsh hen. The vegetation, as might be supposed, is scant, or at least dwarfish. No trees of any magnitude are to be seen.

Near the western extremity, where Fort Moultrie stands, and where are some miserable frame buildings, tenanted during the sum-mer by the fugitives from Charleston dust and fever, may be found, indeed, the bristly palmetto; but the whole island, with the exception of this western point and a line of hard, white beach on the seacoast, is covered with a dense undergrowth of the sweet myrtle, so much prized by the horticulturists of England. The shrub here often attains the height of fifteen or twenty feet, and forms an almost impenetrable coppice, burthening the air with its fragrance.

In the inmost recess of this coppice, not far from the eastern or more remote end of the island, Legrand had built himself a small hut, which he occupied when I first, by mere accident, made his acquaintance.

From "The Monastery of Corbara" by Guy de Maupassant:

The Alps are more imposing than the mountains of Corsica; their eternal white tops, their almost inaccessible passes and dizzy abysses, from which ascends the roar of crashing torrents, make them a sort of Land of Terror.

The mountains of Corsica are smaller and of an entirely different character. They are not as majestic, not as inaccessible, and they do not, even in their wildest parts, present that look of baleful desolation which one encounters everywhere in the Alps.

Then there is always the glorious sunshine; it ripples like water down the mountainsides, which here and there are densely covered with large trees that from a distance resemble moss or else are perfectly bare, their granite flanks standing gaunt against the sky.

From "A Painful Case" by James Joyce:

Mr. James Duffy lived in Chapelizod because he wished to live as far as possible from the city of which he was a citizen and because he found all the other suburbs of Dublin mean, modern and pretentious. He lived in an old sombre house and from his windows he could look into the disused distillery or upwards along the shallow river on which Dublin is built.

The lofty walls of his uncarpeted room were free from pictures. He had himself bought every article of furniture in the room: a black iron bedstead, an iron washstand, four cane chairs, a clothes rack, a coal scuttle, a fender and irons and a square table on which lay a double desk.

A bookcase had been made in an alcove by means of shelves of white wood. The bed was clothed with white bedclothes and a black and scarlet rug covered the foot. A little hand-mirror hung above the washstand and during the day a white-shaded lamp stood as the sole ornament of the mantelpiece.

The books on the white wooden shelves were arranged from below upwards according to bulk. A complete Wordsworth stood at one end of the lowest shelf and a copy of the *Maynooth Catechism,* sewn into the cloth cover of a notebook, stood at one end of the top shelf.

Writing materials were always on the desk. In the desk lay a manuscript translation of Hauptmann's *Michael Kramer,* the stage directions of which were written in purple ink, and a little sheaf of papers held together by a brass pin. In these sheets a sentence was inscribed from time to time, and, in an ironical moment, the headline of an advertisement for Bile Beans had been pasted on to the first sheet.

From "The Three Strangers" by Thomas Hardy:

Among the few features of agricultural England which retain an appearance but little modified by the lapse of centuries, may be reckoned the high, grassy and furzy downs, combs, or ewe-leases, as they are indifferently called, that fill a large area of certain counties in the south and southwest. If any mark of human occupation is met with hereon, it usually takes the form of the solitary cottage of some shepherd.

Fifty years ago such a lonely cottage stood on such a down, and may possibly be standing there now. In spite of its loneliness, however, the spot, by actual measurement, was not more than five miles from a county town. Yet that affected it little. Five miles of irregular upland, during the long inimical seasons, with their sleets, snows, rains, and mists, afford withdrawing space enough to isolate a Timon or a Nebuchadnezzar; much less, in fair weather, to please that less repellent tribe, the poets, philosophers, artists, and others who "conceive and meditate of pleasant things."

Some old earthen camp or barrow, some clump of trees, at least some starved fragment of ancient hedge is usually taken advantage of in the erection of these forlorn dwellings. But, in the present case, such a kind of shelter had been disregarded. Higher Crowstairs, as the house was called, stood quite detached and undefended. The only reason for its precise situation seemed to be the crossing of two footpaths at right angles hard by, which may have crossed thus for five hundred years. Hence the house was exposed on all sides.

But, though the wind up here blew unmistakably when it did blow, and the rain hit hard whenever it fell, the various weathers of the winter season were not quite so formidable on the comb as they were imagined to be by dwellers on low ground. The raw rimes were not so pernicious as in the hollows, and the frosts were scarcely so severe. When the shepherd and his family who tenanted the house were pitied for their sufferings from the exposure, they said that upon the whole they were less inconvenienced by "wuzzes and flames" (hoarses and phlegms) than when they had lived by the stream of a snug neighboring valley.

From "A Simple Heart" by Gustave Flaubert:

This house had a slate roof and stood between an alley and a lane that went down to the river. There was an unevenness in the levels of the rooms which made you stumble. A narrow hall divided the kitchen from the "parlor" where Mme Aubain spent her day, sitting in a wicker easy chair by the window.

Against the panels, which were painted white, was a row of eight mahogany chairs. On an old piano under the barometer a heap of wooden and cardboard boxes rose like a pyramid. A stuffed armchair stood on either side of the Louis-Quinze chimney piece, which was in yellow marble with a clock in the middle of it modelled like a temple of Vesta. The whole room was a little musty, as the floor was lower than the garden.

The first floor began with "Madame's" room: very large, with a pale-flowered wallpaper and a portrait of "Monsieur" as a dandy of the period. It led to a smaller room where there were two children's cots without mattresses. Next came the drawing room, which was always shut up and full of furniture covered with sheets. Then there was a corridor leading to a study.

The shelves of a large bookcase were respectably lined with books and papers, and its three wings surrounded a broad writing table in dark wood. The two panels at the end of the room were covered with pen-drawings, water-color landscapes, and engravings by Audran, all relics of better days and vanished splendor. Félicité's room on the top floor got its light from a dormer window, which looked over the meadows.

From "La Grande Bretêche" by Honoré de Balzac:

At about a hundred paces from Vendôme, on the banks of the Loire, said he, stands an old brown house, crowned with very high roofs, and so completely isolated that there is nothing near it, not even a fetid tannery or a squalid tavern, such as are commonly seen outside small towns. In front of this house is a garden down to the river, where the box shrubs, formerly clipped close to edge the walks, now straggle at their own will. A few willows, rooted in the stream, have grown up quickly like an enclosing fence, and half hide the house.

The wild plants we call weeds have clothed the bank with their beautiful luxuriance. The fruit trees, neglected for these ten years past, no longer bear a crop, and their suckers have formed a thicket. The espaliers are like a copse. The paths, once gravelled, are overgrown with purslane; but, to be accurate, there is no trace of a path.

Looking down from the hilltop to which cling the ruins of the old castle of the dukes of Vendôme, the only spot whence the eye can see into this enclosure, we think that at a time, difficult now to determine, this spot of earth must have been the joy of some country gentleman devoted to roses and tulips, in a word, to horticulture, but above all a lover of choice fruit. An arbor is visible, or rather the wreck of an arbor, and under it a table still stands not entirely destroyed by time.

At the aspect of this garden that is no more, the negative joys of the peaceful life of the provinces may be divined as we divine the history of a worthy tradesman when we read the epitaph on his tomb. To complete the mournful and tender impressions which seize the soul, on one of the walls there is a sundial graced with this homely Christian motto, *Ultimam cogita.*

The roof of this house is dreadfully dilapidated; the outside shutters are always closed; the balconies are hung with swallows' nests; the doors are forever shut. Straggling grasses have outlined the flagstones of the steps with green; the ironwork is rusty. Moon and sun, winter, summer, and snow have eaten into the wood, warped the boards, peeled off the paint. The dreary silence is broken only by birds and cats, polecats, rats, and mice, free to scamper round, and fight, and eat each other. An invisible hand has written over it all: "Mystery."

Using your powers of observation

In seeking your own ways to use setting, you should sharpen your powers of observation. Look around wherever you are and note details of the place, the effects of weather and time, of sounds and feelings. Never assume that a scene you know intimately and take for granted will make dull reading for others. The opposite is true. For if the setting is familiar to the reader, he'll have the pleasure of recognition—and if it's unfamiliar, he will be interested in the newness of an authentic background.

Look at nature carefully for colors and the imagery of landscape or seascape. Take note of furnishings in homes, of equipment used in occupations. If a room has a gloomy effect on you, try to find out why—is it the color of the walls, the placement of the furniture, the cracks in the ceiling, the drab rug?

Look at your own living quarters and rediscover their peculiarities. When you visit another home, note how its details reflect the character of the occupants. Take away useful impressions, recorded in your notebook. As a fiction writer, you will find potential material wherever you go, whether it's a walk down the street, a vacation abroad, a routine visit to office or store, or a flight in a jet-liner. You are now living in another dimension—the dimension of the alert and watchful observer. Soon you'll learn how settings suggest stories, and how to create interesting and effective backgrounds for your characters.

Hemingway uses logic

Professional writers try to plan their characters and situations with such skill that, when a particular point has been reached in their writing, logical things happen as naturally as breathing. This is especially true of fiction.

When Ernest Hemingway was writing *For Whom the Bell Tolls,* he had created a character named Robert Jordan, a guerrilla who blew up a vital bridge during a Loyalist offensive.

One morning Hemingway turned to his wife at breakfast and said: "You know, I think Jordan is going to blow up that bridge today!"

Hemingway had arbitrarily created characters and situation so perfectly that the climax of the narrative—the dynamiting of the bridge—would now *have* to take place and the man who would do it *had* to be Robert Jordan.

Joyce and his "scribblings"

Sylvia Beach states in *Shakespeare and Company,* a book about the Paris writers' group in the 1920's, that James Joyce wrote continually. He loved words, and always wrote by hand. He had to see his work as he shaped it word by word.

Nora, Joyce's wife, grumbled that her husband "never stopped scribbling, reaching down when he was only half awake in the morning for his paper and pencil on the floor beside him, never knowing what time of day it was!"

On one occasion, Miss Beach asked Joyce if, in view of his growing eye trouble (he became blind in later life), he did not sometimes dictate his writing. "Never!" Joyce exclaimed. He liked to be held back because he had a tendency to write too rapidly to see his work as he moulded it into shape. And he "never stopped scribbling."

Editors are people, too

The late George Horace Lorimer enunciated this philosophy in a comment on a story submitted to the *Post.* All of his editors wrote high praises of the story but concluded it should be rejected. "*Post* readers wouldn't understand it," they wrote. Lorimer read the comments and wrote on the manuscript: "Buy! Our editors can't be so different as all this from our readers!"—Edwin A. Peeples in *A Professional Storywriter's Handbook*

Lesson twelve

Fiction writing

course

How to handle situation

As you know, the *situation* of a story is the basic set of circumstances from which it starts. Some writers call it "The Situation," meaning not the "what-happens-next" but the "what" that's happening as the story opens. In any case, situation is irrevocably part of plot since all stories have to move from a given point. *Plotting is the act of storytelling itself.*

Situation presents all the information necessary to tell the reader—in any order the writer chooses—who the character or characters are, what they're like, where they are, what they're doing, what's happening to them at the moment, and what will likely happen next in the story. Situation is the initial action or state of affairs out of which the rest of the story or plot will grow and develop. The what-happens-next is the plot of the story.

As we've said before, suppose a writer's eye were recording life like a movie camera and suddenly stopped at a certain point. The picture caught at this point, if described and explained, would be *situation*. When the camera started turning again and the action began to move ahead from the given situation of the still picture, this would be plotting.

Plot comes in the *development,* not the initial stage, of story-telling. First you have to have a situation from which the plot will evolve. Plot cannot exist, cannot begin to unfold without a situation to start from. A writer creates a plot when he sets a character on a quest. But he has to set the character on his quest from a given point or situation. Hence the name.

Max Shulman puts it this way: "Situation is the problem. Plot is the problem and its solution."

Here's an example of situation that shows how a set of circumstances is recorded for the reader and launches a story into action. It's from "The Liar" by Charlotte Armstrong, which appeared in *The Saturday Evening Post*.

The office had a desk and a girl in it, and some comfortable chairs. The girl said, "Oh, yes, Mrs. Gleeson. Mr. Bowman expects you. Will you please wait a few minutes?"

So Mary Gleeson sat down. Her white-gloved hands were tight on her black handbag. In the bag was the letter, stamped, ready to mail. If she mailed the letter, there would be a wire, a phone call, a plane ticket. A beginning. An end. In perhaps half an hour, she would either mail it or she would not mail it.

The office had a window through which Mary could see a playing field and a huddle of small boys on it. This boarding school was a very pleasant place. This job, as housemother, offering living quarters and small boys to look after, was the one, the only, and the ideal job. Her white gloves clasped each other. Mustn't be nervous. Mustn't care so much. Poise. Calm.

She tried to remember that her dress was dark and decent, her gloves were perfectly clean, no wisps were falling out of her white bun. She was only fifty, well and strong. She had never earned a penny in her life, but she had done one thing, one thing most successfully. She had raised boys.

Mary bent her head. If I do not get the job, I must mail the letter. Help me, help me either way.

Here you've learned that a woman named Mary Gleeson is applying for a job as housemother at a boys' boarding school, that she's clean and neat, fifty years old, healthy, and wants the job very badly. You've learned why she is fitted for it. You have a picture in your mind of the whole scene. This is the situation. The story is ready to proceed. The next lines read:

A door opened. A woman came out of an inner room. Mary's eyes snapped to her. Was this an applicant?

The story has begun to move into its next stage—the second event in a plot sequence leading to an ultimate conclusion.

Situations are not always presented as quickly and inclusively as this, with all the basic information in the first few paragraphs. And yet some authors may be even faster in stating situation, as in "Husbands Are to Love" by Mary Church, from the *Ladies' Home Journal:*

I think the loneliest morning in the world is the morning you wake up on the sofa bed in the study because you quarrelled with your husband the night before.

Stories may be approached in innumerable ways, with authors taking varying times to dwell on the main ingredients. Here's an example of a situation which takes quite a while to create a beginning picture for the reader. It's from "Dead Center" by Judith Merril, which appeared in *Fantasy and Science Fiction* magazine:

They gave him sweet ices, and kissed him all round, and the Important People who had come to dinner all smiled in a special way as his mother took him from the living room and led him down the hall to his own bedroom.

"Great kid you got there," they said to Jock, his father, and "Serious little fellow, isn't he?" Jock didn't say anything, but Toby knew he would be grinning, looking pleased and embarrassed. Then their voices changed, and that meant they had begun to talk about the important events for which the Important People had come.

In his own room, Toby wriggled his toes between crisp sheets and breathed in the powder-and-perfume smell of his mother as she bent over him for a last hurried goodnight kiss. There was no use asking for a story tonight. Toby lay still and waited while she closed the door behind her and went off to the party, click-tap, tip-clack, hurrying back there, too, and she didn't want to miss anything. Toby got up and opened his door just a crack, and set himself down in back of it, and listened.

In the big square living room, against the abstract patterns of gray and vermilion and chartreuse, the men and women moved in easy patterns of familiar acts. Coffee, brandy, cigarette, cigar. Find your partner, choose your seat.

Jock sprawled with perfect relaxed contentment on the low couch with the deep red corduroy cover. Tim O'Heyer balanced nervously on the edge of the same couch, wreathed in cigar smoke, small and dark and alert. Gordon Kimberly dwarfed the big easy chair with the bulking importance of him. Ben Stein, shaggy and rumpled as ever, was running a hand through his hair till it too stood on end. He was leaning against a window frame, one hand on the back of the straight chair in which his wife Sue sat, erect and neat and proper and chic, dressed in smart black that set off perfectly her precise blonde beauty.

Mrs. Kimberly, just enough overstuffed so that her pearls gave the appearance of actually choking her, was the only stranger to the house. She was standing near the doorway, politely admiring Toby's personal art gallery, as Allie Madero valiantly strove to explain each minor masterpiece.

Ruth Kruger stood still a moment, surveying her room and her guests. Eight of them, herself included, and all Very Important People. In the familiar comfort of her own living room, the idea made her giggle. Allie and Mrs. Kimberly both turned to her, questioning. She laughed and shrugged, helpless to explain, and they all went across the room to join the others.

This situation prepares the reader for movement. The movement doesn't necessarily have to be physical movement, but may be dialogue or the thoughts of a main character pushing the story along.

Are there any limits to the situations which create short stories or any fixed rules as to what composes them? The only rule common to all, and this isn't a fixed rule, is that they state the case—in other words, tell the reader what the story is composed of in a graphic, vivid and interest-catching way.

The three general categories

Although any set of circumstances may comprise a valid situation, most situations concern the dilemmas, problems, decisions or crises that confront characters and against which they struggle. The struggle usually falls into one of three categories:

1. Man against forces beyond his control, such as war, the elements, accidents, and what are generally termed "acts of God."
2. Man against other men.
3. Man against forces inside himself.

Within this broad framework come the events caused by the basic traits of a story's character.

First, let's look at a soldier's struggle against forces beyond his control. This example is from "Stalemate" by Bob Bristow, in *Redbook:*

Sergeant Hank Tahsuda understood war in the kill-or-be-killed manner of the mud soldier. It was that simple. He knew the terrible fatigue, the filth, the pain. He knew the smell of powder, of men who had fallen and lay swollen in the sun; he knew the sight of blood on sandy beaches, of demolished tanks, of bomb craters and burned-out buildings.

But as a soldier really knows war, Hank Tahsuda knew the game best by the sounds: the thrust of a jet; the steady, maddening pounding of heavy artillery; and, worst of all, the tense silence while the soldier waited, crouched in a bunker, listening for the rustle in the grass, a slide of soil beneath the foot of an enemy probing closer in the darkness.

Now he lay using all his senses in the faint dawn light, conscious of the biting pain in his leg below his right knee. The edge of the Korean valley was almost silent. The others on patrol, Ernie Long and Chuck Peters, lay dead behind him. Somewhere in the darkness his own rifle had fallen. He could not search for it now.

He stared toward the enemy bunker, where he heard the squirrel-like whisperings of the Chinese. Hank Tahsuda did not have much time. In twenty minutes the sun would illuminate his position and the Chinese would train their rifles on him. A single shot and he would drop into the soil and life would go out of him.

As you've seen, Hank Tahsuda is caught up in war, an event beyond his control. Faced with death, he must act. The way in which he deals with his situation will be the plot, giving the story meaning or theme, and involving the other elements of characterization and setting.

Other stories like this could involve people caught in a hurricane, trapped by a flood, shipwrecked, or, in science fiction, hurled into outer-space conditions. These situations aren't events which the character can bend to his will—he must simply fight for survival.

In the second category—man against other men—situations are based on characters enmeshed in relationships and usually faced with a mutual problem. This doesn't mean the problem is always crucial: it can range from humorous to tragic, as long as it presents the characters with a dilemma which must be resolved to satisfy the reader.

Here's an example in which a character faces a problem arising out of his relationship with another character. It's from "Panic On the Runway" by Alice Lent Covert, from *The Saturday Evening Post:*

"Three on a Match," they were called in their Training Command days, for no good reason save that in off-duty hours they usually knocked about together. The tag stuck, even after two of them took wives and left the third to carry on in single blessedness alone.

Commander of this three-man B-47 jet crew was Capt. Mitch Sprague, a lean hard-muscled young man with sandy hair and level blue eyes. His co-pilot was Lt. Duke Halloran, a homely Irisher with a tall sense of humor. Lt. Jerry Parsons, a lanky Texas boy, was the observer. The three shared a common dream, and now they were SAC crew N-82, sweating out the changing of the prefix N-for-Nonready to the all-important R.

They had spent an afternoon in mission planning, and the crisp autumn evening was cloaking the hangars, blotting out the details of the field, when they came back to the flight-line gate. Jerry drew a deep lungful of the cool, tangy air and exhaled it noisily. "Only one more river to cross. We do good, huh, team? I reckon we're good as the best."

Duke laughed. "Don't give me that jazz, dad. We are the best!"

Mitch said nothing at all. He wouldn't let the way he was feeling spoil their elation. Two days ago they had completed their crew-coordination check flight. The whole crew had to work together on that, but from here on in it was strictly up to Mitch. Duke wouldn't even accompany him on the final check flight tonight; Jerry would ride along only to satisfy regulations that an observer be aboard. Whether N-82 became an operational crew, capable of making an overseas flight on its own, lay on Mitch's shoulders: on his performance tonight, on the check pilot's report.

He felt sick. Major Duckworth, who was to have flown with him as check pilot, was on sick leave. Riding in his place tonight would be one Maj. Bradley J. Thomas—and if Major Thomas had his way, N-82 would be broken up into support personnel! He would be honest in his evaluation, according to his own lights, but he could hardly be expected to admit that he was swayed by a personal prejudice which would never show up in a critique!

You walk into a room, there's a guy there you've never seen before, you're introduced, and in five minutes you can't stand each other. It happens sometimes. It had happened when the major and the captain met for the first time, six months ago; and it had got worse instead of better. One slip on Mitch's part tonight, and all the worry and sweat of the past six months, of having Major Thomas constantly riding his back like a witch on a broom, could be chalked up to experience.

There was irony in knowing that it was his own wife who had first sparked the antagonism between them. The very thought of Kay, now, was like the blow of a hard fist to the belly.

Now let's look at an example of man against forces within himself. In this *Saturday Evening Post* story, "Apache Raid" by John Prescott, a young boy faces an old fear which seems likely to make a coward of him.

After the massacre I came to live with my Uncle Harlan and Aunt Martha Allen. I was their nephew, Uncle Harlan being my mother's older brother when she was living. Since our families were among the early settlers in the valley, coming out from Illinois when the war ended, the places bordered on each other. Yet the ruins of my folks' place couldn't be seen from Uncle Harlan's and Aunt Martha's, and I didn't have to look at them.

They lay deserted a long time. Uncle Harlan now and then rode over to tend the graves and see what time had done, but I didn't. I knew that grass filled the rooms, and that weather had washed the smoke and ash from the walls and fallen vigas, but still I shied off.

I was twelve now, but I was still afraid; and didn't want to have so sharp in my mind all I'd seen on that day, or smelled or heard—what Uncle Harlan called butchery.

Just the word made a picture. Anyone who knows that grassy country along the Sonoita and Babocomari can imagine our life there. Save Tucson, seventy miles around the Santa Ritas, there were no towns. At times, a month or more would pass with no human being even going by, unless it was some Indian skulking through the hills, well out of rifle range.

The main information has been provided here, but the author has reason at this point to establish further the full situation with a flashback and characterization of the scene and people, then to return again to the present and state the final stimulus for action this way:

But one day toward noon, Aunt Martha busted in from outside, slammed the door and drove the drawbar through the brackets. Then she started on the shutters, calling out to me at the same time.

"Get your fire going, Clark! There's Indians over the creek!"

The boy must now face a repetition of his dread experience. Will he or won't he be able to conquer his fear and help to defend his aunt and home? The situation of a story, as you see here, can be the question it poses. People are challenged, are forced or catapulted into some demanding circumstance, and because of their basic character—or perhaps in spite of it—must act. How they act and what happens because of their actions is what the reader wants to know.

Situations arising from character

Faith Baldwin says, about the relationship between situations and characters:

The writer has to set up and devise the situation, but in the best writing the situations and problems grow out of the characters. The student writer should not create—at least not for a long time—improbable situations, insoluble problems.

In devising a situation, in formulating a problem, you should set yourself to extricating your characters and having your characters logically solve their problems.

In the next example, you'll see how the basic trait of a character creates a set of circumstances. It's from "The League of the Old Men" by Jack London:

At the barracks a man was being tried for his life. He was an old man, a native from the Whitefish River, which empties into the Yukon below Lake Le Barge. All Dawson was wrought up over the affair, and likewise the Yukon dwellers for a thousand miles up and down. It has been the custom of the land-robbing and sea-robbing Anglo-Saxon to give the law to conquered peoples, and ofttimes this law is harsh. But in the case of Imber, the law for once seemed inadequate and weak.

In the mathematical nature of things, equity did not reside in the punishment to be accorded him. The punishment was a foregone conclusion, there could be no doubt of that; and though it was capital, Imber had but one life, while the tale against him was one of scores.

In fact the blood of so many was upon his hands that the killings attributed to him did not permit of precise enumeration. Smoking a pipe by the trailside or lounging around the stove, men made rough estimates of the numbers that had perished at his hand. They had been whites, all of them, these poor murdered people, and they had been slain singly, in pairs and in parties. And so purposeless and wanton had been these killings that they had long been a mystery to the mounted police, even in the time of the captains, and later, when the creeks realized and a governor came from the Dominion to make the land pay for its prosperity.

Clearly, many sequences of events might be set in motion by this character.

Although we've illustrated some of the main categories of situation, it's only to explain the chief purpose of this element in fiction and not to set a rigid rule. To familiarize you with situation and allow you to pick it out rapidly from the body of a story, here are more openings in which it has been set forth clearly and succinctly.

From "The Night the Ghost Got In" by James Thurber:

The ghost that got into our house on the night of November 17, 1915, raised such a hullabaloo of misunderstandings that I am sorry I didn't just let it keep on walking and go to bed. Its advent caused my mother to throw a shoe through a window of the house next door and ended up with my grandfather shooting a patrolman. I am sorry, therefore, as I have said, that I ever paid any attention to the footsteps.

From "The Luceys" by Frank O'Connor:

It's extraordinary, the bitterness there can be in a town like ours between two people—more particularly between two people of the same family. I suppose living more or less in public as we do, we are either killed or cured by it, and the same communal sense that will make a man be battered into a reconciliation he doesn't feel gives added importance to whatever quarrel he thinks must not be composed. God knows, most of the time you'd be more sorry for a man like that than anything else.

The Luceys were like that. There were two brothers, Tom and Ben, and there must have been a time when the likeness between the two was greater than the difference, but that was long before most of us knew them.

From "Sudden Life" by Frederick Nebel:

When his kid brother Joe ran away a week after receiving the suspended sentence for wrecking Gus Arkadian's office and running off with two hundred dollars, Frank Lonhart suspected the worst. It took him a couple of days, asking around at Arkadian's chain of poolrooms, to know that the worst had happened. Joe had run off with Whitey Doane, a hoodlum who was only two months out of state's prison.

From "The Regulator" by John Prebble:

The drifters came an hour after dawn. Walter James and his boy heard the nervous beat of hoofs down by the corral, and then a man's laugh, an insanely mirthless sound that scratched unpleasantly on the morning air.

Walter put down the skillet of beans and wiped his hands slowly on his hips. He looked at the Henry rifle that hung on a peg by the door. He looked at it cautiously, moving his eyes only, so that his son might not catch the glance. He knew that most men who recognized that laugh would expect him to take down the Henry and use it.

From "Little Brother," an obvious science fiction story, by D. A. Jourdan:

Elbezed, skimming monotonously through the gray quiet of space in his circular white ship, knew he was over what the Earth people called an ocean when he felt the fear. He was too far out in space to see the water, too far to see even the storm-cloud formations of their atmosphere which overspread that part of the ocean; but he could feel the fear emanations sent out by their flesh.

Although for thousands of years his own people had been hairless, Elbezed could feel the nerves of his skin—like those of the Earth people—quiver in an atavistic effort to raise their fur, in the ancient bluff of making themselves look larger and more frightening to the enemy.

From "Too Young" by John O'Hara:

It was the time of year when once again Bud was made to feel very young. It had happened last year, and it had happened the year before; it seemed as though it had been happening a great many more years than that. It *always* seemed that the Tuesday after Labor Day was around again; Father would be staying at the apartment in town, planning to come out for two or three weekends but not making it. The fathers of the other kids the same way. It just seemed that there were no older men at the beach club, giving you black looks or even coming right out and telling you if you did not get the heck off the tennis courts when they wanted to play their stiff and creaky mixed doubles.

Through the summer, being with your own bunch, you did not think much about being young or old or anything. But then the fathers started to go back to town, and the young married people, only the mothers and the young boys and girls were left, and it made you remember that you were young. Much too young to be in love with Kathy Mallet.

From "The Schartz-Metterklume Method" by Saki (H. H. Munro), the famous English writer whose stories were noted for their satirical humor:

Lady Carlotta stepped out on to the platform of the small wayside station and took a turn or two up and down its uninteresting length, to kill time till the train should be pleased to proceed on its way. Then, in the roadway beyond, she saw a horse struggling with a more than ample load, and a carter of the sort that seems to bear a sullen hatred against the animal that helps him to earn a living. Lady Carlotta promptly betook her to the roadway, and put rather a different complexion on the struggle.

Certain of her acquaintances were wont to give her plentiful admonition as to the undesirability of interfering on behalf of a distressed animal, such interference being "none of her business." Only once had she put the doctrine of non-interference into practice, when one of its most eloquent exponents had been besieged for nearly three hours in a small and extremely uncomfortable may-tree by an angry boar-pig, while Lady Carlotta, on the other side of the fence, had proceeded with the water-colour sketch she was engaged on, and refused to interfere between the boar and his prisoner.

It is to be feared that she lost the friendship of the ultimately rescued lady.

On this occasion she merely lost the train, which gave way to the first sign of impatience it had shown throughout the journey, and steamed off without her. She bore the desertion with philosophical indifference; her friends and relations were thoroughly well used to the fact of her luggage arriving without her. She wired a vague noncommittal message to her destination to say that she was coming on "by another train." Before she had time to think what her next move might be she was confronted by an imposingly attired lady, who seemed to be taking a prolonged mental inventory of her clothes and looks.

"You must be Miss Hope, the governess I've come to meet," said the apparition, in a tone that admitted of very little argument.

"Very well, if I must I must," said Lady Carlotta to herself with dangerous meekness.

"I am Mrs. Quabarl," continued the lady; "and where, pray, is your luggage?"

"It's gone astray," said the alleged governess, falling in with the excellent rule of life that the absent are always to blame; the luggage had, in point of fact, behaved with perfect correctitude. "I've just telegraphed about it," she added, with a nearer approach to truth.

"How provoking," said Mrs. Quabarl; "these railway companies are so careless. However, my maid can lend you things for the night," and she led the way to her car.

From "The Stout Gentleman" by Washington Irving:

It was a rainy Sunday in the gloomy month of November. I had been detained, in the course of a journey, by a slight indisposition, from which I was recovering; but was still feverish, and obliged to keep within doors all day, in an inn of the small town of Derby. A wet Sunday in a country inn!—whoever has had the luck to experience one can alone judge of my situation. The rain pattered against the casements; the bells tolled for church with a melancholy sound. I went to the windows in quest of something to amuse the eye; but it seemed as if I had been placed completely out of the reach of all amusement.

The windows of my bedroom looked out among tiled roofs and stacks of chimneys, while those of my sitting-room commanded a full view of the stableyard. I know of nothing more calculated to make a man sick of this world than a stableyard on a rainy day. The place was littered with wet straw that had been kicked about by travellers and stableboys. In one corner was a stagnant pool of water, surrounding an island of muck; there were several half-drowned fowls crowded together under a cart, among which was a miserable, crestfallen cock, drenched out of all life and spirit, his drooping tail matted, as it were, into a single feather, along which the water trickled from his back; near the cart was a half-dozing cow, chewing the cud, and standing patiently to be rained on, with wreaths of vapor rising from her reeking hide; a wall-eyed horse, tired of the loneliness of the stable, was poking its spectral head out of a window, with the rain dripping on it from the eaves; an unhappy cur, chained to a doghouse hard by, uttered something, every now and then, between a bark and a yelp; a drab of a kitchen wench tramped backward and forward through the yard in patterns, looking as sulky as the weather itself; everything, in short, was comfortless and forlorn, excepting a crew of hardened ducks, assembled like boon companions round a puddle, and making a riotous noise over their liquor.

The old fairy-tale technique

Just as we've suggested that you sharpen your observation of character and setting in daily life, so you will benefit greatly if you watch out constantly for situations. Wherever you go, whatever you do, keep your eyes, ears and imagination working to uncover circumstances that promise interesting foundations for story development.

Perhaps the best illustration of situation comes from the old fairy tales. Remember how they always began: "Once upon a time there was ..." or "There was once a ..."? These introduced the opening facts—in other words, the situation. There was no other way for the author to continue but to state the circumstances.

See how this traditional formula gets right to the point in "The Shoes That Were Danced to Pieces," a classic from Grimms' Fairy Tales:

There was once upon a time a King who had twelve daughters, each one more beautiful than the other. They all slept together in one chamber in which their beds stood side by side, and every night when they were in them the King locked the door and bolted it. But in the morning when he unlocked the door, he saw that their shoes were worn out with dancing, and no one could find out how that had come to pass.

And now another example, "Little Snow-White," also from Grimms':

Once upon a time in the middle of winter, when the flakes of snow were falling like feathers from the sky, a Queen sat at a window sewing, and the frame of the window was made of black ebony. And whilst she was sewing and looking out of the window at the snow, she pricked her finger with the needle and three drops of blood fell upon the snow. And the red looked pretty upon the white snow, and she thought to herself: "Would that I had a child as white as snow, as red as blood, and as black as the wood of the window-frame."

Soon after that she had a little daughter who was as white as snow, and as red as blood, and her hair was as black as ebony; and she was therefore called Little Snow-White. And when the child was born, the Queen died.

Hans Christian Andersen's tale, "The Princess and the Pea," goes even more swiftly to the situation:

There was once a prince who wanted to marry a princess; but she had to be a *real* princess. So he travelled all through the whole world to find a real one, but everywhere there was something the matter.

Although stories no longer begin in this elementary fashion, you can learn a lot from their approach to situation. After all, the approach has satisfied millions of people for centuries. Today it will still satisfy readers, provided you understand what you are working with and present your situations in a more up-to-date style.

Lesson thirteen

Fiction writing
course

How to
handle
theme

Every story makes some point or illustrates some moral or philosophy advocated by the writer. The reason is simple. If the actions of the characters didn't prove anything—whether trivial or profound—then they wouldn't constitute a piece of fiction but merely a record. And simply to record movements and events from one moment to another causes a reader to ask: "So what?"

Mignon Eberhart says you'll find that even the simplest action story has a writer's interpretation set on it, such as the general truth, found in so many Western and crime stories, that right and justice eventually prevail. Thus, if you read stories to find their meaning, you'll soon become familiar with the way writers weave *themes* into their work. You'll see that sometimes they state their theme, their philosophy or truth right at the beginning of the story, then set out to make the characters' actions prove it.

For instance, this is what Somerset Maugham does in his story "Mayhew." If you read the first two paragraphs carefully, you'll note he has set forth his theme in a plain statement, and that this not only gives it first place but emphasizes what he then illustrates through the actions of his characters.

The lives of most men are determined by their environment. They accept the circumstances amid which fate has thrown them not only with resignation but even with goodwill. They are like streetcars running contentedly on their rails and they despise the sprightly flivver that dashes in and out of the traffic and speeds so jauntily across the open country. I respect them; they are good citizens, good husbands, and good fathers, and of course somebody has to pay the taxes; but I do not find them exciting.

I am fascinated by the men, few enough in all conscience, who take life in their own hands and seem to mould it to their own liking. It may be that we have no such thing as free will, but at all events we have the illusion of it. At a crossroad it does seem to us that we might go either to the right or to the left, and, the choice once made, it is difficult to see that the whole course of the world's history obliged us to take the turning we did.

I never met a more interesting man than Mayhew. He was a lawyer in Detroit. He was an able and a successful one. By the time he was thirty-five he had a large and a lucrative practice, he had amassed a competence, and he stood on the threshold of a distinguished career. He had an acute brain, an attractive personality, and uprightness. There was no reason why he should not become, financially or politically, a power in the land.

One evening he was sitting in his club with a group of friends and they were perhaps a little the worse (or the better) for liquor. One of them had recently come from Italy and he told them of a house he had seen at Capri, a house on the hill, overlooking the Bay of Naples, with a large and shady garden. He described to them the beauty of the most beautiful island in the Mediterranean.

"It sounds fine," said Mayhew. "Is that house for sale?"

"Everything is for sale in Italy."

"Let's send 'em a cable and make an offer for it."

"What in heaven's name would you do with a house in Capri?"

"Live in it," said Mayhew.

He sent for a cable form, wrote it out, and dispatched it. In a few hours the reply came back. The offer was accepted.

Mayhew was no hypocrite and he made no secret of the fact that he would never have done so wild a thing if he had been sober, but when he was he did not regret it. He was neither an impulsive nor an emotional man, but a very honest and sincere one. He would never have continued from bravado in a course that he had come to the conclusion was unwise. He made up his mind to do exactly as he had said. He did not care for wealth and he had enough money on which to live in Italy. He thought he could do more with life than spend it on composing the trivial quarrels of unimportant people. He had no definite plan. He merely wanted to get away from a life that had given him all it had to offer.

I suppose his friends thought him crazy; some must have done all they could to dissuade him. He arranged his affairs, packed up his furniture and started.

Capri is a gaunt rock of austere outline, bathed in a deep blue sea; but its vineyards, green and smiling, give it a soft and easy grace. It is friendly, remote and debonair. I find it strange that Mayhew should have settled on this lovely island, for I never knew a man more insensible to beauty. I do not know what he sought there: happiness, freedom, or merely leisure; I know what he found. In this place which appeals so extravagantly to the senses he lived a life entirely of the spirit. For the island is rich with historic associations and over it broods always the enigmatic memory of Tiberius the Emperor.

From his windows which overlooked the Bay of Naples, with the noble shape of Vesuvius changing colour with the changing light, Mayhew saw a hundred places that recalled the Romans and the Greeks. The past began to haunt him. All that he saw for the first time, for he had never been abroad before, excited his fancy; and in his soul stirred the creative imagination.

He was a man of energy. Presently he made up his mind to write a history. For some time he looked about for a subject, and at last decided on the second century of the Roman Empire. It was little known and it seemed to him to offer problems analogous with those of our own day. He began to collect books and soon he had an immense library. His legal training had taught him to read quickly. He settled down to work.

At first he had been accustomed to foregather in the evening with the painters, writers and such-like who met in the little tavern near the Piazza. But presently he withdrew himself, for his absorption in his studies became more pressing.

He had been accustomed to bathe in that bland sea and to take long walks among the pleasant vineyards, but little by little, grudging the time, he ceased to do so. He worked harder than he had ever worked in Detroit. He would start at noon and work all through the night till the whistle of the steamer that goes every morning from Capri to Naples told him that it was five o'clock and time to go to bed.

His subject opened out before him, vaster and more significant, and he imagined a work that would put him for ever beside the great historians of the past.

As the years went by he was to be found seldom in the ways of men. He could be tempted to come out of his house only by a game of chess or the chance of an argument. He loved to set his brain against another's. He was widely read now, not only in history but in philosophy and science; but he had good humour and kindliness; though he took a very human pleasure in victory, he did not exult in it to your mortification.

When first he came to the island he was a big, brawny fellow, with thick black hair and a black beard, of a powerful physique; but gradually his skin became pale and waxy; he grew thin and frail. It was an odd contradiction in the most logical of men that, though a convinced and impetuous materialist, he despised the body; he looked upon it as a vile instrument which he could force to do the spirit's bidding. Neither illness nor lassitude prevented him from going on with his work.

For fourteen years he toiled unremittingly. He made thousands and thousands of notes. He sorted and classified them. He had his subject at his finger ends, and at last was ready to begin. He sat down to write. He died.

The body that he, the materialist, had treated so contumeliously took its revenge on him. That vast accumulation of knowledge is lost forever.

Vain was that ambition, surely not an ignoble one, to set his name beside those of Gibbon and Mommsen. His memory is treasured in the hearts of a few friends, fewer, alas! as the years pass on, and to the world he is unknown in death as he was in life.

And yet to me *his life was a success. The pattern is good and complete. He did what he wanted, and he died when his goal was in sight and never knew the bitterness of an end achieved.*

Another way of handling theme

Here's another example of theme—the *beginning* and the *ending* of a story where theme is presented at the outset as a foundation on which the rest of the story is built and resolved. It's from

"The Patriarch of Gunsight Flat" by Wayne D. Overholser in *McCall's* magazine.

The beginning

The sins of man are many. He will kill. He will take that which belongs to others—money and cattle and all that can be turned into money. Aye, and other things: a good name—a woman's virtue—a man's home—a friend. And who can say with certainty that murder is a greater crime than thievery?

Dave Cray was hitching up when Gramp hobbled out of the cabin and came across the trodden earth of the yard. Sometimes Dave wondered if he hated the old man. The years had made his hair white, had scarred his gaunt face with deep lines. They had brought rheumatism to his gnarled and twisted muscles until there were days when he could not walk. But Gramp didn't hate nor speak ill of anybody.

No, it wasn't that Gramp had ever done anything wrong. It was just that he'd brought Dave out here to Gunsight Flat to dry up with the wind. There'd come a day when Dave's bones would whiten under a hammering sun set in a brassy sky. A million years from now somebody would dig them up like the Gable kids had dug those queer-looking bones out of the sand dunes to the north, bones that must have gone through uncharted eons since some misty day when creatures that were no longer here walked the earth.

"Don't lose your head with Solly," Gramp said in the same even tone he used whether it was a good day or a bad day, whether the rheumatism was giving him its special brand of hell or had for the moment forgotten him.

"I ain't making no promises," Dave replied, climbing into the buckboard.

"You got Luke's list?"

"I've got it."

Dave spoke to the team and wheeled out of the yard, keeping his gaze ahead on the twin tracks that cut straight north through the sagebrush.

He didn't hate the old man. He knew that. You couldn't hate a man who had waited for death with the uncomplaining fortitude Gramp had.

It was just that Dave Cray's life would have been different if Gramp hadn't settled here.

The ending

Then it was just Dave and Ann and Gramp, and the sound of the horses' hoofs dying across the flat. There would come a day when the empty miles would not be empty, when train whistles and the shrill scream of whirring saws slicing pine into lumber would cut the high thin air. There would be people and cities; there would be the echo of children's laughter. There must be compensation, the companionship of tomorrow to replace the loneliness of yesterday, the goodness of the Gramps to balance the sins of the Jim Sollys. It takes time to understand these things; time and human dignity and a willingness to understand.

And Dave Cray did understand. It was a fine land to become a man in, a land where a man could think what it seemed fitting to think.

In other stories which you read for meaning, says Max Shulman, the theme may be stated less flatly:

In these, you'll find that the author's philosophical point evolves only from the actions of characters—made clear entirely from the outcome of events. All through such a story the author is preparing you for a final truth, sometimes by using clarifying thoughts sprinkled into the plot, sometimes with little or no hint of what is to happen until the last paragraphs where, through a speech, an inward musing or a final act, the story is made complete.

If you plan to write a story heavy with theme, you'll want to ask yourself questions before you begin, such as: Is the theme valid? Do I believe it? Can I illustrate it effectively?

But where theme is not the chief aim, you'll find it usually suggests itself from the situation in your mind and arises from a logical sequence of events. Always it's important to introduce theme into your story so that it doesn't slow the pace.

Let's look at some paragraphs from stories showing how hints, clues, themes and promises of a final truth are given the reader, while at the same time the facts and action of the plot progress. The first paragraphs are from "Old Men's Plans" by Oliver La Farge. The italicized passages show how the author put interpretation and meaning into the story's movement.

He was nervous, and he would remain so until they were clear of this dangerous place and out in the wide part of the canyon beyond. He concealed his uneasiness as well as he could, *for the authority of the captain of a wagon train is no more than his personal prestige . . .*

He had not planned to take his ward beyond Santa Fe, nor leave there until the big wagon train with its escort of dragoons was made up. Even letting Susannah come with him across the Santa Fe trace from the East had been unusual enough, *but somehow young people can force a man's hand . . .*

It was a perfect place for an ambush, the Colonel thought. He had made his dispositions with great care, in reluctant consultation with Beaver Jack; he thought them sound, but he felt *the uncertainty of a man who had no real experience and could judge the situation only by guesswork* . . .

The Colonel meditated briefly on *the irritating situations that can develop out of the ardors of young men and women.*

And in the ending, by means of a character's thoughts, the theme is drawn together:

Hurries-to-War lay on his belly, watching the white men, tiny down there in the canyon. They, too, were burying their chief. Buckskin Shirt and the woman stood together. He had not thought of further attack, not only because *of their leader's death, but because there was too much pattern in the way things had gone, his fate and Buckskin Shirt's, the two old men. To attempt more might not be what the Divine Ones intended.* Now he was leader and Cedar Girl was his. The way was clear. They were going back to the wagons down below, Buckskin Shirt and the woman, arm in arm. Hurries-to-War wished them a clear trail and happiness all around them.

When title gives the theme

In the following story, "Time Will Tell," by Harriett Pratt, from *Redbook,* the title—as in many stories—states the theme. We have italicized some of the supporting and emphasizing hints through which the author moves the reader toward a final conclusion:

Grant Reynolds came home in January, and Carla knew that sooner or later she would meet him. A city of a hundred thousand is not really very big. Nevertheless, her heart gave a lurch when, one day toward the end of February, she turned from a shop window and found herself a yard away from *the man she had maybe—and maybe not—misjudged* . . .

She loved her husband. But Grant had been her first love. She had married Oliver on the rebound, and *she supposed it was inevitable that with a part of her mind, she would always wonder if she had missed something wonderful.* Oliver had made her happy. But she had cried so many tears over Grant, and tears were a special sort of bond . . .

Her heart began to pound, and she felt faintly sick. Why would Grant come to dinner—insist upon coming to dinner—unless he really wanted to see her? Unless—unless he was still in love with her? And *if he loved her now, he had loved her then; she had been wrong about him, and everyone else had been right . . .*

And then, to her utter surprise, she began to laugh. She clapped her hands over her mouth and gasped and choked. All she had gone through, *all that soul-searching, twenty-four hours of sheer hell, because Grant—Grant, about whom she had been absolutely right—* wanted to sell them a house.

"We have a lot of good buys," Grant said. "How about taking a look at some of them?"

"Okay by me," Oliver said. "What do you think, honey?"

Carla's first impulse was to say no. Then she looked across the table at Grant. He was, as everyone said, a good guy. *If you didn't love him, it was perfectly possible to like him.*

She pressed Oliver's hand and gave the two men a smile—a real smile. "Sure," she said. "Let's look at the houses tomorrow. I think it's a wonderful idea."

The story illustrates the theme stated in the title and adds a further observation arrived at by the main character. In other words, a set of circumstances is given an interpretation and a meaning by the writer.

Theme as a story foundation

In order to see how a story may rest upon a theme, without the theme intruding upon action, here's a complete short story from *Redbook* entitled "We Can Do Anything," by Keith W. Jennison. (Note again how the theme is stated in the title. Note, too, the italicized sentences.)

Late in the afternoon of the day he had been looking forward to for so long Jerry looked through the storm door at the falling snow. His mother came and stood beside him. "Where are you going?" she asked him, tugging his knit cap farther down over his ears.

"Just out."

She buttoned the top button of his mackinaw. "Don't worry, dear —we'll have a nice birthday party. You'll see. We always do." Her voice didn't sound very certain. "When your father gets home we'll open the presents. There'll be a big one for you and, let's see . . . this year there'll be eight little ones for me." She turned his face up to hers. "Then we'll sing and have the cake. It'll be lots of fun."

"Okay," Jerry said, and opened the door.

"Don't stay out too long," his mother said.

He walked out into the snow without answering. That was the whole thing: "When your father gets home." Since his father had hurt himself at the plant it wasn't fun to have him come home any more, and the way he had been acting made Jerry sure he wouldn't get the puppy. His mother probably wasn't going to get anything she really wanted either.

As he walked, he realized he was on the road to the station, and he thought of all the times the three of them had made the trip in the car. They would go to the train together in the morning, and at night Jerry and his mother would drive back, making sure they got there early so his father could get off and see them waiting. But lately his father had gone off alone in the morning and come back alone at night.

When Jerry reached Mr. Ogilvy's farm he stopped and looked at the white, flat field in front of the cow barn. Only last spring his father had spent afternoons there teaching him how to throw a baseball.

He walked on, thinking of the time they had gathered ferns in the moonlight. His father had smiled mysteriously and had refused to explain when, at home, he had shredded them and put them in a bowl of water. The next morning he'd brought them along on the ride to the station. Instead of driving past the Ogilvy farm, his father had stopped. Jerry's mother had laughed and asked what they were going to do. His father had said, "Pick ferns in the full of the moon, steep them in water overnight, and sprinkle them over cows. It keeps them from getting bewitched."

"Oh, Sam," his mother had said, "you'll miss your train, you idiot."

"I'll get the next train," his father had grinned. "Mr. Ogilvy is a nice man. You wouldn't want his cows to get all bewitched, would you? Besides, we can't have Jerry growing up not knowing about important things like this, can we?"

That was the way his father had been before the accident. But when he came home from the hospital, he had steel clamps where his right hand had been. He didn't smile much, and he never made any jokes at all. Jerry didn't know much about the new job, but it wasn't as good as the old one. He drove the car differently too. Instead of going along relaxed and easy, he hooked the wheel hard with his claw and went fast.

His father didn't seem to care about anything any more. His mother had tried to make him feel like his old self but it hadn't done any good. Now she was sort of sad and quiet, *as though she were waiting, and Jerry didn't know what for.* Maybe they hadn't tried hard enough, Jerry thought. Maybe it would make his father feel better if somebody was there at the station to meet him tonight. If he hurried he could just about make it on time.

It was hard to go fast on the slippery road, and even though he ran the last few hundred yards the train was pulling out of the station when he got there. There were a lot of people piling into cars and taxis, but he didn't see his father. He found their car where his father had parked it that morning, and got in.

"He even missed the train," Jerry said aloud. He knew he should telephone his mother, but he didn't have a dime. And besides, he was sure there was another train in a little while. He got the blanket from the back seat and covered himself up. In only a few minutes he was asleep.

He was awakened when his father opened the door and got in. He wasn't carrying anything at all. "What are you doing here?" he asked.

"I walked over to meet you," Jerry said.

His father started the car. "Does your mother know where you are?"

"No."

"I don't think that's very bright," his father said. "She'll be worried about you. And I'm later than usual, too."

They drove along the curving road without speaking. As they came into a straight stretch, Jerry saw a brown rabbit jump from the bushes. The rabbit started to turn back, but when they got close he tried to cross the road. There was a thud against the front of the car, but Jerry's father didn't slow up.

Suddenly Jerry grabbed the handle of the door and opened it. "Let me out. Let me out!" His voice broke.

His father put on the brakes, shouting, "Close the door, you little fool."

But before the car had stopped, Jerry was out and running back, flashing his light along the side of the road until he found the rabbit. The rabbit's eyes were half open and dull-looking, and one of the big hind legs stuck out at a funny angle. Jerry came closer. The leg was broken and cut and bloody.

His father came down the road from the car, looked at the rabbit and then turned quickly away. *"There's nothing you can do for him, Jerry. Hurt like that, he isn't worth bothering about. I know."*

Jerry tried to stroke the rabbit's ears. "We've got to do something," he said. "He'll die."

"Come on, Jerry," his father said. "*A crippled rabbit isn't a rabbit at all.* Go back to the car. I'll take care of him. It's for the best." Jerry saw the fingers of his father's left hand gripping a jagged piece of stone.

"It isn't," Jerry said, trying to keep his voice steady. *"We've got to try to save him. We've got to."* He bent closer. "If we could stop the bleeding, we could put a splint on . . ."

"No," his father said. "I tell you, there's nothing to do. Go back to the car."

Jerry shone the light up to his father's face. He had never seen it look so white and strange. "Please," he said, "please. We have to save him. *You used to say there was nothing people couldn't do if they really wanted to.*" He shone the light back on the rabbit, put his hand up under the rabbit's forelegs and held him still. "See? If I hold him like this with one hand and the flashlight with the other, you can do something. I know you can."

It was so quiet Jerry could hear his father breathing short and fast. Then he heard the stone crashing into the woods and his father sank to his knees beside the rabbit. Very delicately he took the hurt leg between the steel fingers of the claw. He separated the edges of the cut with his left hand.

"It's not too deep, at that. Maybe if we put some pressure above it we could get him home." He took his tie off and looped it around the leg above the cut. "I'll make a four-in-hand," he said. "It'll look silly but it's easier." He made a tight and dressy knot and wrapped his handkerchief around the cut. "There," said his father. "That ought to hold him."

"Just like you told me," Jerry said. *"We can do anything."*

As they drove the last mile the rabbit became quiet in Jerry's arms. He was looking at his father when his father said, *"Thanks, Jerry. The rabbit and I both needed you tonight."*

They pulled up in the driveway of their house. The kitchen door was open before they got out of the car. "Is it both of you?" Jerry's mother called. "Is it both, and are you all right?"

"Yes, darling," Jerry's father said. "We're all right but we've got *a disabled rabbit here who needs some help.*"

She spread a clean cloth on the kitchen table and watched as they cleaned and disinfected the cut and put a splint on the broken leg. When the bandaging was finished she put a folded blanket in a carton and they laid the rabbit on it. They tucked an old sweater of Jerry's around the rabbit, leaving only the head and ears uncovered.

Jerry's father looked up from the box. "I'll tell you what," he said, "tomorrow we'll get some bark from the dogwood tree and grate it to a powder. Then we'll sprinkle it on the rabbit. You know what will probably happen?"

"Sure," Jerry said. "He'll get well."

"Not only that," his father said. "He'll turn into a puppy."

They went into the living room, and Jerry's father said, "I'm sorry I forgot about the presents."

Jerry's mother put her arms around her husband. *"We've got our present,"* she said.

The italicized words show that the theme of this story is how a small boy's need of his father revived the father's faith in himself and reunited a family. All these italicized phrases are, of course, part of the very plot itself. But they add up to a central theme or meaning.

A writer should develop the habit of looking for themes, truths and philosophical conclusions in daily life. If you reflect over your past, recall events you've observed or experienced, and analyze why people act as they do, even the most commonplace happening may hold a meaning upon which to build a story or to enrich a story idea.

Professional writers know there are meanings in almost every event of life. They also know that if you look for these with a fiction writer's eye, you'll never lack for themes. Faith Baldwin puts it this way:

> We live in one lifetime a thousand years, and we are no more the same people we were half an hour ago than we will be tomorrow. Growth is slow and imperceptible, and you don't notice change from day to day. All experiences leave their marks, like grooves in a record. If we could play them back, how astonished we would be.
>
> It's wonderful to think, however busy, that we share a common lot in the deepest sense with every person living in this world—no matter what their environment, circumstances, race, creed or color. For fundamentally we have the same basic needs. All of us must, each in his own way, worship, love, work and play; all need food and shelter; and each is born, and some day dies.

A classic example from Thurber

In keeping with these words from Faith Baldwin is the classic story with which we end this Lesson on theme. James Thurber's "The Secret Life of Walter Mitty" may seem at first to be merely a humorous portrait of a timid man who escapes his wife's domination by daydreaming of himself as a hero. But it's far more than this.

Walter Mitty is a little like all of us and his wife is a little like the stern realities of the world. From time to time, most of us try to escape the harsh facts of life by imagining ourselves far greater people than we can ever truly be. Therefore we understand and sympathize with Mitty, see ourselves in him, and find a deeper meaning behind the clever and humorous writing of Thurber. Despite its seeming lightness, this story from *The New Yorker* magazine exemplifies theme in story form.

"We're going through!" The Commander's voice was like thin ice breaking. He wore his full-dress uniform, with the heavily braided white cap pulled down rakishly over one cold gray eye. "We can't make it, sir. It's spoiling for a hurricane, if you ask me." "I'm not asking you, Lieutenant Berg," said the Commander. "Throw on the power lights! Rev her up to 8,500! We're going through!" The pounding of the cylinders increased: ta-pocketa-pocketa-pocketa-*pocketa-pocketa*. The Commander stared at the ice forming on the pilot window. He walked over and twisted a row of complicated dials.

"Switch on No. 8 auxiliary!" he shouted. "Switch on No. 8 auxiliary!" repeated Lieutenant Berg. "Full strength in No. 3 turret!" shouted the Commander. "Full strength in No. 3 turret!" The crew, bending to their various tasks in the huge, hurtling, eight-engined Navy hydroplane, looked at each other and grinned. "The Old Man'll get us through," they said to one another. "The Old Man ain't afraid of Hell!" . . .

"Not so fast! You're driving too fast!" said Mrs. Mitty. "What are you driving so fast for?"

"Hmm?" said Walter Mitty. He looked at his wife, in the seat beside him, with shocked astonishment. She seemed grossly unfamiliar, like a strange woman who had yelled at him in a crowd. "You were up to fifty-five," she said. "You know I don't like to go more than forty. You were up to fifty-five." Walter Mitty drove on toward Waterbury in silence, the roaring of the SN202 through the worst storm in twenty years of Navy flying fading in the remote, intimate airways of his mind. "You're tensed up again," said Mrs. Mitty. "It's one of your days. I wish you'd let Dr. Renshaw look you over."

Walter Mitty stopped the car in front of the building where his wife went to have her hair done. "Remember to get those overshoes while I'm having my hair done," she said. "I don't need overshoes," said Mitty. She put her mirror back into her bag. "We've been all through that," she said, getting out of the car. "You're not a young man any longer." He raced the engine a little. "Why don't you wear your gloves? Have you lost your gloves?" Walter Mitty reached in a pocket and brought out the gloves. He put them on, but after she had turned and gone into the building and he had driven on to a red light, he took them off again. "Pick it up, brother!" snapped a cop as the light changed, and Mitty hastily pulled on his gloves and lurched ahead. He drove around the streets aimlessly for a time, and then he drove past the hospital on his way to the parking lot . . .

"It's the millionaire banker, Wellington McMillan," said the pretty nurse. "Yes?" said Walter Mitty, removing his gloves slowly. "Who has the case?" "Dr. Renshaw and Dr. Benbow, but there are two specialists here, Dr. Remington from New York and Dr. Pritchard-Mitford from London. He flew over." A door opened down a long, cool corridor and Dr. Renshaw came out. He looked distraught and haggard.

"Hello, Mitty," he said. "We're having the devil's own time with

McMillan, the millionaire banker and close personal friend of Roosevelt. Obstreosis of the ductal tract. Tertiary. Wish you'd take a look at him." "Glad to," said Mitty.

In the operating room there were whispered introductions: "Dr. Remington, Dr. Mitty. Dr. Pritchard-Mitford, Dr. Mitty." "I've read your book on streptothricosis," said Pritchard-Mitford, shaking hands. "A brilliant performance, sir." "Thank you," said Walter Mitty.

"Didn't know you were in the States, Mitty," grumbled Remington. "Coals to Newcastle, bringing Mitford and me up here for a tertiary." "You are very kind," said Mitty. A huge, complicated machine, connected to the operating table, with many tubes and wires, began at this moment to go pocketa-pocketa-pocketa. "The new anaesthetizer is giving away!" shouted an interne. "There is no one in the East who knows how to fix it!" "Quiet, man!" said Mitty, in a low, cool voice. He sprang to the machine, which was now going pocketa-pocketa-queep-pocketa-queep. He began fingering delicately a row of glistening dials. "Give me a fountain pen!" he snapped.

Someone handed him a fountain pen. He pulled a faulty piston out of the machine and inserted the pen in its place. "That will hold for ten minutes," he said. "Get on with the operation." A nurse hurried over and whispered to Renshaw, and Mitty saw the man turn pale. "Coreopsis has set in," said Renshaw nervously. "If you would take over, Mitty?" Mitty looked at him and at the craven figure of Benbow, who drank, and at the grave, uncertain faces of the two great specialists. "If you wish," he said. They slipped a white gown on him; he adjusted a mask and drew on thin gloves; nurses handed him shining . . .

"Back it up, Mac! Look out for that Buick!" Walter Mitty jammed on the brakes. "Wrong lane, Mac," said the parking-lot attendant, looking at Mitty closely. "Gee. Yeh," muttered Mitty. He began cautiously to back out of the lane marked "Exit Only."

"Leave her sit there," said the attendant. "I'll put her away." Mitty got out of the car. "Hey, better leave the key." "Oh," said Mitty, handing the man the ignition key. The attendant vaulted into the car, backed it up with insolent skill, and put it where it belonged.

They're so damn cocky, thought Walter Mitty, walking along Main Street; they think they know everything. Once he had tried to take his chains off, outside New Milford, and he had got them wound around the axles. A man had had to come out in a wrecking car and unwind them, a young, grinning garageman. Since then Mrs. Mitty always made him drive to a garage to have the chains taken off. The next time, he thought, I'll wear my right arm in a sling; they won't grin at me then. I'll have my right arm in a sling and they'll see I couldn't possibly take the chains off myself. He kicked at the slush on the sidewalk. "Overshoes," he said to himself, and he began looking for a shoe store.

When he came out into the street again, with the overshoes in a box under his arm, Walter Mitty began to wonder what the other thing was his wife had told him to get. She had told him, twice before they set out from their house for Waterbury. In a way he hated these weekly trips to town—he was always getting something wrong. Kleenex, he thought, Squibb's, razor blades? No. Toothpaste, toothbrush, bicarbonate, carborundum, initiative and referendum? He gave it up. But she would remember it. "Where's the what's-its-name?" she would ask. "Don't tell me you forgot the what's-its-name." A newsboy went by shouting something about the Waterbury trial . . .

"Perhaps this will refresh your memory." The District Attorney suddenly thrust a heavy automatic at the quiet figure on the witness stand. "Have you ever seen this before?" Walter Mitty took the gun and examined it expertly. "This is my Webley-Vickers 50.80," he said calmly. An excited buzz ran around the courtroom. The Judge rapped for order. "You are a crack shot with any sort of firearms, I believe?" said the District Attorney, insinuatingly. "Objection!" shouted Mitty's attorney. "We have shown that the defendant could not have fired the shot. We have shown that he wore his right arm in a sling on the night of the fourteenth of July." Walter Mitty raised his hand briefly and the bickering attorneys were stilled. "With any known make of gun," he said evenly, "I could have killed Gregory Fitzhurst at three hundred feet *with my left hand*." Pandemonium broke loose in the courtroom. A woman's scream rose above the bedlam and suddenly a lovely, dark-haired girl was in Walter Mitty's arms. The District Attorney struck at her savagely. Without rising from his chair, Mitty let the man have it on the point of the chin. "You miserable cur!" . . .

"Puppy biscuit," said Walter Mitty. He stopped walking and the buildings of Waterbury rose up out of the misty courtroom and surrounded him again. A woman who was passing laughed. "He said 'Puppy biscuit,' " she said to her companion. "That man said 'Puppy biscuit' to himself." Walter Mitty hurried on. He went into an A & P, not the first one he came to but a smaller one farther up the street. "I want some biscuit for small, young dogs," he said to the clerk. "Any special brand, sir?" The greatest pistol shot in the world thought a moment. "It says 'Puppies Bark for It' on the box," said Walter Mitty.

His wife would be through at the hairdresser's in fifteen minutes, Mitty saw in looking at his watch, unless they had trouble drying it; sometimes they had trouble drying it. She didn't like to get to the hotel first; she would want him to be there waiting for her as usual. He found a big leather chair in the lobby, facing a window, and he put the overshoes and the puppy biscuit on the floor beside it. He picked up an old copy of *Liberty* and sank down into the chair. "Can Germany Conquer the World Through the Air?" Walter Mitty looked at the pictures of bombing planes and of ruined streets . . .

"The cannonading has got the wind up in young Raleigh, sir," said the sergeant. Captain Mitty looked up at him through tousled hair. "Get him to bed," he said wearily, "with the others. I'll fly alone." "But you can't, sir," said the sergeant anxiously. "It takes two men to handle that bomber and the Archies are pounding hell out of the air. Von Richtman's circus is between here and Saulier." "Somebody's got to get that ammunition dump," said Mitty. "I'm going over. Spot of brandy?" He poured a drink for the sergeant and one for himself. War thundered and whined around the dugout and battered at the door. There was a rending of wood and splinters flew through the room. "A bit of a near thing," said Captain Mitty carelessly. "The box barrage is closing in," said the sergeant. "We only live once, Sergeant," said Mitty, with his faint, fleeting smile. "Or do we?" He poured another brandy and tossed it off. "I never see a man could hold his brandy like you, sir," said the sergeant. "Begging your pardon, sir." Captain Mitty stood up and strapped on his huge Webley-Vickers automatic. "It's forty kilometres through hell, sir," said the sergeant. Mitty finished one last brandy. "After all," he said softly, "what isn't?" The pounding of the cannon increased; there was the rat-tat-tatting of machine guns, and from somewhere came the menacing pocketa-pocketa-pocketa of the new flame-throwers. Walter Mitty walked to the door of the dug-out humming "Auprès de Ma Blonde." He turned and waved to the sergeant. "Cheerio!" he said. . . .

Something struck his shoulder. "I've been looking all over this hotel for you," said Mrs. Mitty. "Why do you have to hide in this old chair? How did you expect me to find you?" "Things close in," said Walter Mitty vaguely. "What?" Mrs. Mitty said. "Did you get the what's-its-name? The puppy biscuit? What's in that box?" "Overshoes," said Mitty. "Couldn't you have put them on in the store?" "I was thinking," said Walter Mitty. "Does it ever occur to you that I am sometimes thinking?" She looked at him. "I'm going to take your temperature when I get you home," she said.

They went out through the revolving doors that made a faintly derisive whistling sound when you pushed them. It was two blocks to the parking lot. At the drugstore on the corner she said, "Wait here for me. I forgot something. I won't be a minute." She was more than a minute. Walter Mitty lighted a cigarette. It began to rain, rain with sleet in it. He stood up against the wall of the drugstore, smoking . . . He put his shoulders back and his heels together. "To hell with the handkerchief," said Walter Mitty scornfully. He took one last drag on his cigarette and snapped it away. Then, with that faint, fleeting smile playing about his lips, he faced the firing squad; erect and motionless, proud and disdainful, Walter Mitty the Undefeated, inscrutable to the last.

Why sincerity is important

I have always believed that what you say is more important than how you say it. Certainly it is better to write well than to write badly, but too often I find people worrying desperately about how to say something that isn't worth saying anyhow. I have wished more time was spent on thinking, feeling, knowing people, and less on the thought of style and construction, which has to be second at least.

No amount of technique can repair an engine that isn't under the hood, and no glory of style, knack with words, or fancy writing can conceal the horrid barrenness and vacuum where sincerity, passion, and a great need and desire to tell a story that will make people laugh or cry or fight ought to be.—Adela Rogers St. Johns

The stronghold of the individual

Writing may be the last stronghold of individuality, the place where within reason a man may be himself without being odd or losing status. Indeed, he may gain status if he has a novel as well as a persuasive way of putting ideas. With all our ironclad conformity, most of us still give a man or woman rein when it comes to speech.— Charles W. Ferguson in *Saturday Review*

How the short story has changed

In this country the short story started out by being used for religious and political purposes. The New England preacher, Cotton Mather, is probably the first American short story writer. First, he wrote *The Political Fables*. These were three stories circulated in manuscript form in 1692, warning the Colonists against internal dissension. But Mather really soared off into fiction when, in a frenzy of witchcraft hunting in 1693, he wrote *Wonders of the Invisible World*. This volume is so full of fantastic accounts, so abounding in witches, devils and weird spiritual manifestations that few of the so-called "fantasy fiction" writers of today could hope to equal it.—Martha Foley in *The Best American Short Stories*

Lesson fourteen

Fiction writing

course

Using the elements in a story

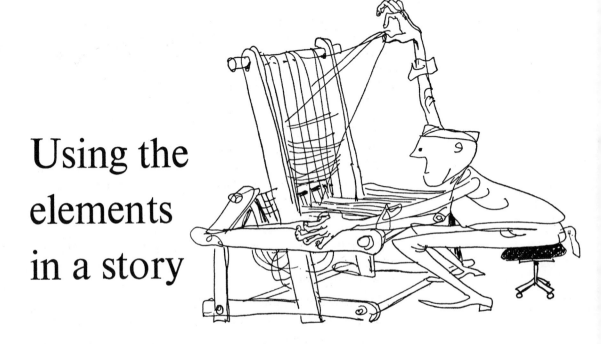

Now that you've studied each element separately, it's time to look at a typical story and see how all the elements—character, setting, situation and theme—are woven together by a skillful author. As a typical story we have chosen "Duel in the Brush" by Ed Montgomery, which appeared in *The Saturday Evening Post*. An excellent example of professional writing, it's aimed at that large American audience which enjoys slick stories of adventure and romance mixed.

The story is presented here in nine sections—each followed by comments to guide you in studying the use of the four elements. Note how the elements are injected so that they blend, with no one element getting in the way of another or holding up the smooth and appealing flow of the story.

I

It's hard to believe now, but when Will Applewhite came to this part of the country he didn't have anything but a pretty good twist-barrel shotgun and an old white mare mule. This was just before he came under the civilizing influence of Mary Martha Barnes, and at first people called him Wild Bill.

Some even called him Wild Bill the Rattlesnake Lover. And anybody who guessed he was on his way to owning half the town and the country around forgot to mention it.

He came to town wearing overalls and a hat that had been used hard for a long time. He hadn't shaved for quite a spell. He got off the mule in front of the bank and went across the sidewalk as far as the door.

"Hello, the bank!" he sang out, in the way you do when you're coming up to a man's camp in the woods and don't want to get shot.

Alf Jenkins, the banker, was standing at the front counter discouraging a new customer who wanted to mortgage a stud-poker game he was organizing.

Let's pause to see what the author has told us so far. He's given us an initial set of circumstances to get the story going. What are they? Does the author include all the elements in these five paragraphs?

We're introduced to Will Applewhite and told several things about him—that he arrived in "this part of the country" with nothing but a gun and mule, that people had called him Wild Bill before "he came under the civilizing influence of Mary Martha Barnes." The author has included a basic trait for the main character, as well as some lesser ones. Will is "wild," he obviously has no fear of rattlesnakes, is altogether indifferent to his appearance—"He hadn't shaved for quite a spell"—is cautious of his fellow men, and is satisfied with the strictly functional equipment of a "twist-barrel shotgun and an old white mare mule." So far, then, we have situation and characterization.

In addition to these two elements, we're told of Applewhite's whereabouts. From the words "this part of the country" and the title of the story, we know the locale is the West. Therefore we now have setting. And the thread which will lead to the final meaning of the story is hinted in the words: "This was just before he came under the civilizing influence of Mary Martha Barnes." So we've been given theme as well.

Applewhite is further characterized by the prediction that he'll ultimately own "half the town and country around." The "town and country around" is added setting, and the phrase that "anybody who guessed . . . forgot to mention it" is another hint of theme. The setting is again brought into closer focus by "He got off the mule in front of the bank and went across the sidewalk as far as the door." And once more we learn about Will from "Hello, the bank!" which indicates he's been living a wild life in wild surroundings.

All in all, the situation presented in these opening paragraphs reveals that an independent and canny man is going to be civilized by a woman. Now the story goes on to show us how this comes about.

II

"Hello yourself!" Alf yelled back. "Come on in."

"No," Will said. "You come out here."

So banker Jenkins got the bank's .41 Colt out from under the counter, put it in his coat pocket, left his hand in there with it, and went out on the sidewalk. The customer went with him, but as soon as he got a good look at Will he turned and went off up the street.

"Howdy," Alf said. "Welcome to Catamount Springs, garden spot of the territory."

"Howdy," Will said. "My name's Applewhite. Whereabouts is there a piece of land so sorry nobody's settled on it?"

"You go west a little better than a mile," Alf said immediately. "As soon as you ford the creek you turn north. Go a half a quarter north and you'll be right in the middle of a hundred and sixty acres just like you're talkin' about. Watch out for the rattlesnakes when you get there."

"Much obliged. Does anybody buy game for the market around here?"

"Right down at the produce house. You a market hunter?"

"Fixin' to be."

"Plenty of game. You might do all right if you can shoot good enough."

"I always could. One time I shot a little too good."

"Huh?"

"Nothin'."

"What else do you do?"

Will considered. "I play checkers."

"Right smart bunch of checker players around here. They're playin' right now, I expect, down in Donaldson's store."

"In the store?"

"Well, sure. This is October."

"I'll wait till spring when they get out on the porch again. Much obliged for the information."

He put the bridle lines over his shoulder and led the mule down the street. He stopped under the post-oak tree in front of the produce house.

"Hello the produce house!" he yelled.

Mary Martha Barnes came to the door. "Come in out of the sun," she said.

Will shook his head. "I'm lookin' for the produce man."

"I'm it."

"Oh. Well, would you come out and look at these chickens?"

She did, and when he got a good look at her, he had a little trouble getting his mind back to prairie chickens. She had blue eyes, like deep water when you see it from a high bluff, and this real light blond hair, and she was as pretty as moonlight on new snow, though warmer-looking.

Will looked away from her and took a deep breath. "I've got a dozen birds here," he said. "Fresh-killed. I missed one."

Mary Martha looked at a couple of the prairie chickens and named the going rate. "Bring the sack of them inside and I'll get you your money," she said.

"I'll wait outside. I don't go in houses."

Mary Martha studied his face, like she was maybe trying to see behind all those whiskers, and then took the chickens inside and came back with the money.

"Ma'am," Will said, "it's a pleasure to do business with you." It wasn't near what he wanted to say to her, but it seemed like about enough for the first time.

In this portion of the story we've learned many more things about Will—that he's "fixin' to be" a market hunter, that he shoots very well ("One time I shot a little too good"). Through Will's own words he's increasingly clarified as a personality: "I don't go in houses . . . I play checkers . . . I've got a dozen birds here . . . Fresh-killed. I missed one." And his vulnerability to Mary Martha is revealed by his words and thoughts " 'Ma'am, it's a pleasure to do business with you.' It wasn't near what he wanted to say to her, but it seemed like about enough for the first time."

Banker Al Jenkins is characterized as friendly, reasonable, yet sensibly armed. "So banker Jenkins got the bank's .41 Colt out from under the counter, put it in his coat pocket, left his hand in there with it, and went out on the sidewalk." We also learn more about him when he says: "Howdy! Welcome to Catamount Springs, garden spot of the territory."

Mary Martha is physically described, and also characterized as straightforward, strong-minded and interested in Will. "Mary Martha studied his face, like she was maybe trying to see behind all those whiskers, and then took the chickens inside and came back with the money."

The setting changes as Will proceeds from the bank to the store, and is merely sketched in like this: "He stopped under the post-oak tree in front of the produce house." And the land Will wants to buy is described by the banker: "You go west a little better than a mile . . . As soon as you ford the creek you turn north. Go a half a quarter north and you'll be right in the middle of a hundred and sixty acres just like you're talkin' about. Watch out for the rattlesnakes when you get there."

III

He backed the mule around and got in the saddle and realized the man he'd seen at the bank was looking at him. The man shoved away from the awning pole he'd been leaning against and came across the street.

"Howdy, Gilson," Will said.

"It's Gilliland," the man said. "Howdy, Applewhite. Just passin' through, are you?"

"No," Will said, and started to turn the mule.

Gilliland moved to stay in front of him and took hold of the bridle. "There's a poker game," he said, "and you're invited."

"No, I guess not," Will said.

"Seems like I heard you used to play some."

"I haven't touched a card in two years," Will said. "And I haven't touched a gun in two years, either, except for the shotgun I use for bird huntin'. But that don't mean I've swore off knockin' people's teeth down their throat if it looks like it needs doin' bad enough. Turn aloose of that mule."

Gilliland turned loose. Will rode on out of town and by the time he came back, a week later, he was famous.

People said his home was the ground under a hickory tree and he didn't even bother to kick the rocks out from under his bed. The bed was some blankets and a piece of tarpaulin. If it started to rain, Will just pulled the canvas up over his head and went back to sleep.

His only kitchen utensils, they said, were a Dutch oven and a pocketknife. The only store-bought food in his camp was salt and corn meal.

Most of the reports came from Bert Higgins, his nearest neighbor.

"One thing you've got to say for him," Bert told people, "he's the gosh-awfulest hunter ever hit this country. I seen 'im shootin' ducks, and he didn't bother to let 'em light, he hit 'em flyin'. And they was these here little blue-winged teals, too, that flies so fast they whistle. The way he finds quail it'd make a bird dog ashamed of hisself just to watch 'im, and he can see a fox squirrel's ear stickin' out over a limb in the top of a tall tree."

Bert said Will wasn't exactly friendly and he wasn't exactly unfriendly. Mostly, he said, old Wild Bill was just strange.

"He told me I was welcome on his place any time," Bert said. "Just so I didn't kill any of his rattlesnakes . . . No, I'm not; he said that! Said he had a lot of rattlesnakes and this warm weather had 'em comin' out like it was the summertime, and he didn't want 'em bothered."

Will came to town with a mule load of quail, prairie chickens and early-flying ducks. But he rode past the produce house and on to the bank. Alf Jenkins came out to meet him.

Will was dressed the same way, but his clothes had been washed and he'd shaved. "Tell me about that girl," he said.

"At the produce house?" Alf Jenkins scratched his jaw. "Nicest girl you ever saw. She inherited that business and she's runnin' it by herself. Mostly she's runnin' it in debt, though."

"I mean is she married or anything like that?"

"Unmarried and disengaged. Though I wouldn't count on her stayin' that way long, girl that looks like that."

"Much obliged . . . Say, you know that man was in the bank the day I came to town?"

Jenkins nodded. "Name's Gilliland."

"It was Gilson, before he changed it. He's a murderer by trade."

"No! Is that a fact?"

"Yes, sir. He'll hear about some old boy keeps all his money in a tin can and he'll go make 'im tell where it's hid and murder him and his wife. Then he'll go on and do the same thing some place else."

"All he's doin' around here is playin' cards."

"He's just waitin' till he hears about somethin'. The last I knew, he had about a hundred and fifty years to serve in the Kansas state penitentiary. He hasn't had time to serve it, so he probably went over the wall."

"I'll tell the sheriff. You wasn't goin' to tell me how you happen to know all this, was you?"

"No, sir; I was goin' to go down and sell my game."

In these paragraphs the unidentified man who's been lurking about the bank is introduced and characterized. ("Howdy, Gilson," Will says, and the reply, "It's Gilliland. Howdy, Applewhite.") The reader knows the man is using an alias, and also knows the way he behaves. ("Gilliland moved to stay in front of him and took hold of the bridle.") Will is shown as fearless when he says: "I haven't touched a gun in two years, either, except for the shotgun I use for bird huntin'. But that don't mean I've swore off knockin' people's teeth down their throat if it looks like it needs doin' bad enough." And the sentence "Gilliland turned loose," shows that Gilson is a coward.

The author continues to characterize Will in the paragraph: "People said his home was the ground under a hickory tree and he didn't even bother to kick the rocks out from under his bed. The bed was some blankets and a piece of a tarpaulin. If it started to rain, Will just pulled the canvas up over his head and went back to sleep . . . The way he finds quail it'd make a bird dog ashamed of hisself just to watch 'im, and he can see a fox squirrel's ear stickin' out over a limb in the top of a tall tree." And again: "Bert said Will wasn't exactly friendly and he wasn't exactly unfriendly—mostly, old Wild Bill was just strange."

We know that Will goes directly for what he wants when he returns to the bank, washed and shaved, and asks Jenkins about the girl. Also that he has no fear of Gilson. But when he doesn't explain what he knows about Gilson, he becomes wary again.

The same settings are repeated, except for the description of where Will has been sleeping. And the meaning is once more suggested as Will asks: "Is she married or anything like that?"

IV

Mary Martha Barnes tallied up the game and did the figuring. "This is more business than I've had all week," she said.

"Things kind of slow?"

"Slow as molasses in January."

"You know," Will said slowly, "there's a lot of money in rabbits. People in big towns eat a world of 'em. You ought to get a batch of old lumber and give it to farm boys around to make rabbit traps out of. You could probably get twice as many as you are gettin'. And you get a better price for 'em if they haven't got any shot in 'em."

"Good idea," Mary Martha said. "Sounds like you've got a good business head on you."

"I don't know. I never tried to find out."

"Maybe if you'd come in and look around you could give me some other ideas."

Will shook his head. Mary Martha looked disgusted.

"Now look here," Will said. "I don't hold it against you because you do happen to believe in houses."

She didn't say anything.

"I lived with the Indians for a spell," Will told her. "I've tried their way and your way both and I use some of both. But mostly the Indian ways."

"Even the Indians have tents."

"They wouldn't, though, if it wasn't for the women. When I get married I'll get my wife a tent, all right."

"You keep on talking like that and you never will get married."

"You're narrow-minded."

"I'm not narrow-minded. You're uncivilized."

"I'm that, all right. But I just got over bein' civilized twenty-four hours a day for two years solid, whether I liked it or not . . . I guess I'd better be gettin' on home."

Will's resistance to civilization is illustrated by his conversation with Mary Martha. Both people are characterized as strongminded. "You keep on talking like that and you never will get married," says Mary Martha. And when he accuses her of being "narrow-minded," her reply, "you're uncivilized," comes straight to the matter. His answer is a further revelation of why he acts as he does, as well as of his stubbornness.

The author doesn't need to tell us where this scene is laid. We know it's the produce house. And the theme has been supported once more through the actions of the two characters.

V

He didn't feel like hunting that night, and he still didn't feel like hunting the next day. He was still sitting by the fire at midmorning when Alf Jenkins rode in.

"Hello the camp!" Alf said.

"Howdy," Will said listlessly. "Light and look at your saddle."

Alf squatted by the fire. "I told the sheriff."

"What'd he say?"

"He jumped Gilliland. And Gilliland told him you was the one. Said you'd been in the Kansas state pen for murder."

"Did he say that?"

"Said the way they caught you, the posse surrounded a house you was sleepin' in. And that's why you won't never go indoors any more, he said."

"Well, he told it all wrong."

"That's what I told the sheriff."

"It was manslaughter."

"Oh."

"The way it was, there was this man in Coffeyville and he tried to palm the queen of diamonds out of the discards because it turned out after the draw he never should have throwed it away. And I jumped 'im about it and he gets this little short-barreled thirty-eight and starts shootin' at me. My gun was in my hip pocket and by the time I got it out he'd already missed me twice and hit me once in the side, and I didn't have time to do anything but shoot at 'im where he made the biggest target."

"Oh."

"There wasn't any posse to it. The chief of police come runnin' in and I give him my gun and went to the jail with 'im. But it seemed like they had this law-and-order crusade on, and cussed if they didn't send me to prison."

"That don't sound so bad to me."

"The next governor come into office looked into it and gave me a pardon."

"Well, I believe you. And the sheriff's done left for Kansas on the mornin' train to find out who's tellin' the truth."

"Did he arrest Gilson?"

"He said he couldn't arrest anybody till he found out more."

"Well, Gilson will be gone when he gets back. If I had a bank I'd be watchin' it."

"Good idea," Alf said. He said it over his shoulder on his way to his horse.

"Watch out for my rattlesnakes!" Will called after him. "Don't kill any of 'em!"

In the first paragraph, Will's actions show again how upset he's been by Mary Martha's forthrightness. Note that the author hasn't told us directly that Will is troubled, but has illustrated it by his behavior so the reader can tell for himself. The author also shows us another facet of Will's character by disclosing his willingness to tell the banker the truth about his past. Because of the careful choice of words, both the banker and reader will believe him.

The setting is merely "the camp." When Will says, "Watch out for my rattlesnakes!" he gives a picture of the kind of land it is. And once more theme is advanced by what transpires. We understand that Will is grappling with the question of becoming civilized.

VI

He sat around thinking for another half hour and then threw his saddle on the mule. When he got to the produce house, Mary Martha came right on out, almost like she'd been watching for him.

"You ought to sell shotgun shells," Will greeted her.

She looked surprised. "I had?"

"Yes, ma'am. The man at the hardware store doesn't have hardly any, because he thinks people will go on loadin' their own forever. But they won't. Why a man that does a lot of shootin', like I do, can't afford to use anything but store-bought shells, figurin' his time's worth anything at all."

"I guess that's a good idea. Look—"

"You ought to sell powder and shot too. You could afford to sell 'em a few cents lower than the hardware store does. Then when a man comes in to sell some hides—why, you could get 'im to take some of it out in trade and—"

"I'll try it," she said. "Look, I don't hold it against you what you believe in. I was wrong about that. Not that I'm not still ready to argue about it, though."

"I'm sure glad to hear you say that."

And that wasn't much to say, so it must have been the way he said it. Because the girl blushed and looked at the ground. Will went down the street to the bank.

He called banker Jenkins out on the sidewalk. Alf looked nervous and he kept his hand in his pocket.

"You don't have to worry about me," Will said. "My shotgun's yonder on my saddle."

"I'm not worried about you, and that's the truth. But if I was you, I'd be worried about Gilliland, same as I am."

"I've got better things to worry about. He wouldn't shoot a man just because he was mad at him. He might have shot me to keep me from talkin' about him, but he wouldn't shoot me after I talked. Not unless he could turn a profit, and he doesn't know he can."

"Could he?"

"For this he could." Will reached in his shirt pocket and took out a folded stack of bank notes. "There's better than two thousand dollars here. He'd kill twenty men for that."

Jenkins whistled. "I'll believe you if you tell me you're not a bank robber. But you'd better tell me."

"I made this money bettin' I was the best checker player in the Kansas state prison. And you don't spend much if you ride an old

wore-out mule and shoot what you eat and don't pay any house rent
. . . How much does the produce house owe?"

"Well—About nine hundred dollars."

"All right, sir. There it is. Business is goin' to start gettin' better,
and I want Mary Martha to start out even."

Alf stared. "What will I tell 'er?"

"Shucks, I'm not a banker. You ought to know what to tell 'er. Say
it's a present from the bank to a good, steady customer. She'll probably believe anything. That girl hasn't got any more of a head for
business than a banty hen."

"I'll try . . . Hey! Look at that scoundrel."

Will turned around in time to see Gilliland slide along the wall
of the grocery store across the street and vanish between two buildings, going toward the alley.

Will finished putting his bank roll away. "You think he saw me
with this money?"

"He was watchin' real close. If I was you, I'd put that money in
the bank where it'd be safe."

"No reflection on the bank, but I'll feel just as good havin' it in my
pocket as in a bank that rascal's got his eye on."

"From what you say, he'd be more interested in your money than
mine. You haven't got as much, but it'd be less of a gamble to shoot
you in the back than to try to rob the bank."

"I'll watch out for him." Will climbed on his mule.

Will now reveals just how much he's been thinking about
Mary Martha by suggesting a practical means of helping her
with the produce house. He also reveals he's a potential businessman himself and implies that at least one of the reasons he
gave the banker $900 is so Mary Martha will be debt-free in case
anything happens to him. And the way Mary Martha quickly
expresses her considered tolerance for his beliefs—"Look, I don't
hold it against you what you believe in. I was wrong about that.
Not that I'm not still ready to argue about it, though"—reveals
how much thought she's been giving him in return.

Will expresses his love for her by straightening out the store
finances with the banker. His own savings, his composure in the
face of danger from Gilson, keep adding to his stature as a man.
The author's skill in characterizing him with each action and
speech makes him real and arouses the reader's admiration. One
small gesture or word out of place and the character would lose
believability.

Here you see a most important lesson in characterization illustrated step by step—*keep your story person in character by ac-*

tions, thoughts, speeches and motives. Know and understand your characters before you begin to write about them, then make every word contribute to their characterization.

The setting is implied again: "Will went down the street to the bank . . . the wall of the grocery store across the street . . . between two buildings, going toward the alley." This is just enough to keep the place in view as the characters move.

The theme isn't mentioned directly here, but it's bolstered by Will's concern for Mary Martha, above the danger to himself.

VII

He started down the street and Mary Martha rode a pretty little sorrel mare out of the livery stable and joined him.

"I thought I'd go for a ride," she said. "The way business has been, I haven't got anything to lose by closing up shop for a few hours."

"I don't know. A lot of runnin' a business is just bein' there in case somethin' does happen, it seems like to me."

"Maybe you don't want my company."

"Yes, I do. I'd like to have your company from now on."

She looked at him sideways. "That could be taken as a proposal of marriage."

Will took a deep breath. "Well," he said, "that's what it is."

She turned her eyes back straight ahead and she didn't say anything more for a quarter of a mile. "Marriage," she said then, "is a big step for a girl."

"I've heard that said."

"A girl doesn't want a man to be just like every other man," she said carefully. "But she doesn't want him to be so all-fired different, either."

Will didn't say anything. They rode on and forded the creek and came to the campsite. Mary Martha looked around and you could tell she wasn't falling in love with the place, but she didn't wrinkle up her nose at it, either.

"Maybe," she said, "if I knew the reasons why you think the way you do—"

"I doubt if you'd understand," Will said.

He didn't really mean to say it, but it was hard to figure out how to tell her he didn't mean it. He turned his mule loose and hobbled the girl's mare and slipped the bridle so she could eat better. He hadn't figured out how to tell her yet when the shot came.

It came from the ridge, maybe sixty yards away. Sounded like a Winchester, and right away Will thought of the rifle he'd seen on Gilliland's saddle. He grabbed his shotgun, got to the girl in a half dozen strides, and swept her behind the hickory tree. "What's the matter with you?" she demanded.

"You stay behind this tree."

"Didn't you ever hear anybody shoot a gun before?"

Chances were, she was right. Somebody was always shooting at something, and this shot probably didn't mean anything. But it was worth finding out about, because Gilliland might have had time to get there ahead of them and get set up for a little bushwhacking.

Will now shows his complete capitulation to Mary Martha in a sincere if inarticulate way, and tries to figure "how to tell her" about his past trouble. His courage, and hers, are revealed in the way they respond to the sudden shot.

The setting is amplified by the introduction of "the livery stable . . . they rode on and forded the creek and came to the campsite . . . the ridge, maybe sixty yards away . . . the hickory tree." The author doesn't detail the settings in this story, mainly because he uses them merely to form a background for action. In other stories, of course, the setting can be more fully described if it has more bearing on the story itself.

The theme is enlarged upon by Mary Martha's remarks: "A girl doesn't want a man to be just like every other man—but she doesn't want him to be so all-fired different, either." Incidentally, note the use of local dialect and speech to characterize Mary Martha and everyone else in the story.

VIII

It wasn't a real big hickory tree, and things would have been real cozy if Will hadn't had Gilliland on his mind. Nothing happened for five minutes and Will got impatient. He started edging his head out from the tree, low down to the ground so he wouldn't make such a clear target, and a shot came and threw dirt in his eyes.

He pulled his head back and got his eyes cleared out. "It's a good thing," he said, "that that Gilson can't shoot very good."

"What's he up to?"

Will thought about it and decided she needed to know. "He's aimin' to kill me first. Then he'll kill you, because that's the way he does. He never left a witness yet."

She looked Will in the eye and nodded her head thoughtfully. "What was that first shot?"

"Must have been some kind of an accident. He's famous for gettin' close and makin' sure before he pulls a trigger."

"What are we going to do?"

"I hate to tell you, but it looks right now like he's got us. We haven't got anything but a shotgun and nothin' bigger than Number Six shot, and he knows it. He'll lay back out of range, you can bet on that."

She was calmer than you'd expect a girl to be. "I hope you can think of something."

"I could let you make a run for your horse while I sprayed a little bird shot in his direction. But I don't think there's hardly a chance you'd make it."

"I'll stay with you."

"Just in case he does get us, I'd like to know what you was goin' to tell me."

"Well—I'd like to know why you won't go in houses and I'd like to know why you take such good care of rattlesnakes and—"

"You mean you won't say. Not even in the fix we're in."

She shook her head stubbornly. "I need more information."

"You're a pretty hard girl to stampede, aren't you?"

"Listen, he'll slip around through the brush and get a side shot at us. You think of something!"

"If I could just get in shotgun range of him. But the ground's too open."

"He's awful quiet," she said.

"I saw a bush movin'. He's aimin' to get to that down treetop yonder."

"Then come on! Move around the tree!"

"No, wait. We can't keep on circlin' 'im forever. Maybe I've thought of somethin'."

Will was searching in his pockets and he came out with a shotgun shell and his knife. He opened the knife and carefully cut the shell almost in half, stopping when only a strand of the outer paper held the two parts together. "Now then," he said. "Might work and it might not. It better, because next time he makes a sneak he'll likely be more careful."

He broke the shotgun, extracted the shell from the right barrel and inserted the mutilated one. He looked up and Gilliland's head was inching up above the trunk of the felled tree.

Gilliland was taking it slow, getting his bearings and making certain he'd get the dead-sure murderer's shot he'd failed to get at first.

Will locked the action of the gun as Gilliland's rifle came into sight. Gilliland took in the situation, but he still didn't hurry. Will cocked the right barrel, raised the shotgun, and shot as the stock hit his shoulder.

There was the crack of the gun and then there was a sound like you can make by hitting a loose board with another board. The second sound was made by an ounce and an eighth of bird shot, all together in one projectile, hitting Gilliland in the head. Gilliland went back and out of sight.

"He's all right," Will said. "I mean he won't be botherin' us now."

Mary Martha shivered. "What did you do? You said it was too far to shoot him."

"Well, you can cut a shell in two between the middle wads, and the entire half of a shell goes out together, just like a great big old rifle bullet. I'd heard about it but never tried it. It can be dangerous. If it puts too much pressure on your gun barrel, the gun blows up in your face. But the shape we were in, it was dangerous not to."

"I'm glad it worked," Mary Martha said in a small voice.

"You wait," Will said gently, "and don't think about it. I'll scout around and make sure everything's all right."

Will's cool courage is emphasized by the words: "Will thought about it and decided she needed to know. 'He's aimin' to kill me first. Then he'll kill you, because that's the way he does. He never left a witness yet.' " And her courage is shown this way: "She looked Will in the eye and nodded her head thoughtfully. 'What was that first shot?' " And when Will explains that he thinks they're doomed, the author writes: "She was calmer than you'd expect a girl to be. 'I hope you can think of something.' " And then we are shown how brave and resourceful Will can be.

The setting isn't actually explained but is conveyed to the reader by phrases like "through the brush . . . that down tree-top yonder."

The theme is gathering force as the plot develops with Mary Martha's insistence on an understanding before she gives her consent to marriage. "You're a pretty hard girl to stampede," says Will wonderingly, but he doesn't get a chance to explain.

IX

Mary Martha was leaning against the hickory tree when he got back. She seemed glad to see him.

"It was a rattlesnake," Will announced. "That first shot, I mean. He came on him sudden in the path and got scared and shot 'im and gave himself away."

"Lucky for us."

"It was, for a fact. I'd warned people to leave those snakes alone. The Indians told me that. You leave a snake alone, and he'll probably leave you alone. But you kill one, and his mate is liable to find you and bite you. Or maybe bite your dog or one of your kids or somebody."

"I see."

"At least that's what the Indians say, and you've just about got to figure they're right because it's their business to pay attention to things like that."

"So that explains the rattlesnake part," Mary Martha said. "Now if I just knew about that not ever going in a house part."

"I spent so much time bein' inside for a while that I just decided it'd take me the rest of my life to get what bein' outdoors I needed to do out of my system."

"You mean you were working in an office? Or a factory? Or maybe you were in a hospital."

"No, ma'am," Will said. "It was a prison."

"Maybe you were a guard."

Will looked her in the eye. "I was a prisoner."

Mary Martha thought about that for just a little while. "That doesn't make any difference," she said.

"I'm glad to hear you say that . . . You go on back to town and I'll bring the body back on the mule. You hadn't ought to see him."

"No," Mary Martha said. "I wouldn't want to see him on my wedding day."

They were married on the front porch of the Methodist preacher's house. After the ceremony, banker Jenkins kissed the bride as much as seemed necessary and then Will took her down the street and to her house.

"I'll wait out here," he told her. "You get what you need, and we can be home by dark."

"No," Mary Martha said, and she sounded an awful lot like a girl with her mind made up. "We're already home."

"I'm not forgettin' my promise," Will said. "I'll get you the best tent I can find."

"I've got a perfectly good house here. You can sleep out there under that old tree if you want to, but I'm not going to."

Will looked at her and then he looked at the sky. He looked stubborn and looked back at Mary Martha and stopped looking stubborn and scratched his head and sighed. "Well," he said, "there is that dead rattlesnake's mate to worry about out there."

The author pits the two characters against each other till the last sentence. But Will tells the reader one more thing about himself—that for the sake of honesty, he can face up to Mary Martha, even if it means losing her. With the setting reduced to the front porch of the "Methodist preacher's house" and "down the street to her house," the theme is completed in the last two paragraphs of plot when Will rationalizes his becoming a civilized bridegroom. The author cleverly leaves him his pride in the words: "Well, there is that dead rattlesnake's mate to worry about out there."

Your reader isn't a mind reader

The inexperienced writer often lets too much happen in a character's mind. Action and dialogue are much more readable than long paragraphs about what the character thinks. Even special points of decision can be handled with action or with a word of dialogue. If the writer has planned properly, then, when his hero gets in a car, starts the engine and drives off in a direction you don't expect him to take, you know what he's decided and why he's going in that direction.—Mignon Eberhart

Adjectives can be dangerous

In 1880 Mark Twain wrote to a schoolboy essayist:

"I notice that you use plain, simple language, short words and brief sentences. That is the way to write English—it is the modern way, and the best way. Stick to it; don't let fluff and flowers and verbosity creep in. When you catch adjectives, kill most of them—then the rest will be valuable. They weaken when they are close together; they give strength when they are wide apart. An adjective habit, or a wordy, diffuse or flowery habit, once fastened upon a person, is as hard to get rid of as any other vice."

Rules for juvenile writing

The Lessons on the short story are a basic foundation for any kind of fiction writing and a necessary preliminary to writing for young people as well as adults. There are, however, some special rules and features unique to the juvenile field, and if you want to enter this field, you must study them with care.

These rules and features will be given later in the Lessons on writing novel-length fiction. Under "Writing Juvenile Books" we will tell you about this young reading audience and how to write for it.

Thurber on the split infinitive

Word has somehow got around that the split infinitive is always wrong. This is of a piece with the outworn notion that it is always wrong to strike a lady.—James Thurber

Section V

Lesson fifteen

Fiction writing

course

Writing

a short

story

Part I

Every writer conceives a story in an individual way and develops it according to his own rules. No one way can be called best, for fiction always remains a completely personal and creative enterprise. However, as we've said, most writers find that planning a story before writing it makes the writing easier and the results more certain.

What exactly goes into the planning of a story? First, some careful thinking about the kind of story you want to tell, the effect you want to make on the reader, and the characters you create for your story people. But chiefly you'll plan the initial situation, the plot, and perhaps the factual research for setting.

You already know that the situation is a basic set of circumstances that launches a story; "what happens next," because of them, is *plot*. Plotting, then, is what we should consider now, for in unfolding the plot we perform the very act of storytelling.

Mignon Eberhart offers this definition of plotting:

The plotting of a story, briefly, is the arrangement of incidents and events in a chain of cause and effect which leads to the climax. In this sense, the dénouement and the climax may be taken as meaning the same thing and should seem inevitable to the reader.

This arrangement goes on almost simultaneously with the selection of characters which fit the plot—that is, characters who might logically be expected to shape and, by their words and action, develop the plot. Sometimes a writer makes a mistake in selecting these characters, with the result that somewhere in the writing he discovers that some particular character is not at all necessary: he is a fifth wheel and has nothing at all to do with the story. When this happens there is nothing to do but rewrite and eliminate this extraneous character.

The plot of a story is likened by Mrs. Eberhart to the track and the stations of a railroad which you, the writer, build. The stations are a series of events or scenes while the track is the logic of cause and effect linking them together. Plotting is choosing the stations and time schedule—in other words, the kinds of events and where and how they take place. And finally, when all this is arranged, the writing is *you*, piloting the train along the prepared route.

Max Shulman says:

A plot is simply this: a problem and a solution. Be sure your people are in a real problem. Be sure the solution is plausible. What you're after in popular fiction is not truth but plausibility. Motivate carefully. Make each event in your story an inevitable outgrowth of preceding events.

One of the first questions in plotting is how to choose the events, occurrences or scenes that take the story from one point to another until the final outcome. Given the same situation to work with, it's safe to say that no two writers would ever strike upon precisely the same plot sequence. This is where the individual writer's imagination, memory and associations come into play. There are, however, ways to guide you in developing plot, to stimulate your ideas and to establish in your mind the habits of story-reasoning that will help throughout your work.

To illustrate, let's go back for a moment to the nature of situation. In situation, you'll recall, are all the facts necessary for a reader to know what is happening *now* to *someone*. And in the Lesson on character, you'll remember that the main character should have basic traits. Also there must be a problem, conflict or crisis which this character confronts and resolves.

Your first guide to a choice of event, therefore, is the way your main character might react to a problem. Here's an example:

A proud Englishwoman is told that her title and properties don't belong to her. There's been a mistake of birthright; actually she is the daughter of uneducated working people. This news is delivered to her by a group of lawyers in the library of her country estate.

Where does the story go from this initial point? Although the writer has a free choice of events, there's a guideline in the fact that the woman is inordinately *proud*. What are some of the reactions this basic trait might produce?

Perhaps she'd refuse to accept the facts and put up a fight for her position. Perhaps she'd be so shocked she would have a nervous breakdown. Or perhaps she'd snatch all the valuables and cash available, change her name, and start all over again in another country. Any one of these reactions could create a scene for the writer. The outcome of this scene would then suggest another plot development from the woman's character.

Also, the way her story is to end will influence the author's choice. If he wants her humbled and defeated, he'll choose her fighting reactions. If he wants her to emerge victorious, he'll have her humiliated in the beginning. But if he wants a satisfied reader, he'll choose events she couldn't foresee because of her blinding pride. Thus, with beginning and end planned, the situation has been taken on, the plot is under way, something has "happened next."

In proceeding from the situation to the first outcome, this story has started to take shape and thus doesn't leave the writer groping in a creative fog. For now he has an outcome to build from. This outcome is the equivalent of another situation, offering a new set of circumstances to be met by the main character —a new problem (or *complication* as some professional writers call it) which makes the reader keep asking: "What will happen now? How will the character get out of this dilemma?"

If a writer wants sympathy for a character, Bergen Evans points out, he shows the character pitting himself against odds. Soon the odds become overwhelming, the character is seemingly defeated, and then, through his own efforts, comes through to a satisfactory resolution. If the writer wants to vanquish his main character he reverses this procedure, has the character seem to win by means of unsympathetic actions, then produces a twist of fate to cut him down at the end.

Naturally, there are infinite ways to finish a story, but an advance decision about the end is a firm step in planning. And in order to create endings successfully, the writer should be able to plot automatically, taking any given idea to a plausible and interesting conclusion.

To show you plotting in action, we have reprinted D. D. Beauchamp's story "The Best Year" below, as it appeared in *Good Housekeeping* magazine. Here again we have inserted our guiding comments between sections of the story.

I

It was the way he always had known it would be. Perhaps he had not actually known it, because it never had been a conscious thought in his mind; but it was a nameless fear that he had lived with for four years, and that became a reality when his father returned from town that morning.

"Millikan's pressing me for the interest on that mortgage," his father said. He stood in the doorway, a gaunt, work-hardened man, thumbing tobacco into the bowl of his pipe and not looking at Ben. Then he went on: "I saw a notice in the county agent's office—seems the Army's lookin' for horses. Some of the Army men will be over at the Coombs' place next Wednesday, ready to buy." He did not say more than that, but he had compressed as much meaning into those few words as though he had made a speech.

We can't know how this story occurred to the author or how the opening situation was decided upon. But once the situation is fully stated, we can see how plot was guided to development.

What are the circumstances that set the story in motion? A country boy, living on a poverty-stricken farm, must sell his beloved horse to help his father pay off the mortgage. We know that the boy has dreaded this for years.

What will happen next? Turning to the boy's basic trait—love for his horse—what's the most likely reaction to the father's subtle ultimatum? The author doesn't have to reach far for the first step in his plot.

II

Ben didn't answer him. He got up from his chair and left the house, to stand for a moment on the back step, staring at the littered yard, the sagging roof of the barn, and the barren fields, which bespoke their own poverty. After a while he moved on down to the pole fence at the edge of the pasture and hooked his elbows over the top rail. Leaning there, he put two fingers to his mouth and whistled.

The answering nicker came from the clump of scrub willow by the creek, and then the horse came in sight, moving at a sharp, effortless trot, his ears up and his tail streaming. It was something Ben couldn't put into words, but the sight of it made him hurt someplace inside. He reached out and tugged at the horse's ears in a sudden, fierce gesture of affection.

"I've had you for four years," he said. "I reckon that's all I was meant to have you."

He climbed through the fence, then, and let his feet take him down the rocky slope, with the horse following him like a dog, until, behind the knoll and out of sight of the house, he lay face down and wept unashamedly into the grass.

It was more than just the selling of a horse. It was a part of his being. In those four years of caring for the horse, breaking and gentling and training, he had imparted something of himself and had taken something in return. It was that much of his life. It had been the source of the only pride he ever had known, and was the only outlet for his affection on that sun-baked farm where all affection had long since disappeared in hard work and poverty.

He could remember clearly when it had begun, in that spring when he was twelve, and the day after the old mare had dropped her foal. He had felt a fierce joy of ownership, and a warm upsurge of tenderness toward the only pet he ever had had. He had laughed secretly at the knob-kneed ungainliness of the colt, as it walked, stilt-legged and unsure of itself, and he had named it.

"You're not white," Ben said, "but I liked that name in the history books, and when you grow up you'll travel some. Your name is Traveler."

He had been repeating the name, with the vision of the colt grown into a horse in his mind, and then he had become aware of the shadow on the ground. He had looked up to see his father, standing unmoved and unmoving.

"I reckon I have to say he's yours," his father had said, "seeing you took the mare in payment for work you done yourself, and seeing you paid the stud fee, but it's time you got over these fancy ideas of yours." He had reached down to pluck a weed, and chewed the stalk in a long moment of contemplation. "Fine horses," he had continued, "ain't for the likes of you and me. I'm a poor man, and nothing can eat off this ground that ain't paid for or that can't earn its keep."

"He'll earn it," Ben had said.

"You can't hitch a race horse to a plow," his father had replied, and turned away.

"I'll pay for him," Ben had said.

He had watched the uncompromising stiffness of his father's back as he had walked across the field. Then he had watched the colt lie down, folding up suddenly at the knees like a jackknife and stretching out on its side while the old mare nuzzled it in worried inquiry. Ben had moved over and taken its head in his lap. He had sat there, gently rocking, with his arms locked in a protective embrace around its neck.

"Don't you worry," he had said. "I'll pay. I'll pay it some way."

But the record of his failure was still there, in the dog-eared notebook on the kitchen shelf, carefully totaled up in his father's scrawling hand. The fixed charge for summer pasturage, the amounts and costs of the hay and the grain and the salt, each entry dated, and the account subtotaled monthly.

The occasional entries of cash paid on account were the only record of how hard he had tried. For his work on the farm he got only his clothing and his board and room, and that work took up most of his time. Sundays he was free, but other farmers didn't work on Sundays and there wasn't much demand for a hand. During the winter he laid out a trap line for muskrats and ran it after dark, trudging the two-mile length of it through the snow and cold and carrying a lantern; but the money he made did little more than pay for his traps and for the kerosene he burned.

Since that first day in the pasture, his father never had mentioned it directly; but frequently the notebook lay open on the table as a mute reminder of what he owed; and in the end it had turned out the way he had known it would, with the amount grown, so that the only way on earth he could square the account was by selling.

It took his father four years to ask for it, Ben thought, but now he'd done it. He turned over on his back, lay staring up at the pale washed blue of the sky. "I reckon the only way I could get out of it would be to saddle up and light out for someplace."

He wouldn't do that, though, and he knew it. It was a debt he had contracted in honor, and he'd pay it the only way he could.

Feeling as heartbroken as he does, it's natural that the boy should find a place to weep unashamedly. And here, he thinks about all the horse has meant to him. The author chooses the flashback technique to tell the reader the past history of the boy and the animal. Once more, given the facts that lead to a fuller understanding of the boy's problem, the story moves on, impelled by the clear statement, "the only way on earth he could square the account was by selling," and by his second trait, honor, which precludes his alternative: "I reckon the only way I could get out of it would be to saddle up and light out for some place."

Note that the author characterizes father and son as he goes along, keeps the setting in view for the reader, and points up theme or meaning.

III

The sale was well under way when he got there. He had topped the last low rise and had come in sight of the ranch buildings sprawled in the valley below him. It looked like a crowd at a Sunday rodeo. Dust lay like fog over the corrals, from the nervous milling of the horses. The rigs were ranked on the flat between the house and the pasture, and the moving figures of men made a restless pattern along the fence.

Ben pulled the horse in and sat for a moment, just looking. For the past two hours he had been content to jog easily, postponing as long as possible the moment of his arrival. The time was running out fast now, and he felt again the lump rising in his throat, and the tight, congested feeling in his chest. Presently he touched his heels to the horse and moved on down the slope and across the floor of the valley.

The men at the fence paid little attention to him when he came up. He was just a tall kid, dressed in sun-bleached shirt and patched overalls, riding a big horse, with a tattered blanket strapped on it for a saddle and a rope hackamore on its nose. The men who noticed him at all looked chiefly at the horse.

Glancing at the rank of buggies, he saw his father's buckboard and the team hitched to a corral post, and his mouth twisted. I might have known he wouldn't trust me, he thought. He had to drive over here to make sure I went through with it.

Looking more closely now at the men grouped along the fence, he saw his father, standing apart, dressed in the rusty black suit he wore on special occasions, with the hard-crowned hat pulled low over his eyes. He glanced at Ben briefly and then turned his gaze toward the pasture.

The horse slowed to a walk, and Eli Coombs strolled across the dusty ground from the corrals. The old mare had been his originally, given to Ben in exchange for the boy's time digging potatoes, and Coombs also owned the stallion that had sired the colt. He looked at the big horse appraisingly, remembering as he did so the ragged youngster who had stood in this same yard five years ago, trying to keep the eagerness out of his voice while he said, "Mr. Coombs, you got an old mare in the pasture. If she ain't worth more'n three or four dollars, I figured I might take her instead of wages."

"He turned out good, didn't he, Ben?" Eli Coombs said now. He made a slow circle around the horse. "I never figured that old mare would drop a colt like this, even if she did have good blood. Looks like you might have outtraded me."

"I reckon I know by now you almost gave her to me," Ben said.

The rancher squinted at him, his eyes alert and kind in his leathery face.

"I don't guess I could have almost given her to anybody better," he said. "You come over to see the sale?"

"I come over to sell."

Eli said, "So?" in a soft, drawn-out voice, but he nodded without asking questions. One look at the boy's face and there was no need for questions.

When he spoke again, his voice was carefully casual. "We all have to do things now and then that we don't like, Ben. You can turn him in the corral while you're waiting, if you want."

Ben dismounted and unstrapped the blanket. Dust had caked in the sweat around the edges of it, and he wiped the dirt off with a handful of grass and turned Traveler into the corral.

Afterward, he kept to himself. There was shade under the lean-to where the tackle was kept, and a cool breeze was moving up from the creek.

He stretched out on the ground with his head on a saddle, staring upward at a shaft of sunlight coming through a knothole in the roof, keeping his mind blank.

He was still lying there when Eli Coombs called him. The sun had moved directly overhead. The intensity of its light burned Ben's eyes after the shade, and the heat came against him in a smothering wave. There was a raw spot on his heel from a wrinkled sock, and he limped slightly going toward the corral. He opened the gate and whistled, and Traveler came out, to follow at his shoulder, out into the pasture where a colonel and a captain of the Army waited for him.

The boy dearly loves his horse, but must now sell him. Since he has no alternative, the second step of the plot leads logically to the inevitable sale. The author might have written more scenes in between, but perhaps keeping the single effect in mind he carefully selected the next action to help move his story along.

This scene is set by having the boy pause as he gets to the "last low rise" and view the details below. We learn again how hard this decision is for him. The author visualizes how the boy looked as he rode up to the men, and shows the reader that the father is there to make sure the boy doesn't change his mind. This points out that the father doesn't really understand how much the horse means to the boy, and adds to the theme of the story which the plot is illustrating.

Once more, the author employs flashback to show how the horse came to be in the boy's possession. The man, Eli Coombs, tries to comfort him. Eli understands, but cannot help to solve the problem.

IV

The colonel took his hat off and wiped his face with a red bandana. He looked hot, but cheerful. "Your horse, son?"

"Yessir."

"What's his name?"

"Traveler."

The colonel smiled. "Good military precedent," he said. "Is he gentle?"

"Yessir," Ben said, and then something inside him broke. "I had him four years, ever since he was a colt, and I broke and gentled him and trained him. He's the best horse—" His voice went out of control. He broke off abruptly, with the color mounting in his face, ashamed of his outburst. His feelings were his own private property, and he preferred keeping them to himself; but his voice had given him away. The colonel, understanding some part of it from the blank, set anguish on the boy's face and recalling his own youth, which was not too recent, and the few things that had been precious then, thought, It's a devil of a note if the Army can't function without buying somebody's pet.

Liking horses—that was a sentiment the colonel could allow himself. He walked around the horse with a studious deliberation, and when he passed Ben, he said softly so that no one else could hear, "If I tried hard, son, I could probably find something wrong with him."

Ben's heart jumped. For just a minute he felt a sudden upsurge of hope, and then it died. He couldn't do it, not honestly, because he knew the cavalry specifications and he knew his horse. He rubbed his nose on a dirty shirt sleeve. "I can't keep him anyway," he said, "not the way he ought to be kept. There's a board bill against him already."

"I see," the colonel said. Then he said: "What's your name, son?"

"Ben. Ben Risteen."

"All right, Ben," the colonel said. He went on with his inspection, impersonal now, doing the job he was supposed to do. He looked at the horse's mouth and measured his height. "Four years old. Fifteen, one."

The captain was squatting in the dust, with a notebook open on one knee, taking down the description.

"Two stockings, both fores. Feet sound, soles intact and properly shod."

The captain went on writing.

"Saddle him up, Ben," the colonel said. "Trot him a little and then run him." He stared at the ragged blanket and the hackamore, understanding then a little more of what he had vaguely understood before, feeling helpless and enraged for a moment at some circumstance that had no relation to him, except through the sight of the boy and the horse. "Dammit," he said.

The captain put the pencil behind his ear. "Did you say something?"

"I said 'dammit,' " the colonel said. "Put it down if you want to."

He stood there while Ben took the horse along the fence at a trot, across the pasture at a long, easy gallop, and brought him back with his belly close to the ground, stretched out in a hard, driving run. The horse pulled up, blowing the dust from his nostrils and panting.

The colonel moved over to his head. "Wind sound."

The captain wrote it down and got up from his crouching position, stretching his cramped legs. The three of them walked back, with Traveler following, toward the cars.

"He's a good horse, Ben," the colonel said. "Would you say a hundred and seventy-five was a fair price?"

There's no price I could think of in money, Ben thought. There are some things you can't buy. He nodded his head.

There was a folding shelf attached to the government wagon, and on it the captain wrote out the bill of sale, with the description and specifications copied from the notebook. Ben read it. On the back it said, "I hereby swear that I am the owner of the horse described on the reverse side, and have this day sold same to the United States Government."

It made it pretty final, Ben thought. He leaned against the wagon, feeling the heat of the wood through his shirt, staring out over the colonel's shoulder at the figure of his father, still standing alone, in the black suit and hard-crowned hat.

"The check will be sent on delivery at the nearest railroad shipping point," the colonel said.

Eli Coombs had come up, to stand with one foot propped on the left front wheel of the wagon. He said, "I'm taking mine down tomorrow, Ben. I can take yours if you want."

One more day, Ben thought. It was a temptation, but it was no good and he knew it. He had his mind made up. The job was done now, and another day would only make it that much worse. He said, "All right, Mr. Coombs."

The captain handed him a pen and ink, and he signed the bill of sale.

Nobody walked with him when he took Traveler back toward the barn. Ben stripped off the blanket and the hackamore, turned him into the corral, slapping him on the rump as he went by, and closed the gate.

When he went away, he heard the low, worried nicker behind him, but he didn't look around.

This sequence also follows logically the process of the actual transaction. The author's use of more kindness emphasizes the boy's dilemma. The hovering figure of the father symbolizes a fate too big to be overcome. The boy goes through with the sale. Although he's offered a delay in parting with the horse, he realizes the futility and lets the animal go.

Now what comes next in plot? What will the boy do now? What will the father's behavior be? He will pay the mortgage and the boy will be bereft. To be guided in the forward motion of the story, keep in mind the boy's basic trait—love of his horse. And also remember that he has honor and pride as other basic traits of his character.

V

The colonel, captain, and Eli Coombs passed him on their way back to the pasture. Ben didn't see them. He was walking with his head down, kicking his boots into the dirt. He stumbled once, the ground only a blurred vision through his tears, and then he walked on, head down, the blanket and the hackamore trailing in the dust.

He had gone beyond the row of wagons, striding blindly through the heat, when he became aware of someone walking beside him.

His father's voice said, "If you're going home, you might as well ride along with me. I got the team here."

Ben came around on his heels with quick anger flooding through him. "I sold him. He won't eat your grass and your grain any longer. That's what you wanted, wasn't it?"

His father stood there unmoving, his voice heavy and patient. "You got to get home some way."

"Yes," Ben said. "I got to get home some way."

The anger had gone as quickly as it had come. Being mad wouldn't get his horse back, and that was the only thing that mattered. He hesitated for a moment and then turned toward the buckboard.

They drove silently for the better part of the trip. His father made a few efforts at conversation, but Ben didn't want to talk. He sat bent forward on the seat, unmindful of the sun and dust, while he thought about it.

He could always pull out, of course. He was sixteen years old and his own man. Whatever obligation he had ever owed his father had long since been squared up in unpaid labor. His mother had been dead for so long that he scarcely remembered her, and, with his horse gone now, there was nothing holding him.

They had left the country road now and turned into their own rutted lane. As the house and barn came into view, his father tried once again.

"I saw you over at Coombs'," he said. "I reckon I know you feel bad about selling your horse." Ben didn't answer.

The man sat hunched over on the seat, groping for words to express some thought that wasn't entirely clear even to himself. "It's something you got to learn," he said. "Some folks are meant to have fine things, and some ain't. People like you and me wasn't made to have luxuries, and that's what a fine horse is. Some day you got to learn it. It might as well be now."

Ben turned his head. It occurred to him that his father was offering him as much sympathy as he was capable of, and that surprised him.

But it was something he hadn't asked for and didn't want. The buckboard rattled into the yard and stopped. Getting down from it, Ben thought, Tomorrow. I'll just pack up and get out. There isn't anything left for me around here.

The horse gone, Ben starts to walk home, a natural action. The author reveals the boy's broken emotions by having the colonel and Eli Coombs pass him without the boy's awareness. And now the author chooses another logical move. The father, too, must go home. It would be reasonable to assume that he had taken the team and would offer the boy a ride. The boy is angry, which is natural. But then he gets over his anger because he realizes "this wouldn't get the horse back."

He looks at his future—it is bleak. He reasons that he could pull out now and leave home, the debt to his father squared. Meanwhile, the father has begun to understand how deeply the loss of the horse has affected his son, and attempts to explain his philosophy to the boy. The boy knows that his father means well, but he doesn't want sympathy now. He decides he'll leave the farm tomorrow.

The author ends this part with the boy's decision. It's a new situation, and the reader once more will look to an outcome. Will the boy go, what will the father do if he does go? The plot moves on without pause, one action leading to the next.

VI

He had his mind made up, but that was as far as it had gone. Lying awake at night and planning it, it seemed free and easy, but that was only the way it seemed. The farm, that one hundred and sixty acres of ground, was all he knew. He had been born on it and raised on it, and he had lived all his life within a twenty-mile radius of it. Anything beyond that was foreign to him, and whether he liked to admit it or not, the prospect of leaving, of packing up once and for all and getting out, scared him to death.

So the days went by, and he had lots of time to think. He still had his work to do, but the days were long, and after the chores were done, the time was heavy on his hands.

The companionship was what he missed more than anything. He never had been close to his father, and since that day of the horse sale the breach between them was wider than before. The bitterness Ben felt was like a wall separating their lives completely.

The sight of the check kept it fresh in his mind. It had lain for weeks now, untouched, on the kitchen table, as a constant reminder of his loss. His father had mentioned it once, at breakfast the day he had brought it in from the mailbox.

"I been thinking," he said. "It was your horse and it's your money. I reckon I can get along some way without it."

Ben got up from the table. "I never asked for the money," he said. "I ain't askin' for it now. You was the one who wanted it." He turned blindly toward the door. He did not see the look of bewilderment on his father's face. He wouldn't have understood it if he had seen it.

Facing the reality of leaving the only home he knows, the boy is scared. He decides not to run away. This is both logical and plausible. What, then, are his days to be like? "The companionship was what he missed more than anything. He never had been close to his father, and since that day of the horse sale the breach between them was wider than before. The bitterness Ben felt was like a wall separating their lives completely . . . *The sight of the check kept it fresh in his mind.*"

This last line may seem an arbitrary thought of the author's, but if you examine the course of events you'll see that they guided him to it quite naturally. The father is not a mean man, as we have been shown, but has become confused by the depth of his son's feelings.

His first effort to put things right is to offer the money to the boy, who refuses it.

The boy is hurt and contemptuous, and the father is further bewildered.

But where does this leave the story? Two lonely people unable to communicate with each other, living out their lives in grim poverty and work. How will the author plot this story to its logical end?

He could leave the characters as they are, but this would be unsatisfactory to the reader. In real life, perhaps this condition could exist for years unchanged. But the story is fiction. The creator of a story must select and bring together events leading to some conclusion of the situation that made a foundation for the story in the first place.

What, then, can this author do with his lonely boy that will be both believable and conclusive? Once more, keep in mind the boy's basic trait, and see how it helps the author to narrow the possibilities.

VII

On the day the envelope disappeared from the table, Ben considered that his victory was won. The night before, it had lain in its accustomed place. In the morning, when he went down to breakfast, it was gone. Ben didn't mention it, but on that day the debt he had contracted had been paid in full, and there was savage satisfaction in that thought.

I guess he knows now, Ben thought. I never would have taken it. He got up from the table and shouldered into his coat. He didn't look at his father or speak to him. He opened the door and stepped out.

It was late in the afternoon when he returned, walking across the field from the wood lot through the fast-settling winter twilight, with his shoulders hunched against the wind. There was no light in the house and no smoke was coming from the chimney. On the way past the barn he noticed that the buckboard was gone, but he paid no attention. He had ceased to pay attention to his father's comings and goings.

He entered the house, lighted the lamp on the kitchen table, and kindled a fire in the stove. He had just finished filling the wood box when he heard the wagon rattle into the yard.

A few moments later the back door opened, and his father's voice said, "Come here a minute, Ben."

He put his coat on without answering and went outside. It was dark by then, and the wind was high and sharp. His father was walking toward the barn, carrying a lantern, the shadows of his legs slashing across the light. Ben followed him.

It was warm inside, out of the wind, and Ben's heels sounded loud and hollow on the plank flooring.

He walked on back, following the light, to the end stall, and then stopped dead, staring.

The colt stared back at him, its head poked inquisitively over the top of the stall door, its ears pointed.

Ben came around on his heels, and his father said, "He's yours, boy. I bought him for you. Him and the mare that foaled him."

The outrage of it showed in Ben's face. He didn't see it as an act of kindness. He saw it only as an effort to thwart him, to take away the bitter triumph he had felt in refusing to take the money. As though any horse, any horse at all, could replace Traveler.

He had opened his mouth to speak when he felt the soft, inquiring muzzle at his neck, and the gentle blowing. And then he turned suddenly, to fumble at the latch of the stall and bury his face in the colt's coarse mane.

He never knew how long he stood that way. But after a while he became aware of his father's voice, tired and regretful, as though he were talking to himself.

"I reckon I never rightly knew how much he meant," the man said. "But even a grown man has to learn. You have something, and you work and care for it, and you lose it through no fault of your own. I lost your mother that way, boy. But I was wrong. You can't quit livin'. And if you go on livin', you got to have something to live for. You got to have something."

Ben looked up then, and for the first time in his life he saw his father for what he truly was. He saw him not as essentially unkind, but as a man who had been utterly and completely defeated by a loss. He did not have anything, and he never hoped to have anything. He had gone beyond resentment and bitterness into a state of passive resignation, in which he denied himself even the right to have anything.

No man ought to be like that, Ben thought. It don't hurt to want fine things.

And suddenly he knew what Traveler had meant to him. The horse had been the one proud thing in his life that had stood between him and his drab existence, not irreplaceable, but more as a symbol of all the things on earth a man could want and live for. And his father was right. A man had to have something. With that realization, all the bitterness he had ever felt was gone, like a ground fog going when the sun comes up.

The idea came to him then. He felt his heart jumping, and there was a new eagerness in his voice.

"Maybe," Ben said, "maybe we could raise 'em. We got the mare and the colt. It ain't much, but it's a start."

The older man turned his head, and some of the tiredness had gone out of his eyes. "Yes," he said, "it's a start." He lifted the lantern down from its peg and smiled uncertainly. "You ain't had your supper yet, son. That colt'll keep till morning."

Ben followed him out. He closed and latched the door behind them, and for a moment they stood uncertainly in the light from the lantern, staring out into the darkness.

His father cleared his throat. "We could grow hay on that land along the creek. If next year's a good year—"

"Yes," Ben said. He stood there, conscious of the sudden awkward pressure of his father's arm around his shoulders.

"It'll be a good year," Ben said, and he knew that was true. No matter what happened, it would be a good year. It would be the best year he ever had known.

It would be an almost inhuman father who could see his son's suffering and coldness without attempting to overcome them. This father is not inhuman, merely hardened by work and poverty.

How can he best bring the boy back and make up to him the terrible loss of the horse?

The author has the father act compassionately, within the limits of his character. He spends part of the money on a mare and her colt.

What would be the boy's natural reactions to this sudden and unexpected act? His first reaction would be outrage over the fact that his beloved Traveler could never be replaced. But the author, steered by the boy's hunger for love, has him won over by the "soft, inquiring muzzle at his neck, and the gentle blowing."

And now, logically and credibly, the author has evolved a change of attitude where it was needed—in the father.

The inarticulate father expresses his feelings humbly, fumblingly. And this leads the boy to a further understanding of himself. The theme of the story is brought into final focus. "And suddenly he knew what Traveler had meant to him. The horse had been the one proud thing in his life that had stood between him and his drab existence, not irreplaceable, but more as a symbol of all the things on earth a man could want and live for. And his father was right. A man had to have something. With that realization, all the bitterness he had ever felt was gone, like a ground fog when the sun comes up."

Note that this is no sudden, convenient change in a character just to make things come out right. The author has used the cause and effect of human nature and circumstance.

The possibility of future improvement in the family's status arises from the boy's plan for the horses, and is a hopeful and happy note, but doesn't diverge from the logic of the story.

As Somerset Maugham says:

The story an author has to tell should be coherent and persuasive; it should have a beginning, a middle and an end, and the end should be the natural consequence of the beginning. The episodes should have probability and should not only develop the theme, but grow out of the story. The creatures of the author's invention should be observed with individuality, and their actions should proceed from their characters; the reader must never be allowed to say: "So and so would never behave like that"; on the contrary, he should be obliged to say: "That's exactly how I should have expected so and so to behave."

In "The Best Year," you have seen how this author achieved his end successfully.

An author analyzes her own story

Now, having been merely an onlooker to one author's plotting, let's examine another short story with closer knowledge. The conception of the idea and the developing of the plot are told by the author herself. "Sheer Enchantment," which appeared in *McCall's,* was written by Faith Baldwin. She'll tell you how she came to write the story, how she evolved the plot, how she used her memory, associations and experiences to construct a complete piece of fiction. But first, read the story all the way through without thought of plot.

For the last week of their trip, Alan and Janey flew from one enchanted island to another. The final one was, as the others, surrounded by a sea of creaming surf, colored in aquamarine and peacock blues. It was a little different, as islands differ, as people do.

This one had a tradition of sailing ships and pirates, legends and many races, lassitude, warm golden sun and a trade wind blowing steadily.

They were not at one of the big hotels but in a guest house, high above the water with steep crooked steps down to a curve of beach, white and gentle as a beautiful woman's arm, and owned by a man who was called variously an eccentric and a character.

Alan's boss had told him about Old Doc. He said, "That's one place you *must* go. Lou and I spent our honeymoon there a decade ago. I tell you, he's marvelous. So is the guest house, the beach and, unless something hideous has happened, his cook. Suppose I write and tell him you'll be there . . . ?"

Old Doc had a name though most people had forgotten it. None knew how old he was . . . seventy, they said. But he'd been on the island for thirty years, and knew more about it than practically anyone. None remembered why he'd come there and bought the big house which either he, or a predecessor, had named "Sheer Enchantment," living in it alone for a time, immersed in his collections, his studies of the sea and shore, shells and corals, and writing his scholarly books. Then he remodelled the house and began to have guests; honeymoon couples, retired folk, elderly people on holiday. None knew how the word got about that Old Doc had a few rooms and baths at reasonable prices he'd rent to people of whom he must approve, offering a fabulous cook, a fishing boat moored to a little dock with a competent fisherman skipper in charge . . . and the beach. He never advertised nor did the travel people know of him commercially. Now and then one said, "Of course if you know anyone who knows Old Doc . . . "

Guests came—by word of mouth recommendation. So now Alan and Janey came, too. But with reluctance; not because it was the final week of the trip but because something had gone wrong. They were twenty-six and twenty-four. He was big, spare, and his eyes were an altering sea blue, his hair was like the golden sands; while Janey was little, dark and quick. She had stopped working when she married Alan, having worked since college in a charity foundation. But Alan's salary was good, he had a small inheritance and the house in Westchester was waiting for them, furnished with love and wedding presents, now overseen by her mother and his—who happened to be good friends.

What had been wrong?

Janey sat at the family table on the screened porch and looked at Old Doc. He was tall and thin. His eyes were hazel and he wore a pointed white beard which cloaked his expression. He was as brown as good toast. He stood as straight as a drink. He had a deep youthful voice. And, mostly, he twinkled.

Janey watched Alan, making conversation. They were the only guests which didn't seem to disturb Old Doc at all. Alan was, she thought, with a turning-over heart, almost too good-looking.

They'd put the best foot forward in the square dance of meeting and during their engagement. They'd adjusted to the waiting period . . . three months. They'd told each other how simple it would be to adjust to marriage. It hadn't been simple, however much in love, for even the best foot forward can show the touch of clay after a week, or two or three.

For instance . . . a spendthrift.

He'd saved for this trip, even before he met her. "I knew that some day I'd find the one and only, so I saved . . . even went without a little, thinking some day I'll take her on the most wonderful honeymoon ever . . ."

She'd saved too; the hope chest brimmed over; for some day she would meet the one and only, and there would be fine linens, gossamer chiffons and all the things a girl dreams about . . .

Now she spoke to Old Doc and Alan listened and looked at his wife. She was very small, with wonderful eyes and sleeked back hair in a pony tail; he could span her waist with his big brown hands. She was honey and dew, she was fire and moonlight, she was quicksilver . . .

But last week was all wrong. It had begun the night he ran into the girl now married to someone with 'steen million dollars, cuffed, girdled and necklaced in diamonds and pearls. So, suddenly, it was a big party on a patio with Alan, brooking no argument, picking up the tab. There went most of the honeymoon dollars except for the last island and (already paid for) the plane tickets home. But he had to show off, just because this blonde creature with whom he'd had traffic in his college days had turned him down for half the money in the world.

Janey thought, if only he hadn't met her! She thought, how dare he spend our money buying food and drink for that artificial creature with her frappéd voice, her diamonds and her Paunch and Judy husband! That was her name: Judy.

It had gone wrong, thought Alan, because Janey wasn't a one-man woman after all; and if you aren't a one-man woman on your honeymoon, Brother, that spells trouble. The Englishman had looked at her, in the way only Englishmen have . . . remote, cool and yet somehow intimate. How he had managed the introduction, Alan couldn't remember, but manage it he had, so he and Janey had danced together, not at all cool nor remote, most of the evening.

Which made Alan feel absurd as well as resentful. How could you exhibit your beautiful little wife to the erstwhile girl who had haunted your senior dreams, if said wife was floating off in the arms of some ha'penny Britisher under the semitropical stars?

Somehow that started it, and all week things had been difficult, the communication so disrupted that they talked, as ordinary people do, just in words.

Old Doc looked from one to the other and said mildly that for their last day on the island, he had planned a beach picnic and perhaps he could time it so the rock pools would be full . . . and perhaps a sailing ship would slide across the water close to the horizon and when night fell and the great stars glittered there'd be a new moon. Perhaps, also, they wouldn't mind if he went along?

They assured him they'd love it! Gratitude and relief were like bells in their voices, Alan's deep and hers husky. For tomorrow was the last day and they dreaded it.

So when it came noon and the sun was high and the trade wind rustled the dry leaves of the palms, they went to the beach the long steep way, and Doc's houseboys carried the baskets and there was a black rock rising from the creaming sea, fissured with time, eroded by blowing sand. In its lee the basket, with the cool fruits and salads, the langouste sandwiches, the thermoses of hot and cold things to drink . . .

So they swam and Old Doc with them; he surprisingly tireless, letting the gentle waves rock, enfold, carry him out, and bring him back.

He said, "I always nap after lunch." So he went off where the sheer hill edged the sand and there was twisted green shade, lay down on a mattress, pulled his straw hat over his eyes, wrapped himself in a robe, and slept.

Alan and Janey were not sleepy. They sat for a time and Janey said, "Put your robe on; you'll burn." She forgot to say "darling" or maybe she didn't but couldn't. So Alan said shortly that he certainly wouldn't burn now. After a while there was nothing left to say, and they went walking idly and silently and looked for shells. But there were very few. They saw antler coral in a patch in the water; a wonderful brown under water, a wonderful lavender when you took it out, at the base; and presently Alan went poking around the big rock with a stick he had picked up.

He took his find to Old Doc . . . it was wedged in the rock, black with age, but metal; it was a coin. And Doc opened his eyes and said, "What's that?"

Janey trailed along, not caring. She hated the sun and wind and water, and the curving tender arm of the beach. She wanted snow and winter. Hers was a winter mood. She wanted to be dead at twenty-four, because when Alan looked at her no sudden spark entered her heart through her answering eyes . . .

And Alan thought, so it's a coin or something and I wish I were back at a desk and going out on a double date, not caring because when Janey looked at him, no sudden spark entered his heart through his answering eyes, and a man's a fool to marry.

The coin was as black as doom. Old Doc looked at it closely, turning it over in his hands. He took from the pocket of his robe a little knife and scraped at the blackness, and something glinted through.

He said, "Pirate gold. It's a doubloon, my boy. Where'd you find it?"

Alan said as Janey drew a sharp excited breath, "Wedged in the rock, sir."

"They dig and dig," said Old Doc, "sometimes they turn up something worth-while; mostly, however, not. Now and then a coin like this washes up and out from God knows where, and comes to rest." He gave it back. He said, "Keep it for luck, you and your wife . . ."

Alan said, "Yes, sir" . . . and then, "is it worth anything?"

"Depends," said Old Doc. "I think it's worth a lot. It's a coin, isn't it? What are you supposed to do with coins? Spend, share, give them. This is like life itself. No matter how dark, or tarnished, life's still a gold coin . . . pure gold," he said, "of the spirit; and of love, like yours and your Janey's."

He smiled a little. He said, "I had a young wife once; she left me long ago . . . I didn't know how to spend the coin nor share nor give it; perhaps she didn't know either . . . I know now, but it's getting very late."

He touched the coin in Alan's hand. He said, "Don't hoard it . . . ever."

He watched them walk up the beach. He saw Alan's arm reach out, and over Janey's shoulder. He saw them disappear around the curve. They would stop there and kiss, and cling to one another.

He had heard them quarreling, almost every night, not loudly but as if hopelessly. He had heard her weep and Alan swear. Tomorrow the bright wings of the plane would carry them home, and they would keep the coin forever.

He put his hand in the pocket of his robe. There was a coin there, there were many in the collection, not of great intrinsic value but often valuable beyond price. He walked to the black rock and wedged the corroded coin in the fissure. Next week or month or year someone would find it, someone who needed it; a couple, perhaps, young and beginning to adjust, frightened by the first little chasm between them; or one on the point of disaster.

Doctor Enoch Fellows, Ph.D., walked away from the black rock, back to the blanket in the sand. He could hear them laughing around the bend. Laughter was like clear sun, like warmed water pouring out, washing away the little accumulations of misunderstanding . . .

Sometimes he wondered why he had never married.

Now here is Faith Baldwin's explanation of how she conceived and wrote "Sheer Enchantment":

I was visiting the West Indies. One day I went down to a boat-yard and ran into an old friend, a non-fiction writer. She wanted to go sailing in spite of a rain storm so we set out together, under a tarpaulin. There, she told me that she wanted to turn from writing non-fiction to fiction. But she didn't have an idea to start with. I asked her if anything of interest had happened on the island lately.

My friend thought a moment, then said uncertainly: "Well, a honeymoon couple found a Spanish doubloon wedged between some rocks the other day."

"There's your idea!" I said. "For some reason they've come to this island—they've been quarreling, making disturbing discoveries about each other. Then they find this old coin. Every coin has two sides. Call the story 'Two Sides of a Coin'—there's the philosophy, the meaning."

My friend murmured something vaguely.

"If you don't write it," I said, "I will."

And that's where the matter was left.

Some time after I came home, I began thinking about the honeymoon couple on the island and the doubloon, and decided I'd like to make it into a story. I wrote to my friend and asked if she'd used the idea, and if not, could I? She replied, telling me to go ahead—with her best wishes.

I began to think about where the young couple would be staying —about their quarreling—about the fact that the story would have a philosophical resolution. I would have to describe the things they were finding wrong with each other. In order to do this I decided that I would have to know what they were like.

Physically, it was easy enough. I made them a sharply contrasting male and female, and attractive. Then, with the problem in mind, I chose to make him a shade too good-looking, a spendthrift, and not immune to other girls, even at this bridegroom stage. For this purpose, I invented an old sweetheart. I gave the wife a similar impulse to flirt—with an attractive Englishman. The young husband, then, also feels that the marriage is off to a bad start.

Now that I knew the direction the conflict was to take, it seemed that another character would have to enter the story—someone to overhear their quarreling and to help with the philosophy. And I decided that a hotel was too cold an atmosphere, so I combined some groping thoughts and came up with the guest house and an aging philosopher who collected coins.

The setting, of course, was romantic and colorful, and I had only to recall it to get the idea of the beach picnic, with all its atmosphere, and the proper mood for the old man to nap and leave the couple to their own devices.

This led to their walk and the finding of the coin. In order to build up to the final twist of the plot, I decided to keep up their resentment toward each other. Then the old man tells them that the coin is a doubloon. They forget themselves with excitement.

The husband's first question would be: "Is it worth anything?"

Quite logically, now, I had found a place for the theme of the piece. The old Doctor makes a speech, profoundly impressive, about the two sides of a coin. As a result, the couple goes off in a mellower frame of mind.

But this wasn't enough. The story needed something more, a twist of surprise. So I decided that not only had the man planted the coin purposely to bring the couple together, but had invented the whole story about himself.

This was the story line with which I began, plotting whatever else the story needed as I went along, and supplying it with the art of words.

Faith Baldwin has illustrated the fact that she thought the story through before writing and knew where she wanted to go with it. In other words, she planned the steps of her plot, used the initial circumstances of situation to get it going, and then developed the problem and the theme through the characters' main personality traits.

How to move your characters around

Beginning writers tend to spend too much time and space trying to move a character from one place to another, or to account for the passage of time. In the first book I ever wrote, all the people did was go in and out of doors. All you have to do to move a character around is to make a new paragraph and then pick up your narrative. For instance:

"I put on my coat and said goodbye.

"When I arrived in Eastport, I met John walking down the street."

There's a simple example of good transition.—Mignon Eberhart

Lesson sixteen

Fiction writing

course

Writing a short story

Part II

So that you'll understand more fully the importance of *basic trait* to plot, here are three different stories evolving from the same situation:

A young career girl, living alone in a big city, gets a call from a married sister, asking her to take care of the sister's three children for a few days. It means the girl must take a day off from work and spend a long weekend confined with active youngsters.

In the first version, let's see where the situation would lead if we made *ambition* the young girl's basic trait. There are, of course, many possibilities, but here's one example:

Taking the day off would cause her to miss an important conference at which an office promotion might be lost. Therefore she turns down the sister. As a result, the sister and her husband are unable to take a vacation that he urgently needs for his health's sake.

During the conference the girl receives an emergency call—the husband has collapsed. Frantic with conflict, she can't forego her chance of advancement and yet she prays she was not a deciding factor in the husband's collapse. She gets her promotion and the husband recovers, but a young man she loves, who has been trying to judge her character, suddenly gives her up. She is left sitting at a big desk, her sister's feelings changed forever, her romance over, her advancement a hollow reward.

Now in the same situation, let's give the girl the basic trait of being *jealous* of her sister's marriage. She has sold herself on the idea of living alone and liking it, so she turns down the sister's pleas to baby-sit. The husband calls to plead that the sister is near a breakdown. The girl counters by saying the couple should have weighed in advance the penalties of having children.

But when the sister does collapse, the girl is the only person who can take over. Through the sister's sudden claim of dependency and the children's new-found affection for her, the heroine overcomes her jealousy and is a much warmer and kinder person. Soon she captures the attention of a young man and becomes a bride herself.

In a third version, the girl's basic trait is *love* for her sister and the children. Because she wants to help, she is forced to tell her new beau that she is baby-sitting on the night they had planned a dancing date. To her surprise, he offers to go with her to the sister's house and give a helping hand. But she's fearful of the outcome. The children are noisy and active. How can she be glamorous amidst the clutter and complication? Yet she is determined to succeed—if possible.

Now see how this situation and this third trait were actually used in plotting a story called "Michael and the Dragon" by Lois T. Henderson, which appeared in *Woman's Day*.

Two months ago, I was a career girl. Oh, maybe not the highly polished, smoothly suave young thing who earns such a fabulous salary that she can afford white iron furniture and aquamarine velvet cushions even in the bathroom. But I was doing all right. I earned enough to keep me in nylons, and I liked it the way it was. I went to work every morning and put up with Mr. Varner's grouchiness, because underneath he was kind of a nice guy, and I knew it was only his ulcers that made him snarl. And I came home at night to my one-room apartment which maybe didn't have aquamarine cushions, but it was warm in the winter and not too warm in the summer. What's more, it was quiet and private and gave me time to read and do my nails. And I liked it, the whole setup, the job and the apartment and being on my own.

One hot evening in June I was sitting in my room wearing only a halter and some watermelon-colored shorts and feeling fairly sophisticated, if the truth were known. The telephone rang, and I had the arrogance to think, "I wonder what man is calling me now?" As if I had dozens of them panting after me. Don't misunderstand me, I wasn't lonesome exactly, but then I wasn't Marilyn Monroe, either.

Anyhow, it wasn't a man. It was my sister Ruth. Now, Ruth is a nice girl, and I love her. Or at least, I'm very fond of her most of the time. But she is one of these addle-headed females who never knows up from down, and when things get completely beyond her, she comes to me. Oh, I suppose she goes to her husband first, but if he doesn't have any bright suggestions, then it's little Lucy who gets called. So I'm always a trifle wary when I hear her voice.

"Hi." She sounded so friendly that she scared me to death.

"Hi," I answered, trying to sound a million miles away.

"Lucy," Ruth said. She has a husky, soft voice, and you always have the feeling she's going to break down and cry the next minute. "Lucy, I'm in a mess."

"When aren't you ever?" I said ungraciously.

"Oh, no, this is different. I'm not in trouble now, but I will be if you don't help me. I mean, not trouble exactly, but my heart will be broken. Really shattered."

I was familiar with how easily Ruth's heart gets shattered, so I didn't exactly go into convulsions at the prospect.

Her voice hurried on. "Listen, Lucy, Carl has to go out of town on business, and we've decided we can afford for me to go, too, if you'll come and stay with the kids." The last eight words were said all in a blurred rush, like one long word.

"You're mad!" I said flatly.

"Oh, Lucy. They're good kids. They won't be any worry."

"I work, you know," I said, still in a cold tone. Now, don't judge me harshly. It isn't that I don't love Ruth's children. It was simple self-preservation that brought about my reaction.

"We won't leave until Thursday evening, and you'd only have to take off one day. Couldn't you? Just this once? I've never asked you to stay with them before."

Well, that was true. She had only asked me for advice, money, the loan of my best suit and little things like that.

I hesitated, and her voice got huskier and trembled a little. Ruth is older than I am, but I have always been a sucker for the wavering voice bit.

"Please," she said. "Just three days. It would be like a second honeymoon for Carl and me, and we'd never be able to afford to go anywhere if the company weren't paying his way."

This was logical, and Mr. Varner owed me some time off, because of all the extra hours I had put in lately, so that part didn't trouble me too much. It was just that . . . well, Ruth's oldest is seven, a boy, and the girls are five and two. You can see what it would be like. And I was a career girl, not a housewife.

"Please, Lucy," Ruth said, and her words were eloquent with tears.

"Okay, okay," I said. "I'll do it."

After I hung up, cutting short Ruth's tearful thanks, I decided that my mind was softening and I probably needed a long, long rest. I'd need it more, however, after next Sunday night, so there was no use getting worked up about it now. I got a Coke out of the refrigerator and sat cross-legged on the couch to drink it. From that position, I could see the latest picture of Ruth's three, and I frowned at them.

"You'd better be good," I threatened and waved the Coke bottle at them. I sounded very fierce, and I wished Michael, in particular, could hear the fierceness. He is a monster and smarter than any seven-year-old I have ever known, so, as a result, he can think up many things that aren't on the accepted list of Things for Little Boys to Do. The last time he visited me, he built the Sahara Desert on the floor of my tiny kitchenette alcove. Brown sugar made very fine sand, he informed me, when I inadvertently stepped on one of his dunes. This was two weeks ago, and I was still digging brown sugar out of the cracks in the floor.

There was, really, a sort of running feud between Michael and me. I was ahead by a nose. The little girls, Sandy and Lynne, were younger. Not better, just younger. Oh, it promised to be a jolly weekend.

When the phone rang again, I brightened, thinking maybe Ruth had suffered a change of heart and wouldn't be able to leave her darlings, after all. But it was a man. A very special man.

Peter Bartlett was a young architect, with a very good firm and definitely On His Way Up. He was tall and slender, his hair was dark red and his eyes were awfully blue. My plushest daydreams which included sophisticated apartments done in smart decorator shades, dinner for two by candlelight and hi-fi music in the background, always had as the hero of the piece a man who looked exactly like Peter Bartlett. We had gone out together a number of times, and those evenings I had been very smooth and suave and witty because I felt certain Peter liked his girls that way. I had no desire in the world to get married and be a housewife. But to get married and keep on with my job and live in a smart apartment with Peter! Ah, that was something altogether different.

"Hi," Peter said. "How're you?"

"Never better," I said sounding like a phony Britisher. "You?"

"Fine."

We talked, brightly, of several things, and then Peter said, "If you're not busy Saturday night, I thought we might go out. Dinner, dancing. How about it?"

My heart skidded right down into my shoes, except I was barefooted, so it just kind of plopped on the floor. I wondered, for one awful second, if Peter had heard it. A million plans zoomed in and out of my head with the speed of light. I could tell Ruth I was sick, dying, I had leprosy. I could hire a baby sitter for Saturday evening, couldn't I? But my conscience, which also evidently moved with the speed of light, jeeringly commented on my sense of responsibility, and *that* was out. I knew I had to answer Peter, and I didn't know what to say. If I gave a flimsy excuse, he'd probably never ask me again. It was a mess.

I searched in vain for the right, smooth, answer, and then I stammered stupidly, "Gosh, Peter, I'd love to. But I have to . . . baby-sit."

"Oh?" The question was a cool one, and I felt certain it implied I was a moron.

I hurried on sounding less and less like a sophisticate and more and more like a teen-ager being asked for her first date. I explained Ruth's request and my promise to her. And all the time, I was thinking that I was really too nice to deserve this.

Peter interrupted me at last. "Tell you what," he suggested. "I'll spend the evening with you and help you baby-sit."

My reply was a startled squawk. I could just visualize the whole evening. Cute children, continuous chatter and clamorous confusion. It would probably be worse than that, but I had run out of c's.

I couldn't visualize Peter in Ruth's house. I had seen him only in elegant restaurants and the thought of him in conjunction with Michael's hobbies (he's a would-be zoologist, and the place crawls with turtles, mangy dogs and stray cats) and Sandy's and Lynne's dolls, blocks, mudpie equipment ad infinitum was simply incredible.

I tried to dissuade him. I told him he would be bored, but he wouldn't listen. I was afraid to be too discouraging, for fear he'd stay permanently discouraged. So at last I gave him Ruth's address and hung up, feeling that I must be serving penalty for some horrendous childhood crime. Why else would I be in such a situation?

Somehow, the week went by. I wasn't sure whether I was hoping Thursday would come quickly so I could get this mess over, or whether I was hoping it would never come.

It didn't make any difference, because it came anyhow. I packed a few sturdy clothes that could stand the buffetings of children and one fragile dress that might appeal to Peter, and off I went, feeling utterly desperate. Ruth and Carl had their suitcases in the car and their hats on, evidently taking no chances on staying around long enough for me to persuade them not to go. With a wave of their hands, they were gone.

The three children stood staring fixedly at me for one long minute, as though gauging my strength, and then with a whoop, they flew into my arms. I guess, in telling of their less desirable traits, I have failed to mention the fact that they are the most lovable kids in the world. Which is part of the trouble, of course, for who can discipline, with any firmness, a freckle-faced boy who is hugging you fiercely and saying, "I love you, Aunt Lucy" or two little girls who are staring at you with wide blue eyes and saying practically in unison, "Pretty, pretty aunty." I'm not pretty and they know it, but they're smart.

Thursday evening and Friday went by, and somehow I was able to cope. That is to say, nothing went smoothly and we ate cereal three times a day (who can cook with three mons . . . er . . . children underfoot) but it wasn't too horrible. However, by 10 P.M. on Friday, I was utterly exhausted. Ruth claims she gets the children in bed by 8:30, but she's either lying to me or she has access to tranquilizer pills. When I finally got them all settled, I was too tired even to watch television. I just threw on a pair of pajamas and fell on my face in bed.

I was awakened by a great thump in the bed, and I opened blurry, puffy eyes to see Lynne and Sandy beaming at me. Michael was at the door and he held something in his hands. "I brought my dragon to say good morning," he announced cheerfully.

"Dragon?" I was groggy but instantly on the defensive. "What dragon?"

"Sir Launcelot," Michael said, opening his hands enough to show me the ugliest horned toad it has ever been my misfortune to see. I felt a scream building up in me that would blast the covers right off the bed.

"Ah," Lynne crooned, reaching for it.

I swallowed the scream and spoke in a hoarse croak, "Michael, you take that thing out of my room this instant."

Michael looked surprised. Lynne and Sandy looked at me as though I were Bluebeard, and Michael disappeared.

We all got dressed and ate cereal again, although I found Sandy surreptitiously dumping hers into the dishwasher. When I scolded her, she quavered, "I'm tired of cereal." That did it. I picked her up and cuddled her. Anything to stop the tears.

"Okay," I said. "Tell you what. We'll all go out this noon and have hamburgers."

This created joy all around, and in such a cheery atmosphere, even digging soggy cereal out of the dishwasher was not too impossible. I tried to get beds made and the house straightened up in the morning, but somehow, I got talked into watching cowboys on television. Well, not watching, exactly, but I held Lynne while she watched. She informed me, with her eyes very big and blue, that she liked laps better than chairs.

The promised jaunt in search of hamburgers was hectic, but it absorbed a couple of hours, and I had reached the point where I was merely waiting numbly for evening to come so Peter could arrive, be thoroughly disillusioned and go home.

After supper, I raced around like a mad woman trying to make the house look presentable for Peter. At seven-thirty, I herded them all upstairs and began to run bath water. I was still in shorts and a jersey, my lipstick was eaten off, and my nose shiny. If the kids hurried, I'd have time to dress and be relaxed by nine when Peter would probably arrive.

The doorbell rang, and I ran down wondering who on earth could be there. I stared stupidly through the screen door, too stunned to say a word. Peter, immaculate and smiling, stood on the porch.

"You're too early," I gasped at last.

"I wanted to see the kids," he announced, not at all put off by my ungraciousness.

I wanted to drop dead, but life doesn't grant all our wishes, so, reluctantly, I opened the door.

"I brought ice cream," Peter said. "I thought we'd have a party."

I still couldn't say anything. All three children were standing in a silent semicircle around Peter, staring at him.

I broke the silence. "Children," I said, "this is Mr. Bartlett. And Peter, this is Michael, Sandy and Lynne."

Peter said "How do you do" very formally and politely. Lynne and Sandy began to dimple shyly. Michael grunted, then, man-fashion, spoke to Peter.

"Is Aunt Lucy your girl?"

I could feel the hot blood staining my face, and I wanted to wallop my nephew. But instead, I spoke hastily to all three youngsters.

"Come on, hurry up, it's time for your bath." The word was hardly said when I headed a mad dash for the upstairs, because it had occurred to all of us at once that the bath water was still running.

There was only a little water on the floor when I skidded into the bathroom and twisted the faucets. I pulled the drain and drained out part of the water and mopped the floor and I began to think some very nasty thoughts about Ruth. This was all her fault. I looked up to see Peter standing in the doorway.

"Can I help?" he said.

I wanted to say, "Yes, go home." But I didn't. I just shook my head mutely.

After a minute he wandered over to Michael's room, and I heard him exclaiming over the turtles and the bird's nest and the old fossil that looks like a skull.

I only got more hectic-looking as the baths progressed, but eventually, miraculously, the children were all in bed, and there had been no more mishaps. I suggested to Peter that he go downstairs and relax while I got cleaned up.

"Well, all right," he agreed, "but I think you look cute just the way you are."

My heart bumped around, and I started to smile shyly when Michael stuck his head out of his door. "I'll bet she *is* your girl," he said accusingly.

I fled into Ruth's room and shut the door before Peter could answer. This was awful. Peter would feel that he had not only been drawn into a dreadful, child-crammed evening, but he was being involved in a way he had not intended.

There was no time for a bath, of course, but I had been pretty well soaped and soaked when I washed the girls, so I just put on fresh makeup, combed my hair and put on the fragile dress and high-heeled shoes. I gazed at myself in the mirror. I did *not* look sophisticated, in spite of the finery. There was the imprint of children all over me.

Peter was waiting for me in the living room. He didn't look bored, but I figured he was too courteous to let it show.

"We forgot the ice cream for the kids," he said.

"They're asleep," I answered quickly.

"I'm not." Michael's head popped around the banister. "Only the girls."

Did Peter sigh? I couldn't tell. I did.

So we had ice cream . . . Peter and Michael and I. It was about as glamorous and romantic as a pile of dirty dishes.

But, at last, Michael went to bed. I prepared myself for Peter's staying only long enough to be polite and then leaving. To my way of thinking, it was inevitable.

I let the two dogs out and the cat in. And Peter watched me. I wanted to say, "This isn't what I'm like . . . dull and domestic. I'm gay and young and witty."

I was trying to think of a way to phrase it, when suddenly, there came a scream from Michael's room. It was a sound of pure tragedy, and I ran upstairs as swiftly as I could. Michael was standing on his bed, pointing with a trembling finger to where the cat crouched on the floor. I saw, in the dim light, that something was held prisoner between the cat's paws.

"My dragon," Michael roared. "He's got my dragon."

The cat's eyes gleamed at me in the semidarkness, and I reacted with instinct. I grabbed, without thinking, and I put the toe of my shoe, with no gentleness, against the pussy's backside. With a loud startled yowl, the cat went sailing out into the hall, and still automatically, I turned and handed the horned toad to Michael.

It was only after the thing had left my fingers that I realized what I had held in my hand. Involuntarily, I screamed and stepped away from the bed to find myself in Peter's arms.

But Peter wasn't looking at me or even thinking about me. He was looking past me at Michael who was crouched, sobbing, in the middle of his bed.

It occurred to me, as it apparently did to Peter, that this was Michael's first brush with violence and death and cruelty. Peter's arms let me go, and in one stride, he was beside Michael's bed, holding the little boy in his arms.

"My dragon," Michael gasped. "My dragon."

Peter looked at the toad, and his words were calm. "It'll be all right, Mike. The cat hardly hurt it at all. See? Your Aunt Lucy will take him down and put him in a box, safe, where the cat can't get him."

Michael's Aunt Lucy nearly fell over, but somehow, with Peter's eyes looking at me so confidently, I managed to take the loathsome thing in my fingers.

"I'll be right down," Peter said. "After I've talked to Mike a minute."

His voice was a soothing murmur, talking to the child, as I hurried down to the kitchen to find an empty box, a cereal box, of course, in which the toad would be safe.

It seemed a long while before Peter came down, but finally he came into the living room, sat down beside me on the couch, stretched out his legs and sighed.

It was on the tip of my tongue to say, "Aren't they horrible?" when something hit me, like a blow to the solar plexus. It was a sudden realization that they weren't horrible, they were darn nice little kids, and I loved them, and if Peter Bartlett wanted sophisticated women with aquamarine hair he could just go and whistle for one. I would not stand for any abuse of *my* sister's children.

This was utterly ridiculous, considering the way I had felt a week ago, but I only knew I was tired and oddly upset by the pain I had seen on Michael's face.

I started to get up from the couch, but Peter's hand detained me.

"Michael might need me," I said, while my heart thudded at his touch.

Peter's voice was lazy. "Mike's okay. I explained to him that cats can't help the way they act. He understands."

I turned to face him, seeking boredom in his eyes. But there was warmth on his face and a sort of excitement.

"They're great little kids," he said. "But their aunt is even greater."

I stared, my mouth open, looking about as lovely as the horned toad, I imagine.

Peter said, "I've always liked you, Lucy, only you scared me. But not any more. Any girl that could handle a horned toad . . . well . . ."

He shook his head admiringly and then he started to kiss me and my mind went blank . . . except for a brief, bemused reflection that who cared about being a glamorous career girl when she could be Peter Bartlett's girl. Certainly not me.

He was kissing me for the third time when a sound made me turn toward the steps. Michael stood there, his dragon in its cereal-box lair, cradled in his arms.

"She *is* your girl," he said again. And then, "I'm glad," he announced and headed for bed.

I gazed after him fondly and then turned to smile at Peter. As I've said before, Michael is a very smart little boy.

The same trait in different situations

Another way to show how plot is guided by basic trait is to present different characters with the same trait in different situations and see the varying results.

Suppose we choose *a deep sense of duty* as a basic trait. The writer has a clue to creating situation for this character because there's bound to be a conflict of emotion between duty and personal problems. Unless the choice is made difficult, the reader will not be interested. In other words, a strong basic trait logically calls for a strong situation, a strongly plotted story.

Let's see how the trait would work in a hypothetical situation:

A dedicated young scientist is on the brink of a discovery that may bring tremendous benefits to mankind. Working without thought of effort or hours, at times he feels strangely dizzy. As he comes closer to success, his health grows worse. A doctor tells him he must either take a long vacation—or die.

Driven by his basic trait of duty above self, what would the young scientist do? He might temporarily succumb to his wife's concern and his doctor's warning. But in the brief time that he's forced into idleness, he may also start thinking about the value of his life as compared to the value of the health of all mankind.

Unable to overcome his sense of duty, he struggles from his bed and returns to the lab. Ill and depressed, he goes to work. His wife discovers his absence and, together with the doctor, rushes to him. How might this story end? Does the scientist force them to understand what he must do, even if it costs his life? Does he complete his discovery and then collapse? Or does he literally work himself to death? These are questions for the writer to plot out in his own way.

Now let's put another character with this same trait in a totally different situation:

A young woman with a strong sense of duty has a chance to marry, but in the opening situation her widowed sister has just died, leaving the heroine in charge of four small children. Very much in love with her fiancé, a law student with years of study and financial struggle ahead, she's faced with the choice of giving him up or putting the children in foster homes.

The fiancé would like to care for them, but how can he? He doesn't have the means. The girl is ready to marry him and live simply and frugally. But what about the children?

In an attempt to harden her heart, the girl might try to find homes for the children. But in the process she finds that the children love her, and her sense of duty toward them becomes stronger than her desire to marry. She cannot harden her heart. So she gives up her hope for marriage. She and the law student have a long, long wait ahead—perhaps they'll never be able to marry.

In this same situation, the writer might want a sense of duty to bring its reward. For example, an older woman who's aware of the girl's sacrifice decides to give a helping hand. She talks to friends in the neighborhood: someone offers a house, rent-free; someone donates money for the children's education; an elderly widow offers to care for the house and youngsters so the girl can take a paying job. All in all, the young couple decide they can manage the domestic problems—if they're brave and resourceful. So the story ends happily, led to its outcome by the girl's basic trait.

To show how the basic trait used in the above illustrations was actually put to work, here's a story called "Death Warrant" by David Karp, which appeared in *The Saturday Evening Post*.

You'll see how the author's plot has been guided by the character's decision to place principle above self.

It couldn't have happened at a less eventful moment during the General Assembly's proceedings. The newsmen were out having coffee at various places along First and Second Avenues. The press-association men had a bridge game going in the delegates' lounge with some minor English Foreign Office people. On the floor of the great assembly hall an aged, leathern-faced member of the Indian delegation was solemnly reading a long report on the Kashmir dispute. More than a score of headphones dangled over the arms of chairs and delegates chatted. The visitors' seats were filled with a sprinkling of people, mostly groups of young students, solemn-faced out-of-town visitors who were waiting out the rainy afternoon before dinner and the television showplaces opened.

Apparently only one person had noticed the softly heated discussion, and that was the woman who sat alone in an aisle seat near the front of the auditorium. Apparently only she noticed the tall, hawk-faced man rise, his face deeply flushed, showing up the gray hair at his temples. His eyes sought hers, and she followed his unspoken command by rising and walking to the rear of the auditorium.

On First Avenue she waited in the faint drizzle of the fall afternoon, pulling up the heavy coat collar of the European coat with the oddly unmodish cut. The coat was a sharp contrast to the flimsy, expensive shell pumps of kidskin she wore on her feet and the sleek new nylons on her surprisingly good legs. Her hat, like her coat, was made of excellent material poorly cut and fitted and oddly old-fashioned in appearance.

The tall, hawk-faced man came out on the sidewalk wearing a long European coat, belted, with squared shoulders and a sturdy double row of buttons. A few passers-by glanced at him because of the familiarity of his face. They passed on, not sure of his name, but certain that they had seen his picture in the newspapers.

The man came up and took the woman's elbow. She looked at him with enormous, questioning black eyes that seemed larger and blacker in the milk-white complexion of her face.

"Let us walk," he said in an odd blend of Oxford and middle-European accents on his precise English.

"Why did you leave?" she asked, falling in beside him as he hurried across First Avenue.

"A man may bear so much and then no more. Do you understand that?" he asked, glancing at her with those proud, eagle-fierce black eyes.

"What will Doctor Hoxa say?"

"I am no longer interested," the man said, staring ahead as they walked quickly through the rain toward Second Avenue.

"To get up and just walk out," the woman muttered as they waited for the light to change on Second Avenue. She bit her lip. "Was it wise?"

He glanced at her obliquely for just an instant, and then said softly, "No, my darling, it was not wise."

They walked in silence through the rain most of the way across town, and because they were both chilled and soaking, they went into a coffee shop of a hotel on Lexington Avenue. The place was quiet and empty in the way that only a midtown coffee shop can be around three-thirty on a rainy afternoon. A busboy sat at one table folding napkins, while a waitress filled sugar bowls. The manager of the coffee shop sat at a distant table in earnest conversation with a man who kept both his hat and coat on while he chewed a dead cigar and listened.

The waitress left her task long enough to bring them two cups of black coffee. The man gave her a dollar bill. She smiled, and came back bearing silver, which she put down beside him. He nodded his thanks and began idly to fan the silver in front of him with his long fingers.

"What a strange country," he said, looking at the coins. "I don't know the value of any of these coins. Which is the English equivalent of a penny?"

The woman pointed out the copper coin with her finger in an abstracted manner.

"The shilling?" He nodded. "Do they have a half crown?" He turned over a nickel. "There's an animal on the obverse of this one. Is it a cow? A bull?" The man smiled. "Jan would know what animal it was. He has such a mania for American movies. I think he misses them more than anything else in the world. It was a stupid regulation, banning them. They were so innocently violent. Men were shot, but they never died—not truly. Such innocent movies, really." The man hit the table softly with his fist. "Stupid."

The woman looked at him for a long moment, and then decided not to ask the question that had to be asked.

The man sipped his coffee. "I like their coffee—it is innocent too. No brandies, no whipped cream. They're all innocents. Even their delegate. Such a young man. I understand it was his grandfather who was responsible for the death of the League. Poetic justice, is it not, Anna?"

"I had a letter from my mother today," Anna said softly. "It came in the diplomatic pouch."

"Oh?" the man said mildly. "Doctor Hoxa did not mention it."

"I ran into him before the Assembly convened, and he had it in his pocket. He asked me to send my parents his kindest wishes when I wrote in reply."

"What did your mother write?"

"I have the letter," she said, and reached for her purse. The man shook his head as he lowered his eyes. "Not now, my darling." He looked up and tried to smile. "You tell me yourself."

"Well," she began hesitantly, "for one thing, she and my father are well. The children are well. They miss us, send us their love. Jan has won some sort of badge for musketry, and is very anxious for you to know about it." The man's mouth tightened a bit. When Anna hesitated, he put his hand out to cover hers and nodded encouragingly for her to continue. "My mother says she is sorry she did not have time to thank you for the extra winter bed clothing you sent them. The weather has been exceptionally cold for so early in the year."

"And the coal ration has been exceptionally low," he said with faint bitterness. "That was never a problem with them before the war, Anna, was it? It was you and I and Lisa and little Anna who froze, and your parents who sent us warm bed clothing. They had that fine house on Rajek Street where that fabulous *Konditorei* used to be—remember? I was a starving counselor with the wrong political affiliations. Those were cruel winters, Anna." He lapsed back into their native tongue: "Remember the old gang? Everyone church-mouse poor, but burning inside with ideals, ambitions, dreams, plots, plans. Between the smoke of cigarettes and the smell of printer's ink, you and the children always had headaches. Do you remember the mice who made themselves cozy winter homes in the middle of the leaflets we kept hidden in the air space under the roof?" He smiled. "The opportunistic little vermin. They gnawed holes through Lenin's noble forehead." He paused, smiled softly again, and then the smile disappeared.

"Shall I go on?" she asked in her precise English.

"It was my fault, Anna, wasn't it?" he asked her.

"I don't know."

"I and the others. We thought we were bringing a cleaner, sweeter, fairer world for ourselves and for our children. We were the innocents, Anna—the simple-minded, kindhearted innocents. And I led them, Anna. I." He poked a stiff finger at his chest. "What was poor, honest Buldov but a cab driver? A man without education, without parents, without someone to love him, without anything but the party. And I was the whole party to him. I've never told you this—but he was killed last spring."

She nodded. "Yes. I had heard that."

"How?"

"My father told me."

"He will not live to a ripe old age, Anna," he warned her softly.

"Will any of us?"

His eyes dropped again when he could no longer meet his wife's gaze. "Go on with the letter."

She rolled her eyes upward and sighed unhappily. "Let me try to remember. Oh, yes. She said Vladek came to visit them on his way to his brother's farm."

"No," he exclaimed with a sudden surprised smile. "He's not really alive and well?"

"My mother said he was. She said he had a good job too."

"But not with the party's knowledge. That's a certainty." He shook his head in awe. "Astonishing how he's managed to survive all that's happened. With my own eyes I've seen his death warrant signed."

"Perhaps the party isn't so powerful as it seems."

"No," he shook his head. "It is laxity. Our Russian comrades will start an administrative survey next spring. Poor Vladek—he won't get away this time."

"He could be warned," she said softly.

"Through your father?"

"Or someone else."

"I won't permit your family to risk its members so rashly."

She looked at him significantly. "Your walking out—"

"It is on my head," he said stubbornly, as if to convince himself.

"There was no more to the letter," she said finally, and they both lapsed into silence. It was a silence that grew deeper between them, as if they both knew they were waiting. Again and again she saw ghosts drift through his eyes, saw the tiny workings of his mouth and jaws as he resaid the ten thousand things he had said in the years of their marriage. Her own mind was filled with the pictures of those she loved—her daughters, her son, her parents, her brothers and sisters. As if they were mounted on the edge of a wheel, their faces spun past her, first one, then another, and another and another.

She caught herself repeating their names—the names of her children, her parents, her family, her friends. There seemed so many of them. So terribly many of them.

They waited, and what they waited for happened soon enough. The two men came into the coffee shop and instantly saw them.

The taller, leaner, fairer one came over, sat down and spoke directly into the man's face, "You lousy, stinking traitor. I'm surprised you're not spilling your guts out in an American police station."

The heavier, darker man with the pince-nez sat down beside Anna and spoke softly, "Be still, Yussef."

When the waitress approached the table, the man with the pince-nez shook his head and waved her away.

"Don't think you can come back now," Yussef said, leaning closer to the man, his eyes chilled with cold blue hatred.

"I asked you to be still," the man with the pince-nez said softly. Yussef leaned back in his chair, his face white with rage, his eyes narrowed with hatred. "Now," the man with the pince-nez said in a quiet, conversational tone, "let us make several things clear. What you said, your behavior in the auditorium are inexcusable. I do not intend to forgive nor to forget, and I am, of course, required to file the necessary official report on all that's happened."

"Doctor Hoxa—" Anna began.

"Please," Doctor Hoxa said softly, "this is not a matter for a woman. But since you have joined him here, I presume you are of the same opinion as your husband, so what I have to say to him will apply to you with equal force."

"I am not returning home. You cannot compel me," the man said with soft defiance.

"I cannot and will not compel you or your wife to return," Doctor Hoxa said smoothly. "As Yussef has said, you've acted the traitor. It now remains to be seen whether you will also act the jackal. You may consider yourself safe, but have you thought of your wife's parents, your wife's brothers and sisters and their wives and husbands and their friends? You see, when you drop a pebble into the water, the ripples spread quickly and widely. A traitor may betray his country and his party, but only a jackal prizes his skin over everything and anything else in the world."

"You wouldn't," the man said hoarsely. "I'll create an enormous uproar in the American press. World opinion—"

"Don't be a fool," Doctor Hoxa cut him off quietly. "World opinion is a childish fiction, and I am surprised that a man as sophisticated as yourself takes it seriously. I have been thoroughly disillusioned about you; please don't also disgust me."

"Can't we come to some understanding?" Anna asked quietly.

"I'm sorry, madam. Neither you nor your husband is in any bargaining position. I have no intention of striking any bargains with you. My only promise," he said, turning to the man, "is that if you return home quietly, without creating any further vulgar disturbances, you will be discreetly dealt with." Hoxa's mouth twisted faintly. "At least you won't have any lingering prison sentence to complete."

"And my wife, my children, my wife's parents and the others?" the man asked.

Doctor Hoxa shrugged his shoulders. "Those matters will be decided after your case has been disposed of."

"You will kill my husband," Anna said, without any questioning tone in her voice.

"I thought that implication was plain enough, madam," Hoxa replied, taking off his pince-nez and exhaling on the lenses before he polished them.

"You will not touch the others?" the man asked insistingly.

"No promises," Hoxa said as he fixed his glasses on the bridge of his nose and frowned.

"I've never known the party to be reluctant about making promises before," the man said wryly.

"It is a matter of principle," Hoxa replied flatly.

"It was also a matter of principle that made me walk out," the man replied.

"Your principles are of no interest to me," Hoxa said. "The question is: Have you completely funked your manhood or is there some scrap of it left in you?"

The man's eyes dropped, but Anna lifted her chin, her face cold and her voice sure. "My husband will not go back, Doctor Hoxa."

Hoxa looked at Anna for a moment. "Does your wife speak for you?"

The man raised his eyes to stare at Anna.

"He will not go back," Anna said flatly.

"It is your parents who are still alive, madam. It is your three children, your two brothers and two sisters and their husbands and wives and children. You are rather cavalier with the lives of innocent people, madam."

Anna reached over and squeezed her husband's hand hard. "He will not go back."

"This is ridiculous," Hoxa said with a soft sneer. "You don't even know why he walked out. Or are you perhaps more politically aware than I had realized? Are you perhaps the inspiration of this betrayal?"

"No, no, no," the man insisted quickly, quietly. "She knows nothing of what's happened. I didn't discuss it with her. She doesn't actually know why. Believe me, Hoxa. She does not know."

"She must know," Hoxa said coldly, looking at Anna. "Else she would not be so determined to uphold your betrayal . . . I fear I have underestimated you, madam. It seems that you are your husband's evil genius. Well, it won't be the first time a woman's undone a man too weak to know his own mind."

"Anna, Anna," the man pleaded softly, "let me decide, please. I'll go back."

"You will not," she said.

"Make up your minds," Hoxa said briskly. "I despise domestic quarrels." Hoxa looked at Anna sharply. "You haven't the faintest idea why your husband left the country of his birth, the party of his choice, the comrades whom he has fought beside for so many years. Admit it."

"Yes," her voice was barely audible. "I do admit it."

"Then how can you pretend to decide for him? If you had anything to say, you would say, 'Save my parents, my children, my family.' Those are the normal, natural instincts of a true woman. Even a sow will not let her young be taken from her. Are you no better than an animal, madam?"

Anna's eyes were glimmering with tears, and her husband saw her heart breaking, but her voice had no quaver in it. "I love my husband and I want him to do what he thinks is right. When he walked out, he knew what he was doing." She looked at her husband and clenched his hand tighter. She spoke now so softly that only her husband could tell what she was saying, "Even if it means my children, my parents, my family, everyone." He swallowed hard as he looked into his wife's face and felt the desperate grip of her fingers.

Her trust, her love moved toward him like an enormous, bracing wave of certainty. It could bear him upward and outward toward freedom, toward a world that had dignity, hope. To be free of them, he thought, his heart contracting with the sheer joy of such a life—a life that Anna offered him over the bodies of all she loved.

"And Abraham offered the Lord his only son," the man said softly. Anna understood. Her eyes dropped; she pressed her husband's hand harder. "It is enough you love me and believe that freedom is worthy of the sacrifice." He pressed her hand with enormous strength. "It is," he said with terrible, burning-eyed insistence. "It is."

Hoxa spoke coldly, "Well?"

"Yes," the man said softly, certainly, "I will go back with you."

"Mind you," Hoxa warned, "I've made no promises."

"Your promises are as unimportant as your threats," the man said. He rose, holding his wife's hand. "Whoever holds principles must be prepared to die for them—the first to die for them." He moved ahead of Hoxa and Yussef with Anna, his back straight and stiff with pride. Yussef nudged Doctor Hoxa and indicated his watch. "From defection to surrender—just forty-five minutes."

Doctor Hoxa, who was following the progress of the husband and wife across the room, nodded perfunctorily in agreement, but was not nearly so sure he had won.

The plot of this unusual story is based on the husband's belief in principle above self, which led him to turn his back on communism, even though he knows it means his death. Without this basic trait in the main character, the plot development and outcome would be different.

The purpose of keeping notes

I'm always working at a book. I have a little davenport beside my table and it's got a few drawers in it, and I have notes for two other books in there. When I get an idea I write it down and put it into one of the two drawers. It's very restful from the book I'm working on.

The reason why it is possible for me to do that is that all my ideas are part of the same system. I'm continually getting impressions, usually of a character in a situation, and I generally get it down as a sketch, with a little monologue or dialogue and some description. I have hundreds of them put away in the davenport drawers.—Joyce Cary in *The Writer Observed*

Minding other people's business

The majority—I should say 85 per cent—of short stories are in some degree reportorial. They are sparked by something the writer saw, heard, felt or read. Therefore it is necessary for the writer to have a nose like an anteater for everybody's business, a rubber ear that hears what people say, a spyglass that sees what's going on, a keen faculty of observation for little things, all motivated by a burning, unquenchable curiosity about people.—Adela Rogers St. Johns

Editors keep looking ahead

Most editors look ahead. They don't ask themselves what do people want to read today; they ask what will they want to read in, say, three months, since it takes that long for a magazine to appear on the stands. You have to keep looking ahead. The writer who knows what people will want to read in three months, six months, or a year will probably never have a rejection.—Faith Baldwin

Lesson seventeen

Fiction writing

course

Writing
a short
story

Part III

Another vital aid to successful plotting, apart from characters' traits and motives, is to understand the difference between an incident or incidents and a story.

An incident can seem very much like a story. And a series of incidents strung together can seem very much like a plot. But the difference, however subtle, is the difference between readers gained and readers lost. For an incident, no matter how intriguing by itself, often lacks the essential ingredient of fiction. If undeveloped, it has no suspense and thus fails to stir the reader into asking: "I wonder what'll happen now? What's the outcome of all this?"

Let's look at some typical undeveloped incidents and see why they fail, in themselves, to constitute a story.

An elderly woman is walking along a crowded street, wondering at the changes made in the town since she was a girl. She thinks about her school days and the girls who were then her friends. Bumping into someone, she snaps: "You might look where you're going!" The other woman simply stares, then walks on. Suddenly they both turn: they have recognized each other as childhood companions. They laugh at the fact that the years haven't stopped them from having spats.

This incident is deceptively story-like. But if you study it a moment you'll see why it doesn't meet your plotting test. The main character has no problem; she's not confronted by a crisis; there's no urgency to her act of walking. She's musing about the town, but without emotion. The clash with the other woman is merely an occurrence without significance. No suspense is created. There's nothing to cause the reader to ask: "I wonder what will happen next?"

To make this incident into a story, we would have to know more about the woman to begin with—about her basic traits. We would have to give her a problem to solve, provide her with a set of initial circumstances to interest the reader, and then impel her into another situation with new complications. There would have to be some related significance in the encounter of the women and in their recognition.

A series of incidents can be illustrated with the same two women. If, after they recognize each other, they have a cup of tea and talk over old times, and discover that their sons are soon coming home for a family reunion, there's still no story. Even if —to take an extreme example—the home of one of the women catches fire while she's eating dinner at the other's, it is still only another incident.

On the other hand, if these two women no longer find their spats amusing and start to fight, and the first woman wishes the other would once more vanish from her life, except that her son has now become engaged to the other's daughter—a conflict is created, a plot takes shape.

In developing incidents into stories, Bergen Evans warns:

Be sure the added complications are valid to the situation. Sometimes delays are mistaken for complications, just as incidents are mistaken for stories. A delay in the movement of a story, caused by some unrelated complication, merely irritates readers. A complication must make the character's goal more difficult, put hurdles in his path—but these obstacles, whether within the character's mind or coming from outside, must always contribute to his conflict and intensify it to an eventual crisis.

For instance: a farmer's son wants desperately to go to the city and become a businessman, but as the story opens his father has died and left him saddled with the farm, too run-down to sell. Furthermore, his mother loves the place too much to leave it. The initial complication has been set.

The first question is: What will the son do about the situation? His basic desire is to get away and become a businessman. Now he's in conflict with two forces—one from outside: the run-down condition of the farm, and one from inside: his mother's love of the homestead.

Now plot reasoning goes to work. If the son is a businessman at heart, he'll know that he must first make the farm a going concern. After which he could hire another man to run it for his mother. His main goal, then, is to make the farm pay.

The first step in the plot has been set. The son must now do something. Just what he will do must come from the writer's imagination. At this point, the writer should decide if the new farmer will succeed in making the farm pay, proving that he's suited to the business world, or if in the end he'll decide he's really a farmer at heart and loves the place the more for having given it his wholehearted attention.

Whatever the writer decides, he now has situation, plus the first step of the plot. Now the complication sets in.

The farmer begins to reorganize the farm. He's partially successful, but at this point the writer must provide opposition, must increase the difficulties between the hero and his goal. What shall the complication be? Broken machinery? Bad weather? Remember, this is not to be merely a delay in the story but an added complexity.

Broken machinery can be fixed—this would merely require patience and endurance rather than resourcefulness.

Bad weather? This is better. Just as the son gets a new crop sown, flood threatens. What does he do now? The right question has been asked: "What happens next?"

Wouldn't it be logical for the young farmer to remember things his father attempted to teach him against his will? Anyway, let's try this. In plot reasoning you try all possible combinations until you find one that seems most valid for your particular story line.

Now the writer would have to seek information about floods and crops so his details would be authentic. Armed with this information, the writer has the farmer go into action again—but the end of the story can't come yet. He can't succeed too easily. And so on to another complication.

What will it be this time? The farmer has a pretty girl whom he hopes to marry. But she doesn't want to be a farmer's wife. So wouldn't it be a good complication if she issued an ultimatum —told him to abandon the farm and take a job with her uncle in town? The farmer tries to win her over. Reluctantly she agrees to wait another six months. Now he has a time element against him as another obstacle to overcome.

He works and works to make the farm succeed. Events pave the way for a profitable crop. But at this point the farmer must receive the worst setback of all: his efforts must be doomed. Or so it must seem to the reader, who will say: "How will the writer end this?"

What event brings the crisis about? A sudden illness? A bid from the State to buy the farm for part of a superhighway? A fire which destroys the crops? Which of these complications would most logically bring about the hero's eventual triumph?

If the farmer is to succeed with the farm, a sudden illness would merely lay him low and leave the solution to others. An unsatisfactory way to end the story.

The State's bid to buy the land would solve everything financially. The only flaws are the mother's loss and the fact that the farmer has put in all his effort for nothing. Another dead end.

But what about a fire that destroys the crops? Imagine the despair, the heartbreak! What a test of courage and endurance!

So in this plot step, the writer shows the farmer ready to

market his crop. He's intensely happy: he'll be able to marry the girl: the future looks promising indeed.

Then the writer creates a terrible scene of fiery destruction, unexpected and devastating. When the fire is over, the farmer's reaction is one of intensified hatred for the farm. Why? Because the writer is leading up to an opposite discovery.

What happens next? As a result of the situation the girl would reject him. Grimly he would start to sow again. Time would pass, the farmer's increasing desire for escape making him bitter, a stranger to his mother. Then spring would come again, with nature covering the damage, and by summer the farmer has a crop of even greater richness than before. Now, as we head for a solution, we need no more complications.

The farmer is now free to go to the city. But instead, he is awed by new emotions. He looks over his land and feels a sudden, deep kinship with it. As he gives himself to it, it gives itself to him. At last he knows he belongs here—forever.

Further thoughts on complications

The story we have just discussed could be approached from almost uncountable directions, but the main object was to show the nature of a complication. Now we'll show complications that have no direct bearing on character and situation.

A city girl is meeting her date at a restaurant at 6 o'clock. At 5:25, she's in a department store, but the saleswoman is slow in adding up the bill. The afternoon closing bell rings. The girl hurries to a booth to phone her date. The booth door sticks, imprisoning her. When a watchman finally rescues her, the store is closed and he unlocks a rear door to let her out.

She can't find a taxi so she starts to walk. She's now 20 minutes late for her date, and upset. Finally one of her shoe straps breaks and she limps into the restaurant at 7 o'clock. Her sweetheart is worried, but when she explains, he's sympathetic and amused.

Or let's say a man is rushing to meet his wife at a suburban railroad station. On the way he has a flat tire and hurriedly hires another car. But when he reaches the station, he finds the train is late, so he has a full hour to wait.

Complications of this sort, greatly exaggerated here for illustration, are unrelated to the plot of a story and merely serve to impede it and provide suspense.

Sometimes, in order to provide a solution, the writer will employ coincidence. A person suddenly turns up, just at the right time and place to make a situation work out. Coincidence, however, must be approached with extreme care, says Mignon Eberhart:

A specific trap into which a beginning writer may fall is that old bugbear, coincidence. This happens in real life. It may be unusual and entertaining but it is unusual and entertaining only in *real life*. The events *of a story* must develop from the characters, and must be brought about *intentionally* by the characters. It cheats and disappoints the reader (and it shows up the writer's lack of skill and fertility of invention) if coincidence is lugged in either to advance or resolve the plot.

There is one rather amusing exception which Carl Brandt, my literary agent, once pointed out to me: he said that where coincidence may never be employed *for* the hero, that is to help him, it may sometimes most entertainingly and helpfully be used *against* the hero.

Here, for example, is coincidence used in such a way that the reader will be let down and disappointed. A girl is trying to make her reluctant boy friend jealous. She asks another boy to act possessively with her. Very conveniently, that same night they go into a restaurant and there, at a table, is the boy friend with another girl. He's furious, and of course the other girl turns out to be his sister.

In reality, a situation like this would not be credible, unless the writer has told the reader that this was a restaurant frequented by the girl and the boy friend. And the event would have to occur in a small town, for the likelihood of this happening in a big city would be remote indeed.

The same principle applies if the writer has his characters killed off conveniently, come into fortunes, sent to war or offered a sudden job in far-off Borneo. Be careful of story people that fall in love at first sight, or of invalids who recover in the nick of time. Coincidence should at all times be tempered by logic, and conveyed to the reader in an acceptable way.

There's one major reservation to keep in mind when planning a story before writing. Although plotting is of invaluable benefit, you should never feel you must follow your plan exactly—or fail. You are using plot to lead you to your own story—not to restrict or limit you. At the very least, plotting is a stimulus. At most, it's a safeguard against wasted time and effort. When an idea refuses to stand up to any kind of plot test, it indicates you'll run into trouble with the writing.

There's no surer way to prove this than to sit before your typewriter with unplotted and unstudied ideas and try to shape them into successful stories. *Think first, write second,* is not the only way to approach a story, but it comes close to being so. Here's what J. P. Marquand has to say about the problem:

I sit around and think about the story. The more leisure and freedom a writer has to sit around and think about his characters, the better. The physical business of writing is secondary to contemplation. I used to write right off. Now I like to know everything in advance—certainly everything about my characters.

And Roger H. Garrison in *A Guide to Creative Writing*, says:

Stories must be architecturally sound. They should be absorbing. They need strong plots. It often seems to me that learning writers fail to ask themselves this crucial question: "Would people really be interested in this story? Would they find it absorbing right from the start?" Too often writers think: "Will they admire the writing, my cleverness with words, my subtlety of thought?"

In the preliminary phase of story writing, remember:

1. If you have an understanding of your characters;

2. Know roughly where you're heading them;

3. Can provide alternate twists to fall back on in case of difficulty with your plot;

4. Can see the high spot where the characters reach the crisis of their problem; and

5. Can plan a logical way out of it that will be interesting and perhaps meaningful to your reader . . .

Then you're well on your way to plotting a successful story.

Lesson eighteen

Fiction writing

course

Writing a short story

Part IV

Creating your plot before you start writing is not all you can do to make your work easier. There are other advance decisions that free your mind and give direction to your flow of words and images.

One of the main decisions is what *kind* of story do you want to make of your idea—slick, pulp or quality? Referring to Lessons Six, Seven and Eight describing the kinds of stories, you'll note that this decision affects the audience or reader, and so to some extent directs the language you use, the handling of subject matter and length.

Next comes the decision as to which *element*—character, setting, situation or theme—will be most important. For instance, if you choose to write a character story, then you devote most of your effort to details of characterization, telling the reader everything you can to focus his interest on the person or persons in your story.

When situation plays the major role, ideas and complications guide your thinking. With setting, the atmosphere of your story leads your characters into their actions. And, with theme, the meaning you wish to convey molds your story line. To illustrate the way in which these decisions help to form your imagery and language, here are four different ways of handling the same initial circumstances. The style and pace of these four examples have been highly and purposefully exaggerated to make the points quickly:

Richard Denham, pursued by his business partner who believes he has embezzled the company's funds, is hiding in an old, deserted mansion. In the first version of the story, let's assume the writer has decided to make *character* the central drive, and thus is more interested in Denham than the other elements. This, roughly, is one way the story could be told:

Richard Denham was suddenly impervious to the gloom of the great, ruined mansion into which he had fled. Through a doorway he had caught sight of massive bookshelves, miraculously stacked with books. Wonder and excitement overcame the urgency of his flight from his pursuer. Why, he asked himself, had these books been left, and might there not be some rare ones among them? He could barely wait to strike a match and pass it before the cobwebbed titles. Thinking of a priceless addition to his collection, the fact that a man was closing in to kill him lost significance as he saw the words *Lost Tribe* by T. Van Orme.

Seizing the volume in trembling fingers, wiping it clean on his jacket, he lit another match and studied the text, hearing the approaching footsteps but wanting to make sure this was the original edition he believed it to be . . .

Naturally, this character would have to be built up with more and more details as the story progressed. But the fact that he puts book collecting above a threat to his life is a rich source of characterization. How did he get that way? What kind of a person is he in other respects? Is he tremendously brave or insanely driven; will he turn in the nick of time and become a resourceful fighter; will he kill his pursuer or talk him out of attacking? You can see that character shapes the choice not only of the plot but of wording.

Now let's see what help the writer would obtain from emphasis on *setting:*

Although his pursuer was close behind, as Richard Denham pushed through the creaking iron gate into the garden of the deserted mansion he was swept more by a mood of foreboding than by the danger to his life.

It was the pervading gloom of the place that immobilized him. A thick mist hung over the ruined masonry, the trailing willows, the broken statues, the waist-high weeds, the gnarled vines. There was a pungent odor of rotted leaves, of soil long hidden from air and sun.

"Go! Turn away!" the black windows seemed to say to him. "Don't seek asylum here!"

Still unable to cast off the spell, he heard the approaching steps of the man intent on killing him. Surely, here, in this vast, mysterious place, he could elude him. Surely . . .

A chill wind moaned through the willows. He drew back involuntarily, sensing an evil more horrible than death—and now the steps, running softly, came closer, closer . . .

Now let's take *situation* itself as the chief interest of the writer:

Richard Denham crouched in the shadows behind the rusty-hinged door. His breath came harshly, giving away his presence in the deserted mansion. As his pursuer's footsteps ceased momentarily, Richard tried to hold his breath. If only the door would close! The heavy oak panels would halt both his pursuer and the bullet . . .

But now the footsteps came on again. Richard's breath burst from him with a choking sound. He made a frantic effort to close the immense door. The steps quickened. Richard heaved again, perspiration running down his face.

"You made a mistake coming into this house, my friend," said a drawling voice. "I know every inch of it. You're in the storage room. There are no windows here. You haven't a chance."

A flashlight beam followed his words, cutting through the gloom between door and wall. As Richard braced himself for a last desperate heave at the door, a bullet whistled through the opening.

In this instance, situation is important, and character, setting and theme are secondary to "what happens next."

For the next example, let's assume that *theme* has stirred the writer to create a story around the same initial circumstances. What the story is to prove or mean overlays the other elements, which are used mainly as support.

As Richard Denham crouched in the gloom of the ruined mansion, he heard the footsteps of his pursuer coming closer, closer . . . If he was discovered here, then his life was but a step away from those who had once inhabited these silent, dust-shrouded rooms. How many of them would have died for the same reason, he wondered, and who would care why, once the act had been done? No final justice was to be found here. It might almost have been better had he actually stolen the money, and thus was to die for a real crime rather than an imaginary one. What *was* the meaning and significance of existence, he asked himself, as the footsteps shuffled nearer, backing him into final moments of his life . . .

No one can put words into another's mind, but the guidance that comes from knowing in advance what kind of story you want to write helps greatly to shape your plot and give your work momentum.

Your choice of viewpoint

Another decision to make before you start your story is the imperative one of choosing *who* shall tell it—that is, from whose point of view will the events be recorded or felt? You may wonder why it's necessary to choose a viewpoint, but if you remember what we've said about the nature of fiction—that readers like to identify themselves with a character, to share an emotion or experience—you'll see why it's impossible for them to jump from one character to another and feel a strong response.

In a novel, where there's room to develop fully more than one character, several viewpoints can be handled. But in a short story, the reader only has time enough to respond to one.

How does a writer go about choosing a viewpoint? Is it entirely a free choice or is it dictated in part by the kind of story you hope to create? Faith Baldwin answers: a little of both.

Certainly you try to choose the viewpoint that will make the most of your initial idea. Think over your story—ask yourself how it can best be made graphic, intriguing, suitable to mood and goal: (1) through the viewpoint of the main character; (2) through the viewpoint of a minor character; (3) through the viewpoint of an observer?

First, look at the advantages and disadvantages of each of these viewpoints.

The single viewpoint of a main character is the one most often used in short stories. It gives the writer a good chance to make a character known by his thoughts and actions, and thus ensures the reader's interest. This viewpoint can be that of the Third or the First Person. The Third Person, or the "he-and-she" of a story, is more widely used than First Person, "I." This is because the Third Person gives the writer more leeway in describing a character. For instance, consider this sentence:

She was an enchanting girl of twenty with startlingly blue eyes, a fair, transparent skin, and soft butter-colored hair.

Obviously it would sound conceited if a character said: "I am an enchanting girl of twenty," etc., unless the author was seeking an amusing effect. Or, to take another example, it's simpler for a writer to say, "He was a man of high moral principle, despite his easygoing charm," than it would be for an "I" to convey the same fact. This is not to say, however, that a skilled writer can't surmount such obstacles. In fact, here's an example of one who has. This is from "Seed of Wisdom," by Sarah Litsey, which appeared in *Cosmopolitan:*

I had never thought of my brothers as separate from me. We liked games, we had our sailboat. When I started going out with Tom Traynor, it was still like that. But that morning when I came out of my cabaña, Monsieur Guillard turned toward me with a strange expression, and everything changed. I could feel my bare feet pressing the cool bright sand; I saw that Peter and Luke were just gangling boys and that I was a grown-up girl with blonde hair under a wide-brimmed hat, in a green swim-suit.

In this short example, the "I" has obliquely described herself as a maturing young girl about to experience the sensation of attracting the opposite sex. There's a suggestion that she's lovely indeed. In Third Person, however, the writer could have given a detailed description of her and hence a clearer outer picture.

Which brings us to the viewpoint of the *observer*. The observer may be anyone, present or absent, involved or uninvolved with the story itself. Sometimes it's a child seeing a grown-up world, sometimes a parent through whose eyes we see a child's world. In some stories the observer is affected, in others he only watches the effect.

For the writer, this is the most difficult viewpoint to handle because the reader must see through the eyes of a character standing by and also through the eyes of the character whose story it is. It's much harder to reach the reader's emotions this way, since he may feel that he's a spectator, not a participant. Nevertheless, if the writer is skilled, this can be the most effective method of telling certain kinds of stories.

To help you further in selecting points of view, here are some examples of each. The first, told in Third Person, is from the story "Hank and Julie and Dylan Thomas," by Nelia Gardner White, published in *Ladies' Home Journal:*

At the rear of the dean's house was a basement room, which had an outside entrance down three steps, and in which was domiciled each year a student who took care of the dean's furnace, shoveled his walks and mowed his lawn. The room, the dean often said, was one of his few good investments. This year it was occupied by a junior named Henry Woodridge, but called Hank. It was a plain, snug room with a pine dresser, unpainted pine bookshelves, a cot, a card table, two chairs. It also had a gas plate on which the tenant could cook if he chose. Henry Woodridge so chose, for he was an exceedingly poor young man. Also he was an exceedingly appealing young man, with a quick smile, thoughtful dark eyes and untidy hair.

On an afternoon in late January, a girl came down the three steps, knocked on the door impatiently. She had on a short plaid skirt, a pillbox of a plaid hat with a strap under the chin, long woolen socks and a green jacket. Over her shoulder were slung skating shoes. Her face was impudent, charming, young. She stood there knocking for only an instant, then she opened the door, stepped inside. Hank was sitting at the card table, his back to her, working away at something or other.

The girl—she was Julie Lankton, the dean's daughter—stood there an instant, scowling at Hank's back, then said humbly, though she was not humble, "I thought you might like to go skating."

Note the freedom with which the writer is able to describe girl and boy, setting and situation. She can simply say that Hank is appealing, has a nice smile and thoughtful eyes. She's able to characterize him from the outside by stating that he's poor, has untidy hair, chooses to cook for himself, shovels the walk and mows the lawn for his keep, and is an industrious student. She's also able to describe the girl fully, and remarks that though she does speak humbly, "she was not humble." In other words the author can look all around a story from this viewpoint, can enter the situation from any angle, and make any observation about the characters that creates a vivid picture for the reader.

A story told from the viewpoint of First Person is represented here in an excerpt from "Attack," by Alec Hudson, published in *The Saturday Evening Post:*

The admiral was standing behind his desk when the aide escorted me into the room. The admiral had been talking to the others, but immediately he turned to me and said, "Commander Dorsky, what is said in this room today is secret. You will in no way divulge it or discuss it with anyone without my express permission to do so."

The words he uttered were so simple it was impossible to misunderstand them. He wasn't trying to be dramatic. I don't know why I was so tremendously impressed, but I know I shall never forget that moment. I recalled then, and I don't know why, a similar scene some twenty years before. Another admiral, long since dead and probably forgotten by everyone but me, had looked up from his desk to find twenty of us gawky kids assembled in an embarrassed mob before him. He had stood up and said, "Raise your right hands." He waited for just a brief instant for a hush to descend upon us. Then from memory, clearly and distinctly, he had repeated the oath of allegiance to the United States.

There wasn't any ostentation and there wasn't any attempt to be dramatic, but each phrase of that oath meant something to the man who was administering it, and ever afterward each phrase of it meant something to me. Somehow I felt that this was an occasion just as solemn.

I only gulped and said, "Yes, sir."

"Well, sit down and we will go on with the discussion," the admiral invited. "Ask questions whenever you feel it necessary."

In this example, only the descriptive word "Commander" is used to form a physical picture of the man through whom the story will be told. As the tale goes on, the reader learns through the Commander's actions, not from any straightforward statement, that he has extraordinary courage. This kind of viewpoint often leaves physical description to the reader's imagination, thereby avoiding the problem of self-flattery in the First Person narrator. It's good for describing *how* a character feels, but not for showing what he does to illustrate that feeling outwardly.

For instance, let's say a young man in a story is extremely nervous. In Third Person, it's possible to picture this for the reader in words such as: "He had a mumbling way of speaking, kept licking his lips and avoiding everyone's eyes. When someone spoke to him, he would stiffen and lock his fingers so tightly that the knuckles whitened." This outward picture would be difficult to convey in First Person because gestures and signs are unconscious. If the character knew about them, it would change the whole effect.

Interchanging points of view

On the other hand, First Person does have some advantages that at times makes it more effective than Third. In most stories the two points of view can be interchanged. Write a paragraph in Third Person, or pick one from a printed story, and then substitute First Person, or vice versa. You'll see that the change doesn't alter the sense in most instances. However, there's a shading to be considered, a greater intimacy that can sometimes be conveyed by First Person.

In the following excerpt from "I Broke My Back on a Rosebud," by William March, the main character is a corporal, marching up Fifth Avenue on Armistice Day, 1919, when a pretty woman tosses a rosebud at him. He slips on it, breaks his back, and is bedridden for life. The emotions described here *could* have been put in Third Person, but would have lost some of their immediacy for the reader.

Hope dies hard in a man, but it does die finally . . . Am I telling you something new? Am I telling you something you haven't heard before? I don't know how hope died in me, but one morning I woke up wise to myself. I knew, then, what the doctors had known all along, and that was, I'd never be any better, no matter what they did for me. That's when I started to see the woman's face again. I'd close my eyes and try to shut it out, but I couldn't. I cursed her and damned her from morning to night, like a crazy man. "Why wasn't she home, where she belonged, cooking her husband some dinner?" I'd say. "Why did she have to show herself off like she did?"

I'd known from the beginning, you see, that she didn't come out that morning to look at the soldiers. She came out to have the soldiers look at her . . . And she didn't throw me a rosebud because I was a returning hero in her eyes. Oh, no! Not that one! She did it so people could see how nice she looked throwing a rosebud! That was the worst thought of all, and when it came to me, I'd close my eyes and lay my head deep in the pillow . . .

Next, let's look at an example of the observer viewpoint

(either First Person or Third Person) in which a detached spectator tells a story as he sees it, understands it, feels it or thinks about it. In this viewpoint, the person observed emerges as the main character, leaving the spectator in a role ranging from someone who has heard a story worth telling to someone who actually participates in the story in a minor capacity.

This excerpt is from "When the Light Gets Green" by Robert Penn Warren:

My grandfather had a long white beard and sat under the cedar tree. The beard, as a matter of fact, was not very long and not white, only gray, but when I was a child and was away from him at school during the winter, I would think of him, not seeing him in my mind's eye, and say: He has a long white beard. Therefore, it was a shock to me, on the first morning back home, to watch him lean over the dresser toward the wavy green mirror, which in his always shadowy room reflected things like deep water riffled by a little wind, and clip his gray beard to a point. It is gray and pointed, I would say then, remembering what I had thought before.

He turned his face to the green wavy glass, first one side and then the other in quarter profile, and lifted the long shears, which trembled a little, to cut the beard. His face being turned like that, with his good nose and pointed gray beard, he looked like General Robert E. Lee, without any white horse to ride. My grandfather had been a soldier, too, but now he wore blue-jean pants and when he leaned over like that toward the mirror, I couldn't help but notice how small his hips and backsides were. Only they weren't just small, they were shrunken. I noticed how the blue jeans hung loose from his suspenders and loose off his legs and down around his shoes. And in the morning when I noticed all this about his legs and backside, I felt a tight feeling in my stomach like when you walk behind a woman and see the high heel of her shoe is worn and twisted and jerks her ankle every time she takes a step.

The grandfather is the main character in this story and the child remains in the background while the grandfather emerges more and more clearly in the telling. Throughout the story, the child participates only to the extent that he observes from an indistinct vantage point.

In all these single points of view, the minor characters are handled objectively. Remember, the *objective* view of a character is one told from the outside without thoughts, while the *subjective* gives the thoughts and emotions from within the character. The reader evaluates the minor characters only by what they say and do. They react outwardly—and the writer must give a very clear picture of what they are thinking, without actually stating their thoughts.

Another viewpoint used by writers is worth mentioning—the *omniscient* or over-all viewpoint—in which the reader is taken into the thoughts of any or all characters in the story, the switching being arbitrary. But this is seldom if ever used in the short story, and will be gone into more explicitly in the later Lessons on the novel.

All in all, the Third Person viewpoint is recommended to the student writer as the safest and surest means of handling short story material. John Erskine has this to say on point of view:

The body travels more easily than the mind, and until we have limbered up our imagination, we continue to think as though we had stayed home. *We have not really budged a step until we take up residence in someone else's point of view.*

Nothing truer could apply to the fiction writer.

Making an outline for a story

Now that you've been told about the steps preliminary to writing, you may want to put them in order by preparing an outline. Preparing an outline for a short story is as highly individual a procedure as any in fiction, and there are innumerable ways of going about it. We suggest making a simple outline, more like a list of ingredients than a detailed chart. In fact, going back over the decisions you have made and numbering them may be as effective an outline as you need. For instance:

1. *Kind of story:* Slick, pulp or quality.
2. *The situation:* All the initial circumstances.
3. *Chief element:* Which element to emphasize—character, setting, situation or theme?
4. *Plot complication:* Chief obstacle to character's solution of problem.
5. *Climax:* The crucial complication.
6. *Outcome:* How is the plot problem resolved?
7. *Viewpoint:* Which viewpoint will tell this story most suitably?
8. *Theme:* What does the story have to say, if anything? What truth or moral or message does it convey?
9. *Emotional effect:* How do you want the story to affect the reader's emotions?

To show you how such an outline might work, we're reprinting a short story below from *McCall's* magazine—"Half a Man" by Marjorie Worthington. At the end you will find what might have been the outline the author made before she began writing. Read the story through first, and then go back over to check it against the hypothetical outline.

The lighthouse had been abandoned for a long time. It stood on a point of land on the North Shore of Long Island, near a little town called Midford. It was a grim, square building with stone walls a foot thick. Clustered behind it were a few smaller buildings, one large enough for a barn or a garage. Farther out toward the sea was a conical tower in which a light, controlled by mechanical devices, still functioned.

The Moores discovered it almost by accident in their desperate search for a house they could afford. The rent was nominal. The only catch, so the real estate agent told them, was that the town would have to approve of them. They didn't want anybody like the last tenant.

"What was the matter with him?" Tom Moore asked.

"He was a morose kind of fellow," the agent said. "Kept to himself. One day they found him dead. Hanged himself in that barn there. They don't want that kind out here any more."

Gwen looked at her husband—at his broad shoulders, stooped now as if he were making apologies; at his stocky body in the old tweeds he had dug up; at the unruly hair with the cowlick that made him look even younger than his thirty-three years; at the high cheekbones; and the new lines that ran from his nose to the corners of his mouth, giving him a strained expression.

She took his hand and squeezed it, and said to the agent, "We'll be very happy here. I know it."

It took until the middle of October for the people of Midford to consent to the Moores as tenants for the abandoned lighthouse, though there was nothing to show that they wouldn't be exemplary. He'd been an advertising copy writer earning a good salary when he became ill. Heart trouble, something everybody could understand. The doctors had advised a quiet place to live, away from the noise and hustle of New York. They'd find quiet enough out on the point. Everyone felt sorry for them now and wanted to help. They were an attractive young couple; too bad they had this trouble. But she looked like a cheerful soul, and as if she could take care of him. The sea air might make him well; it had been known to work miracles.

On an Indian summer day the Moores arrived at the lighthouse with a truck and all their possessions. A few asters and chrysanthemums were still blooming, and there was a warm, golden sunset to greet them. They stacked everything in the two lower rooms, and when the truck drove off they went outside to look over their estate.

"The only thing I don't like," Gwen said, "is that barbed-wire fence around the place. It looks so unfriendly. We should tack up a sign saying 'Visitors welcome.' "

Tom frowned. "I don't want people to get the idea they can barge in on us whenever they feel like it. It's too bad we can't have a telephone."

"Well, we can't get on a party line, and a private line costs too much. Maybe later," Gwen said, trying to sound promising. "And of course we'll want company—I don't want you to get bored with me. Besides, the people here seem nice, and they'll expect to come calling on us as soon as our curtains are up."

Tom's expression was one she had come to dread. He said, "They don't have to think that just because they had to pass on us, they own us. I don't want their charity and I don't want them snooping. Let's have that understood from the start."

"We're not going to be hermits, are we?" Gwen asked, trying to make it sound as if he were joking.

"I don't want to meet anybody," Tom said. "Not for a while, anyway. Not until I get used to being half a man."

"Tom, don't!" Gwen cried. She looked away from him toward the Sound. "Look, aren't those porpoises?"

They ran to the rail that marked the edge of the land and a steep drop to the rocks below. Tom watched three porpoises arch through the gray water. "We could be in the middle of the ocean," he said with a return of interest. "Not such a bad place, is it?"

"We're going to love it," Gwen said enthusiastically. "Let's go inside before it gets dark, and I'll see what I can cook up for supper."

They didn't do anything about the little building a few yards from the main house. It was there that the former tenant had died, and they didn't want to go inside. They hardly talked about it.

They painted the walls and the beams of their house and arranged their furniture as attractively as they could. Tom enjoyed doing things with his hands and Gwen kept finding things for him to do. When the weather was good he fished from the rocks. The doctor had advised a hobby and fishing was as good as any.

But even that benevolent Indian summer came to an end. The days grew shorter and it became too cold to stand on the rocks below and cast. Tom watched the local fishermen enviously. They went out regularly in their boats and caught enough fish to support their families. If only he had a boat, he might at least be able to feed his wife occasionally. As it was, he could only sit around and watch what little money they had saved dribble away. He grew moody again, so Gwen started looking around for an old rowboat that would be both seaworthy and cheap.

She came back from the village one day with two pieces of good news. She'd located a boat—and a job for Tom. The job really had been offered to her, but she'd managed to get it for her husband. It was the sort of thing he could do without any strain on his heart, and although it didn't pay much, it would give him the feeling he was earning money again.

As Gwen drove around to the back of the house, she noticed a light in the front room. It was only four o'clock, but on these cold, sunless days the daylight went fast.

Gwen pushed open the door to the kitchen and dumped her groceries on the wooden table. She heard voices in the next room. Tom had company—that was good. The visitor arose as Gwen, her cheeks pink from the cold, entered the room.

"This is . . ." Tom began, then he frowned and the stranger said, "My name is Robert Bassett. How do you do, Mrs. Moore."

"How do you do," Gwen said cordially.

"I'll get to the point at once," he said, smiling. "I'm a painter, and like you and your husband, a fugitive from the city. I've been asking your husband if you'd consider renting me the building in back for a studio. It's just what I've been looking for."

He was tall and thin and quite well dressed. His manner was charming and his voice cultivated. And yet in spite of the smile, his eyes were cold and gray—like the winter sea outside. Penetrating, too, like the wind.

Gwen hesitated, trying to catch her husband's eye for a cue. "Well," she said, "we haven't really thought of renting anything. We've barely got settled ourselves."

"I'd promise not to be a nuisance, not to sit in your pocket," the stranger said. "Only by invitation if you get lonely. And you might, you know, during the long winter."

There was a silence which Tom didn't help. He sat in his chair, adding nothing, only drawing on his pipe. He was leaving the decision to Gwen—throwing it in her lap.

She did some rapid figuring. If they asked fifty dollars a month, that would help considerably. And fifty was such a ridiculous figure to ask for that cold shack, he'd probably say no, and that would settle it. But suppose he jumped at it? He looked as if fifty, or even a hundred and fifty, meant nothing to him if he wanted something. Gwen thought hard. He mightn't be any trouble at all; he looked as if he had a great deal of tact. And it would be good to have someone on hand to help in case—well, in case Tom became ill suddenly. That contingency had occurred to her, of course, and it had frightened her.

"We'll think about it," Gwen said. "It's something we hadn't considered. Will you have a cup of tea with us?"

"No, thanks," Mr. Bassett said. "I'll be getting back to the inn. You can reach me there any time for the next few days."

Gwen saw him to the door and they shook hands politely. When she returned, she said, "Everything seems to happen at once." She went over and kissed Tom and put her hand on his shoulder. "I've got lots to tell you . . ."

She always did have when she went to the village. She scraped up a lot of trivia and spun it out to amuse him.

"First," she said a little breathlessly, "we've got a boat. It's a dory, I think, or a dinghy. Belonged on a big boat, you know. The kind of thing they have on hand in case of shipwrecks."

He looked interested. "Probably a wreck itself," he said with a half-smile. "Where is it and how much?"

"Not very much—thirty dollars. Mr. Mesner said it was a bargain. He's bringing it over tomorrow on his truck for your inspection. If it's a nice day, you can go out and try it."

"Sounds all right. We can't be lighthouse keepers without a boat, that's certain. Now I can dash out onto the high seas and rescue people. Might even catch some fish and peddle them."

"No rescues," Gwen said sternly. "Remember, doctor's orders. And the second thing—you've got a job."

"No!"

"Yes. The town of Midford wants you to be an assistant post-master. Four hours a day, three days a week. Pay very small. But pay."

He tried not to show any eagerness, but it·was there, giving him backbone again. "What about civil service exams?" he asked.

"Not for an assistant. Mr. Bowles is postmaster, but he's also a lot of other things in town, and he needs a substitute for times when he has to be away. He calls it helping out in rush hours—that means if more than five people come for their mail at once. Twenty-five dollars, that's all. But . . ."

"No wear and tear. Fine. I'll take it."

"Isn't it wonderful the way everything falls into place?" Gwen said. "Like in a double acrostic. I'll fix supper."

She had to go into the kitchen because she had an outlandish need to cry. Everything was going to work out well now. Tom would be too busy to get depressed, and the doctor had said that half the battle would be keeping him interested in living. And how little it took—just a secondhand boat and a boy's job! Tom, who had been one of the most successful copy writers in New York, a bright young man with a future.

"Stop it," she told herself through the tears. "Happiness is the most relative thing in the world—if you go on using a yardstick, you're sunk. All that matters, anyway, is for Tom to get well."

The subject of Robert Bassett didn't come up until they'd finished supper, although it was there in the back of their minds. It was almost as if they dreaded talking about it, as if they both understood they were building something very intimate and the intrusion of a stranger might spoil it. And as if they both knew they should be practical and realistic, and that what they really felt wouldn't be a strong enough argument against the idea because neither of them could put it into words.

"It would be fifty dollars a month as good as found," Gwen said, bravely taking the lead. "And he might really mean it about keeping to himself. There's a separate entrance and the width of the back yard between us. We'd have to put in a kerosene stove and he could cook his own meals. I'd hate to turn down his offer. We'd never find fifty dollars as easily as that—"

"You don't have to be mercenary," Tom said with unusual sharpness. "We've been managing to get along all right."

"Yes, of course," Gwen said quickly. "But it would be nice to count on a little extra that we could put aside—"

"For my last sickness and the funeral," Tom said.

Gwen stopped him. "Don't talk that way! You're going to live forever if you're just a little bit careful. The doctor said so. Besides, unless you deliberately want to be horrid to me, you'd know how that sort of talk makes me feel."

"Darling, I'm sorry." Tom put out his hand and touched hers. He got up slowly. "Think it over yourself. If you're sure it won't be any extra work, let's tell Bassett he can move in."

"I'll tell him tomorrow," Gwen said, "when I go to the village." She turned on the radio. She wanted suddenly to fill the house with cheerful music, to drown out the everlasting sound of the waves washing over the rocks below.

Good weather came back, and Tom took the boat out almost every day and fished. His job at the post office kept him busy enough to enjoy his leisure, which was what Gwen had hoped for. She was busy herself with her house to care for and meals to prepare and various community activities in which she'd begun to take part. She liked being with other women, sharing their housekeeping problems and hearing about their husbands and children. She liked feeling part of the world, the normal world, liked feeling that she and Tom were normal people too. The more she held on to other people, the more she felt she was helping Tom to go on living.

The tenant had moved in quietly, with furniture of his own in addition to his painting materials. He came and went in his car, and they hardly ever saw him.

One day toward the middle of December Gwen returned from Midford a little later than usual. On the way home she had felt happier than she had in a long time. Every day Tom seemed stronger and in better spirits. The doctor had been so right when he told her that if she kept her husband cheerful and full of hope, nature might work a miracle.

She put down her parcels, then listened. Tom was talking earnestly with someone. She recognized the other voice as that of their tenant, Robert Bassett.

"Men no longer have a need to think," she heard Bassett say. "What we have become is a race of robots, material for armies, manpower for factories that turn out weapons for our own destruction. Civilization is doomed. Its last chapter is being written."

Tom said, "Have another drink?"

"Thanks. What I mean to say is that the time for the artist, for people like us, individualists with our sentimental ideas of love for each other and for our so-called fellow man, is over. There is room for a few on top, trampling with big boots over the rest, pushing them farther toward the cliff: but for us, what is there left? To go off by ourselves and hug our last vestiges of private ambition? Rot. If I thought there was anything better in store for us in hell, I'd take off in my own time as a last gesture of individuality."

Gwen stiffened, and then a surge of anger sent her quickly into the next room. She glanced from one man to the other and saw the half-empty bottle between them. The atmosphere in the room was thick with gloom.

"Hello," she said, and lighted the table lamp. "Nice of you to drop in, Mr. Bassett. I saw you go out this morning with your paints and was glad you had such a fine day. It's been wonderful weather, hasn't it?" She emptied an ashtray and put it back on the table with a bang.

Bassett had risen politely and she didn't ask him to sit down again. She looked at him as if she had suddenly discovered a cobra. The lean, dark face she had thought rather attractive now looked evil. She wanted him to go away and keep away from them with his poisonous talk.

"Gwen," Tom said, "why not ask Robert to supper?"

"Thank you very much," Robert Bassett said, "but not tonight. Do ask me again. I'll drop over tomorrow with those books, Tom. Thanks for the drinks and good talk. Good night."

Gwen went to the door with him. "Are you sure you're comfortable in the studio?" she asked. "The heating arrangement isn't much. I'm afraid you're going to be awfully cold this winter."

"Everything is perfect," he said with a smile. "I'm quite contented."

She closed the kitchen door and stood against it for a moment, watching through the glass as he made his way into the other building. I must talk to him alone, she decided. He mustn't come here feeding that poison to Tom. He can keep his sour old philosophy to himself. We don't want any of it!

She started preparing supper and went into the other room to set the table. Tom was still in his chair, but his head was in his hands.

"Are you feeling all right, dear?" Gwen asked, trying to hide her anxiety.

He looked up and his face was gray and haggard—the way it had looked when he'd first become ill. "Is anybody feeling all right?" he asked bitterly. "Or can I be the only one who feels this way?"

"What way?" Gwen asked, gathering the glasses and the bottle and trying to keep her voice and hands steady. "What are you talking about?"

"Oh, I don't know. Just that we might as well face the fact that we're licked. The whole world is in a mess too, if that's any consolation, which it isn't."

"We're not in a mess," Gwen said sharply. "Maybe we were, but we're getting out of it."

He shook his head. "Let's not go on fooling ourselves, Gwen. I'm sick. I'll never be anything but a burden to you. Do you want to go on living on the edge of the world this way, waiting for God knows what?"

Gwen held the glasses close to her so she wouldn't drop them. Then she said, keeping her voice calm and clear, "I certainly want to go on living, if that's what you're asking. If there's anything more wonderful than waking up each morning and facing a new day, I can't imagine it."

"You don't understand," Tom said, misery in his eyes. "All you have to do is pick up the morning paper. All you have to do is read and think—"

"I do think," Gwen said. "I think all the time—of you and of us, and of all the beauty there is in the world handed to us free if only we know enough to recognize it. There are sick and tired people who try to make trouble, but we don't have to listen to them. We've got so much, Tom, and we're happy because we love each other and because we've found peace. Don't let anyone come in here and try to destroy us because he's unhappy."

Tom put out his hand, touched hers and withdrew his hand again. "I'm sorry," he said. "Go on and get supper. I'll wash the dishes." She felt his eyes on her as she left the room, and she knew he was making an effort to conquer his despair.

She tried to get rid of Robert Bassett. But it wasn't easy now that he had broken the ice and become friendly. He brought them presents —a bottle of Scotch, an imported cheese, flowers for Gwen. His manner was suave and charming, and he brought a breath of the sophisticated world into the lighthouse. He might have been a welcome guest were it not for the bitter streak in him that came to the surface from time to time. And to Gwen, who was fighting for Tom's life, he became a dangerous foe, a mortal enemy, but one whom she had to receive with at least the gestures of hospitality.

Winter settled over them. The winds blew more strongly from the Sound now, pounding against the lighthouse and the rocks below. There were fewer ships passing, and frequently there were heavy storms, turning day into night. Tom's rowboat lay below, carefully secured and covered with an old tarpaulin. No one, no matter how ardent a fisherman, would go out in such choppy seas.

One cold January afternoon as Tom and Gwen returned from the village, they saw their tenant sitting before his easel on a point of land that jutted out to sea. He was wearing a heavy Mackinaw and seemed too engrossed with his work to mind the cold. The sky was overcast and there had been storm warnings over the radio all day, but the cloud effects were magnificent.

"If he gets any of that on canvas before the storm, he's good," Tom said as he and Gwen got out of the car.

They saw Bassett put down his brushes and pick up a pair of binoculars which he pointed somewhere between the rocks and the horizon.

Then, apparently having seen them arrive, he turned and signaled them to come nearer.

"Looks like a small boat out there with two men in it. They seem to be having trouble," he called. "Take a squint at them through these, Tom."

Tom strode over and took the binoculars. "Couple of fishermen," he said. "Must be fools not to have listened to the storm warnings. They probably know what they're doing, though. The fish must be running well today, and they can't afford not to pick up an honest dollar. They'll be pulling for shore soon. I don't think we need worry about them."

Tom and Gwen were just sitting down to cups of steaming tea when the storm broke. There were flashes of lightning and accompanying claps of thunder, and then a deluge. But it was warm and cozy in the house. Tom had taken off his heavy shoes and put on slippers and an old jacket. Gwen, watching him relax, told herself that he looked well, almost like his old self.

The next clap of thunder was followed by a sharp rapping at their door. Tom opened it and Robert Bassett, soaked and dripping, came in.

"Get your stuff stowed away before the rain?" Tom asked.

"Yes," Bassett said, "but I went out again to watch what was happening. That boat with the two fishermen had me worried. I stood on the point and there was a flash of lightning that filled the sky with brilliance. Lord, it was magnificent! Made everything clear as day, though it only lasted a split second."

"What about the fishermen?" Tom interrupted.

"They'd capsized, and the two of them were clinging to the boat. At least, I could make out one of them—I'm not sure of the other. Darn fools—they'd deserve to drown! What are storm warnings for but for them and their stupid tribe? But just the same—" He stared at Tom. "You're the lighthouse keeper, more or less, aren't you? I suppose something has to be done for them. There's your boat down there. I'll help you get it in the water."

"But Tom can't take a boat out in this weather," Gwen protested. "His doctor would never permit it. It might—"

"Kill him?" Bassett said calmly. "Maybe not. If we had a telephone, we could call the Coast Guard. But we haven't. And by the time we drive to a phone and get help, those fools will have drowned. I'll start getting the boat ready. No time to lose now."

He was gone. Tom went to the hook where his slicker hung and dug around for his rubber boots.

"But you can't go!" Gwen cried in alarm. "It would be absolutely crazy for you to try to row against that sea. Bassett doesn't understand. And if he did, what would he care? He's the coldest, most inhuman—" She turned her fears for Tom into rage against Robert Bassett. She wouldn't let Tom risk his life for a couple of strange fishermen. "Tom, you mustn't," she said. "I won't let you."

He had put on his slicker and was pulling on his boots. He looked up at her and said simply, "I have to."

She put on her raincoat and went down the steep cliff with him. Bassett already had the tarpaulin off the boat.

"I'll take the oars," he said crisply. "Tom, all you have to do is bail and take it easy. Don't try to help those idiots get aboard. I'll manage that. Shove us off, Mrs. Moore, and watch out for that rock —it's slippery."

The icy water came up to her knees before she got the boat pushed off into the breakers. She stood there watching them until they were lost in the blackness. From time to time the lighthouse beam swept the angry water, but she couldn't make out either the capsized boat or the one with Tom and Bassett. They'll be capsized too, she thought in agony. That old boat hasn't a chance . . .

Her wet hair was slapping against her face; her wet skirt dragged against her legs; a large wave nearly pulled her into the sea. Carefully she climbed back over the rocks until she was safe on land. "Oh, God, keep him safe," she said over and over as she walked back to the house.

She got busy at once, starting a pot of coffee and kettles of hot water. She brought spare blankets from the closet and hung them next to the stove. And from time to time she ran to the window that faced the sea and looked out, though there was nothing visible.

When the coffee was made, she threw on the clammy raincoat again, picked up a lantern and ran out. She slid down the cliff to the rocks and waited. And she prayed. By now her anger was gone; only anxiety remained. She prayed for all of them, Tom and Bassett and the two fishermen. Tom will be all right, she told herself. His heart will find the strength to keep going. And Bassett? Bassett who talked of his contempt for the human race and who had taken it as a matter of course that he and Tom should risk their lives to save two un-known fishermen? God will take care of him too, she thought. He understands Bassett better than I do.

Then she heard the sound of oars and of high waves slapping viciously at the sides of the small boat. She heard the scraping of the boat's bottom on the rocks, and she waded into the icy water again to pull them to shore.

Tom was the first man out; then he helped the others, who seemed exhausted. Bassett made the boat fast and Gwen, holding the lantern, led the procession to the house. Nobody had said a word. They drew up chairs in the kitchen and Gwen filled the cups with coffee while Tom passed around a bottle of rum. Gwen brought towels and dry shirts and went to the bedroom to put on dry things herself. She could hear their voices as she dressed.

"Why in blazes did you want to put out today in the face of the storm warnings?" Robert Bassett demanded.

One of the men answered, "The fish were running and they bring good prices this time of year. We've done it before."

The contempt in Bassett's voice made him sound more like him-self. "You mean you were ready to risk your lives, to say nothing of ours, for the sake of a mess of fish that would net you thirty cents?"

"You don't think of that when you've got a living to make," the other man said. "Thanks for what you've done. We'd better be get-ting along now."

"Have some more coffee?" Tom offered. "Another shot of rum? Do us all good." He sounded cheerful, as if he were enjoying himself. Gwen entered the kitchen and stood watching him. His face was glowing and he looked handsome. She felt a rush of pride in him.

The two fishermen stood up. "We'll be back tomorrow to look for our boat," one said. "She wasn't insured."

Then Bassett spoke. "She'll be driftwood by tomorrow. Come along—I'll drive you back to the village."

When they were alone Gwen sat down and poured herself some coffee. "Was it awful?" she asked.

"Awful?" Tom lighted his pipe and squared his shoulders. "It wasn't too bad. They had strength enough to yell out so we could locate them. After we got them into our boat I took the oars and rowed back. Bassett seemed all in." He began to laugh. "It's a good joke on the doctors, isn't it? They give me up, tell me not to lift a finger or else. Yet when it comes to something like this, I can pull it off like nothing at all. Never felt better in my life, as a matter of fact."

"Being a hero becomes you," Gwen said, and found she could smile.

"Hero, heck," Tom said, but he looked pleased with himself. "It was all Bassett's idea, wasn't it? Queer duck. Goes around saying how much he despises people and then goes and saves a couple of them from drowning. You never can tell, can you?" He yawned comfortably and decided to go to bed.

Gwen washed the cups and glasses and set the table for breakfast. When she heard Bassett's car she threw a scarf over her head and went outside.

"Mr. Bassett," she called softly.

He came toward her, looking very tired. "Yes?" he asked.

"I—I just wanted to tell you how splendid I think you were tonight."

He shrugged and said, "Reflex action, that's all. Commonly called instinct. If I'd thought about it, I suppose I'd have let them drown. No business of mine, after all. How's Tom?"

"He's fine," Gwen said with enthusiasm. "I guess he needed something like that to prove to himself he was a whole man."

She held her breath, then blurted out, "Thank you. Thank you for giving that to Tom, for saving him as much as you saved the others."

He stood looking down at her for a few seconds. Then he took her hand and kissed it. "Good night," he said.

"Good night, Robert. Come to breakfast, won't you? Or lunch?"

"Lunch will be fine," he said. "Thanks a lot."

She returned to the house and stood at the window till she saw the light go on in the studio. She wasn't afraid any more. Not of anything.

Now, here's how an outline could have helped to guide the author of this story.

1. *Kind of story*. Slick. The author probably reasoned that the subject matter—a problem faced by a young married couple—would be best suited to a mass audience.

2. *Situation*. Tom Moore, a prosperous advertising copywriter, has been stricken with a heart ailment. The doctor has advised a quiet place to live, away from the bustle of New York. Tom and his wife Gwen have searched desperately for a place they could afford to rent, and have finally found an abandoned lighthouse. The people of Midford have had to pass upon the Moores as tenants, because they don't want another tenant like the last, who committed suicide. Finally they've approved of Gwen and Tom, who are moving in as the story begins.

Gwen is determinedly cheerful and optimistic in the face of difficulties, for she's bent on helping Tom regain his health in the bracing sea air. Her task is not an easy one, for Tom is depressed, considers himself a burden, and is under great strain.

3. *Chief element*. Character. Although setting is important,

too, the story is primarily about people, especially one person.

4. *Plot complication.* Gwen is doing fairly well until a man asks to rent an outbuilding on the property. Robert Bassett, an artist, negates her good work with Tom by exposing him to a bitter philosophy of life. Tom gets more depressed than ever.

5. *Climax.* Two fishermen are drowning in a storm. Bassett, in spite of his cynical view of humanity, sets off to save them, and Tom finds that he, too, in spite of his weak heart, must risk his life on the rescue mission. Gwen is frantic with worry.

6. *Outcome.* The two men, Tom and Bassett, save the fishermen. Gwen wades out in the icy water to pull the rowboat to shore and finds Tom in glowing spirits. Obviously he no longer feels like "Half a Man" but one able to cope with life.

7. *Viewpoint.* Third Person. Because this story needed plenty of action and switching of scene, it required the greater range and freedom of this viewpoint.

8. *Theme.* Through a selfless act we often redeem ourselves.

9. *Emotional effect.* Sympathetic participation of the reader in Gwen's problem.

Having read both the story and the outline, you'll see that the actual writing—the author's professional skill—provides the "soul" of the story.

Methods of outlining differ

Although many professional writers use an outline like the one above, their methods of outlining differ. Here is Mignon Eberhart's method:

I do not outline the exact events and incidents; my experience is that an attempt to cling to an exact and detailed outline in fiction makes my story inflexible. But I do make many notes before I start to write—the names of characters, their relationships to each other, the general circumstances of the story, many details which I may or may not use. I do know what the story is to be about, where I am going to start the story, the ending of the story, and (in a general way) how I hope to arrive at that ending.

I cannot make a detailed, chapter-by-chapter outline but every day when I start to work I have a fairly firm idea of what point in the story I hope to reach at the end of the day's work—that is, what I am going to write about that day and how I hope it will advance the story. In general the incidents which advance and develop the story emerge during the writing: if you are very lucky (or if you have given enough thought to the story), these incidents derive from the characters as they come alive on the typewriter.

Other notes which I find helpful are thumbnail biographies of the characters. I usually put these on paper. I also find that I must know accurate facts concerning the background for my story, not only the setting but the various pursuits and professions of the characters in the story. For example, I could not write a story, say, set in a ranch in Australia. I have never so much as set foot in Australia. But I have written stories set in Chicago because I have lived there.

I could not possibly write a story in which, say, a prime minister took a leading role. My daily routine does not include chats with prime ministers. But I could write and have written stories in which a doctor, a banker or a businessman took leading roles for all of us, in our daily lives, have had occasion to observe, or are able to discover by immediate observation, something of these backgrounds.

Whether or not the plan for a story is on paper seems to me unimportant, but the plan *must exist*. The goal at which you expect to arrive and the working structure of how you are going to arrive at that goal are not only important, they are essential.

But there's one more step in planning before you are ready to add the "soul" to your practical foundation. That is *research,* or gathering the facts you'll need for story authenticity.

Earlier in the Course, you've read of ways to go about researching. In short stories, you may need only facts from your own knowledge and experience—or you may need a great many more. In the latter case, it's wise to collect them in advance so you'll have them available the moment your story calls for them.

For instance, in a prison-escape story called "The Blue Wall," author Bill Corcoran has this to say of how he came to write it:

The essential situation in this story is one that actually happened. Such an escape was planned and executed a generation ago in Charlestown Prison in Boston. Upon that basis of fact I built a tale that is, of course, straight fiction.

Thus you know that Corcoran did some research to get his facts straight. Otherwise, letters of protest would have come to his editor, an always embarrassing occurrence for the author.

Here are excerpts from "The Blue Wall," showing some of the details and facts the author had to know to write the story:

Tip had first been put to work on the coal pile, the usual thing for beginners. That accounted for his meeting Gallagher. Con Gallagher was an engineer and he ran the boilers. It was a practice of Warden McCloud's to shift convicts from job to job at intervals, to prevent them from plotting or consolidating unscheduled privileges. Very logically Tip was installed in the prison offices after his initiation, and there his deft hands proved so useful in filing papers and disposing of routine that he retained the post for many months.

He was there when McCloud ordered a housecleaning. Ancient, bulging files of duplicate records, orders, bills, were to be cleared out and burned. Tip tossed stacks of dusty, brittle papers into wicker baskets and carried them down to the boilers. On each trip he chatted with Gallagher a moment while the refuse roared to ashes on the coals . . .

Recreation came at 2:30 P.M. For two hours the 1,500 inmates of Graymoor had the run of the great bare enclosure within the walls. Mostly they spent this time walking in pairs or small groups. Everywhere they talked, ardently and incessantly. A few walked alone, but even these talked to themselves; they were the stir bugs, the nuts who "had missed too many boats" . . .

The punishment cells at Graymoor are no worse than those of any penitentiary the country over. They express the corrective ideas of two generations back, and express them well. They were in the basement of the main building, a single line of narrow coops walled with stone, windowless except for a small grille in the solid steel door, ventilated by a pipe running from one corner of the low ceiling to the main vents a couple of stories above. There is no cot, there is no light, there is no sound; there are only a couple of moldy blankets, a low stool, and twenty-four hours of reflection on a diet of bread and water. The occupant of a cell remains there at the pleasure of the warden.

In a story in *Argosy* called "Stilled Are the Guns," by George Taylor, only a careful investigation of facts and details could have created plausibility and the right Civil War atmosphere. Here are some excerpts for illustration:

Then came the second day of fighting at Gettysburg, the fighting on the slopes of Culp's Hill, so verdantly and gently rising out there in the middle distance. Elliott breathed deeply, and once more his nostrils seemed to draw in the smell of sweat and rot and humid dampness.

He and the quiet-spoken Vermont men and boys had crouched behind the stone wall following the backbone of the ridge. Johnson's men had surged yelling out of the woods like a prairie fire. Elliott had felt immortal. But in the midst of the hand-to-hand fighting he had taken a Minié ball in the leg. Rising to his knees he caught a glancing blow on his forehead, probably from a rifle butt. The ensuing darkness, he thought wryly, was the only undisturbed peace he was granted during the whole damned war . . .

Still carrying the Minié ball in his left leg, he picked up another in his side at Spottsylvania Courthouse, and a long bullet crease across the top of his head during an unimportant skirmish somewhere in the Virginia woods in the closing days.

Researching for authenticity isn't always necessary. Often you'll have lots of facts in a notebook and can build a story from them. Your notebook—if you establish the habit of jotting down useful information, including the way things smelled, looked, felt, tasted and other details which are apt to escape the memory later—can be a constant research source.

Different ways of collecting facts

Different writers have different ways of collecting facts. Their notes may be based on firsthand experience and knowledge, or gained from books, or taken from conversations with others who've had certain experiences.

Faith Baldwin, as have many writers, discovered early in her career the wonders of the public library:

At the time I wrote *American Family,* which was practically a million years ago, I haunted the New York public library and when I sprained my ankle sent a friend to haunt it for me. For much of the book was laid in China and some dealt with clipper ships. I had a lot of source material from the journals of my missionary grandfather and my own father's letters but how I needed clipper ships' logs!

At the library I was able to get a photostat of the very ship upon which grandfather had sailed on his second voyage; and in the files of the newspapers discovered what the weather was like on that day, also the winds, and who was at his lookout post at Sandy Hook.

Much of the Chinese part came from libraries too. A friend, China-born, and in the same missionary compound, whose husband was then teaching at Ohio Wesleyan, sent me a great number of books—part of one was written by my grandfather—dealing with the section in which this part of the story was laid. Without her, the New York library, and the University library, I could not have written the book.

In the *Adventure* story, "The Sea of Night" by Robert Edmond Alter, the author had to use research sources to create a realistic atmosphere. On the following page is an excerpt.

Someone lit a cargo lamp. It swung lurchingly overhead, smearing the passengers' waiting faces a pale orange, chasing the shadows into brown corners. They were Malays for the most part, traveling freight, like Dave, from Padang to Djakarta. The *Mula Mulai* was a schooner-rigged prau or palari. Her hull, with the high poop deck, resembled her model, the Portuguese galleon of four hundred years ago. Her cargo was tobacco and a large shipment of empty arrack casks. She was a trim little sailer, but she wasn't meant for an Indian Ocean hurricane.

In the next excerpt, it's also easy to imagine that the writer used a notebook. It is from "Day of Vengeance" by Noel Langley, published in *The Saturday Evening Post*.

Lt. Torbal Medwin, of the Queen's cavalry, was twenty-three when the Zulu rebellion broke out in South Africa. Being all that a young cavalryman should conform to in the 1870's, he left a young wife behind him; and the parting seemed vast and everlasting, even before the troopship entered the Biscay . . .

The Zulu regiments, circling out in their huge pincer formation, rattling their shields and roaring their battle chants, struck awe and terror into young Medwin's heart by their pure magnificence, but the first cavalry charge, well-covered by rifle fire, cut through their ranks like a knife through butter, and drove them off. They fought with stabbing spears and huge oxhide shields, with a raging courage and utter indifference to death. Young Medwin had seen nothing like it before, and found his imagination perpetually boggling, like a child's overwhelmed by Arabian Nights fantasia . . .

The unit's chief scout was an old Boer hunter called Sannie Verster, nearly seventy, but as wiry and chipper as a thirty-year-old. He shuffled along beside the dapper officers, seated on the saddleless rump of a Basuto pony, a pipe in his mouth, and a flow of white whiskers splaying out over his chest and drifting over his shoulders in the wind. He had no love for the British militia, but he had less for the Zulus, who had ravaged and massacred his own families when they had thrust through from the south on their great trek forty years earlier.

He knew every strategy and tactic of the Zulu impi attack; it was upon his advice that the colonel abandoned the old square and used the Boer laager, a makeshift fort of supply wagons, end to end, like a snake with its tail in its mouth; from behind which his men loaded, fired and reloaded like automatons.

These kinds of stories, requiring detailed facts, are less likely to contain a technical error than the everyday type in which minor details, seemingly familiar, may be glaringly wrong to a reader who happens to know more about them than the writer.

For instance, if you write of a farm, an opera, a horseshow, a walk in the wood, a night club, a business office, a hunting trip, a golf game—be sure your description passes muster with those who know exactly what you're writing about, down to the smallest item.

As Mignon Eberhart puts it:

If someone is to be poisoned, do you know exactly how the poison would affect the character's speech or actions? If there's to be a doctor or policeman or judge in the story, are you sure you have the right terminology at hand? Is your costuming correct for the period in which your story is set? Are there details about your characters' social background, geographical environment, education, work or nationality that would add color and authenticity to your story?

Do you know the proper names for the trees, bushes, flowers in the locale you've chosen to write about? Are you sure of the dialect of the people in your story? If children are to appear, will they speak in a manner appropriate to their age? If you mention an illness, will it be properly described, with medically correct symptoms? If you are to use slang, have you brought it up to date? Do you know the music and dances of the time and place of your story?

In other words, do your research *first*. In this way you prepare yourself as much as possible for the big, important step—which is *to begin writing!*

The endless lure of entertainment

A piece of fiction is rarely read because a reader wishes to be informed. All fiction, no matter how profound, must contain a certain entertainment quality. I don't mean entertainment in a light sense but in the sense that it will hold a reader's interest. Dickens was a great social reformer, but did anybody ever read his books for that? Hardly. They wanted to know what was going to happen to David Copperfield when he got to the sweatshop. They didn't want to read statistics on child labor—they wanted to know what was going to happen to the boy.—Mignon Eberhart

Section VI

Lesson nineteen

Fiction writing

course

Choosing

titles

and names

In the preceding four Lessons, we sought to establish these foundations clearly in your mind:

1. Situation.
2. Plot outline.

3. Kind of story.
4. Point of view.

Now the time has come to consider the art of weaving them together—of creating out of them the unified design of a story.

This setting down of words—the act of writing itself—eludes fixed rules. It springs from each individual in a blend of imagination, inventiveness, experience, taste, interest, philosophy and state of mind. But even so, many questions asked by student writers can be answered with the knowledge gained over the years from the response of many readers to many stories. Some of the questions are these:

1. *Titles.* How are they selected or created? Is there any definite procedure for titling a story? What should I know about titles in general?

2. *Names.* How do I go about naming characters or places in my stories? Are names important or unimportant to the success of a story?

3. *Scenes.* How can I create the most effective scenes to move the plot along? Is there a way of putting scenes together that will help me visualize them and thus save me time and effort in writing?

4. *Selectivity.* How shall I select what to write and what not to write about my characters, their backgrounds and histories, the setting of my story and the details of action? Is selectivity an innate talent or can it be learned? Is it essential to my craft?

5. *Style.* What style shall I choose for my story? How will I know whether or not it is the best choice? How do I develop my own style? What should I know about the style of other writers and of the importance of style in telling a story?

6. *Dialogue.* What should I know about using dialogue in a story? How much or how little should be in it? Is dialogue important to a story or merely incidental? Is there any difference between the way dialogue is used in a short story and in a longer piece of writing?

7. *General information.* What general information do I need about writing that will help me to write an interesting story? How, for instance, do I create: (a) Suspense? (b) Emotion?

8. *Motivation.* What is motivation, and how does it enter the structure of a story?

9. *Technicalities.* Are there any technicalities of writing that I should learn and put to use? For example:

(a) The flashback?

(b) Planting clues? Why are they important, and how are they incorporated into a story?

(c) Transitions? Just what are they, and how are they achieved?

(d) Length? How shall I decide how long or short a story should be?

10. *Devices.* Are there any mechanical devices that would help to make my story more successful? What, for instance, should I know about:

(a) Repetition? Why is it an important part of creating a story effect, and how will I know when to apply it?

(b) Implication? What is implication, and is it useful to my story?

11. *Beginnings.* How about beginning my story? What should I put in the opening paragraph? What is a *narrative hook,* and how is it used?

12. *Crisis.* After I am launched into my story, what about the crisis I am leading up to?

13. *Ending.* And then, how about the ending? Are there specific ways to bring a story to its conclusion? Are there different kinds of endings that I should know when and how to use?

Listed together, this may seem like an overwhelming number of questions to consider before you get into the creative writing. If, however, you pause to examine the answers one by one, you'll not only avoid discouraging delays and unsuccessful attempts, but will also give the greatest freedom to your creative urge. In fact, once they're set in your mind, you may never have to pause to consider them again, for they'll become automatic processes in your writing.

Choosing your title

Going back to Question No. 1, here are some suggestions on *titles* from Bennett Cerf:

Many writers like to decide upon a title before commencing a story. It not only changes the look of a piece of blank paper but often helps to set up or clarify the story. A title with meaning can form a guidepost for your words.

On the other hand, some writers don't care whether they have a title or not, and come back later, after the story is finished or half-finished, to think of one. They may find an apt title in the text of the story, or the writing itself may bring out new meaning in the original idea and thus produce an appropriate title.

Sometimes a title springs to the writer's mind ready-made like an inspiration. At other times a title simply won't present itself. Even searching through books of quotations fails to yield just the one the writer is looking for. So he'll give up for a while and try to write the story without a heading of any kind.

Titles vary in importance. Sometimes they are vital to the story, sometimes not. But they are worth real consideration, both for what they can do for your story and in the various functions they perform.

Some titles are designed chiefly to capture the reader's attention or curiosity. They may startle with their idea or phrasing, arouse a question, perhaps a puzzle. Because of this, the reader may be hooked into the opening paragraphs of the story. Titles in this category are:

"Weather or Not"   "Ride on a Short Dog"
"Trigger Sudden"   "Two Bottles of Relish"
"Among the Dangs"   "Bitters Neat"

These titles don't tell you very much about what to expect, so you have to read the story to find out what it's about. But don't use this kind of title unless you want to approach the reader obliquely.

Another kind of title is an intriguing comment or observation, sometimes philosophical, sometimes ironical, often humorous, such as in the following:

"The Daring Young Man on the Flying Trapeze"
"What a Thing, to Keep a Wolf in a Cage!"
"Never Take No for an Answer"
"The Picture Wouldn't Fit in the Stove"
"How the Devil Came Down Division Street"

These are statements that challenge the reader's imagination and hint at the story's nature, but avoid being specific or descriptive.

Titles that describe the story or give a fairly direct clue are likely to trap readers intrigued by the subject. Here are some typical ones:

"The Other Wise Man"   "The Man Who Would Be King"
"Home From Camp"   "Revolt of the Machines"
"The Way of the Hunted"   "Happy Anniversary"
"Tip on a Dead Jockey"   "A Cup of Coffee"
"The Last Kill"   "The Most Dangerous Game"

Titles sometimes describe the setting in which the stories take place, a main character or group of people, or a special time, and in this way give the reader a clue to the subject. Here are titles dealing with setting:

"A Table at Ciro's"	"The Other Side of the River"
"An Odyssey of the North"	"Weekend at Grimsby"
"Lost on 44th Street"	"Night Club"
"House of Many Rooms"	"No Room in the Inn"

The following examples tell the reader that the story is about a person or people, using dominant personal traits to arouse interest:

"The Healthiest Girl in Town"	"Children on Their Birthdays"
"A Thief by Choice"	"All the Dead Pilots"
"The Non-Marrying Male"	"The Undefeated"
"The Amazing Mrs. Mimms"	"The Summer People"
"The Doctor's Son"	"The Excursionists"

Using the name of a character as a title has valid purposes. According to the kind of name chosen, it may convey a wide range of impressions about what the story holds. The title "Belle Starr," for instance, denotes a story about the famous heroine of the Old West, while "Klondike Mike Mahoney" tells the adventures of a gold prospector. But when the connection is not so obvious, a phonetic association is helpful. For instance, a strong-sounding name usually denotes a strong main character, such as "Masterson" or "Markheim." Likewise, a title like "Mrs. Confedrington" promises a strange or unusual female character, thus arousing reader curiosity. The title "Grenville Fane" suggests a male of some note, while in contrast, "Mr. Nab" suggests a hero with mental or physical eccentricities.

The time element in a title can be used to create suspense, nostalgia and other moods. Here are samples taken from published stories:

"One Hour to War"	"The Five-Forty-Eight"
"The Long Night"	"The Day It Rained Forever"
"The First Morning"	"Between the Halves"
"Back for Christmas"	"Hold Back the Dawn"

Perhaps the most frequently used titles emphasize the outstanding situation, object or event of the story. They are both direct and informative, and arouse the reader's anticipation.

Some examples of titles of this kind are as follows:

"The Monkey's Paw"	"Fall of the Hero"
"The Beating of Jim Pope"	"The Snapshot Mystery"
"Flight Through the Dark"	"Robot's Return"

The use of a theme, sometimes as a quotation, is often effective in titling. It indicates to the reader that the story will attempt to illustrate some truth of life—ironical or thought-provoking, uplifting or satirical.

The following examples show a variety of ways in which such titles have been employed:

"Act of Faith"	"Some Like Them Cold"
"The Law of Life"	"Kneel to the Rising Sun"
"In Sickness as in Health"	"Loved I Not Honor More"
"Substitute God"	"The Lark's on the Wing"

In many a short story written around a person, place or thing, the author has used the name of that person, place or thing as an effective title. For example:

"Araby"	"Herself"	"Portrait"
"Harvest"	"Widow"	"Chickamauga"
"Champion"	"Pardner"	"Fighter"
"Rain"	"Haircut"	"Carrie"

Finally, an alliterative title does wonders in luring your reader. The following titles rhyme or, at the least, repeat a single sound, usually a consonant, to fix them by alliteration in the reader's mind.

"Mrs. 'Arris Goes to Paris"	"Big Blonde"
"The Willow Walk"	"Love Is for Lovers"
"Silent Snow, Secret Snow"	"A Summer Shower"
"Success Story"	"The Honey House"
"The Devil and Daniel Webster"	"Brahmin Beachhead"

How to choose names

Finding a name for a character is the first and most important step in identifying him or her for a reader. A name with just the right sound and tone can do a great deal to establish a character's background, while a carelessly chosen name creates a hazard in the reader's mind and dilutes the details of the author's portrayal.

Writers who make a real study of the subject know how helpful names can be in denoting a dominant trait, an age, an occupation, a nationality, a race, an education level, an emotional quality, a physical characteristic. Often the mere length or spelling of a name evokes a vivid image for the reader. On the other hand, a name created in contrast to the character's dominant trait can be useful in achieving a humorous, eccentric or strange effect. Max Shulman says:

If finding names to suit your characters is difficult, the telephone book or city register is a big help. But before turning to such sources, you might make a list of character traits and then choose names that seem to fit them appropriately.

The same principle of matching names to people can be also applied when you are seeking names for towns, cities or streets. Give careful thought to the mood, geography and main characteristics of the place, then choose a name that to you evokes a clear picture.

To show how people's names are important to characterization, here are some examples paired for contrast. Note the different picture the reader would receive:

Mark Steele entered the crowded room and looked around.
Egbert Sniffen entered the crowded room and looked around.

Sonia wiped her hands on her apron.
Cynthia wiped her hands on her apron.

Chauncey Tremaine gave a small bow.
Mike Higgins gave a small bow.

Mrs. Irma Schlumpf paused at the store window.
Mrs. Prudence Hetherington paused at the store window.

Brett Ashley ate hurriedly.
Joe Kranz ate hurriedly.

Babe Kelly hurled the ball.
Hermann Ludwig hurled the ball.

Wendy danced for the grownups.
Carlotta danced for the grownups.

Using the same method, note contrasts in names of towns, cities or streets:

Sweetwater was filled with strangers.
Schweinfurt was filled with strangers.

Black Eagle was chosen as the site for the event.
Charlestown was chosen as the site for the event.

Each summer we go to Cool Harbor.
Each summer we go to Mosquito Cove.

Plain, familiar names are often exactly right for a character, but different effects can be achieved by taking well-known names and giving them a new twist. *Sarah,* for instance, is made more exotic by changing the *ah* to *i,* creating *Sari.* Adding an *a* to *Ann* making it *Anna* seems to change her characterization. Or, to reverse the procedure, dropping the first letter from *Elizabeth* makes *Lizabeth* which, in another variation, can become *Lizbeth.*

You can change first letters in a surname as well as final letters, thereby creating a different characterization. For instance, a *G* could replace the *H* in *Higgins,* making *Giggins;* an *F* could replace the *H* in *Harris,* making it *Farris;* a *B* could replace the *T* in *Taylor* making it *Baylor.*

Let's try other changes at the end of names. A *t* in place of the *h* at the end of *Smith* makes it a strange name, *Smitt;* the *f* in *Wolf,* replaced by a *k,* making *Wolk,* evokes another character; the *e* in *Rose* changed to a *t,* making *Rost,* provides yet another variation. Bergen Evans says:

In studying names, remember that in real life people don't always bear a name that characterizes them, while in fiction a valuable means of characterization is lost if they don't. It's wise, therefore, to consider carefully each character in your story before you start, for a thoughtlessly conceived name may lead your characterizing astray, causing you to write according to the name chosen rather than to the person you originally had in mind.

What professional writers have done with the names of characters is an invaluable guide to the beginner. Some who've given deep thought to characters' names are Zane Grey, Rex Beach, Jack London, Robert Louis Stevenson, Joseph Conrad, Conan Doyle, James Michener, John Galsworthy, Sinclair Lewis, William Faulkner, James Warner Bellah, Dashiell Hammett, Raymond Chandler, Paul Gallico, Mickey Spillane, James Cain, Irwin Shaw, Kay Boyle, Max Shulman and many others whose work is found in current magazines and in story anthologies.

If you turn back to some of the story examples given in this Course, you'll find enlightening hints about naming characters. Villains and heroes, heroines and villainesses, even minor characters are carefully differentiated. It was not by chance that

Charles Dickens called one of his most despicable characters *Uriah Heep,* for the very name sounds like the detestable sneak he was in *David Copperfield.* Willa Cather correctly called one of her most lovable foreign-born characters *Neighbour Rosicky,* while P. G. Wodehouse, famous for name choices, created an English butler named *Jeeves* and a lovable old scamp named *Uncle Fred.* Robert Louis Stevenson called his merciless pirate *Captain Flint.*

With careful selection you can give tough men names that sound tough—*Wolf Larsen* is Jack London's brutal sea captain, for instance. Or, gentle women can be given names that convey gentility—*Beth* in the Louisa May Alcott story, *Little Women.*

Picking two stories reprinted in this Course, "The Best Year" and "Company Cast-Off," let's try to guess why the authors chose the names they did.

In "The Best Year," the main character is a young farm boy who's never known anything but hard work and poverty. The name the author chose is *Ben.* Why? Well, Ben is a short, simple name without color or vigor, but straightforward, honest and appropriate to the boy's environment. When the author gives the name in full, we find it is *Ben Risteen.* Did the author perhaps think in terms of age—teens?

The boy's parent is not specifically named, but by constant references to "his father" the author clearly shows the man's lack of intimacy with the boy, his detachment, his authority. The rancher is *Eli Coombs.* Could anyone but a rancher be called this? In real life, perhaps—but in a story this name carries associations that create a picture for the reader. Had Eli Coombs been called Hugo Martin, the writer would have had to work harder to establish the image of a rancher.

The Colonel doesn't have to have a specific name in order to be characterized. He needs only to be an Army man. In his dialogue with Ben, the reader learns what *kind* of Army man he is, but the Colonel still doesn't need a name. Had he been given one, it would have been irrelevant to the story. The name of the horse is *Traveler* like the famous mount of General Robert E. Lee. *Traveler* must be a fast, nicely gaited, sleek animal ideal for an Army officer.

In "Company Cast-Off" the main character is *Talbot Brand.* Guessing at the author's associations here, we sense that Talbot has been selected to convey dignity and quality, while Brand brings the somewhat unbusinesslike first name into the realm of business by its association with products. Thus we have a prominent man in big business.

Belle, an old-fashioned name, is suitable for an older wife. It also denotes prettiness in her youth—"Belle of the Ball"—and characterizes her physically as still pretty. The shoeshine boy is simply called *Joey.* The name is both cocky and endearing.

Talbot Brand's superior is *J. C. Tanner.* The initials sound vaguely powerful, and the name Tanner sounds as if he is capable of "tanning," in a business way, anyone who opposes him.

Glance through current magazines and note the trends in names. You'll see that names once popular with authors have changed with the times. For instance, men's names like Hiram, Wilbur, Orville, Roscoe, Theodore, Elmer, August, Rufus, Percy, Homer, Horace, Eugene, Silas, Clarence, and dozens of names from ancient history and the Bible, once typical for men in fiction, sound pretentious nowadays. They've been replaced by Bob, Dick, Jim, Joe, Al, Gary, Mike, Rex, Tony, Eric, Larry, Max, Bill, Tom, Craig and others.

Female names like Abigail, Elvira, Prudence, Fanny, Maude, Bertha, Lena, Hannah, Pearl, Gussie, Flora and Violet are seldom used for modern heroines. Their places have been taken by Mary, Betty, Cynthia, Anne, Linda, Pam, Carol, Ava, Debbie, June, Diane, Susan, Barbara, Joan, Judy, Sandra and others.

Furthermore, there are subtle differences in the names used in slick, pulp and quality stories. The pulp names, for instance, are generally plain. The slick names often are slightly more stylized, with fewer bluntly descriptive nicknames for the men and a greater degree of ornateness for the women. In quality stories, names may be used in a purely symbolic way or may be more like names in real life, as truthfully blunt as the characterization demands or exaggerated for irony.

The choosing of names should provide you with many fascinating moments in the process of characterizing, and will prove more than worth the effort you expend. After all, in real life, names are and always will be our chief form of identification for each other—the first question we ask or respond to when we meet, and the first item of information in the formal record of our existence.

Getting rid of characters

You should think carefully about the four elements in a story—character, setting, situation and theme. But the time always comes when you've just got to get words on paper, and when you transfer your ideas into words, your characters, settings, situations and themes are bound to change somewhat. Many things come out of the typewriter that you hadn't imagined. But as they develop clearly, they give the whole project better focus.

I know for my own part that I seem more and more likely as my characters come out of the typewriter to understand what that kind of person would do. I also find, occasionally, that I have created a character who has no relation whatsoever to the plot. He's a fifth wheel. I thought of him, I put him into the story. But he never came alive; he proved to have nothing whatever to do with the story. So I had to remove him.—Mignon Eberhart

Women make successful writers

Any woman, given some talent, the urge to express herself and the will to work, can write successfully—and her sex will not deter her. There are as many successful women fiction writers as men. One factor attributed to women which has often been (as far as the critics are concerned) a detriment in other professions does not hold true in writing. Women lawyers and doctors, for instance, are always accused of being "too emotional." Yet in writing, emotion is certainly no drawback. Instead, it's an enormous help. For you have to *feel* in order to write.—Faith Baldwin

Through a writer's eyes

No writer should be afraid to describe the world he sees, even if it is different from the world of others. He is the only one who sees it. After all, all a writer has to give is himself.—Somerset Maugham

Lesson twenty

Fiction writing

course

How to pick scenes

By this time you've established your story line or *plot*. You have your foundational situations—your *plot outline*—mapped out. Added to this you have a *title*, and your characters have been given their identifying tags, *names*.

Now, how do you go about illustrating your situations, putting your people into action? How do you actually translate your story outline into words to show your reader what is happening?

This next step requires you to look at your technical material from a new point of view—the visual and imaginative. The material guides and launches you, but now you must create the actual scenes that bring the story to life for your reader. Bergen Evans says:

A scene is a unit of action. A story is a series of units linked together. These units or scenes illustrate one by one the points in a story that move it along. Each scene is complete and has its own function, yet leaves the way open for another unit to follow.

The chief value of scenes is that they allow a writer to break down a mass of impressions and ideas into a reliable design for his imagination. In a short story, one scene leads the writer's imagination to another, since each scene not only illustrates and advances the story but leaves material for another scene to resolve. In other words, by grouping your story into scenes, you find out which material moves it forward and which doesn't.

The art of smoothly joining your scenes together will be covered later in Section VII. At this point, it's sufficient for you to end a scene simply where it ends in your imagination. When you come to the end, stop—then switch to the next scene. Although you may one day abandon any conscious thought of creating scenes, the habit of thinking out your stories this way will greatly stimulate your imagination. Stories will present themselves in visual terms, whether in logical sequence or not, and scenes will occur to you as a major part of your inspiration.

For proof of the way in which stories are composed of scenes, let's examine some action units and see what has gone into them in the form of information and narrative, the two main essentials for advancing a story. First, we're giving you a published story which we have reduced to a synopsis: the mere facts of what takes place. Read it slowly and carefully so that the story line becomes sharp in your mind. Immediately after the synopsis the full story is printed as it appeared in *McCall's*. You'll see for yourself exactly how one author's imagination went to work to shape his plot into scenes.

No two people would imagine scenes for this particular plot in the same way, so as you read "And One Was Loyal" by Stanley Abbott, compare your own visualizations with the author's. Although of course they will differ, you'll note there's logical material in each of these units, and that they follow the principle of telling the reader what he should know, then illustrating an action that changes the situation and advances the story.

We have put Summaries at the end of each scene so you'll not only be able to note where a scene ends and another begins, but the way in which an insignificant scene (which may be necessary to illustrate an action) can be slipped into another without emphasis, and even bolster a bigger scene. The Summaries also show what information the writer has used and what portion of the situation in the scene he has left unresolved.

Synopsis of story

An English writer, while in New York on a visit, notices a familiar painting in an art gallery window. He goes inside and finds that a woman he once knew in Malaya is having a showing of her work. They arrange to meet later that evening.

Meantime, he recalls the events that brought their lives together and sees himself as he travels the Kelantan River in Malaya, doing research on a jungle book . . .

Coming upon a rubber plantation, he seeks lodging in a planter's bungalow. Grudgingly, and only in exchange for whisky, the ill-tempered planter admits him.

The writer finds that the planter's wife is mute from some past shock. He feels sorry for her, and in conversation discovers she's an excellent amateur painter. He encourages her, and she is pathetically grateful. A bond is formed between them.

One night the planter is awakened by a snake dangling over his head. Concluding that his wife is trying to kill him, he rushes for her, but confused by terror he plunges through a veranda railing to his death. When the writer goes to shoot the snake, it has vanished. Meanwhile, the shock of the planter's death has brought back the wife's voice.

The police learn that someone intent upon killing the planter had paid $120 to the hero's boatman to put the snake in the bedroom. The police suspect that the writer gave the money to the boatman. But the writer, knowing the planter's wife had saved this exact amount from winning at cards with her husband, and that she had recorded it in a notebook, steals the notebook to protect her. Then he leaves. . . .

Now, a year later, in New York, he finds the planter's wife having a first exhibit of her paintings. At their arranged meeting, it is revealed that she was not responsible for her husband's death. She knew the $120 had been stolen by the houseboy. But because the boy had always been loyal, she wouldn't tell her husband, for he would have beaten the servant mercilessly. Then, that night, fate decreed that the husband should die in an accident.

So much for the synopsis of Stanley Abbott's "And One Was Loyal." Now we reprint the story just as it appeared in *McCall's,* with our summary comments appearing at intervals throughout.

I

Experience has taught me never to let my friends in New York know when I am arriving. This may sound churlish, but as a Londoner I find it absolutely necessary for survival. At one time I used to announce my arrival well in advance, and the moment I set foot in New York I'd be snatched up in a mad race. Friends would have every minute of the day arranged for and most of the night.

It was all meant kindly and it nearly killed me. I found the answer in not letting anyone know I was in New York for two or three days, at least. I would wander about at leisure—go to the theater, eat where my fancy took me, or walk along the sidewalks pretending to be a native. And all the time I was picking up speed—it was as though my motor were revving up just before going into high gear.

And that's how I felt that afternoon as I strolled along Fifty-seventh Street, when my eye was caught by a painting as I passed an imposing-looking art gallery. It was a study of the jungle and seemed strangely familiar, so as I'd nothing in particular to do, I went in. There was a well-dressed crowd, with the usual sprinkling of not so well dressed but more intense.

I was making my way through the crowd when I came on a large group gathered about a tall girl with auburn hair—Anne Howard! But she looked very different from the girl I'd known almost a year before in a bungalow miles from anywhere in northern Malaya. She wore a smart black silk suit with some frothy nonsense on her head and was laughing gaily, obviously enjoying the adulation of her admirers, and I wondered if any of them knew that her husband had recently died under most peculiar circumstances. She came toward me with hands outstretched.

"George Manson—I can scarcely believe it!" she cried. "How did you know I was here?"

She was smiling up at me and I fancied for a moment there was a hint of mockery in her wide blue eyes. I told her that I hadn't known, that I'd just come in by accident, but I could see she didn't believe me.

"I simply must talk to you, George." She laid her hand lightly on my arm. "But I can't leave—this is my first showing in New York."

"How's it going?" I asked.

"Marvelous—absolutely marvelous. I'll tell you all about it later."

She talked very fast, and there was that typical American quality of excitement about her which was most infectious.

She was having a few people in for cocktails and going on to dinner—would I join them? I told her I would like nothing better.

"I'm at the St. Regis. Come early—at six, before the others do." With a wave of the hand she was gone.

In his first scene, the author has decided to start his story in New York City. This choice of order or sequence of scenes is a writer's privilege—there's no rule about it. To this author the flashback device seemed the most compelling way of illustrating his situation and the most satisfying to his own sense of story telling.

For initial information, the author has visualized the hero arriving in New York, has provided some reasons for his presence on 57th Street, and has thought up the art show to introduce the woman in his story, Anne Howard. To capture the reader's curiosity, he brings in the jungle painting to make contrast with the woman's chic appearance. He wants the reader to know there's been an intriguing situation connected with her, so he has the hero (his name revealed through dialogue is George Manson) remember "a bungalow miles from anywhere in northern Malaya" and the fact that the woman's husband died there "under most peculiar circumstances." He tells the reader that the girl was very different when the writer knew her a year ago. In the dialogue, a bond between them is suggested.

If you think over this information, and examine the creative process by which the author has set it down, you will see that the story is competently launched. Of course, there are other ways of achieving the same end. Why not compare what you might do for a beginning and what information you would supply, and then visualize a scene of your own to replace this author's?

The questions left by this scene are: What was this woman doing in Malaya? Why did she paint a picture of the jungle? What was Manson doing there? Why does she look "very different" now? What was the bond between them? And, the main question, what did this woman, now a successful artist, have to do with her husband's death?

These questions are material for future scenes.

II

When I got back to the hotel I searched through my luggage for a small red leather notebook that belonged to Anne. I'd picked it up in the bungalow on the Kelantan River where we first met. I'd come downriver from the interior and was on my way to the coast to take ship to England.

It was a tedious journey, lying in the bottom of a proa on a dirty mattress during the day and camping each night on the riverbank, and I'd have given anything for a bath and a bed with cool, clean sheets. For hundreds of miles the river cut through the jungle—a wild extravagance of tall, strange-looking trees, intertwined by fast-growing parasites with huge, fleshy leaves and violently colored flowers, all growing out of a floor rank with the decay of centuries.

I'd been wandering about Malaya for many months, picking up material for a book I had in mind, and I was sick of it.

I was consoling myself with the thought that it was only about another day to the coast when the jungle gave way to rows of gashed rubber trees standing in formation. I have always found rubber plantations strangely melancholy, but now it was a relief after the everlasting jungle and it meant a bed when we came to the home of the planter.

It was nearly dark when Kassim, my Dyak headman, gave an order to the paddlers and the proa was brought smartly alongside a landing stage. The plantation bungalow stood on the brow of a hill some fifty yards from the river. I sent my Chinese boy Wong up with a message requesting the kindness of a bed for the night. It seemed no time before he returned; the answer was no. I was completely taken aback.

Planters on the whole lead lonely lives, and apart from its being the custom, are only too pleased to welcome a stranger. I was wondering whether to invite another snub by going up myself when a lantern came swinging down the path.

"What's your name?" a voice shouted, and at the same time the lantern was thrust into my face.

"I'm George Manson. I'm sorry to trouble you, but I was hoping you might be able to put me up for the night."

"What do you think this is, a hotel?" The voice was deep and rasping.

"I thought at least an Englishman would observe the custom of the country." I was annoyed, and gave orders to cast off.

"Wait a minute!" he shouted. "There's no need to lose your temper. Have you got any whisky with you?"

"I suppose you've run out."

"Yes—and if you've got any, I'll pay for it."

"Well, we'll see about that. I've got a case of Scotch."

"Come on up, then," he said. "Tell your boys to bring your things along to the house."

He led the way up a steep path and across a wide veranda into the living room, brilliantly lighted by pressure lamps.

"I'm Roger Howard," said my host. He was a tall, powerful figure

—well over six feet. His face was burned brick red, with a pugnacious nose, and small blue eyes a trifle bloodshot.

"We're not used to visitors," he continued, "so the spare room isn't ready. However, I'll have the boys make it up while you have a bath."

For the second scene, the author begins using the flashback technique to introduce the significant "small red leather notebook" that belonged to the woman. But note that this sentence is not a scene unit in itself, but merely bait to whet the reader's curiosity. It leaves material to be resolved later, and raises interesting questions.

Having dispensed with the notebook, the author is ready to take the reader to the jungle. He now answers some of the early questions. Visualizing the boat coming down the river in Malaya, with details of how Manson feels and why he is there, and the meeting between George and Roger Howard, the author presents a scene remote from the art gallery and exciting by contrast.

By way of new information, he characterizes Howard as uncouth and sets up reader antagonism toward him; shows the setting and creates its atmosphere, and introduces native boys who seem irrelevant at the time but whom you find to be important later. The scene has achieved the purpose of informing the reader and advancing the story in a complete unit of action. Unresolved in this scene is the reason for the husband's ill will and his special interest in whisky.

III

When I had bathed and changed, I went into the living room. It was larger and more tastefully furnished than most of the planters' homes I'd stayed in. The walls were of a dark native wood relieved by brightly colored, full-length curtains. On the walls hung several well-chosen paintings and scattered about on low tables were some fine pieces of Brunei brass and Malayan silver. A long, low bookshelf held a mixed collection of books and periodicals. It was easy to see a woman's touch.

Presently Howard came in, followed by a native boy carrying a tray of drinks.

"Put them on the veranda, Allas—and watch what you're doing, you clumsy idiot!" he shouted as the boy caught his foot in the matting and nearly fell.

"I've been admiring your house," I said, mainly to divert attention from the boy.

"I'm glad you like it. I designed it myself. D'you notice the interior walls don't go up to the roof?"

"Is that for ventilation?"

"Yes, and you've no idea what a difference it makes. You get a free flow of air over all the rooms."

We had an excellent dinner; but I was surprised to find that we dined alone, for the whole place had that indefinable air of a woman about it. Most planters' houses have a rather beaten-up look, but this was beautifully kept. The napery was spotless, the cutlery gleamed and the white uniforms of the houseboys were immaculate.

After dinner we stretched out on long chairs on the veranda. I noticed that Howard drank heavily and steadily, but I made no attempt to keep up with him.

Naturally enough, a fine whisky combined with the novelty of a visitor was not without its effect. As the evening wore on, he became very talkative. He told of strange adventures in the East Indies and of adventures with strange ladies in the West End. London made him sentimental and he started to sing a song from a show he'd seen six years before. I could hardly keep my eyes open.

"I'm afraid I'm going to have to turn in," I said.

Howard swayed when he got to his feet and had a silly look on his face.

"All good things come to an end, old boy, don't they?" he said, putting a hand on my shoulder to steady himself. "I haven't had such an interesting talk for a long time."

Which was very human of him, considering I'd hardly uttered a word.

"I suppose you get up early, don't you?" I asked.

He made a large gesture. "Like the lark, I rise with the sun." He beamed on me with fatuous pride.

"Well, I'd better say good-by to you now. You'll no doubt be gone by the time I'm packed and away," I said, holding out my hand.

"What d'you mean, good-by?" he said, ignoring it. "You don't have to go, do you?"

"Well, I only intended staying the night. I don't want to make a nuisance of myself."

"Forget it—stay as long as you like. After all, you're providing the whisky." He laughed uproariously and gave me a slap on the back that nearly knocked me flat.

He staggered into the living room. I was following him when he turned suddenly and put his face close to mine. "You haven't met my wife," he said in a hoarse whisper. "She doesn't talk."

"Really?" I said, surprised in spite of myself.

"Lost her voice. Had a little accident."

He turned and shouted "Anne!" at the top of his voice. "Anne!"

"Don't bother to disturb her now," I said anxiously. "She's probably gone to bed."

I didn't want to meet her with Howard in this condition. I imagined she would feel I was to blame, and I was wondering how I could sneak off to bed when the door opened and she came in. My eye was caught immediately by her hair reflecting the light from the lanterns; it was a deep shade of auburn and fell nearly to her shoulders. She was tall and wore slacks and a smock stained with paint.

Howard introduced me, and she gave a polite little smile. His speech was slurred, and I noticed that when she looked at him her face was utterly devoid of expression, her wide blue eyes empty, as though she did not wish to see him. It gave me the shudders.

"I hope my staying won't put you out," I said. "By the way, I see you're a painter."

Her smile was more friendly now.

"I'd like to see your work sometime, if I may."

She nodded and held out her hand, so I said good night and she left without looking at Howard.

I decided that it would do no harm to take Howard at his word and stay on for a couple of days. After all, I'd had a hard journey.

In the introduction to this scene, the author's imagination has created a detailed description of the bungalow, and thus brings in the first hint of a woman's presence. The reader becomes expectant. He knows it will be Anne Howard because of the information in the story's opening.

In order to justify later material, the author builds up the cruel nature of the husband. He does this by having the planter berate the helpless houseboy. Also, because the author wants Manson to stay longer than one night, he emphasizes the husband's interest in liquor.

Also in this scene, to get the story moving along, the author creates a means of introducing Anne Howard and the shocking fact that she can't talk. It's quite natural that she and Manson would be drawn to each other: the author explains this to the reader by such words as "her face was utterly devoid of expression, her wide blue eyes empty, as though she did not wish to see him . . ." The reader knows, without anything being said, that there's a link between her inability to talk and the husband's cruelty.

Unresolved material is left in the questions: What has happened to her? What will the hero find out as he stays on at the bungalow? The scene, a complete unit of action, has informed us and advanced the story.

IV

Next morning I breakfasted alone; Howard had left earlier to make his rounds of the estate. Afterward I took a book and walked around the veranda, where, as I hoped, Anne was sitting reading. She smiled and motioned me to a long chair. For a while we sat in silence, looking out over the river. Presently she took a pad from her pocket and scribbled on it, "What do you do? Tell me about yourself."

What more invitation could anyone want? I told her of my plays and novels and was delighted to find she knew one of them. She had a lively sense of humor and I spoke of the things I guessed would interest her most—of books and the art shows I'd seen in London and Paris before coming East. Though of necessity I did the talking, I was amazed at the ease with which we exchanged ideas and sensed each other's thoughts.

When I asked if I might see her paintings, she rose and led the way through a double door off the veranda into a large room. It was pleasantly furnished, but the overwhelming impression was the paintings. Unframed, they covered the walls and were stacked in heaps in odd corners and leaning against pieces of furniture. A large easel stood in the center of the room, but what caught my eye immediately was an enormous canvas on one wall. It was a study of the jungle and it was staggering—a powerful piece of work. It conveyed an unmistakable sense of the relentless struggle for life—of the stark cruelty of nature's underworld.

She was watching me intently, obviously concerned about what I thought, so I told her. When I added that in my opinion her work should be shown, she dropped into a chair with her hands to her face.

I am always at a loss to know what to do when a woman cries and usually end up by doing nothing, which is generally the best thing. All I could do was wonder what had caused this. She was attractive and talented and I could understand that being shut away in this Godforsaken place must have been almost more than she could stand.

But I couldn't escape a feeling that there was more behind it and I left quietly, wondering what it was.

Now the author creates a scene to show us more of Anne Howard, to establish the fact that she's an excellent artist, and to strengthen the bond between her and Manson. Here also he injects the jungle painting already mentioned in the story. He pictures all this as taking place on the veranda of the bungalow and in the room where she paints.

This complete unit has moved the story forward, kept the reader sufficiently informed and left unresolved the reason why an attractive, talented woman lives in the jungle with a brute for a husband.

V

Anne joined us for dinner that evening, and I noticed her manner toward Howard remained aloof and detached. As far as she was concerned, he didn't seem to exist. Howard appeared accustomed to it.

After dinner he suggested that we play cards. From his conversation I gathered that they played regularly and that Anne usually won. Howard tried to be light about it but I could see it rankled a bit. It was easy to understand why she won, for she was not only a good player but cool and detached, while he was inclined to bluff. She caught him several times with nothing in his hand and he became sulky.

I finished even, but Anne won seven dollars from Howard. He paid up grudgingly, and after she'd put the money in her bag she made an entry in a small red leather notebook.

"Well, what's it amount to now?" he asked.

She appeared not to have heard him. Suddenly he shouted, "Gimme that," and grabbed it out of her hands. She jumped to her feet, giving him a scornful glance as she swept out of the room.

"A hundred and twenty dollars," he said. "What do you know about that!" He threw the book on the table. "What the hell—I'll get even someday. Come on, let's have a drink."

We sat on the veranda and Howard shouted, "Boy!" When Allas appeared, he ordered a jug of water.

"This is a remarkably fine whisky, Manson. What am I calling you Manson for—mind if I call you George, old boy?"

"Not at all." I smiled. "I'm glad you enjoy it. I'm going to leave the rest of the case with you."

"Oh, no, you can't do that—I'll pay you for it," he protested.

He was making a gesture of some sort when Allas returned silently with the tray. Howard's arm struck it and the jug upset over him. If it was anybody's fault, it was his own, but he jumped up with an oath and caught the boy across the mouth with the back of his hand. Allas lost his footing and fell heavily. I jumped up to help, but before I could get to him Anne was there.

"You don't have to help him. Get one of the boys to do that," Howard cried, pushing her out of the way. For a moment I thought he was going to hit her.

Fortunately Hamid, the number-one houseboy, came running.

"Get him out of here!" Howard shouted, his face livid with rage.

He seemed to have lost all control of himself. "Get him out or I'll thrash him!" he screamed at Hamid.

I went to bed, but it was a long time before I slept. I was upset over what had happened; I felt inclined to tell Wong to pack, and leave in the morning, but was held back by the feeling Anne needed help, I could not understand how she could stay with Howard, for it was obvious that she loathed the man. I wondered if it were a question of money. Well, there was one way to find out and that was to ask her.

At this point the author wants a scene that will pave the way for a climax. Events must speed up a little. So here he concocts a card game through which he reveals the purpose of the notebook, and establishes the sum of money entered, $120, and how the woman has accumulated this amount. Another outburst of cruelty by the husband heightens the tension. Manson decides to come to the point and ask Anne why she stays on with Roger Howard.

One more complete step is achieved in advancing the story. The reader will learn in another scene why the woman is there, and if she wants help. Note how one scene both settles a question and raises others, leading the way for the writer's imagination.

VI

I awoke late the following day and had brunch with Howard when he returned from his rounds. He was taciturn, almost sullen. No one likes a stranger about when the skeletons are rattling in the closets, I thought.

"I think I'd better be off tomorrow," I said. "I'll go down and warn my boys to be ready."

He growled something about "If you must, you must, I suppose."

Without a doubt the civilities had worn decidedly thin.

Later I went along the veranda to Anne's room. The double doors were open and she was painting a scene of the native kampong on the other side of the river. For a while I sat watching her work. I wanted to say something but did not know quite how to put it.

"Anne, you may say it's none of my business, but I want to talk to you."

She put down her brushes and came and sat on the floor beside my chair. I knew I was taking a chance but I felt my guess was the right one. As tactfully as I could I told her I had a large house in England, that I was rarely there, and that my old housekeeper would look after her if she'd like to use it until she'd established herself. For some moments she didn't move, then I saw her eyes were swimming with tears. She took my hand and laid it gently against her cheek. It was one of those moments when anything can happen, but just then we heard Howard shouting to a groom. I saw a flicker of fear in Anne's eyes. I told her I was leaving in the morning but would see her before I left, and went to my room.

The author has visualized a touching moment between George and Anne. To bring events closer to a climax, he has George decide it's time to leave. But since he wants the hero to be tactful, he has him offer Anne a sanctuary, thereby recognizing her need and leaving the rest up to her. The author then shows that love could exist between them—if circumstances were different.

The reader, in this short but vital scene, learns of Anne's fear and gratitude, is led further along by a complete action unit; and is given questions to which he will want answers.

VII

The evening passed quietly. Anne did not join us for dinner and Howard, still in a taciturn mood, drank heavily. I was relieved when it came time to turn in. I said good-by and thanked him for his hospitality.

I seemed no sooner to have fallen asleep than I found myself bolt upright with the most terrifyingly inhuman screams ringing in my ears. I tore through the mosquito net and grabbed a flashlight. Someone was running on the veranda, and I rushed out to find Allas coming from the opposite direction. The screaming came from Howard's room. The double doors stood wide, and a dim light was burning on a side table. The mosquito net had been torn away and Howard lay on the bed as though paralyzed, his arms outstretched and his eyes bulging. Suspended a few inches from his face was a huge cobra as thick as a man's forearm. It was a horrifying sight as it lashed about in the semidarkness. One move and Howard would have been finished.

I was wondering if I could shoot it without risk of hitting Howard when something caught my eye. I turned the flashlight toward the roof and could scarcely believe what I saw. The cobra was hanging from a leather thong secured to its tail and passed over a beam. For a moment, but only for a moment, I thought of climbing into the roof. There was only one thing to be done—I'd have to shoot it.

Howard hadn't stopped screaming for an instant, and the veranda was crowded with wide-eyed natives as I rushed to my room for a gun. I loaded it and went back. There was no sign of a cobra. I flashed the light up toward the roof again, but for all I could see there might never have been one. I was wondering if I'd been seeing things when Wong shouted, "Look, tuan—look!" I turned in a flash, thinking he'd seen it, to find Howard lifting himself. His lips were drawn off his teeth in a snarl and his eyes blazed at Anne, who was watching from the veranda.

"Hold him!" I shouted, dropping the gun and jumping for him— but we might as well have tried to hold a full-grown tiger. Howard leaped from the bed, throwing us all aside, and hurled himself toward Anne. She appeared too terrified to move. Suddenly she let out a terrible scream and crumpled to the floor. Howard, unable to stop himself, fell over her and crashed through the veranda railing.

I rushed to Anne and knelt beside her. She'd fainted but did not seem to be hurt. Shouting to the others to look for Howard, I was lifting her when she started to struggle and cried out, "No, no—don't let him . . ."

I felt my heart leap—I couldn't believe it was her voice. I talked to her gently, reassuring her, until she stopped struggling and lay quietly in my arms. As I carried her from the veranda I glanced over the edge where the railing had gone. The bungalow was on a hill and the ground fell away steeply. It was impossible to see anything and there was not a sound.

Here again is an example of a small, unimportant scene tucked into a major one . . . "The evening passed quietly," etc. Three or four lines take care of a dinner and a farewell, and launch Manson into action.

This is the crisis the author has been preparing for. Remembering the plot synopsis, you know the husband's life is to be threatened by a snake dangled over his bed. Now the author imagines just how it happened, taking care of the facts as he creates the sounds, smells, feelings and setting in a dramatic and exciting manner. He has used words to bring an imagined scene to life. Blending imagery and information, he has advanced the story to its peak of action.

When he comes to the end of this unit, he says: "It was impossible to see anything and there was not a sound." In other words, when he comes to the end he stops. He does not trail on, but cuts off to another time, another place, another mood.

VIII

From where I sat on the veranda I saw Jack Simmons, the district officer, talking to the headman of the native kampong on the other side of the river. I'd sent a message to him, and when he arrived in the government launch he'd questioned Anne and me and then gone over the place with his police boys. He was a breezy, cheerful sort and didn't seem at all put out when he heard that Howard had broken his neck. But for that matter everybody seemed more cheerful; even the houseboys were all smiles as they went about their work.

I noticed Simmons returning, and soon he came up the path and I heard him go through the living room. He was evidently talking to Anne, for occasionally I heard their voices. He came out shortly and joined me on the veranda. He slumped into a chair.

"Phew! I could do with a drink." He looked at his watch. "No, it's too early."

"There's some tea coming up—how about that?" I suggested.

"That's just the ticket."

He dropped a battered old topee on the floor and mopped his head with a large red handkerchief.

"Life's a rum business, isn't it?" he commented.

I nodded and wondered what had prompted the remark.

"I was thinking about Anne," he went on. "You know, I never thought she'd be able to speak again. Mind you, I've heard of cases of people being shocked and recovering, but I've never come across one before."

"No, neither have I."

He took out a villainous-looking pipe and proceeded to fill it.

"There's a touch of irony about it, too, you know."

"In what way do you mean?" I asked.

"I thought you knew what had happened. I mean when she lost her voice—a terrible experience."

I waited for him to go on.

"There was a young chap going up-country, and they put him up for the night. Oh, let me see—this must have been about six months ago. Bill Neville's his name—he's a planter. Well, he got the shivers in the night and found he hadn't any quinine. He saw a light under a door and knocked—it was Anne's room. Well, she gave him some and everything would have been all right, but Howard heard them. He flew into a towering rage, knocked Neville down and threw him out."

"He was certainly a violent customer."

"Just wait till you hear the rest," said Simmons. "When he got in from his rounds at noon the following day he started to drink—a mistake in this climate anyway. My police boys got all this from the houseboys, incidentally—they know everything that goes on. Well, he was trying to get Anne to admit what wasn't true, and he started knocking her about. Then in a blind rage he dragged her out and tied her to a tree on the riverbank."

Simmons paused to relight his pipe.

"Well, he hid behind the tree and she didn't know he was there.

Then when a crocodile came lumbering out of the water you can imagine what she went through. Of course he shot it before it could do any harm, but she nearly went out of her mind. When she recovered, she couldn't speak."

"Good God—he must have been a maniac!"

"The strange part about it," said Simmons, "was that he wasn't a bad fellow in some ways. He and Anne used to come down to the club once a month for tennis and bridge and he was liked well enough. Of course, everybody loved her—it isn't often we get such a good-looker out here. However, the liquor got him and the worst side of his nature came out—he became a sadistic brute. It's the old story," he added. " 'They shall sow the wind and they shall reap the whirlwind.' Isn't that how it goes?"

I glanced at him in surprise. He was the last man I would have expected to hear quoting the Bible.

"Wasn't there anything you could do about it?"

"Not officially," he replied, "unless Anne put in a complaint. Of course, when I heard of it I came up immediately, but she wouldn't do anything. It wasn't that she was in love with him; that was over long ago. She's got that hardheaded New England pride and was determined to see it through on her own. Added to that was the fact that she'd no money and no relatives left in the States."

"She could have got a divorce, of course. But I don't suppose she'd have got much, would she?"

"No—a mere pittance, barely enough to live on."

The slap of bare feet echoed on the veranda and a native police boy came up to Simmons and gave a smart salute. Simmons talked to him in a Malay dialect which I couldn't understand. When the boy had gone we sat for a while looking out over the river. What breeze there was had dropped and the air was heavy.

I was lighting a cigarette when I felt Simmons watching me. There was a speculative look in his eyes that made me oddly uncomfortable. As much for something to say as anything, I asked him how the sleuthing was going.

"Nothing to it," he replied, knocking out his pipe. While he filled it, he grinned at me like an overgrown schoolboy. "I know what you're thinking, Manson—how the Scotland Yard inspector spends weeks eliminating the suspects and searching for clues. I love that stuff, but I must admit it's easier out here."

"How do you mean?"

"You've got to know your customers—that's the secret." He paused to light his pipe. "Take this case, for example. We don't start by looking for a motive. We start at the other end, the weapon. In this case, a cobra. Now, a Malay wouldn't pull a trick like that. If he wants to avenge something, he'd use a kris, and then usually only in a passion. So even though Allas and several other Malays on the plantation had felt the strength of Howard's fist, we can safely rule them out. The Dyaks are a different kettle of fish. They have a number of cunning tricks and this is one of them, though I must admit I've never heard of its being done to a white man before. So you see, that narrows it down quite a bit."

I nodded and waited for him to go on.

"Now, whoever did it would have to be an expert to handle a cobra, especially up in that roof, and there's only one among the Dyaks here that I know of who could do it—and that's Kassim."

"My boatman!" I cried in surprise.

Simmons nodded. "He'll catch 'em and handle 'em any time. Used to bring 'em down to the coast for collectors when there was a demand. Anyway, I got my police boys busy, and just to make certain we searched the whole crowd. Sure enough, Kassim was hiding a lot of money in a bellyband."

"How much?"

"A hundred and twenty dollars—and if you know anything about natives, you'll know that's a lot of money."

"That's true. Could he account for it?"

"Said he won it gambling, but that won't wash."

Allas came padding along the veranda with the tea tray and set it on the table between us. Simmons poured himself a cup and drank it.

"Assuming you're right," I said, "who could have paid him that sort of money?"

He gazed at me for a few moments and a quizzical little smile played around his lips.

"Well, since you ask, who else but you, Manson?"

I jumped in my chair as though I'd been shot. "Was that meant to be funny?"

"Not in the least, old boy," he said coolly. "I know Anne didn't do it; I've already talked with her. She hasn't a penny of her own. She told my missus months ago that if she had, she'd have been off long since."

"And so by your simple process of deduction you hit on me. Even though I've no possible motive," I said acidly.

"Well, not exactly. After all, you must admit she's not a bad-looking girl."

I lighted a cigarette and tried to hold on to my temper.

"What do you mean by that?" I asked coldly.

But Simmons wasn't at all put out. He smiled imperturbably. "To put it simply, Manson, anyone with a pair of eyes couldn't help but see the way she looks at you."

This time I knew I was going to blow up. I could hear my voice rising. "If you're suggesting that Anne—"

"Don't misunderstand me," Simmons interrupted. "There's no evidence to make a case for Singapore and I'm glad there isn't. I mean that. If anyone deserves a chance, it's Anne—she's had four years of hell and Howard had it coming to him. But I still hold to my opinion."

I waited a few moments till I'd simmered down, then I leaned across the table, giving my words all the weight I could.

"Listen, Simmons," I said quietly, "I'll give you my word that I know nothing about this. That I had absolutely nothing to do with what happened to Howard."

He looked at me for a few moments, then got to his feet with that schoolboy grin on his face. "All right, old boy—have it your own way." He patted me on the back. "I'm going to have a bath," he added, "then we'll have a drink."

The author now skips forward to the point where the district officer has already been called and has questioned George and Anne. Whatever might have taken place since the husband's death hasn't seemed as important to the author as this next step, perhaps because it wouldn't advance the story but merely pad it out.

In another story, where length was required, the author might take time to go into the matter of Anne's returned voice, the question of the snake's disappearance, or perhaps the relationship between George and Anne.

In this instance the author wants to "get on with it," so each scene must do as much work as possible. At this point the reader has to be told a few of the deliberately withheld facts, or he will begin to question the plausibility of the tale.

So now the author, with good craft, has the district officer enlighten George as to the reason for Anne's lost voice, her presence in the jungle and her marital relationship, as well as why and how the snake came to be dangling over Roger Howard's head. This is an expository scene: there's little action but the necessary exchange of talk achieves the same effect as action by moving the story forward with information.

With equally good craft, the author doesn't tell the reader everything, but just enough to maintain suspense. Knowing how to keep the reader reading on avidly, he creates a misunderstanding on the district officer's part and switches the burden of suspicion to George himself. With all the facts of the notebook established for the reader, the author has conceived a nice twist of plot by having the district officer smilingly disbelieve George's statement of innocence.

The end of the scene leaves the question: What will George do about this?

IX

I was furious as I paced up and down the veranda. That maddening grin and the patronizing pat on the back. I could have strangled him cheerfully. It wasn't until I'd calmed down and was thinking it over that the penny dropped—or rather, the one hundred and twenty dollars. I hurried into the living room, to the corner where the card table stood. The cards were on it and Anne's little red book was where Howard had thrown it down that night. It looked like a diary, but in the back pages Anne had entered her winnings. It wasn't owing to her—she'd been paid—but she'd kept a record of it. It was totaled at a hundred and twenty dollars. Simmons believed she had no money, while all the time she had. I'd have given anything to have shown it to him, just to watch his face. I slipped it into my pocket.

By the time I joined them for a drink I was in a much better mood. I didn't care now what Simmons thought—after all, I had an ace up my sleeve. But I had no intention of using it to prove that he was wrong. Though he'd been sympathetic, largely because there was no real evidence, you never can tell what the military mind will do when presented with a solid fact; it's apt to sacrifice anything to duty.

And I wasn't going to expose Anne to that risk. It had shaken me considerably to think she could have done it, but the facts all pointed that way.

While I was having a drink it occurred to me that Simmons might very well be leaving soon, which meant I'd be left alone with Anne. I didn't want that to happen now. I was very much attracted to her and wanted to see her again—but under different circumstances. When I mentioned that I would have to leave if I was to catch the next boat for England, Simmons's mouth literally fell open. I could hardly conceal a smile. Before I left I asked Anne where I could write to her, and she gave me the address of a bank in New York.

It wasn't until a few weeks later at sea, when I was changing into warmer clothes, that I came on the red leather book and packed it carefully among my papers.

You know now that the author will create a scene to answer the unresolved question of the preceding scene: What will George do now?

The author pictures George pacing the veranda, furious, then calmer, and finally coming to a conclusion of his own. The author doesn't explain the conclusion right away but shows George hurrying to the card table and retrieving the book. Now the reader knows that George thinks Anne was responsible for her husband's death. Once more, this scene is preponderantly informative, with a suggestion of action in the brief exchange between George and Simmons.

The author remembers to plant the notebook in George's baggage, and ends the scene there.

X

I must have packed it too carefully; it was some time before I found it. I dropped it into the pocket of my dinner jacket and looked at my watch. I would have to hurry to be at the St. Regis by six.

Anne was waiting when I was shown into her apartment.

"I'm so glad you came early. Now we can talk before the others get here," she said, leading me over to a sofa.

She was wearing a beautifully cut dress and she looked stunning. We had a drink and she talked excitely of her show. Four of her pictures had been sold and it was only the first day. I could not resist the impulse to say "I told you so."

"You were perfectly right." She smiled. "What you said at Kelantan gave me the courage to show them."

She reached for the cocktail shaker.

"Tell me, George," she asked, "why did you leave Kelantan so suddenly?"

I took the red book from my pocket and handed it to her. She looked at it and then back at me in surprise. For some moments she leafed through it until she came to the pages at the back. Her expression didn't change.

"Where did you find this?" she asked.

"I picked it up in the living room and slipped it into my pocket."

"Why did you do that?" she asked quietly.

"Well, I thought I'd better if Simmons wasn't to get hold of it."

Her eyes widened. "Oh, now I see!" she cried. "That's why you left so suddenly." She threw back her head and laughed. "You thought that I had done it."

Somewhat piqued, I said, "Well, I must say everything pointed to it."

"And you were trying to protect me, weren't you?" She gave me a gentle smile. "And I was protecting Allas," she added quietly.

For a moment I didn't understand. "What did you say?"

"I was protecting Allas," she repeated. "You see, it was Allas who did it, George, but I couldn't give him away. He'd been devoted to me for years, and what good would it have done?"

"But how did you know?"

"I saw him creep into the studio that night while I was on the veranda. He stole my winnings. I kept them in a box in the bureau. Of course he knew where everything was."

I was dumbfounded. "Didn't you try to stop him?"

"I couldn't. Roger was with me, and you can imagine what he'd have done to him. Later that night I realized that Allas must have paid Kassim to do it."

I couldn't help laughing. "And Simmons was so sure I'd done it."

"And still is," added Anne with a laugh.

"I won't lose any sleep over that."

Just then I heard the buzzer and a maid going to the door.

"Do you think we could get away and go on alone somewhere later?" I asked quietly.

She smiled up at me. "I'd like nothing more."

She came close and made a pretense of straightening my tie. There was a hint of mockery in her eyes.

"George, how did you know where to find me today?" she asked softly.

I told her that I hadn't known, that I'd walked into the gallery quite by chance. She wasn't at all put out, and I wasn't surprised when she smiled and said, "You know, George, I shall never believe that as long as I live."

And such is the vanity of women, she never has.

The author has brought the story around full circle and now returns the reader to the Manhattan hotel where George is looking for the notebook. He decides to take care of this moment of action briefly and to get George to his appointment with Anne quickly. In this way he keeps the story going at a swift tempo, wastes no words on extraneous material, and creates the scene of conclusion.

The author now has the task of tying up all the threads left dangling and of creating a final emotion in the reader. How does he do it?

He decides not to waste time describing the hotel apartment but describes briefly the way George and Anne look. His emphasis is on the people themselves and what transpires between them. Dialogue, then, must be the means of communication, between the story characters and the author and reader.

A very simple and straightforward exchange of conversation clears up the missing information. All is neatly tied together, and the author leaves the reader feeling satisfied with both the plot and the promised relationship between Anne and George.

This complicated story has been made easier to write, and

more interesting to read, by the process of dividing or grouping it into ten main scenes.

Now that you have studied this example of a published story, read others to see how their scenes are handled. Practice marking the end of each action unit and listing what it contained. Although you may eventually discard this conscious habit of visualizing your stories in scenes, doing this exercise now will sharply stimulate your visual powers and imagination. The chances are that you will soon automatically group your plots into these units, which is by far the most effective way of actually *telling* a story.

The importance of background

Background is not only up to the writer but to the people he's writing about. If they'd be happy living in a luxury resort, in a slum, in a walk-up or a penthouse, put them there. If they are country people, they belong in the country. If they are city folks, in the city. You have the world to choose from and it's better for you to choose that part of it you have seen.

In the modern story or novel, background is chiefly important as it relates to the people in your story. You can take your people out of their normal background and put them in one alien to them and that, in itself, is a story. In historical and period novels, the backgrounds go with the periods.—Faith Baldwin

Wise words from an editor

I met and talked with George Horace Lorimer, the famous *Post* editor, only once or twice, early in my writing life. I was so dazzled and awed that I honestly cannot remember a word he said but I do remember his kindliness and wisdom.

His precepts have made writing legend. One, of serial writing, went like this:

"The break at the end of an installment is not when your hero is hanging over a cliff, clutching it with his fingernails. It is when he has pulled himself up on the narrow path above and turned around to face a grizzly bear."

And another: "A reader may be led by a silken thread," meaning that the barest suggestion, well placed and worded, is more effective than beating the reader over the head with repetition or explanation. Overemphasis is the bane of any writer. This is particularly true in a mystery story; it is fatally easy for an event which is intended to be one of credible suspense to cross a fine line into utter incredibility and turn itself into a kind of horrible, slapstick farce.

I know because I have done this. Overemphasis is an insult to the reader and a pitfall for the writer.—Mignon Eberhart

To help you in revisions

Constant revision is one of the keys to successful writing, whether the revising is done by the author or the editor. For the writer, one simple device will make revising easier and more effective. After you've finished the first draft of a piece, put it away in your desk drawer for a few days, even longer. You'll be amazed at what comes to light when you read it again.

Phrases and sentences that seemed quite adequate when you wrote them will now obviously stand in need of repair. Paragraphs, pages, perhaps the entire piece will reveal flaws that need fixing. There's nothing like putting copy in the "deepfreeze" for a while. Not only will the flaws crystallize but also become so obvious that you'll wonder how you made them in the first place.

No professional writer is ever satisfied with his first draft. But if you correct this draft *immediately* after writing it, you are too close to the words to see the errors. That's why we suggest the deepfreeze method. Try it on your next piece of work and you'll be both surprised and pleased at the results.

Lesson twenty-one

Fiction writing

course

How to
select
material

A writer uses *selectivity* when he decides which of his story material to use, which to leave out. This form of writing economy is overlooked by beginners, and learned by most professional writers only after years of trial and effort. It's therefore worth understanding, particularly in relation to the short story, where there is no room for wasted words. Faith Baldwin says:

The first thing to know about selectivity is that it's not cutting or revising *after* the story is done but is a considered choice—*before* you write—of what is essential to the most effective telling of your idea. It's the way in which you leave yourself elbow room for the writing of some special description or detail, or time to enter a character's thought or to inject a note of philosophy.

Selectivity aims to give the reader all the information and facts he needs for plausibility, while keeping his attention on the principal action of the story. This applies equally to the fast-paced or leisurely-told story. It's not a matter of speed, but of economy; the less you spend on what is unimportant to your story, the more you have to spend on what *is* important.

Exactly how do you make your selections? Once again, rules can't be fixed, but we can offer a list of selectivity guides and later illustrate to you by example the way in which they've been used successfully in a published story. Here's the list to guide you in making your choices:

1. *Selectivity in characters.* Use no more people in your story than it needs and give them no more space than is necessary to support your main character. And don't try to tell any more about your main character than you need to advance or enhance your story.

2. *Selectivity in actions.* Use actions to create only meaningful incidents or crucial situations. Give as little space as possible to unimportant actions, in order to be able to give more to the important ones.

3. *Selectivity of settings.* Make settings real and clear, but don't allot to them more or less words than their importance warrants. Too few words may tax the reader's credulity, but too many will reduce the space you'll have left when you get to the main setting or settings.

4. *Selectivity of scenes.* Keep space to a minimum for the lesser scenes, in order to give maximum effect to the larger ones.

5. *Selectivity of expression.* The right word, sentence and paragraph are the ultimate test of selectivity. (Later in these Lessons we shall cover the subject in detail.) The primary purpose is to tell your story with as few and yet effective words as will carry the story forward vividly and realistically.

6. *Selectivity of time.* A certain time in your story will be the turning point. Keep the reader aware of each time span in your story but with no more words than necessary. Remember that

the shorter the story, the shorter the time span it should cover.

7. *Selectivity of mood.* Select the mood best suited to your story, then write of it sparingly where you don't need to emphasize it so that you can enlarge upon it where mood counts most.

8. *Selectivity of length.* After you have applied every form of selectivity listed above, you'll be able to judge whether you have material for a short-short, a short story or a longer length. Practice in this appraisal will eventually enable you to judge the approximate story wordage before writing.

And now, so you can see selectivity actually at work, we print a story a shade longer than a short-short and therefore one requiring the utmost selectivity. "You're Not My Son!" by Betty Kjelgaard, appeared in *This Week.* Read it through first to familiarize yourself with the plot and emotional effect, then study our list of comments to see how this author has kept room to say all she wants and needs to say, and then said it with maximum effect.

The boy entered their lives one June evening, against Jim Talbert's will. Barbara Talbert had answered the ringing telephone and come out to the porch where Jim sat, the two Irish setters behind his chair.

It had been Clayt McConnell, the county commissioner, she'd said. The county had had to take over five children whose parents had deserted them. Clayt had them all farmed out to responsible people except the oldest. Would the Talberts take him for a couple of months? They had this big place outside of town and Jim had been saying at the last Lion's club meeting that he needed help with the lawn and the shrubs . . .

"How old is he?" Jim asked.

"Almost sixteen," Barbara said. The blur of her face was turned toward him in the twilight. She was very still.

He looked straight ahead at the mountains. "What did you tell Clayt?" But he had the feeling he already knew.

"I told him—" her voice faltered, then steadied—"I told him we did need someone. Clayt's bringing him out tonight."

Well, she's half the household, Jim thought; she's got a right to assert her wants, too.

Quietly, Barbara said, "You can't stay in a cave forever because we lost Rusty."

That's what everybody said; that's why Clayt had saved this boy for them. Well-intentioned people could be cruel; and you were helpless against that kind of cruelty. "If that's it, then," he said, "why, that's it."

So he had been prepared for the boy's arrival half an hour later. But not for the terrible identity that leaped in him when the boy got out of the car and walked toward the porch. Or the irony. After a year and a half of avoiding the school and the football field and any place where boys might hang out, he had to sit there and watch one approach with that awkward grace of all teenagers who have grown too tall too fast. Clayt introduced him as Richard Dodd, better known as Tick. His face was indistinct in the deepening night, but he was obviously very uncomfortable until one of the watchful setters moved behind the chair. His quick eyes saw them both then, and he dropped down on his heels, all uneasiness gone.

"Oh, golly," he breathed, "oh, golly."

That was Rusty, too. Jim turned away so harshly that an ash tray went clattering to the floor. "I've got work to do," he said. "See you, Clayt."

Out of the silence behind him, Barbara's voice came, bright. "This is Lady and this is Reb," she said. "They're hunting dogs, Tick."

When Jim went into the kitchen the next morning, Tick was sitting at the table and Barbara was fixing bacon and eggs.

"Good morning, Mr. Talbert," Tick said, in a quiet way.

"Good morning," Jim said politely. He let his glance flicker over the boy. Brown hair, blue eyes too big for that thin face, a good enough chin.

"What would you like me to do today, sir?" Tick said.

Jim turned with a deliberate gesture to Barbara. "What would you like him to do today?"

Her look met his. She understood; he was denying any association between himself and Tick. "I thought we might work in the rock garden," she said. Her voice was level.

"Fine."

A little while later, driving to his insurance office in town, Jim decided he had set the best possible course. He had no grudge against the boy; it was just that he couldn't be expected to lavish love on every waif who stumbled along. He had no love to lavish, actually. Rusty, his only son and child, had gone with dreadful swiftness, dying in the bud without ever having a chance to unfold. Because he seemed to have merely a mild sore throat, Jim had not been alarmed. Then meningitis struck, sweeping Rusty out before anyone could help. Though he was technically blameless, Jim in his ravaged mind had said, over and over, if only I had known, or been more alert. By that time it was too late, and so his spirit was imprisoned forever when his son left him. But boys had an uncanny way of resembling each other, and for that reason you had to build up a defense. If you didn't, memories could be stabbing all the time.

Tick had done a good job on the rock garden. He did a good job on the lawn, too, and on the shrubs. He ran errands for Barbara, helped her with the dishes and the housework. And spent all his free time with the setters. Jim was driving in one August afternoon when Tick came loping around the corner of the garage with Lady and Reb. He stopped short when he saw Jim.

Jim got out and fondled the leaping dogs, noting the super brilliance of the dark red coats. "You brush 'em?" he asked Tick.

"Yes, sir." The boy hesitated, then said, "They're great hunters, Mr. Talbert! We were in the woods and two grouse flew up and—"

"That's what they're trained for, Tick," Jim said shortly, and walked away. The boy's rare eagerness had broken through his precious guard for a moment, so that he had had a flashing picture of himself teaching Rusty to hunt behind the dogs. The cheerful insults would have flown back and forth across the brush and the sedge, that special language of father and son; and always the bridge of closeness would have been there, warm, binding . . .

Barbara was in the kitchen. She kissed him and said, "I was watching you and Tick. If you could have seen the way he curried those dogs today!" She laughed. "He keeps whispering to them, like someone with a deep secret."

"Yeah," Jim said. He had seen that, too, the soft absent look on Tick's face. "Saturday Doc Egan and Sam Hawke are coming out with their pups and we're going to start getting them and Lady and Reb in shape for the hunting season."

"Jim," Barbara began.

He had gotten to the back stairs, the small burr of pain still jabbing. Now he turned.

Her eyes searched him skillfully; then she moved toward the cupboard, saying over her shoulder, "Do you want iced coffee or iced tea for dinner?"

"Coffee," he said, puzzled, and went on up the stairs.

At five o'clock Saturday morning he waited for Doc and Sam to arrive. Because the leashed dogs were impatient, he walked them into the field across the road. Coming back, he could see his house, clean and pleasant in the opal dawn. His look climbed up to Rusty's room and clung there until a flicker at another window made his glance swerve. That was the room Tick had. Jim frowned. Was Tick standing behind the curtain? Everything was still as still.

Then Doc Egan's station wagon came into view and Jim went to meet it. It was nothing, he thought; just wishful thinking; a desire to see a boy I'll never see again except in mind and heart.

They worked the dogs until the thick heat of midday drove them home. But they went again the following Saturday. The next Friday Jim was sitting on the porch before dinner when Barbara appeared.

"Are you going to take the dogs out tomorrow?" she asked.

"Doc and Sam can't make it," Jim said, "but I thought I would."

Barbara said, "Will you take Tick along?"

No, something inside him said instantly; almost anything but that. "Why?" he asked.

"Well, not only because he would love to go," Barbara said, "but because Clayt McConnell was here today. School starts week after next, and Tick has one more year. Clayt said if we weren't going to —to keep him, there's a farmer out at Dry Run who'll give him room and board in exchange for Tick's helping with the chores. That means he'll be leaving us in a few days."

Jim looked at Barbara, slender and lovely in her simple dress. She wasn't pleading, and yet she was. Women were funny and wonderful. Give them some kid—any kid—to fuss over and they could do it wholeheartedly without losing one shred of devotion for their own offspring.

"Would it mean a lot to you if I took Tick tomorrow?" he said.

"Yes," she said evenly.

He put on a smile for her. "Okay."

Tick was in the kitchen when Jim got down the next morning. "I've got breakfast nearly ready, Mr. Talbert," he said.

"So I see," Jim said. "I didn't hear your alarm go off."

"It didn't," Tick said, almost shyly. "I was awake."

Jim poured coffee with steady hands, thinking of how Rusty would come in and nudge him at four-thirty, his eyes aglow, as he whispered, "Hey, time's awasting; get up!"

They ate in a silence that was not painful because they were both used to it. Then they piled the dogs in the car and drove away.

"Now keep me in sight," Jim instructed, "so you can get my signals. The dogs will range afield. When they come to a full point, be careful. Move very slowly and very quietly. I'll break the point by shooting my pistol. Do you understand?"

"Yes, sir," Tick said.

Jim parked at the edge of a field which was full of old corn shocks and stubble. Ahead was a thicket. Tick's thin shoulders were trembling a little. Jim told him to wait, walked fifty yards to the left, loosed the dogs, and motioned Tick forward. They followed the questing setters across the field and into the thicket until Jim saw Lady alert herself in the familiar way that told him she had sighted birds.

He glanced across at Tick, intending to signal caution because the dog would close in for the point. But the boy was watching Lady with fascinated eyes and walking forward eagerly. Jim felt a peculiar jar, as if a chink had come open. That was Rusty's trouble too, he thought: jumping the gun. His heart began to pound then, and suddenly it was another day in another year and a brown-haired boy was there and everything was all right with the world. Something long controlled let loose in Jim, pouring out in a joyous gush.

"You lop-eared, blockheaded, lollapaloozing young ape!" Jim

yelled. "I told you to hold up when the dogs began to point!"

And back came a boy's happy, exultant laughter. "Okay, Dad!"

Complete silence fell. They stared at one another. Tick licked his lips and swallowed. He said that, Jim thought, as if he'd been thinking it for a long time. Okay, Dad! The words filled him, eased him —and released him from a past to a future. Get a little more meat on his bones, he thought, and he'll start growing up to his eyes. We'll see to that, Barbara and I.

"You'll learn," he called to Tick, his voice not quite steady. "Let's try it again."

"Okay—" Tick called back, and shut his mouth.

He almost said it again, Jim thought. He grinned at Tick and shyly the boy grinned back. The bridge of closeness was beginning between them, warm, binding . . .

Now let's check the selectivity guide list to this story:

1. *Selectivity in characters.* The only characters the author has used are the ones absolutely necessary to act out her story— Jim; Barbara, his wife; the boy, Tick; and Clayt McConnell. She might have written in a grandmother living with the Talberts, who missed Rusty and was glad of the new boy to talk to. A grandmother would have fitted nicely into the story, but hundreds of words would have been needed to characterize her sufficiently and give her room in scenes. By leaving her out, the author has more room to write about the essential characters.

McConnell could have had an assistant, Tick could have had friends, there might have been neighbors. In each case, however, the story would have had to be longer or run the risk of crowding. Revision would have been made a major job instead of a minor one. This is the difference between cutting and selectivity.

2. *Selectivity in actions.* The goal of the story is to bring about Talbert's acceptance of the boy. The action to illustrate and resolve this could take many forms. The author makes her first guiding choice from the cause-and-effect of the plot, but this still leaves a wide choice of action. She might have introduced a disaster: for instance, there could have been a picnic at which the boy nearly drowned, or Tick might have set a fire by accident. Perfectly good action, but in order to accommodate more words than the author used, the story would have been overcomplicated, and when the high spots came, such as the hunting action, she would have lacked space for them. Again, effort is saved and the over-all effect is simpler to achieve.

3. *Selectivity of settings.* If you note the author's settings, you'll see that she needed each one she used, and kept them to a minimum. The boy and Barbara might have gone to a market. Their work in the rock garden setting might have been described instead of merely mentioned. The boy could have been shown in the setting of the yard or porch where he brushed the dogs. In that way, many extra words would have been used. No matter how effective each setting might have been, the story would have become too long. Also note how the author passes quickly over settings that are necessary yet don't play an important part in the foundation of an action unit:

Tick had done a good job on the rock garden. He did a good job on the lawn, too, and on the shrubs. He ran errands for Barbara, helped her with the dishes and the housework. And spent all his free time with the setters . . .

At five o'clock Saturday morning he waited for Doc and Sam to arrive. Because the leashed dogs were impatient, he walked them into the field across the road. Coming back, he could see his house, clean and pleasant in the opal dawn . . .

They worked the dogs until the thick heat of midday drove them home. But they went again the following Saturday . . .

In this last instance, two settings are summed up in two sentences. The third sentence: "The next Friday Jim was sitting on the porch before dinner when Barbara appeared . . ." launches a setting that holds an entire scene.

A study of your story material before you write, a selectivity of setting like this, will save much needless work and space.

4. *Selectivity of scenes.* Action and setting are held to a minimum in this story, and so are the scenes. They require no more words than are needed to paint them swiftly and vividly, to inform the reader and advance the story, to complete a unit of action. Many more scenes could have been visualized, but the author chose from among those in her imagination, kept them to a crucial few, and had, when the time came, enough space to give them full play.

5. *Selectivity of expression.* If you go over each paragraph of this story and study what it says, you'll find that although there are as many ways to say the same thing as there are people in the world, this author has said it with admirable economy and effect. She has used selectivity to judge the subject matter and decide

where she'll need terse, swiftly explained passages so that she can expand a little when she wants to be leisurely. In this story, the author moved action and dialogue at a brisk clip, but allowed herself room to enter the thoughts of Talbert at some length.

6. *Selectivity of time.* As we pointed out in the Lesson on the single effect, the shorter the story, the shorter should be its time span. The author here has handled this well. Choosing a span of roughly two months, she compresses some of these days into a sentence, and pushes them ahead like this:

> They worked the dogs until the thick heat of midday drove them home. But they went again the following Saturday. The next Friday Jim was sitting on the porch before dinner when Barbara appeared. "Are you going to take the dogs out tomorrow?" she asked.

The author has moved the reader swiftly to the time of the main scene, and thereby given herself plenty of room to write dialogue, action, setting and final resolution. Selectivity of time is one of the chief means of spacing a short story. If the author here had made the span longer, once more she would have been involved in extraneous passages.

The old quotation, "There's a time for everything," is a good one for writers. There's a time to talk of time; there's a time to speed up its passing. You might, for instance, want to show the excruciating slowness of waiting for important news or the passing of an enforced confinement. For this, you would have to make the time that preceded go quickly, so that you could slow up and create for your reader the details of the agonized minutes and hours.

7. *Selectivity of mood.* The mood the author has chosen here is one of loss and yearning. She creates it with carefully placed emphasis. She doesn't inject it where it would overload the story with words but bears down in passages like:

> Coming back, he could see his house, clean and pleasant in the opal dawn. His look climbed up to Rusty's room and clung there until a flicker at another window made his glance swerve. That was the room Tick had. Jim frowned. Was Tick standing behind the curtain? Everything was still as still.

The injection of too many references to what Jim feels, the clinging memories of the boy, the wife's obvious hunger to keep Tick, would slow up the direct moving line of the story. It would alter the simple goal of the story and present unnecessary complications. The reader could perhaps be misled into thinking the story was mainly about the Talberts' lack of a child rather than the acceptance of Tick. They might think that Tick was to create a major conflict between man and wife. All these shadings of meaning would have caused confusion, requiring much revision afterwards.

8. *Selectivity of length.* Having written with a careful eye to selectivity, the author brings off a story of appropriate length for the material, and vice versa. If she hadn't written with economy, her story would have trailed off or perhaps collapsed from lack of effective construction. Ask yourself: Would this story have been better if longer? Would it have been better shorter? Should it have been expanded to a novelette? Should it have been reduced to a short-short?

The chances are, you'll agree the story is essentially a simple and uncomplicated one that couldn't have stood up under much expansion, and perhaps too emotional to resolve in a condensed version. To recognize selectivity, put it into your working thoughts, read many stories with this in mind, then try it on a few of your own plots.

Sincerity is always important

The basic principles in writing are, apart from the academic knowledge you learn yourself, based on the student's own attitude. In the first place, sincerity. Writing with your tongue in cheek always shows through; it isn't good writing. You are saying in effect: "This is a silly story and I know it. But I'm really superior to this sort of thing." The reader doesn't like your being superior and can usually spot a phony a mile off.

In the second place, you have to like what you are doing, no matter how hard and how often you are discouraged. This rule applies to every career, including homemaking. If you don't like what you're doing, the reader won't either.

And thirdly, you have to *want* to write more than anything else in the world. You have to condition yourself to sacrifice, disappointment, even despair. You have to realize there is no royal road to success and that it's uphill most of the way and strewn with obstacles.

In short, you have to have the will to write as well as the desire.—
Faith Baldwin

Storytelling is an ancient craft

As a writer of fiction, I go back through innumerable generations
to the teller of tales round the fire in the cavern that sheltered neo-
lithic men. The delight in listening to stories is as natural to human
nature as the delight in looking at dancing and acting, out of which
drama arose.—Somerset Maugham

Write to please yourself

I am not sure that it is a good idea to try to tailor short stories to
anybody's measure. Any issue of any magazine will give you some
idea as to the kind of stories that its editors have liked enough to buy
and publish, but every good editor is always looking for the good
story that will be unlike all the other good stories that he has previously published.

I think it is pretty generally true that nobody can write for an
audience to which he does not himself belong, and the best work, I
firmly believe, has always been done by people who were concerned
only with pleasing themselves. Given a reasonable degree of competence in the mechanics of the craft, there is an audience, large or
small, for anything that any of us writes to please himself, since none
of us is unique, however much our egoism tries to persuade us that we
are.—Hugh McNair Kahler

Be careful with exposition

I do not like to start a story with exposition, although there are times
when exposition just can't be avoided. I think that to start with a
long description of a day, or a setting, or the weather is dull and un-
dramatic. Most of these things can be told in a flashback or dropped
into the action from time to time. But don't lead off with them. For,
while a bit of straight exposition never hurt any story, to start with it
may be dull and lose you your reader right off.—Mignon Eberhart

Lesson twenty-two

Fiction writing

course

How to
handle
words

When artfully used, words and phrases strengthen the magic
link of communication between writer and reader. This is
because words and phrases have associations for both writer
and reader, and on this mutual awareness the successful author
builds the illusion of reality called fiction. A survey of this subject is given in Volume I, Lesson Seven, "Ways to Use Words,"

and you should reread this Lesson to refresh your memory about word values in general.

In fiction, words and phrases aim to achieve an effect on the reader as well as inform him correctly, Bergen Evans points out.

The more closely allied to real life that effect can be, the better the writing. Words that do the most to achieve this are:

(a) Those defining or describing the exact quality of an object, person, place or feeling;

(b) Words carrying associations that readers share, thereby increasing their understanding of the writer's idea;

(c) Words comparing or replacing one object with another to sharpen the idea or image in the reader's mind or senses.

Let's take the above listing one by one:

(a) Words that define or describe the exact quality of an object or character, atmosphere or state of mind, usually make the difference between dull and interesting writing. Take a sentence like this:

His wavy hair looked unreal.

Is there a way to define "his wavy hair" more exactly and thus create a sharper image for the reader? (In the following examples we don't claim to supply the best or the only improvement, but merely a suggestion or possibility.) How about "his wavy hair looked wig-like?" Doesn't the word "wig-like" sharpen the image? If you pause in your own work to sharpen definitions, you'll give your words increased power as well as the flavor of professional writing.

Here are other sentences, together with an improved definition or description:

The pastry was soggy.
The pastry was limp and wet.

I looked at the big heap of dirty clothes.
I looked at the mountain of dirty clothes.

The boy stared at her with narrowed eyes.
The boy stared at her craftily.

(b) In these sentences the meaning is kept but the image is heightened by words that have associations for the reader:

Another dawn came up.
The pink glow of morning lighted the sky.

The kittens played happily in the sun.
The kittens leaped and frolicked in the sunshine.

He gave me a funny look.
His gaze measured me.

She could see he was angry by his eyes.
She could see anger in his fixed stare and set mouth.

He rode into town, watching everyone in case of trouble.
He rode warily into town, alert for trouble.

(c) Words that compare or replace one object with another to sharpen the idea or image fall into several categories which can be combined under the heading of *figures of speech*. If a writer says a sunset looks like "molten gold spilling over the horizon," he's using a figure of speech. He's not only telling the reader that the sunset is beautiful, but giving him an imaginative comparison that makes a more vivid image. Readers enjoy these similarities and take pleasure in recognizing them. Although a story shouldn't be overloaded with too many figures of speech, their presence gives charm and life to writing.

The best way to create effective figures of speech is to catch yourself when you have written such phrases as: "He had a longish face . . . The evening was . . . She wore a blue dress . . . Her eyes were merry . . ." and ask the question: "What does his longish face remind me of *exactly*? A horse? A clown? A face elongated by a trick mirror? And what *was* the evening . . . ? Moonlit? Murky with clouds? And if it was moonlit, what does the moonlight remind me of that I could picture for the reader? *Neon lights cast over the trees and lake? Silver rain? Silver radiance pouring over the sleeping earth?* And the blue dress: Was it just a blue dress, or a particular shade of blue? *A blue like a summer sky? Like cornflowers in the sun?* And "her eyes were merry . . ." Is there a resemblance or comparison that would say this more vividly for the reader? Her brown eyes were as merry as—or looked like . . . *what?*

What do merry eyes look like? They seem to twinkle, to sparkle, to have glints of gaiety in them, don't they? Dancing eyes is a cliché, so avoid it. What else, then, twinkles, sparkles or glints? Stars seem to. Water glints in sunlight, particularly when it has ripples. Diamonds sparkle, but they are a cold image —merriment is warm. Starlight does not suggest merriment as much as sunlight—the word *sunny* is gay in itself. (The similarity does not come to you at once, perhaps—this is the creative work that distinguishes fiction writing from other kinds.)

Well, we'll see what can be done with sun and water. *Her eyes were merry as twin pools sparkling in the sun?* A bit wordy—let's shorten it. *Her eyes were as merry as twin pools sparkling with sunlight.* Now, further reducing it, let's see if we can't eliminate the *merry* and let the comparison speak for itself. How about— *Her eyes were pools sparkled with sunlight?*

To help you understand the full range of figures of speech, here's a list of their various forms under technical headings. You don't have to memorize these rhetorical terms—just understand their uses for your writing.

1. *The simile.* We have just shown you the process of creating similes. A simile is the comparison of one thing with another. This is the most flexible, adaptable and therefore most commonly used figure of speech. While similes are comparisons, all comparisons are *not* similes. The simile compares two things that are essentially different in all but one or two ways—the comparison is made on the basis of those ways.

For instance: comparisons between two objects or people that are basically alike, such as—"The glass was as clear as crystal—" or "She had a disposition like her mother's—" don't point up a sharp enough contrast to be good similes. If the glass were to be made to resemble motionless water, and the disposition that of lemon-and-sugar, then they would be based on fundamental differences with points of likeness—similes.

A simile is an effective tool for defining feelings and actions. "He was ever at her side . . ." might seem a more true-to-life observation if it were told with a simile, such as: "He was like a guardian shadow beside her." "The snow blew coldly on his face . . ." comes to life as: "The snow blew against his face like cold cobwebs."

And here are some examples of a basic character trait given reality by a simile:

The man was insincere . . .
His promises were as bland as olive oil.

She was not aware of us in any way.
She was as oblivious to us as a burrowing mole.

She was a skinny little thing, with quick, darting movements.
She was a skinny little thing, quick and darting as a sparrow.

Perhaps the clearest understanding of similes comes from noting them in published stories. Pencil a line under them and observe how they have elaborated a point, made a description more visual or true to life, and try to apply what they teach to your own work.

2. *The metaphor.* The metaphor doesn't say one thing is *like* another—it says it *is* another. The metaphor is a strengthened simile, in that it's more forceful or direct. A metaphor is, actually, a word with one literal meaning, used to replace or refer to another. The two things must have something in common which the reader can perceive immediately. In that sense the two are compared. The italicized words or phrases below are metaphors; some of them, you'll see, are quite slangy:

The *breadwinner* took the 7:37 train every morning.
I liked her at first but she was a *chameleon.*
His home is no *bed of roses.*
He brought home the *bacon.*
He is the *hare* and his brother the *tortoise.*
Screaming headlines announced war.
He *spouted* poetry to every girl he met.
We *sweated out* our appointment.

Much slang is metaphorical. But overuse soon kills its imaginative and metaphorical qualities. To use such figures of speech effectively, think up new ones—don't fall back on the tiresome old expressions you've heard so often.

As you've seen, in a *simile* there is a resemblance—in a *metaphor,* identification. Metaphors are worth the time they take to create, for they add quality and force to your writing.

3. *Personification.* In personification, you give human qualities to inanimate objects or forces of nature to increase a dramatic effect or mood. For instance, if a person were driving to a hospital with great urgency, the car and the traffic might present obstacles. With personification you might say: "His car chose this moment to be perverse, to spit and cough, and finally come to a stubborn halt in the middle of the thruway. When it decided to start again, the traffic had grown into a great surging monster that blocked his path with roaring indifference."

In another example, perhaps a character wants to scale a

mountain, but is afraid. The effect of fear might be strengthened if the writer said: "The mountain scowled down upon him, a black, forbidding giant of rock."

Here is a Biblical example showing the personification of a virtue: "Charity suffereth long, and is kind; charity envieth not; charity vaunteth not itself, is not puffed up."

Here's another example, one that gives human powers to the ocean. "The arms of the ocean were open and ready to receive them the moment their strength failed."

Now let's take a look at a description without personification, and then add it to increase mood and effect.

In her grief, she could not sleep. She could hear the rain, and the far-off whistle of a train.

In her grief, she could not sleep. She could hear the steady weeping of the rain, the lonely wail of a far-off train.

Personification has given facts much more vivid imagery for the reader, and therefore has drawn greater response. Personification can be used to inject humor, as in the following:

He looked in the mirror. He did not like what he saw, so he stuck out his tongue at his reflection.

He looked in the mirror, did not like what he saw, and was about to turn away when the mirror stuck its tongue out at him.

Personification is another tool to improve your writing and hence you should learn to use it well.

4. *Irony*. A way of implying the opposite of the literal meaning of words. Correctly used, it's of great value when a writer makes a point or emphasizes a situation. For instance:

It was just a little house, fourteen bedrooms, eight baths and three living rooms, but it would do until Nancy had time to look around and get something livable.

The writer has slipped in some effective characterization of Nancy by the use of irony. Had the same facts been presented literally, they would have required explanation.

It was a huge house, fourteen bedrooms, eight baths and three living rooms, yet to Nancy, used to even bigger mansions, it was only makeshift until she could find one she considered more suitable.

Here's another instance of irony:

He turned up his coat collar with a smile of apology for his weakness—after all, it was only twenty below and he loved Alaska, had absolutely no desire to be back in Florida basking in the sunshine!

And here are some more brief samples:

He was never busy, just frantic.
She was gentle as a wrestler with a hammerlock.
She had nothing to do—just keep twenty-five rooms cleaned, the furnace stoked, and the meals on time.
He believed in short engagements—not longer than three or four years.

Irony differs from sarcasm in that it's not derisive or bitter. When sensibly used, it can be an excellent means of conveying your ideas in stories.

5. *Metonymy.* This figure of speech calls a thing by the name of one of its attributes or characteristics, such as "The Crown" for "The King." Or you might say: "The school rose and cheered," when you mean that the students of the school rose and cheered. Some other instances would be:

The company issued a statement of policy.
We welcomed the press in our home.
The White House opposes the idea.

Metonymy is seldom mentioned in writing circles and few authors are aware of its technical name, but it's widely used because of its conciseness and adaptability to every form of writing. Not only will it reduce several words into one sharp image, but it is especially serviceable in characterization, where a minimum of words must exert a maximum effect on the reader, such as when a new character, about whom the reader knows nothing, enters the story and must be characterized without loss of pace. Here are more examples:

She opened the door and a freckle-faced Mercury grinned, "Miss Smith?" and handed her a yellow envelope.

The Voice of the Ladies Sewing Society rose to her five-feet-two, plus three inches of feathered bonnet, and protested.

Feet stampeded into the room. Steel gleamed. A manacle snapped. Authority had caught up with him.

If you master the use of metonymy, you'll find that it gives your work extra power and originality.

6. *Hyperbole.* Hyperbole is an exaggerating figure of speech,

an overstatement of fact to the point where it stresses an effect you wish to make or the trait of a character, as in this sample: "Tom would rather be dead than eat beef stew." From this, the reader knows that Tom not only dislikes stew, but is apt to make a terrible fuss if it's placed before him. However, it would be a gross distortion to say he would not eat stew under penalty of death. Nevertheless, the exaggeration or hyperbole makes the point of Tom's dislike much more emphatic than if the writer had said: "Tom does not like stew at all, and will not eat it."

Here are some other examples of hyperbole:

The boy made a dash for the other side of the street.
The boy shot across the street.

He laughs a good deal.
He never stops laughing.

She can be real catty.
She'll scratch your eyes out as soon as look at you.

At the drop of a hat, he'll perform for you.
He doesn't wait for the drop of a hat to perform.

The pain was bad.
The pain tore me apart.

Hyperbole is never an exaggeration that could be logical. It is excessive, but it gives a true impression, often truer than the exact facts. Although this figure of speech shouldn't be used too frequently, at the right place in a story it can be most effective.

7. *Paradox.* A paradox is a statement that seems at first glance to be nonsense or to contradict itself. It's a tricky figure of speech for the writer, since good paradoxes are not easily come by. The writer shouldn't strain for them but be alert to their sources in everyday life, particularly in the lessons life teaches you, for there is underlying instruction in a paradox. You may choose this figure of speech to tell a reader something you've learned and he'll accept it freely, because it is hidden in seeming contradiction rather than in preachment.

Here are some paradoxes that may lead you to your own:

Robert put all his energy and strength into avoiding work.
The less he knows, the nearer to wisdom he grows.
In surrendering to him, she conquered him.
Now that we are really desperate, we cannot afford desperation.
She gave the little boy her last dime, and counted herself rich.

8. *Onomatopoeia.* Like metonymy, this is a formidable word, but it names a helpful figure of speech for the fiction writer. Onomatopoeia is the use of words that fit a sound to a sense, like this:

The small bird on the window sill went cheet-cheet-cheet!
The wind went whooooeeee around the eaves.

Or it can be the description of a character's speech, such as: "Her voice clacked and squawked over the telephone wire."

Onomatopoeia helps the writer to characterize and create a strong sense impression for the reader. Here are a few more samples:

The soprano warbled and the basso rumbled.
The doors whined and groaned as the gale approached.
There was a sharp rat-tat-tat on the front door.
Her heels made an imperious tattoo down the hall.

Onomatopoeia (or fitting words to sounds) should be used sparingly and carefully. A sound description here and there can add greatly to the effect of your writing, but too many of them can create a forced tone.

Now, to recapitulate what we've said about figures of speech, here is a helpful list:

1. *Simile*—A simile says one thing is *like* another: "Her hair was like spun gold."

2. *Metaphor*—A metaphor is a word used in other than its literal meaning: "All the world's a stage."

3. *Personification*—Personification gives human qualities to inanimate objects or forces of nature: "The old engine puffed and grunted up the hillside."

4. *Irony*—Irony expresses the opposite of the literal meaning of words: "He was not a conceited man, but he considered himself superior."

5. *Metonymy*—Metonymy uses one word for another associated with or suggested by it: "The pen is mightier than the sword."

6. *Hyperbole*—Hyperbole is an exaggeration, an overstatement of fact: "My relatives are arriving in swarms."

7. *Paradox*—A paradox is a statement that seems contradictory or nonsensical but has a deeper meaning: "She never invented a lie without learning a truth."

8. *Onomatopoeia*—Onomatopoeia is a way of making words match sounds: "The dog's tongue lapped steadily at the water—slosh, slosh, slosh."

Lesson twenty-three

Fiction writing

course

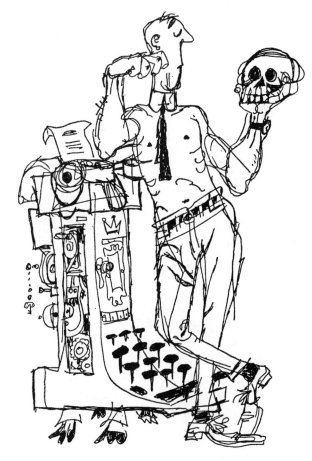

How to
develop
style

Style, or the over-all tone or effect made by words themselves, comes to each writer after much practice. Most writers eventually develop a style of their own, whether deliberately or not. It's a natural compound of impressions made in your formative years by reading the works of others, by the speech habits you developed from education and home surroundings, by your own special interests and pursuits, and the particular way you express yourself to others.

No matter what individual style you develop, you can be helped by experimenting, by studying masters in your chosen field, and by knowing as much as you can about each story before you write it. There's one vital rule to keep in mind: Never strain in your efforts to create a writing style. As Arthur Sullivant Hoffman once said:

There is always danger in the temptation to copy or adopt some device used by a successful author. In his skilled hands it may be effective; in yours disastrous. Or it may be merely an experiment that he will abandon later as not worth-while. Or it may be effective in that particular story but not at all effective in most others . . .

Beyond any question, writers often can gain from some study of the masters of their art, and even of authors who have attained only moderate proficiency, but there are dangers and your eyes should be open to them. It is safer to fix your main attention upon developing the ability to get *yourself* on paper and to your readers; later you can turn to models for whatever tools and devices you can adapt to your own needs and skill without denaturing your own product.

If you turn back to the subject of *style* in Volumes I and II, you'll see famous writers compared through excerpts from their works. Note that many authors use a different style for a book than for the more compact short story, not always purposely but because pace and tempo play a stronger part in stories. Also the era in which a story is written must be watched carefully, as writing styles too will vary with the times.

Prose styles have changed a great deal in recent years, says Bennett Cerf.

Modern short stories are molded with an economy of words. Ornate and flowery language has become old-fashioned. Long, wordy passages of description are no longer favored. Comments and asides from the writer are to be used only with great skill, if at all, for every sentence these days should move the story forward. Writers don't adopt the lecturer's tone but keep themselves out of their stories and let the characters say whatever needs to be said.

Observations are never lofty in tone but simple and direct, slipped in, as it were, rather than delivered. Subtlety of thought or phrasing, however, should never be confused with obscurity or with contrived wording. The art of writing is saying what you want to say in words that communicate clearly with the reader. Style should not hamper this, but rather should sharpen the effectiveness of mood and interest.

There's no better way of describing a definite style than by seeing it in use. Here, then, are a few examples of sharply different styles taken from published short stories.

The first one is from "Palo," by William Saroyan, in the magazine *Tomorrow*.

The old boy himself, bored worse than ever, and annoyed because something was the matter with the brakes, something more was the matter with them that was going to cost more money, more of the stuff he'd been having too much trouble trying to get all his life, and because the windshield wiper wasn't wiping, the cars coming in the other direction weren't dimming their headlights—they ought to know enough to dim their headlights—so that slipping through the hills, he could not see, he could not see the white line on the edge of the road.

The radio, which ordinarily helped dispel the boredom, was no help at all now, although it was tuned to the proper station, the one that played records of good music from six-thirty in the morning to midnight. Now, though, it was the half-hour for children, which was something else again.

He was late, too. He was supposed to see Doc at Doc's office at six-thirty, but it was almost that already. His neck, where it was attached to his head, was hot, and he knew that meant he was tired. He was especially tired of looking at the frosty windshield and not being able to see past it.

Saroyan has presented an initial set of circumstances in a special language. Note that although there's repetition in the easygoing flow of words, the situation holds together and keeps moving steadily towards an outcome and a new turn of plot.

Here's another excerpt of style, taken from "The Face Is Familiar, But—," by Max Shulman:

You never can tell. Citizens, you never can tell. Take the weekend of May 18. From all indications it was going to be a dilly, a dreamboat. Saturday night was the fraternity formal, and Sunday night Petey Burch was taking me to the Dr. Askit quiz broadcast. Every prospect pleased.

At 7:30 Saturday night I got into my rented tux and picked up my rented car. At 8:30 I called for my date and was told that she had come down with measles at 7:30. So I shrugged my rented shoulders, got into my rented car, and went to the dance alone.

This humorous effect is derived from an adolescent's simplicity of word choice. The reader knows that it doesn't represent the author's own state of mind, but is done deliberately to amuse those reading his story.

Here's a totally different style. Conrad Aiken, in his story "Strange Moonlight," blends an individual way of thinking with a special method of expression. Frequent reading of authors like Aiken makes their styles easily recognizable.

It had been a tremendous week—colossal. Its reverberations around him hardly yet slept—his slightest motion or thought made a vast symphony of them, like a breeze in a forest of bells. In the first place, he had filched a volume of Poe's tales from his mother's bookcase, and had had in consequence a delirious night in inferno. Down, down he had gone with heavy clangs about him, coiling spouts of fire licking dryly at an iron sky, and a strange companion, of protean shape and size, walking and talking beside him.

For the most part, this companion seemed to be nothing but a voice and a wing—an enormous jagged black wing, soft and drooping like a bat's; he had noticed veins in it. As for the voice, it had been singularly gentle. If it was mysterious, that was no doubt because he himself was stupid. Certainly it had sounded placid and reasonable, exactly, in fact, like his father's, explaining a problem in mathematics; but, though he had noticed the orderly and logical structure, and felt the inevitable approach towards a vast and beautiful or terrible conclusion, the nature and meaning of the conclusion itself always escaped him. It was as if, always, he had come just too late.

There's the quality of poetry in Aiken's style, both in the imagery and in the inner groping for transient thoughts. Compare this with the style of Thomas Wolfe, in "A Portrait of Bascom Hawke":

During the first twenty-five years of this century, business people who had their offices in or near State Street, Boston, no doubt grew very familiar with the cadaverous and extraordinary figure of my uncle, Bascom Hawke. Shortly before nine o'clock of every working day he would emerge from a subway exit near the head of the street and pause vaguely for a moment, making a craggy eddy in the tide of issuing workers that foamed swiftly about him while he stood with his enormous bony hands clutched comically before him at the waist, as if holding himself in, at the same time making the most horrible grimaces with his lean and amazingly flexible features.

These grimaces were made by squinting his small sharp eyes together, widening his mouth in a ghastly travesty of a grin, and convolving his chin and cheek in a rapid series of pursed lips and horrible squints as he swiftly pressed his rubbery underlip against a few enormous horse teeth that decorated his upper jaw. Having completed these facial evolutions, he glanced quickly and, it must be supposed, blindly, in every direction; for he then plunged heedlessly across the street, sometimes choosing the moment when traffic had been halted and pedestrians were hurrying across, sometimes diving into the midst of a roaring chaos of motor cars, trucks and wagons, through which he sometimes made his way in safety, accompanied only by a scream of brake bands, a startled barking of horns, and the hearty curses of frightened drivers, or from which, howling with terror in the center of a web of traffic which he had snarled hopelessly and brought to a complete standstill, he was sometimes rescued by a red-faced and cursing young Irishman who was on point duty at that corner.

This is straight narrative style, unaided by dialogue but heavily detailed with long sentences that seem to unwind from a limitless knowledge of the subject matter.

In contrast, read the beginning of "The Short Happy Life of Francis Macomber," by Ernest Hemingway:

It was now lunch time and they were all sitting under the double green fly of the dining tent pretending that nothing had happened.

"Will you have lime juice or lemon squash?" Macomber asked.

"I'll have a gimlet," Robert Wilson told him.

"I'll have a gimlet too. I need something," Macomber's wife said.

"I suppose it's the thing to do," Macomber agreed. "Tell him to make three gimlets."

The mess boy had started them already, lifting the bottles out of the canvas cooling bags that sweated wet in the wind that blew through the trees that shaded the tents.

"What had I ought to give them?" Macomber asked.

"A quid would be plenty," Wilson told him. "You don't want to spoil them."

"Will the headman distribute it?"

"Absolutely."

Francis Macomber had, half an hour before, been carried to his tent from the edge of the camp in triumph on the arms and shoulders of the cook, the personal boys, the skinner and the porters. The gunbearers had taken no part in the demonstration. When the native boys put him down at the door of his tent, he had shaken all their hands, received their congratulations, and then gone into the tent and sat on the bed until his wife came in. She did not speak to him when she came in and he left the tent at once to wash his face and hands in the portable wash basin outside and go over to the dining tent to sit in a comfortable canvas chair in the breeze and shade.

Hemingway's economy of words has won him fame and established a trend in writing which penetrates deep into modern fiction. He goes directly to the telling of a story, using simple words and sparse but always explanatory dialogue.

Quite another style is the approach of Jean Stafford, in "A Reasonable Facsimile," which appeared in the *New Yorker:*

Far from withering on the vine from apathy and loneliness after his retirement as chairman of the Philosophy Department at Nevilles College, Dr. Bohrmann had a second blooming, and it was observed amongst his colleagues and his idolatrous students that he would age with gusto and live to be a hundred. He looked on the end of his academic career—an impressive one that had earned him an international reputation in scholarly quarters—as simply the end of one phase of his life, and when he began the new one, he did so with fresh accoutrements, for, as he had been fond of saying to his students, "Change is the only stimulus."

He took up the study of Japanese (he said with a smile that he would write *hokku* as tributes to his friends on stormy days); he took up engraving and lettering (designed a new bookplate, designed a gravestone for his dead wife); he began to grow Persian melons under glass; he took up mycology, and mycophagy as well, sending his fidgety housekeeper off into shrill protests as he flirted with death by eating mushrooms gathered in cow pastures and on golf links. He abandoned chess for bridge, and two evenings a week played a cutthroat game with Miss Blossom Duveen, the bursar's blonde and bawdy secretary, as his partner and as his opponents, Mr. Street, the logician, and Mr. Street's hopelessly scatterbrained wife.

In another vein, familiar to most American readers, is the deliberately illiterate style of Ring Lardner. Here's an excerpt from his "The Golden Honeymoon":

Mother says that when I start talking I never know when to stop. But I tell her the only time I get a chance is when she ain't around, so I have to make the most of it. I guess the fact is neither one of us would be welcome in a Quaker meeting, but as I tell Mother, what did God give us tongues for if He didn't want we should use them? Only she says He didn't give them to us to say things over and over again, like I do, and repeat myself. But I say:

"Well, Mother," I say, "when people is like you and I and been married fifty years, do you expect everything I say will be something you ain't heard me say before? But it may be new to others, as they ain't nobody else lived with me as long as you have."

So she says: "You can bet they ain't, as they couldn't nobody else stand you that long."

"Well," I tell her, "you look pretty healthy."

"Maybe I do," she will say, "but I looked even healthier before I married you."

You can't get ahead of Mother.

These examples represent the styles of individual writers, but there are also styles consciously adopted to suit your story or the editorial flavor of a particular magazine. This is deliberate stylizing and can't be achieved without a thorough knowledge of the craft.

Variations on the same theme

To give you an idea how the same subjects can be handled in different styles, here are some variations. The first subject calls for scenic description. The simple facts involved are these:

The farmhouse is big. It is located on the Illinois plains on the outskirts of a village called Paraguay. Its Lutheran church spire and some buildings can be seen on the horizon. The country roads stand out clearly because it is winter.

In the first variation, we show you a style that's extremely economical, says just what has to be said in as few words as possible, yet creates a vivid picture:

You saw it suddenly. A farmhouse, giant-like on patchwork plains. On the horizon were other houses, other barns, then the final jut of the Lutheran church spire and the three-story buildings in Paraguay, Illinois.

The second variation arranges the same facts in a loose, chatty manner:

The farmhouse was a big place, all right, way out there in the wintry Illinois plains, and because the grass and corn were withered now, the land, as far as you could see, seemed to be cut into small, neat squares, like a chessboard. And then, if you went on thinking like that, the other houses and barns could be knights and pawns, only no one ever moved them. Way, way off, at the very end of the land, where the sky and the earth came together, you could see the village of Paraguay, see the red brick spire of the Lutheran church there, and some of the three-story buildings on Main Street.

For the third variation of this scene, we reprint the version written by the well-known American writer, Victoria Lincoln, from her story, "Morning Wishes." Note the use of similes and imagery:

The farmhouse rode at anchor in the center of the vast circle of earth and sky, like a ship on the sea. The village of Paraguay, Illinois, was just beyond the horizon, the roofs of its three-story buildings and the brick tower of the Lutheran church riding the skyline like a fleet climbing into view over the curve of the world. In winter, when the grasses were withered and the corn was down, you could see that the land was marked out with roads in exact square miles, like Alice's chessboard; and the farms, the big barns, so widely spaced on it, appeared to be set with deliberate intent to show, by their diminishing proportions, the curious blank majesty of the plains.

In the next set of variations, we give you the physical facts about a man and show you several ways in which they're presented in different styles. The facts are these:

The man is not big, but thin and hard, with the face of a killer.

The first variation states these facts briefly and economically, but creates a distinct characterization:

He was not a big man and he had small, almost delicate hands and feet. He was thin to the point of gauntness and his windburned face was taut and hard, the face of a killer.

Now the style becomes chattier, with a few similes and more descriptive words:

No one could say he was a big man, because he wasn't. In fact, he was a real small one, thin and hard as a post, with hands and feet so delicate as to be ladylike. Not that you'd think about this after you'd seen his face. That face of his was burned to leather and taut as a whip. You could just tell when you looked at him that he was a killer. Don't know how you told—you just knew.

The following is a more formal, more literary style with some interpretation of the facts:

The impression of power that he gave did not stem from his size. He was not a big man. Far from it: he was lean and smallish. His hands and feet were delicate, and his frame bone-thin. Perhaps it was his wind-darkened face that conveyed the formidable quality. It was hard, gaunt, grim—the face of a man who would kill.

Overdoing the style

So that you can see how styles sometimes err too far in the wrong direction, here are three to avoid. Each is based on the man described above.

1. *Slang.* Seldom use it except in dialogue.

He wasn't a big bruiser, just a skinny little guy with dinky hands and feet, and a cold, hard mug that told you he was mean, would kill you as soon as look at you.

2. *Verbose and pompous.* Be careful of using unfamiliar words that send your readers to the dictionary when they should be getting on with your story.

He was not in any sense a mammoth man of imposing demeanor. He was, quite to the contrary, a diminutive and skeletonized creature. But his wind-ravaged countenance was as impervious as granite, as thin, stark and intractile as the weapon with which he killed.

3. *Cliché-ridden.* Be careful of your comparative expressions. Try to think them out each time for yourself.

He wasn't a giant, he was thin as a rail, with hands and feet like a girl's. His face, burned brown as an Indian's, was thin and hard as a steel trap, and you saw he would kill you at the drop of a hat.

In order to achieve ease with style, you should consistently read books by authors who use varied approaches, and see why and how they differ. Also, and most important of all, experiment with your own writing. Take plenty of time for this. Try doing descriptions in many styles. You may be surprised to find yourself suddenly at ease in one that's quite unfamiliar, just as you'll find that some are not suitable to your talent.

Nothing, however, will take the place of practice, so that ultimately your work will bear the stamp of your own personality and your own powers of expression.

When editor and writer agree

I have always felt that an editor wants a story that will please the readers. Since the writer wants a story that will please the readers, editor and writer really want the same thing.—Mignon Eberhart

This volume of the
Fiction Writing Course
is set in Times New Roman type.

The format and binding were designed by
Bradbury Thompson.

The illustrations are by
Ric Estrada.